T0206885

Game Programming with Unity and C#

A Complete Beginner's Guide

Second Edition

Casey Hardman

Apress®

Game Programming with Unity and C#: A Complete Beginner's Guide, Second Edition

Casey Hardman
West Palm Beach, FL, USA

ISBN-13 (pbk): 978-1-4842-9719-3   ISBN-13 (electronic): 978-1-4842-9720-9
https://doi.org/10.1007/978-1-4842-9720-9

Copyright © 2024 by Casey Hardman

This work is subject to copyright. All rights are reserved by the Publisher, whether the whole or part of the material is concerned, specifically the rights of translation, reprinting, reuse of illustrations, recitation, broadcasting, reproduction on microfilms or in any other physical way, and transmission or information storage and retrieval, electronic adaptation, computer software, or by similar or dissimilar methodology now known or hereafter developed.

Trademarked names, logos, and images may appear in this book. Rather than use a trademark symbol with every occurrence of a trademarked name, logo, or image we use the names, logos, and images only in an editorial fashion and to the benefit of the trademark owner, with no intention of infringement of the trademark.

The use in this publication of trade names, trademarks, service marks, and similar terms, even if they are not identified as such, is not to be taken as an expression of opinion as to whether or not they are subject to proprietary rights.

While the advice and information in this book are believed to be true and accurate at the date of publication, neither the authors nor the editors nor the publisher can accept any legal responsibility for any errors or omissions that may be made. The publisher makes no warranty, express or implied, with respect to the material contained herein.

Managing Director, Apress Media LLC: Welmoed Spahr
Acquisitions Editor: Spandana Chatterjee
Development Editor: James Markham
Editorial Assistant: Jessica Vakili

Cover image from Freepik

Distributed to the book trade worldwide by Springer Science+Business Media New York, 1 New York Plaza, Suite 4600, New York, NY 10004-1562, USA. Phone 1-800-SPRINGER, fax (201) 348-4505, e-mail orders-ny@ springer-sbm.com, or visit www.springeronline.com. Apress Media, LLC is a California LLC and the sole member (owner) is Springer Science + Business Media Finance Inc (SSBM Finance Inc). SSBM Finance Inc is a **Delaware** corporation.

For information on translations, please e-mail booktranslations@springernature.com; for reprint, paperback, or audio rights, please e-mail bookpermissions@springernature.com.

Apress titles may be purchased in bulk for academic, corporate, or promotional use. eBook versions and licenses are also available for most titles. For more information, reference our Print and eBook Bulk Sales web page at http://www.apress.com/bulk-sales.

Any source code or other supplementary material referenced by the author in this book is available to readers on GitHub. For more detailed information, please visit https://www.apress.com/gp/services/ source-code.

Paper in this product is recyclable

Table of Contents

About the Author

Casey Hardman has been a programmer and hobbyist game developer for over eight years. He found inspiration in the capacity for immersion and interactivity provided by games and has nurtured a passion for video games since he was a child. In his early teens, this interest led him on a journey into the world of programming and game design. He works with the Unity game engine, the Godot game engine, and web development technologies.

About the Technical Reviewer

Simon Jackson is a longtime software engineer and architect with many years of Unity game development experience and is an author of several Unity game development titles. He loves to create Unity projects and help educate others, via blogs, vlogs, user groups, or major speaking events. Currently, his primary focus is the Reality Toolkit project, which is aimed at building a cross-platform mixed reality framework to enable both VR and AR developers to build and distribute efficient solutions in Unity.

Introduction

Welcome to the start of your adventure into game programming with Unity. This book is designed to teach you how to program video games from the ground up, while still engaging you with plenty of hands-on experience. It's not focused on completing ambitious projects, and it's not about fancy graphics. We're learning how to program and how to use the Unity engine. Once you have a solid understanding of these integral topics, you can expand your knowledge and make more and more complicated and impressive games.

These may not be the kinds of games you want to work on right away, but I encourage you to follow along in the order that the chapters are presented. You'll learn important tips and tricks for coding that will set you up to advance much more quickly than if you attempted to jump around within the book or tackle lofty game projects on your own.

Unity is cross-platform, meaning you can run it on a Windows, Mac, or Linux computer. This book will mostly stick to Windows-based terminology, but you can still follow through with the other operating systems with little to no extra trouble.

As for system requirements, any modern computer purchased within the last five years or so should be totally capable of running the software we'll be working with. Since we aren't fiddling with high-end graphics or computing long-winded algorithms, the example projects we develop should run fine on most systems. However, older systems may run the Unity engine itself slower, which can be frustrating. You can find the system requirements for the current Long Term Support version (2022.3.6) of the Unity editor here:

`docs.unity3d.com/Manual/system-requirements.html`

In Chapters 1–5, we'll begin with a primer for the essential concepts of the Unity game engine itself and get all our tools set up and ready for action.

In Chapters 6–12, we'll get into the core details of programming. You'll start to write your own code and learn the fundamentals to ensure that you understand not just what code to write, but why you're writing it and what it's actually doing.

In the remainder of the book, we'll tackle individual projects one at a time, making playable games that you can polish and add features to later if you please. This is where you'll get much of your hands-on experience. We'll implement actual game mechanics and tackle the hurdles and little hang-ups that come with a beginner's approach to the world of game programming.

Game Project 1, "Obstacle Course" (Chapters 13–25), will be a top-down obstacle course where the player moves their character with WASD or the arrow keys to avoid touching hazards of various forms: patrolling and wandering hazards, traveling projectiles, and spike traps in the floor. We'll get practice with basic movement and rotation, setting up levels, working with fundamental Unity concepts like prefabs and scripting, and coding basic UI.

Game Project 2, "Tower Defense" (Chapters 26–35), will be the basis of a simple "tower defense" game, where the player places defensive structures on the playing field. Enemies will navigate from one side of the field to the other, and the player's defenses will attempt to fend them off. We'll explore basic pathfinding (how the enemies navigate around arbitrary obstacles) and further expand on fundamental programming concepts.

Game Project 3, "Physics Playground" (Chapters 36–44), will be a 3D physics playground with first- and third-person camera support for a player character with more intricate mouse-aimed movement, jumping, wall jumping, and gravity systems. We'll explore the possibilities of Unity's physics, from detecting objects with raycasts to setting up joints and Rigidbodies.

PART I

Unity Fundamentals

CHAPTER 1

▪ ▪ ▪

Installation and Setup

Installing software is somewhat simple – download an installer, run the installer, a menu (sometimes called a "wizard") pops up, you agree to some terms of use, it asks you where you want to install the program on your computer, maybe it offers some additional options, and then it starts installing. Easy, right? So I won't go into painstaking detail over the installation process. I'll just show you what to install.

Unity Hub

Unity is frequently releasing new versions with new features, bug fixes, and little improvements. Because of this, they offer a lightweight little application called Unity Hub that lets you install the actual Unity engine, including older versions of the engine. It also lets you manage older versions of the engine already installed on your computer and view all your Unity projects from one place.

Sometimes it's useful to keep an old version of Unity around even after you upgrade to the latest version. You may want to work on an older project with the same version you started with, in case some new features or changes aren't compatible with your old project – things change, and sometimes the new stuff breaks the old stuff. Sometimes the old stuff just gets reworked and isn't valid in a newer version. In those cases, you might decide to stick to the old version until you finish a project, to avoid spending unnecessary time changing the way you did something to the "new way."

So we're going to install the Unity Hub first, and then we can install the Unity engine itself through the Hub. To download the Hub, navigate to this link in your web browser:

`unity.com/download`

This page should show a download button, which may vary based on your operating system. I'm on Windows, so it shows a button titled "Download for Windows," as shown in Figure 1-1.

Figure 1-1. *Download for Windows button*

Click this button to download the Unity Hub installer. Once it finishes, run the installer and follow the prompts.

© Casey Hardman 2024
C. Hardman, *Game Programming with Unity and C#*, https://doi.org/10.1007/978-1-4842-9720-9_1

Once the Hub is installed, run it. You may be prevented from getting very far by Unity asking you to accept a license, which may involve creating an account with Unity. This is a little one-time setup that pretty much stays logged in and accounted for afterward. It won't bother you much once it's done – but still, if you're prompted to make an account, don't forget your password and username!

Unless you're working with a big company that's making money off of products they create with Unity, then you can just choose the free "Personal" license and be on your way. Unity describes this license as being for "individuals, hobbyists, and small organizations with less than $100K of revenue or funds raised in the last 12 months."

Once you've got a license and an account, you should see an "Installs" tab on the left side of the Hub (see Figure 1-2).

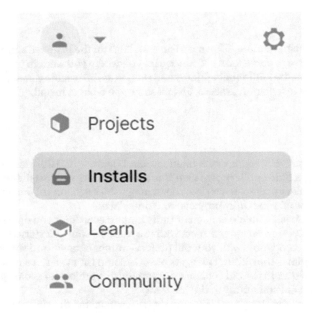

Figure 1-2. *Top-left corner of the Unity Hub, with the Installs tab selected*

This is where you can see all the versions of the Unity engine you have installed on your computer. You can also install new versions – although installing many versions can quickly use up space on your hard drive, so you may want to uninstall old versions to avoid this.

Before we get into that, let's discuss options for code editors. One can be installed right here through the Hub with our Unity installation, but there are a few other options that may better suit some users.

Installing Our Code Editor

You don't write code in the same sort of software that you might write a book or a resume in. Code editors are text editors that are fine-tuned for writing code. They have special highlighting for words and symbols, they know how to format code, and they often come with a slew of features that make it easier and faster for us to write and work with code.

One such feature is **debugging**, which is when our code editor "attaches" to Unity while our game is running. We can then designate points in our code that we want our game to pause upon reaching. This will freeze the game as it's running in the Unity editor, as soon as the code hits that point. While the game is paused, we can see the state of our code, run it step by step while keeping the game frozen, and resume whenever we please. This can be very useful in pinpointing why something is going wrong with our code.

Let's briefly go over the options for code editors:

- **Microsoft Visual Studio** is a free, feature-packed editor that supports Windows and Mac. It can be easily installed with debugging support through the Unity Hub. Unfortunately, it does not support Linux users. It has paid versions for commercial and professional use, but the free, Community version will be more than enough for most hobbyist users.

- **Microsoft Visual Studio Code**, or just Code, is a more lightweight version of Visual Studio that can operate on Windows, Mac, and Linux. Unfortunately, its latest versions do not support debugging with Unity, and older versions only supported it experimentally. It also has a much smaller file size than Visual Studio, which is great if you're cramped for space on your computer.

- **JetBrains Rider** is an editor that supports Windows, Mac, and Linux, as well as debugging for Unity. Its features are similar to Visual Studio, but unfortunately, it is not free to use. At the time of writing, it offers a 30-day free trial, after which users must pay monthly or yearly to continue using the product's latest version; however, paying the yearly price once will allow you perpetual access to the version of Rider that was available at the time, although you will have to pay again if you'd like to use any newer versions released since your first yearly payment.

Personally, as a Windows user, I use Visual Studio Code for a lot of purposes, as I enjoy its lightweight, "getting out of the way" design. However, Visual Studio (not Code) can debug Unity out-of-the-box if you install it through the Hub with your Unity installation, assuming you're on Windows or Mac. Due to this, I also have Visual Studio installed for use with Unity and C# specifically.

We'll be learning how to debug our code using Microsoft Visual Studio later on, in Chapter 12, so if you'd like to follow along with that chapter, Visual Studio is a fine pick.

Debugging can be a very useful feature, but if you'd like to stay simple for now, or if you're running Linux and don't want to pay for Rider just yet, then you can always pick up Visual Studio Code and learn about debugging later if you'd like, once you've gone through the book and have started branching out on your own.

To summarize...

- **For Windows and Mac users**, I recommend using **Visual Studio** due to its debugging support and ease of installation through the Hub; however, if your computer is pinched for space, know that Code will eat up much less space on your hard drive, so it may prove a better option.

- **For Linux users**, I recommend **Code** if you want to stay simple and wait to learn about debugging later, or **Rider** if you'd like the full kit of tools and don't mind that you'll have to pay after the free trial.

To download Code, head on over to this link in your favorite web browser:

```
code.visualstudio.com/download
```

From there, you can select the correct button to download the software based on your operating system (Windows, Mac, or Linux). The installer should begin to download. Once it completes, run it and follow the instructions it provides.

To download JetBrains Rider, here is the link to the homepage at the time of writing:

`jetbrains.com/rider`

From the homepage, you should find "Download" buttons sprinkled about in clear view, so give one a click and follow the instructions.

Installing Unity

Okay, with that settled, let's install a version of Unity. With the "Installs" tab selected, as shown before in Figure 1-2, click the "Install Editor" button in the top-right corner. A popup will offer a list of versions you can choose from.

Unity's versions are numbered by their year of release, followed by a period and additional version numbers, such as 2021.2 or 2022.1.

The topmost version will be the latest "**LTS**" release, which stands for **Long Term Support**. The LTS versions are meant for projects that are already in production or are close to release: they won't have any changes that will break your project or make you refactor anything, and they are frequently updated to fix minor bugs or improve performance and stability.

Below the LTS versions, you'll find "other versions," which will likely have a more recent version number. These will have the latest features and changes.

If you're committing to a project, particularly a large one with a team of developers behind it, Unity recommends using the LTS version to ensure that the engine doesn't experience any major changes during your development cycle. If you're just experimenting and learning, or just want to see the latest stuff, you can use the other versions. You can even try beta or alpha versions, although these are likely to be less stable than the others.

For our purposes, the latest of the "other versions" (below LTS) will do. Click the "Install" button for that version number. It will be off to the right side of the version number.

You'll be asked to select what Unity Hub calls "modules" to install with the engine. These are extra little features to add to the installation, which take up some more space on your computer if you choose to install them. You can always add modules later, after installation completes, if you find that you want them.

By default, Unity Hub may have already checked a box to install the module called "Microsoft Visual Studio Community." If this is the case, you can leave it checked or uncheck it based on the decision you made earlier regarding which code editor you'd like to go with.

Other notable modules are the Build Support modules, which allow you to build a Unity game project to different operating systems, environments, and hardware.

"Building" a game project is the process of turning it from a Unity project, playable only through the Unity engine, to an actual application used to play the game.

Some of the platforms that Unity projects can be built to are

- PC, with support for Windows, Mac, and Linux

- Android

- iOS

- WebGL (played in a web browser)

- Xbox One

- PS5 and PS4

- Nintendo Switch

Unity also supports building to various extended reality (XR) platforms.

As I said, if you need to build to these platforms down the road (we won't get into them in this book), then you can always install them through the Hub.

You can also select to install the Unity documentation locally as a module. The documentation can be immensely helpful. It's available online as well, and I myself tend to use the online resources, but if you plan on using Unity offline, you may want to install the documentation so it's available without an Internet connection.

Once you're finished, click the button in the bottom-right corner. If you've chosen to add any modules, that button may say "Continue" to offer further options relating to the chosen modules. If not, it will instead just say "Install."

Once it's done installing, you can now create a Unity project with that version of the engine. Another nice feature about the Hub is that it will automatically run the correct editor version of Unity when you open a project (assuming the version is still installed on your computer), so if you have projects spread across multiple versions of Unity, you don't have to remember which version of the engine to run – you just start up the Hub and click on the project you want to open.

Creating a Project

We can now use the Unity Hub to create our first project, so we have an environment to play around in as we learn. In the Unity Hub, click the Projects tab on the left side, and then click the blue "New project" button in the top-right corner.

A dialog box will appear, allowing you to select a template to base the project on.

The template is just a simple starting point for your project. The most bare-bones and simple templates are the first two, titled "2D" and "3D." These are pretty much blank slates, one set up for 2D games, and one for 3D.

We'll start with a blank 3D project, so select the 3D template by clicking it. It will have a blue border around it if it is selected, as shown in Figure 1-3.

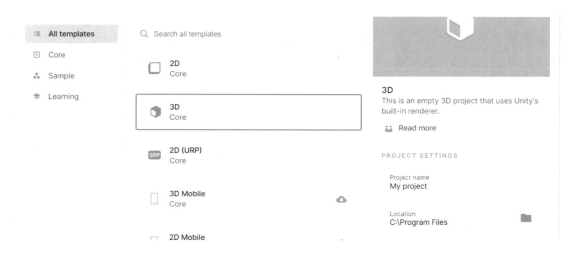

Figure 1-3. *Dialog box for creating a new Unity project*

On the right side, there's a description of the template. Beneath that description, there's a "Project Settings" header where you can supply a name for your project, as well as select where you want to store it on your computer.

We'll name our project "ExampleProject" – note that we aren't using a space between the two words, because file paths aren't always fond of spaces.

You can change the directory to save the project wherever you like. Whatever file path you choose, a folder named after the project will be created there. That folder is the "root directory" for your project, and all your project's files and resources will be stored in that folder.

Once you've selected the path you want, click the "Create project" button in the bottom-right corner, and wait for Unity to create the base project files. This may take a few minutes. When Unity finishes, the editor itself will pop up with your brand-new project opened and ready for editing.

Summary

The following is a recap on what we learned in this chapter:

- The Unity Hub program will be used to download new versions of the Unity editor, uninstall old versions you no longer need, create new projects, and open existing projects.

- Opening a project in the Unity Hub will start the Unity editor, which is where we'll actually use the engine to develop our game.

- A Unity game project is stored on your computer, with all the related files – including stuff we make ourselves like art and code – stored in a "root directory" named after the project name.

- Our code will be written with a text editor designed specifically for writing code. This offers us useful features that normal text editors don't have, making it easier to format and navigate our code.

CHAPTER 2

Unity Basics

Now that we have Unity set up and a new project to work with, let's get comfortable with the engine. This isv the user interface we will be interacting with quite a lot as we develop our games, after all, so we ought to get to know it early.

Windows

Unity is separated into different windows that serve different purposes. Each window has a little tab at its top-left corner where the type of the window is written.

Each of these windows is a separate piece of the program that can be positioned and sized how we want it, or even altogether removed. There are a handful of other window types in Unity that aren't being used now, so we don't see them on our screen – but if we ever wanted to use them, we could add them with a few clicks.

You'll notice that if you left-click and drag one of these window tabs, the window can be picked up and moved to a different spot in the program. Doing this, you can split one window's space to cover some of it with a different window. If you ever want to rearrange your windows in a certain way, chances are you just need to start dragging stuff around and see how Unity reacts.

You can also dock windows beside others to place their tabs side by side (see Figure 2-1). Whichever tab you clicked last will gain focus and fill the space of the window.

Figure 2-1. *Two window tabs docked side by side in the same space. The Project window has focus and will fill the space, but the Console window can be given focus instead by clicking its tab*

Unity also lets you save all your current windows and their sizes and positions in a **layout**, which you can assign a name to. This is done with the little drop-down button in the top-right corner of the Unity editor, with the text "Layout" written on it. Click this button to see all of the built-in layouts you can choose from, as shown in Figure 2-2.

© Casey Hardman 2024
C. Hardman, *Game Programming with Unity and C#*, https://doi.org/10.1007/978-1-4842-9720-9_2

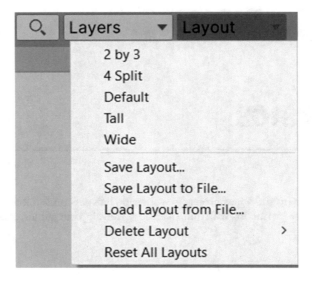

Figure 2-2. *The Layout button in the top-right corner of the Unity editor, after it has been clicked to show its options*

By default, it will be set to a layout very aptly named "Default." Try clicking a different layout, and you'll see Unity automatically restructure all its windows for you. You can also select the "Save Layout..." option in the drop-down list to save your current layout under a new name to keep it around, once you've set things up the way you like. That way, if you ever unintentionally close a window or accidentally cause some catastrophe to your window setup, you can just reset it to the way you had it by loading your layout with the drop-down.

Layouts can also be useful when dealing with different aspects of game development. Certain activities might be easier to do with a different set of windows in different positions. The ability to save layouts makes it easier for us to hop back and forth between activities – we can do it with just a few clicks.

The default layout has all the most important windows, so you don't have to change anything if you don't want to. Let's go over these windows to learn about what they do.

Project Window

The Project window can be found in the bottom-middle section of the editor by default, paired alongside a window called Console – which we'll learn about later, as it relates directly to code. The Project window shows us all of our **assets**. An asset is the game development term for some piece of work we can use in our game – art, sound effects, music, code files, game levels, things like that.

Once we get around to making assets, we'll see them here in the Project window. It pretty much functions like your computer's file system. You store assets in folders, also known as directories. You might have a folder for all your sound effects, another for all your code files (called "scripts"), and so on. We organize it all however we like in this window, and it's from this window that we can find, select, and use our assets within the engine.

Our project has been set up with some folders for us by default: the Packages folder – which we don't need to pay any attention to right now – and the Assets folder, which is the root folder inside which all our assets will be stored. The arrow beside a folder can be clicked to hide or show its contents (if it has anything inside it). If you unfold the Assets folder, you'll see it already has a "Scenes" folder inside it and an asset named "SampleScene".

Scene Window

The Scene window can be found dominating most of the screen space, docked in the upper left with the Game window. It lets you see the environment your game is taking place in. What we might call a "level" in our game is a "**scene**" in Unity. Scenes are saved as assets, so we'll see them in our Project window when we save them – this scene is the "SampleScene" asset we have in our project by default.

Each scene has its own collection of objects in it. The Scene window lets you view a scene and navigate through it, like a floating camera observing your game world. It's your main viewport into the game environment.

The sample scene we have open now doesn't really have anything inside it yet – just a light, which is an invisible object that casts light over everything in the scene, and a camera, which is the object through which the player will see the scene when the game is being played. It should also have a basic sky and horizon showing.

If we had other scenes, which we will later, we would store them all in our Scenes folder, and double-clicking one of them there would load a different scene, letting us view and edit that scene instead.

Within the Scene window, moving your mouse while holding right-click will turn the camera, much like looking around in a first-person game. While holding right-click, you can use the WASD keys to move the camera around – once again, much like in a game: W to move forward, S to move backward, A to move left, and D to move right. You can also use Q to move directly down and E to move directly up. Holding down the middle mouse button while dragging will pull your camera without turning it.

Hierarchy Window

The Hierarchy window, in the bottom left by default, allows you to see the objects contained within the current scene. As we just covered, a scene is pretty much just a collection of objects. When we switch from one scene to the other, we're just tucking away all the objects in the current scene and pulling out all the objects in the new scene instead.

You can see that those two objects we mentioned in our scene are listed in the Hierarchy: a "Directional Light" and a "Main Camera." By default, we'll have a light source and a camera in our scene, so we'll see them both listed here in the Hierarchy (this camera isn't the one we're viewing the scene through in the Scene window – rather, it's the camera that the player will be viewing the game through).

These are **GameObjects**. Simply put, a GameObject is some object in your scene. It could be a prop, like a box or a plant or a tree. It could be the player character, an enemy, a power-up on the ground, or a disembodied light. It could even be a GameObject that does nothing: it just exists, invisible in the scene. At their simplest, they're just a point in space with a name.

Inspector Window

The Inspector window, covering the right side of the editor by default, is a very important window that we will use extensively in our adventures with Unity.

As we just went over, the Hierarchy window shows a list of all GameObjects in the scene. Click one of these GameObjects in the Hierarchy window to select it. You will notice that this causes the Inspector to change. It's now showing you information about the selected GameObject. At the top of the Inspector, you can see a box containing the GameObject name, which you can click to type a new name in if you please. There are also a few drop-down buttons, one for the "tag" and one for the "layer" – we'll learn what those are for later.

But the main functionality of the Inspector is to show us all the **components** attached to the selected GameObject(s).

Components

A component is a Unity term for a feature, some single piece of game functionality, that is attached to a GameObject. A component cannot exist without a GameObject to attach it to.

There are many different kinds of components that serve different purposes, all included in the Unity engine by default. There's the Light component to cast light, whether it's a sunlike light that covers the whole scene or something like the beam of a flashlight.

Let's look at a Light component. Since the Inspector is designed to show us the components of the selected GameObject, try clicking the Directional Light in the Hierarchy window to select it. You'll see the Inspector update after you do this, to look something like Figure 2-3.

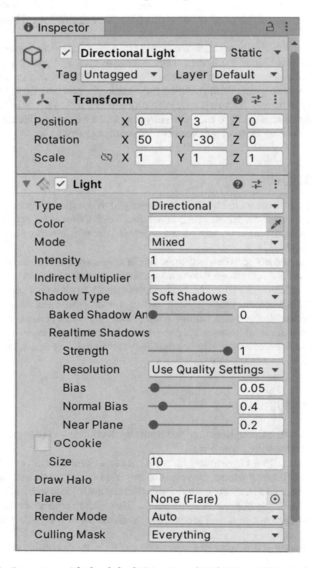

Figure 2-3. *A view of the Inspector with the default Directional Light GameObject selected*

Beneath the basic information at the top, like the GameObject's name, you'll see a heading for each component attached to the GameObject. This GameObject has two components attached: Transform and Light. You can click the headings of these components (where the component name is) to hide them (also known as "folding" them) or show them. Beneath the header, the various properties of the component are listed as value fields that we can change to affect the component – make the light more intense, change its color, change the way it casts shadows, and so on. The field name is on the left side, and the field value is on the right side. Some of these field values are numbers, and some are little "sliders" that let you click and drag a dial with your mouse – you'll come across many kinds of fields designed to edit different sorts of values.

This is the major functionality of the Inspector: viewing and editing the properties of components on a GameObject.

Another example is the Camera component. It's essential. It's what renders ("render" means "draw to the screen") the scene to the player's screen when the game is playing. If you select the Main Camera GameObject in the Hierarchy window, you'll see the Camera component listed in the Inspector.

When we start making things ourselves later in the book, we'll be getting some hands-on experience with using many kinds of components. Unity also has helpful official documentation, and this can be easily accessed by clicking the little icon that looks like a "?" symbol, located on the right side of each component header in the Inspector. This will open the documentation for that specific component type in your default web browser.

Our code will be attached to GameObjects in the form of components as well. They're called "scripts" in this case: that is to say, a script is a component which runs our code when it's attached to a GameObject. So when we write code, the way we get it into the game is by attaching it as a script component to a GameObject.

This means we can reuse and mix different pieces of functionality, if we're smart about how we write and define our scripts.

For example, our first example project is a game where the player must avoid various obstacles. Let's say you're making a project like this, and you want to make different kinds of obstacles to keep the game interesting. You want obstacles that shoot fireballs, blades that spin in a circle, and rolling spike balls that move back and forth between two points.

Each of these pieces of functionality can be made into a separate script component: Shooting, which periodically fires projectiles in front of the GameObject; Spinning, which makes the object constantly twirl around; and Patrolling, which makes the object pace back and forth between two or more points. Then, we can have a component called Hazard that we attach to the fireballs, the spinning blades, and the patrolling spike balls, which makes them kill the player when they touch.

The cool thing about components is that we can then mix them with each other to create new types of obstacles.

Because each different piece of functionality is contained within its own component, we can make anything shoot, spin, patrol, or kill the player on touch. And since we aren't limited in how many components we can add to a single GameObject, we can make a fireball-shooter that spins in a circle by attaching both the Shooting and Spinning components to a single GameObject. We can attach a blade to its opposite side which acts as a hazard. We can make a patrolling spike ball that shoots fireballs in front of it.

You get the point. As long as each piece of functionality is part of its own script component, we can simply throw any combination of script components onto one GameObject to fuse all the different things we coded onto that object.

This is one of the major advantages of Unity's component system. It provides a system where we can mix different features however we please.

Adding GameObjects

Let's start getting familiar with using Unity to create and manipulate some GameObjects. We won't be making character models, spaceships, guns, or anything fancy like that from within the Unity engine. Unity is not a modeling package (to create 3D objects) or an image editor (to create 2D objects). It's a game engine; you make the models and animate them in other software, and then you import them into Unity by simply putting them into your project folder, where Unity makes sense of them and lets you drag and drop them into your scenes.

For the sake of learning the engine and learning to program, we won't be messing around with fancy art. However, Unity can create GameObjects of basic shapes for us on the fly with just a few button presses.

Just beneath the top of the Unity editor (the title bar), you'll see a bar with a selection of different buttons: File, Edit, Assets, GameObject, Component, Services, Window, and Help. These can be clicked to drop down a menu with further options.

The GameObject drop-down menu can be used to create simple, frequently used GameObjects: basic 3D shapes, cameras, lights, and so on.

Using this menu, we can create a cube through GameObject ➤ 3D Object ➤ Cube, as shown in Figure 2-4. Alternatively, you can also right-click anywhere in the Hierarchy, but not on the name of an existing GameObject, and use the context menu to select 3D Object ➤ Cube.

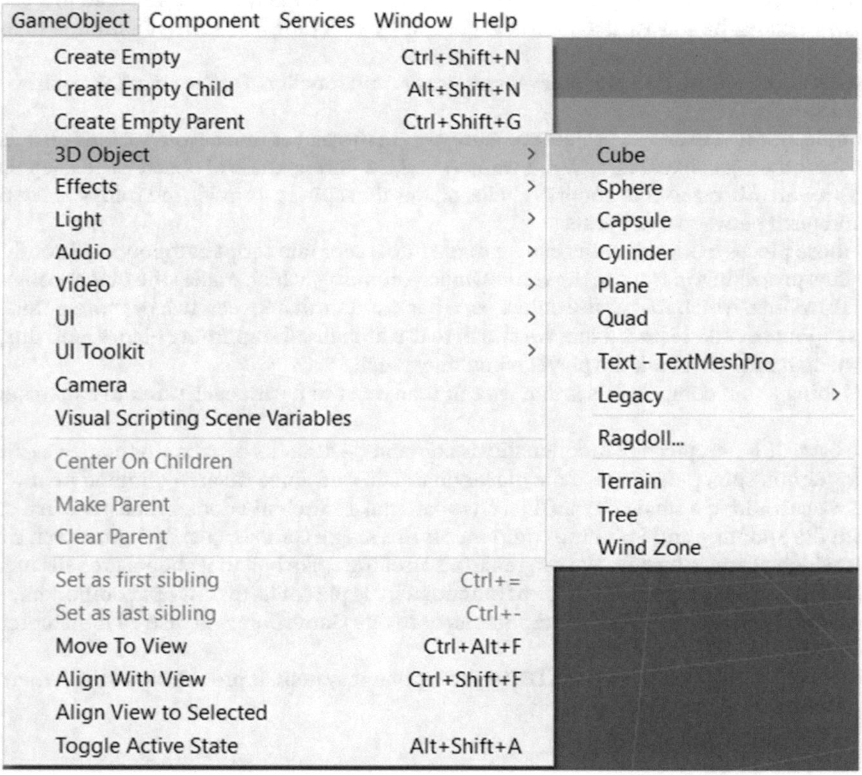

Figure 2-4. *Creating a Cube using the GameObject menu*

After doing either of these things, you'll notice a Cube will be added to our Hierarchy and will show up in the scene if your camera is pointing at it.

If you can't see it in the scene, your view is probably out of whack. You can easily navigate your view to a GameObject in the current scene by clicking the object in the Hierarchy window to select it, then putting your mouse over the Scene window so it has focus, and then pressing the F key. This is a handy shortcut that moves your view over to the selected objects so you can see them. If you ever move so far away from your objects in the Scene window that you get lost, just use this.

To expand on our talk about components earlier, let's check what components are present in this cube we just made. Making sure the cube is selected, look at your Inspector window.

The topmost component will always be a **Transform**. Every GameObject has a Transform component. A Transform is a position, size, and rotation. It's essential to a GameObject. You can remove components on the fly with code, but you can't remove a Transform. You have to delete the whole GameObject if you want to destroy its Transform component. Every object that exists in your scene must have a position, right? It has to *be somewhere*.

Aside from the Transform, you'll notice a few other components. There's a Mesh Filter and a Mesh Renderer.

The word **mesh** is pretty much synonymous with "3D model" as far as we're concerned. It's an asset that defines the surfaces that make up a 3D model. Again, we won't be making our own meshes – we'll be using the default shapes provided by Unity, like cubes, capsules, spheres, and cylinders. **Render** is just a fancier-sounding word for drawing or displaying something on the screen.

So a Mesh Renderer is a component that allows a 3D model to be drawn, although the drawing of it is done by a Camera component.

The Mesh Filter is a component that holds the mesh you want to pass to the Mesh Renderer. Pretty much whenever you see a Mesh Renderer, you'll see a Mesh Filter as well, because the Filter tells the Renderer what to render.

You'll notice a little check mark beside the Mesh Renderer component in the Inspector. Components like this can be enabled and disabled by clicking this check mark. Just in case you don't believe that the Renderer component is actually drawing the cube to the scene, try clicking that check mark to uncheck it. You'll notice that the cube stops rendering to the screen in the Scene window. Check it again, and it'll pop back up.

Summary

In this chapter, we learned the following:

- The Unity editor is made up of various **windows** that serve unique purposes. Any window can be rearranged and resized by clicking and dragging the tab at its left-top corner.

- An **asset** is a file for use in our game, such as art, audio, or code. These are viewed in the **Project window**, and often we'll incorporate them into our game by simply dragging and dropping from that window.

- A **scene** is an **asset** that resembles a game environment, like an individual level. We can double-click them in the Project window to load them, allowing us to view and edit them in the **Scene window**.

- A **GameObject** is an object that exists in the scene. Their functionality is driven by **components** that we attach to them. Unity provides many built-in components for fundamental things like displaying a 3D model, casting light, providing physics and collisions, and so on.

- The components attached to an individual GameObject are viewed in the **Inspector window**. Here, we can customize their functionality by editing fields that relate to them, such as how bright a light is. Each component is a unique instance with its own values associated with it, and these values can be customized to provide different functionality.

- Every GameObject has a **Transform**, a basic component that resembles a **location**, a **rotation**, and a **size**. Other component types can be added and removed on the fly through code, but the Transform cannot – there can only be one per GameObject and it cannot be deleted.

CHAPTER 3

■ ■ ■

Manipulating the Scene

We've learned the basics of the most important windows in the Unity engine, and we know how to create simple objects and view their components through the Inspector. Now let's get familiar with moving, rotating, and sizing GameObjects in our scene.

Transform Tools

We learned in the last chapter that a Transform is the component type that all GameObjects have, which provides them with a position in the world, a scale (size), and a rotation. The **Transform tools** in our Scene window allow us to interact with the Transforms of selected GameObjects.

The Transform tools are docked at the top-left corner of the Scene window by default, although you can drag the two lines at their top to move them around within the Scene window. Doing this, you can also drag and drop them under the Scene tab to lock them in place with the other buttons at the top of the window, as shown in Figure 3-1.

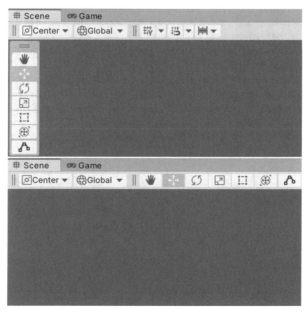

Figure 3-1. *The Transform tools popped out into the Scene window (top) and locked in under the window tab (bottom)*

© Casey Hardman 2024
C. Hardman, *Game Programming with Unity and C#*, https://doi.org/10.1007/978-1-4842-9720-9_3

There are six buttons for six different kinds of Transform tools, and depending upon what GameObject you have selected, you may also see a seventh button for custom editor tools – but we don't need to concern ourselves with that right now. If you don't see a seventh button, don't worry about it.

Each of these buttons can be clicked to switch to a different tool. Only one tool is ever active at a time, and they all serve different purposes.

From top to bottom (or left to right), you can use the hotkeys Q, W, E, R, T, and Y to toggle between these tools.

The first tool, with the hotkey **Q**, is the **hand tool**, which lets you left-click and drag on the screen in the Scene view to drag your scene camera around. It doesn't edit the scene. It just helps you navigate it. Clicking and holding the middle mouse button while dragging will automatically employ the hand tool, if you'd rather use it that way.

The other tools will allow you to edit the GameObjects you are selecting. In the Scene window, the transform tool you have selected will provide little "gizmos" on or around your selected GameObjects. These gizmos are simple tools that we click and drag to use the Transform tool to interact with the GameObject. You will notice, if you select a GameObject and toggle between these tools, that the gizmo drawn around the object changes as the selected tool changes.

W is the **position tool**. While active, it shows arrow gizmos on your selected GameObject. You can drag the object in specific directions by clicking and dragging the arrows. You can also drag it along two directions at once by clicking the square shapes between arrows.

E is the **rotation tool**. It shows circle gizmos on the selected GameObject. Clicking and dragging the circles will spin the object, and each circle turns it along different directions. You can also click in the middle of the gizmo, between the circles, to turn the object in multiple directions at once. Clicking the outer, gray circle will spin the object relative to your camera.

R is the **scale tool**. It shows gizmos like the arrows, but with cube-shaped ends. Click and drag these boxy arrows to change an object's width (red), length (blue), or height (green). Click the cube in the center of the gizmo and drag to scale the entire object at once – that is, raising or lowering the width, height, and length evenly at once.

T is the rect tool ("rect" being short for "rectangle"). It is most applicable to 2D projects, but can have its uses in 3D as well. The gizmo shows a rectangle around the selected object, with circles at the corners. The edges or corners can be clicked and dragged to expand or shrink the object as a rectangle, affecting both the position and scale at once. This can be useful to make an object larger or smaller on one side only, since the scale tool will affect the scale on both sides.

There's also a circle at the center of the gizmo which can be clicked and dragged to reposition the object along the two directions that the rectangle is aligned with. You'll notice that the rectangle gizmo operates on two directions at any time. Attempting to move your camera over to the side of the rectangle will cause it to flip around and face the camera again.

The **Y tool** combines the W, E, and R tools, showing the arrows for moving, the circles for rotating, and the cube at the center for scaling, all at once.

Positions and Axes

So how does positioning work in 3D space? It might take a little getting used to, but a position in 3D space is defined by three number values, referred to as X, Y, and Z.

The **X** position is **right and left**.

The **Y** position is **up and down**.

The **Z** position is **forward and back**.

These positions are often written as (X, Y, Z). For example, (15, 20, 25) would be an X value of 15, a Y value of 20, and a Z value of 25.

If you have a position of (0, 0, 0), you are at the "world origin," so to speak – the center of the universe, or at least the center of the scene.

Add 5 to your X position, and you've moved 5 units to the right.

Subtract 5 from your X position, and you've moved 5 units to the left.

It works similarly for the Y and Z values: adding moves in one direction, subtracting moves in the opposite.

Adding to the Y will take you up, and decreasing it will take you down.

Adding to the Z will take you forward, and decreasing it will take you backward.

It is the combination of these three values which defines where something is in the world. Each of these is called an axis (plural "axes"). So you might hear people say "the X axis" or "the Y axis" or "the X and Z axes."

The scale and rotation work in much the same way: they have the same three axes, each one determining a different direction.

The **X scale** is the **width** – left and right.

The **Y scale** is the **height** – up and down.

The **Z scale** is the **length** – forward and back.

I'm sure you can imagine how rotation works pretty much the same way. The object's orientation is defined by three angle values between 0 and 360, which determine how it is turned on each axis.

You'll notice that the gizmos of the Transform tools that we use to position, rotate, and scale objects (W, E, and R, respectively) are all color-coded.

The X axis is always red, the Y axis is always green, and the Z axis is always blue.

This is pretty much universally accepted. Get into making 3D models, and you'll see the same thing – although some programs consider the Y axis to be forward and back and the Z axis to be up and down, which is opposite to how Unity does it.

Making a Floor

Let's use what we've learned to make some cubes, position them, and scale them. But first, let's make a floor.

Create a Plane, using the same method we made the cube in the last chapter: GameObject ➤ 3D Object ➤ Plane.

A plane is like one surface of a cube – a paper-thin, flat surface that has no thickness. They're one-sided: you can't see them at all if you look at them from the backside. Try navigating your camera beneath the plane and looking up at it. You won't see anything, as if it never existed. Still, it'll serve fine for our floor, because we don't expect to be looking at it from below.

Because we know exactly where we want our floor to be, we can set it up using the Inspector. With the new Plane selected, look to its Transform component in the Inspector.

As stated before, the Transform has a position (where it is), rotation (how it's turned about), and scale (how large it is).

Remember, the Inspector's primary purpose is to interact with components, not just to view their data: it exposes the actual values of the position, rotation, and scale of the Transform to us. We can edit the individual axes to our liking, simply by clicking these fields and typing in the numbers we want.

This is a useful way to set things up if you know exactly how you want to set them up, because getting precise values for positions and rotations using the Transform tools can be very tedious. We want our plane to be at the world origin (the center of the scene), so use the Inspector to change its position to 0 on all three axes, if it isn't already. As for the rotation, it should be (0, 0, 0) already, so leave it as is.

Scale and Unit Measurements

Now for the scale. "What is a unit of space?" you might be asking. What does it actually mean when we change a GameObject's position from 0 to 1? How much space is that?

This is a slightly confusing concept for some. You probably expect a straight answer. The Unity developers decided what it is, right? It's a foot, or maybe a meter – perhaps a yard.

But that's not how it works. Don't worry, though. It's still quite simple: we must decide what a unit is ourselves. Let's say we decide that 1 unit is 1 foot. So be it. As long as we follow this in every measurement we make, then that's what 1 unit means. We make our people between 5 and 6 units tall, roughly. If we want something to be just one inch, we make it a twelfth of a unit (roughly 0.083). If we want something to be a yard, we make it 3 units.

But one more thing we need to note about the scale of a Transform is that the scale is not "how many units wide, long, and tall something is." It's actually a **multiplier**. It multiplies the size of the mesh (the 3D model).

The mesh itself has its own size, and then the scale value of the Transform just multiplies that size.

This is fine for a cube. The cube mesh is 1 unit wide, tall, and long. So if we set its scale to 5, it's going to be 5 times 1 on each axis, so it's still just 5 units large.

But a plane is trickier. The mesh itself is 10 units wide and long (and it's paper-thin, so it really has no height). So when we have a scale of (1, 1, 1) with a plane mesh, it's actually 10 units wide and long already.

You can see this if you create a Plane and a Cube, leave the scale of each one at the default value of (1, 1, 1), and position them both in the same place. Note how much larger the Plane is than the Cube, as shown in Figure 3-2.

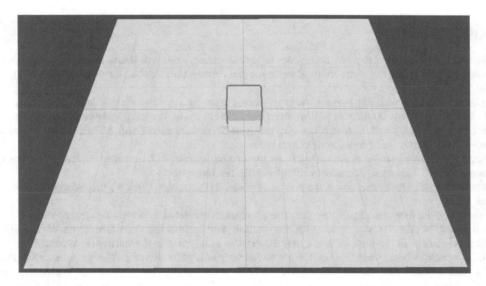

Figure 3-2. *A Plane and a Cube, both with scale (1, 1, 1) and positioned in the exact same spot*

This is because the size of their actual meshes is not the same. Even if their scale is the same, the cube mesh is 1 unit wide and long, while the plane is 10 units wide and long. Since their scale is just a multiplier of the mesh size, not a depiction of the actual size of the object, the scale of (1, 1, 1) is not affecting the mesh size at all. It's multiplying by 1, so of course, it's leaving them as is.

Now, if we change that cube to have a scale value of (10, 1, 1), it will become 10 units wide, which matches the plane exactly, as shown in Figure 3-3.

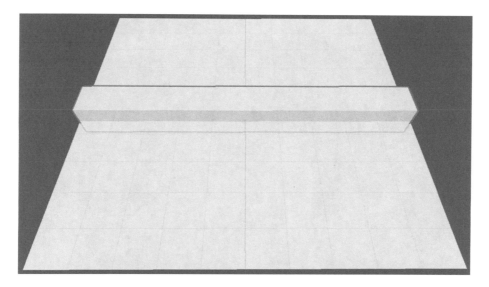

Figure 3-3. *A Plane with scale (1, 1, 1) at the same position as a cube with scale (10, 1, 1). The cube is exactly as wide as the plane*

To sum it up, just remember this: the mesh has its own size, and the scale is merely a **multiplier** for the mesh size. It is **not** a flat value depicting "how big the mesh is."

All that aside, let's press on and finish setting up our floor. We want a large floor so we don't have to worry about making it bigger every time we want to put some more stuff on it. Let's set its scale to 10 on the X and Z axes – which, mind you, is actually 100 units wide and 100 units long. Of course, it'll be easier to just set the X and Z scale values to 10 in the Inspector rather than using the scaling tool.

Summary

In this chapter, we learned the following:

- How to manipulate the position, rotation, and scale of GameObjects using the transform tools (hotkeys W, E, and R).

- Positions are resembled as an X, Y, and Z value. Adding to a value moves in one direction, while subtracting from it moves in the opposite direction. X is right (positive) and left (negative), Y is up (positive) and down (negative), and Z is forward (positive) and back (negative). By combining all three values, we can define a 3D point in space.

- Scale is a multiplier for the size of the actual mesh that the GameObject is rendering. It's not the number of units wide, tall, and long a GameObject is. Rather, the X, Y, and Z scale of the Transform multiplies the size of the mesh that's being rendered.

- A single unit doesn't correspond to a particular number of feet or inches or meters by default in Unity. We have to decide what a unit means ourselves, and as long as we stay consistent with that decision, our objects will end up properly sized in proportion to each other.

CHAPTER 4

Parents and Their Children

Now that we have our floor set up, let's dive into some very important concepts employed by game engines. Unity allows us to attach individual GameObjects to each other in a system known as "parenting," where "children" are attached to a "parent" GameObject and thus move, rotate, and scale with it. This creates a distinction between two ways of looking at an object's position: its **world position**, which resembles where it is in the scene, and its **local position**, which resembles where it is in relation to its parent. This also gives us an option to define parents and children in a way that lets us set up **pivot points** to change the point around which objects rotate.

Child GameObjects

There's a reason why the Hierarchy window is called a hierarchy. We haven't exhibited that reason yet, but we're about to.

A GameObject is capable of storing any number of other GameObjects "inside it." This system is called **parenting**: one GameObject may be the **parent** of many others, and those GameObjects stored inside it would be called its **children**.

Technically, Unity looks at this as the Transform components being attached to each other, because that's where the actual relevance of the concept is seen. Making one GameObject the child of another is like physically attaching it to its parent. Because the Transform deals with the physical position, rotation, and size of an object, this essentially means attaching the Transforms to each other.

When the parent Transform moves, its children move with it. When the parent rotates, the children pivot as if they were attached to the parent, even if there are miles of open air between them. When the parent becomes smaller or larger, the children follow suit proportionately.

Let's play with this concept so you can see it in action.

Create two cubes and position them anywhere apart from each other. It doesn't really matter where, as long as they aren't directly on top of each other – they can touch or overlap if you want. Use the position transform tool (hotkey W) to do this.

Now, scale one cube up a little. You can do so in the Inspector by setting its scale to something like 1.5 on all axes, or simply puff it up a little with the scale transform tool (hotkey R). When you're done, it should look something like Figure 4-1.

© Casey Hardman 2024
C. Hardman, *Game Programming with Unity and C#*, https://doi.org/10.1007/978-1-4842-9720-9_4

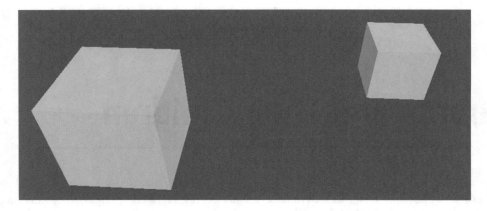

Figure 4-1. *A cube with (1.5, 1.5, 1.5) scale (left) and a second, unchanged cube positioned off to its side (right)*

That larger cube will be our parent. Select it to see which cube it is in the Hierarchy (it will be highlighted, since it is selected). Using the Inspector, change its name to "Parent" so it's easy to recognize.

Now, click the other cube in the Hierarchy to select it. Then, click and drag this cube in the Hierarchy, and drop it over the "Parent" cube.

Once you've dropped it, the Hierarchy begins to look like a hierarchy for the first time. The dragged cube is now a child of the "Parent" cube and is now "inside" its parent in the Hierarchy. This is shown by its indention: the children will be offset to the right a little further than their parent GameObject. In Figure 4-2, you can see our Parent cube, a Cube child inside it, and another GameObject beneath which is not a child. Notice that the "Cube" child is pushed to the right side a little bit, denoting that it is a child of "Parent."

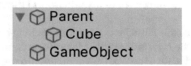

Figure 4-2. *View of our two cubes in the Hierarchy window. The "Cube" GameObject is a child of the "Parent" GameObject. The third GameObject is not a child, as seen by its indention*

You'll also notice that the parent now has a little arrow icon on its left side, which can be clicked to hide or show its child GameObjects in the Hierarchy. This can be useful to tuck away a complicated hierarchy of GameObjects that's cluttering your view.

Now that the cube is a child of the parent, any Transform changes we make to the parent will affect the child cube. The opposite is not true – the child can be moved, rotated, or scaled without any changes applying to the parent, but any movement, rotation, or scaling you apply to the parent will always affect the child as well.

Try it yourself. Select the Parent cube, go to the Scene view, and use the Transform tools (W, E, and R) to move, rotate, and scale the cube. If your transform tool gizmos are showing between both cubes, this is because the Tool Handle Position setting is set to "Center." Press Z to set it to Pivot instead, which should make the gizmos be centered on the Parent cube.

When moving and rotating the parent, the child will move with it and pivot around it, as if some invisible bar is attaching them to each other. When scaling the parent, the child will scale as well – they will both grow larger or smaller, and the distance between them is kept the same proportionally to their new size.

We aren't limited to a simple parent-child relationship. We can have grandchildren, great-grandchildren, and so on – as many layers as we want. We could add another cube and make it a child of the child cube – which would make it a grandchild of the cube we named "Parent." Then, moving the Parent cube would move its child, and as a result, it would also move the grandchild.

If you ever want to "unparent" a child (make it no longer have a parent), you can do so in the Hierarchy window by clicking and dragging the child above or beneath the parent object. Note that while you're dragging a GameObject around in the Hierarchy, any other GameObject that you pass your mouse cursor over will be highlighted in light blue. This means you'll be assigning the dragged object (the one you're "picking up") as a child to that highlighted object. If there is no object directly under your cursor, you'll instead get a blue line with a circle at its left side. This is how you move the object around in the hierarchy: you can unparent it, place it among the children of another parent, or just move its place among the other children for organizational purposes.

Pay attention to the left side of the line: that circle will indent further to the right when placing a GameObject within the children of another. This behavior can be a lot easier to observe when you have more complicated hierarchies of GameObjects, with multiple levels of children. For our purposes, you can pretty much just drag an object into the empty space below the others and release to make it have no parent.

World vs. Local Coordinates

Let's learn the distinction between world coordinates and local coordinates. The position of an object that has a parent can be depicted in two ways:

- Its **world position** is its **absolute position in the scene**.

- Its **local position** is its **position relative to its parent**.

When an object has no parent, the Inspector will show us its world position. Once we give it a parent, the Inspector will instead show us its local position.

A position of (5, 0, 0) in world coordinates is "5 units to the right of the center of the world."

But in local coordinates, that same position instead means "5 units to the right side of the parent object." And that corresponds to the parent's rotation: notice that I wrote "to the right side of the parent," not "to the right." Rotate the parent, and the local position of the child doesn't change. Adding 1 point to the X axis doesn't move the object 1 unit "to the right" in world space – it moves the object 1 unit to the right of the parent object.

This is why even a direction can use local coordinates instead of world coordinates. If you're shooting out a projectile from the player character in a game where the player is rotating around, such as pointing their character with their mouse, then you would use the player character's local forward direction, not the world forward direction.

A good way to look at it is that the world directions are something like directions on a compass. You could consider world forward to be north (positive along the Z axis), world backward to be south (negative along the Z axis), world right to be east (positive along the X axis), and world left to be west (negative along the X axis). A projectile that's coming out of a gun, or the flaming hands of a magician, shouldn't just "go north," right? It should go forward along the local direction that the gun or the hands are pointing.

Another complication of local positions is that they're affected by the scale of the parent. So if the parent doesn't have (1, 1, 1) for its scale, then adding 1 unit isn't actually adding 1 unit, so to speak. The **local position** is **multiplied by the scale of the parent**. For example, if your parent has an X scale of 2, then adding 1 unit to the X is really adding 2 units in world space.

A Simple Building

Let's use cubes to assemble a shape similar to a building – picture a blocky skyscraper, with no detail on the outside whatsoever, just flat surfaces. We'll learn a little about how to position objects when creating them, and we'll practice the concepts of parenting while we're at it.

Our building is going to be made of three cubes. The bottom one will be the base – thicker and shorter. The middle and top will each be thinner and taller than the last. We'll center the cubes so they all have the same X and Z positions (forward/back and right/left) but raise and lower them so that they make a sort of tower, almost like a stack of blocks. In the end, it will look something like Figure 4-3.

Figure 4-3. *A look at our Skyscraper GameObject*

First, before you embark upon this quest, make sure you're not lost in some awkward orientation within the Scene view. You can use the little gizmo in the top-right corner to see how your camera is rotated, almost like a compass (shown in Figure 4-4). The arrows are color-coded by axis, as we mentioned before. If you'll recall

- The **X axis** is **red**, and it corresponds to **right** and **left**. Increase the X to go right. Decrease the X to go left.

- The **Y axis** is **green**, and it corresponds to **up** and **down**. Increase the Y to go up. Decrease the Y to go down.

- The **Z axis** is **blue**, and it corresponds to **forward** and **back**. Increase the Z to go forward. Decrease the Z to go back.

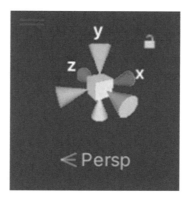

Figure 4-4. Gizmo in the top-right corner of the Scene window. The axis that the arrow corresponds to is written beside it, and each arrow is color-coded by axis

The colored arrows, with the axis letter written beside them, all point along the positive direction of their axis. The gray arrows point in the opposite direction, which is the negative direction of the axis. In other words, the colored arrows point to the actual world direction of right, up, and forward. So the green arrow, corresponding to the Y axis, is always pointing up. This means if that arrow is pointing down for you, then your camera is upside down. The gizmo is telling you where "up" really is. If it's not already, realign your camera by holding right-click while moving the mouse until you have the green Y arrow pointing up, as it is in Figure 4-4.

Now create a cube. Make sure it's selected and change its name to Cube Base at the top of the Inspector. We'll make it thick, but short. Using the Inspector, set its Transform scale to something like (10, 4, 10). That's 10 on the X and Z axes, but only 4 on the Y axis (height).

There are several ways to ensure that one object is aligned with another when you create it. Every object you create is placed at some certain spot in front of the camera. If you create another cube without ever moving your camera since you made the first one, they'll both be in the same spot.

If you ever use the shortcut that we described earlier to center your camera on a selected object, which is done by pressing F, you've also positioned your camera such that any new object created will have the same position as the object you've focused on. It puts the camera in a place where the objects you create will go exactly on top of that focused object.

So if you've moved the camera since creating your Cube Base, you can simply make sure it's selected and then press F while your mouse is over the Scene window. This will put focus on the Cube Base, moving the camera to look at it. Any new objects you create will be placed in the same position of the Cube Base, so create another cube now, and it should be in the same spot. You can also simply copy-paste the values from the Cube Base position to that of the new cube using the Inspector.

But all of these objects are meant to be attached to each other, so we know we're going to use parenting anyway. It makes sense that the upper cubes would be attached to the lower cubes, right? So when you create your new cube, name it Cube Middle and make it a child of the Cube Base. This makes it even easier to see if they're aligned correctly, since the Inspector will now be showing us the local position of Cube Middle. If they're in the same spot, Cube Middle will have a position of (0, 0, 0).

We want to make sure it's centered on the X and Z, so if the X and Z position values of Cube Middle are not 0 already, set them to 0. Now you can simply use the position and scale Transform tools (W for position and R for scale) to move the Cube Middle up above the Cube Base and scale it up until it's a good size, if you want to go by eye.

Do the same thing for a third cube, named Cube Top. If you want, you can copy-paste Cube Middle (Ctrl+C, Ctrl+V) and then rename it, so that it starts right at the same position, or start fresh with a new cube and set its local position to (0, 0, 0) to center it again. Make it a child of Cube Middle, not Cube Base, because the Cube Top is technically attached to the middle cube – that is to say, if we wanted to just rotate or move the middle cube, we would expect the top cube to rotate or move with it.

You can once again scale and position the Cube Top, just as you did for the others. Leave its local X and Z positions at 0 so it's centered, and raise it so its bottom rests on the top of the cube beneath it.

Now you have the Cube Base, which is the parent of Cube Middle, which in turn is the parent of Cube Top. You can make those upper cubes look however you like. It isn't really important. If you want them to look just like our version of the Skyscraper in Figure 4-3, set their **world scale** to

- (10, 4, 10) for Cube Base
- (5, 6, 5) for Cube Middle
- (2, 5, 2) for Cube Top

Note that I say **world scale**. Like the position, the scale can also be portrayed either as local or world. The local scale is relative to the scale of the parent. The X, Y, and Z values of the child are multiplied by the corresponding X, Y, and Z values of the parent. This can make it a bit harder to work with, since you have to do some extra math to figure out exactly how many units the scale actually comes out to.

Instead of doing that math, you can just unparent the cubes so they go back to using world scale, set the scale, and then parent them again. You'll notice when you parent or unparent a cube, its scale values will change, although its size doesn't appear to be any different. Like with the position, that's just the scale going from world to local (or vice versa). They still represent the same physical size; it's just a matter of whether it's relative to the parent or not.

Pivot Points

With our cubes all put together, let's demonstrate another important concept when it comes to hierarchies of objects. A pivot point is the point around which an object will pivot when it is rotated.

Select your Cube Base and switch to the position Transform tool (hotkey W). As I mentioned before, the Transform tool handle position can be toggled between "Center" and "Pivot" by pressing Z. There's also a button you can press under the Scene window tab, which will either say "Center" or "Pivot."

Center means the gizmos will draw at a point between the object and all its children. **Pivot** instead draws the gizmos at the pivot point of the selected object.

This doesn't just affect the drawing, though: it also affects how Transform tools like rotation and scaling work. If you select a parent object and use the Center mode to rotate it, the parent and its children all rotate around a point centered evenly between them. If you use Pivot, they all rotate around their parent.

For a cube, the pivot point is at the center. This means if we rotate it, it rotates around its center.

The pivot point is also the point on the object that will be positioned at the exact point that the Transform position is set to. So if the cube is positioned at (5, 5, 5), then that means the center of the cube is at (5, 5, 5), not one of its sides, not its bottom or its top. This can be a pretty important detail to know when positioning objects.

Every mesh (3D model) has a pivot point. For these simple shape meshes that Unity provides us, like cubes, spheres, planes, or cylinders, it's always the center. But at some point, you might use meshes you find on the Internet or meshes designed by artists you're working with or even meshes you made yourself. If the pivot point is somewhere weird, it's usually pretty obvious once you get to using the mesh.

For example, let's say your artist provides you with a mesh to use for a gun that your player character is supposed to hold in their hand. You make a GameObject for the gun, and your code positions the gun at the position of the player character's hand. But the gun isn't showing up in the player character's hand. It's somewhere off to the side.

This is a pivot point problem. Remember, the object's pivot point is the point of the mesh that actually goes where the object is positioned. If you're going to position the gun at the player's hand, then the pivot point should be at the handle of the gun. That way, wherever we position the object, that's where the handle is – not the barrel or some random sliver of air two feet away.

Lucky for us, we aren't dealing with anything but the basic shape meshes, so everything should be pretty predictable. Still, there will be times where we'll want to adjust a pivot point for an object ourselves – and it's not hard to do this.

Let's say, in our game, we had buildings like this skyscraper that we just made, and we wanted to let the player purchase and place these buildings wherever they liked on the playing field. Our skyscraper is going to have a pivot point at the center of its base cube (the biggest cube on the bottom, which is the parent of all the rest).

This pivot point becomes a problem for us, because we can't just use the surface position of the floor to place our building there – we'd only be placing the center of the bottom cube on the floor, which would cause half of it to clip through the floor, sticking out beneath it and not showing on the camera. We would have to always position them upward by half the height of their base cube to get them neatly placed on top of the floor. But if we have different buildings, each with a different height for its base cube, this becomes a hassle to code.

We want its pivot point to be at the center on the X and Z axes, but at the very bottom on the Y axis, so that when we say "place the building at this point on the floor," the bottom of the building is at that point. This way, no part of the building ends up sticking through the floor.

This is a simple fix. We can make an "empty GameObject." This is a GameObject with no components except for the Transform – nothing but a point in space, with a scale and rotation. Of course, we could add components to it afterward, but we don't need any in this case.

Create an empty GameObject with GameObject ➤ Create Empty or Ctrl+Shift+N. Name it something accurate: Skyscraper. It's the root GameObject of the building hierarchy – that means the master parent, the GameObject that holds all the rest. When we move it, we move the whole building. So it makes sense to name it what its children make up: a skyscraper (albeit a simple one). Accurate names are a good practice to get used to!

Now we just position it where we want the pivot point to be and then simply make this empty GameObject be the parent of the Cube Base. I'll show you a trick to position it correctly.

Remember how I said that local positions are based on the scale of their parent? If the Skyscraper has a parent that has, say, 10 scale on the Y axis, then each point in the Skyscraper's Y position will count for 10 units. It's multiplied by the scale of the parent. We can use fractions too, so 0.5 would count for half the Y scale, 0.25 would count for a quarter of it, and so on.

We can use this to our advantage. For now, make the Skyscraper empty GameObject be a child of the Cube Base. Now the Skyscraper is using local positioning, meaning its position is relative to the Cube Base.

Going by what we just discussed, this means that a single point in the Skyscraper's Y axis will count for the whole height of the Cube Base. We know that if we position the Skyscraper at (0, 0, 0), it's at the exact position of the cube. Since the cube's pivot point is its center, this means the Skyscraper is placed at the center of the cube. So all we need to do is "go down" by half the height to reach the bottom of the cube. To do that, since we're using local positioning, we just give it a Y position of -0.5. You'll recall from the preceding text that adding to the Y value goes up and subtracting from it goes down. That's why it must be negative, so make sure you put that "-" in there.

After we apply that position, the Skyscraper object should be at the exact bottom of the Cube Base, with the other axes centered on it. You can now just make the Cube Base a child of the Skyscraper object: first, unparent the Skyscraper so it has no parent at all, then drag the Cube Base onto the Skyscraper.

Now the Skyscraper is the root GameObject, as we intended, and it's positioned at the bottom of the whole building. This makes it the pivot point. When we rotate the Skyscraper object, everything is spinning around it, so it's all pivoting at the bottom, not the center of the bottom cube as it would before. And now if we position a Skyscraper at some point on the floor, the bottom of the building will go there, just as we would like it. We'll be demonstrating another reason for that to come in handy in the next chapter.

Of course, you could just position the pivot point by eye with the Transform tools in the Scene window and save yourself some trouble messing with the numbers and the parenting and unparenting. You won't get it right on the dot that way, but a little inaccuracy is unlikely to affect you in this situation – but there may be times where complete accuracy is important, so it's nice to know you have things exactly as they should be.

Summary

In this chapter, we learned the following:

- GameObjects can be the **parent** of other **child** GameObjects. When the parent position, rotation, or scale changes, the children move, rotate, and scale with it as if attached to it.

- **World position** is the position of a GameObject in the scene, without any relation to other objects. **Local position** is the position of a GameObject relative to its parent. They both can be used to resemble the same position in different forms.

- The **pivot point** is the point on an object that goes exactly where the object position is set. For example, if you want to set the position of a gun to put its handle in the player's hand, you want the pivot point of the gun to be at the handle. If it's somewhere else, like the barrel of the gun, positioning the gun at the player hand position will instead place the barrel of the gun there – not the handle.

- When rotating an object, all of its children pivot around the pivot point. This can change the way an object rotates in a significant way.

- To reposition an object's pivot point, you can create a new empty GameObject, place it where you want the pivot point to be, and then make the object a child of that empty GameObject.

CHAPTER 5

⬛ ⬛ ⬛

Prefabs

A **prefab** is a type of **asset** you'll store in your project. They act something like a blueprint for objects. You set up a prefab for some kind of object in your game and then add instances of the prefab to your game, in any of your scenes. This connection to the prefab will remain across all the instances, and you can then change the prefab itself to automatically change every instance you've placed.

For example, you might make a prefab out of a certain enemy type. You place that kind of enemy throughout your game levels (scenes) possibly hundreds of times. Somewhere down the line, you want to make some change to this enemy type – make it a little bigger or give it a little more health or make it move a little slower. If you had simply copy-pasted your enemy GameObject through all your scenes, you would have to change each one individually and make sure you kept them all consistent. This can be very tedious! But since you made a prefab for the object, you can just change the prefab itself. As an asset in your project, you simply find the prefab in the Project window, edit it, and make the changes you desire. Those changes automatically reflect across all the prefab instances in all your scenes.

Making and Placing Prefabs

To create a prefab out of an existing GameObject in your scene, you can just drag that GameObject from the Hierarchy window into the Project window and drop it into a folder where you want to save the prefab asset. This creates a prefab and automatically associates that GameObject in the scene with that new prefab. In other words, the object you dragged and dropped is no longer some random, one-off object in this scene. It's now an instance of the prefab, and it now exists as an asset in your project. Even if you delete it from the scene, you can still get it back through the Project window.

We'll create a prefab out of our Skyscraper GameObject we created in the last chapter. Drag the Skyscraper GameObject from the Hierarchy and drop it in the Project. Don't just drag one of the children, though. It must be the root GameObject, named Skyscraper.

The new prefab asset will be named the same thing: Skyscraper. To place further instances of the prefab – exact copies of our Skyscraper – we can just left-click to drag and drop the prefab asset from the Project window into the Scene window. As you're dragging the prefab over the Scene, you'll notice that Unity lets you see where it's going to be placed, showing the new Skyscraper where your mouse is pointing. It will automatically be placed on the surface of other objects you're pointing at, whether they be another instance of the Skyscraper or the floor we created earlier. Once you release the left-click, the instance is officially placed in the scene.

Remember what we were learning about pivot points in the previous chapter? If we had left our pivot point in the center of the Cube Base of the Skyscraper, it would not be placed so neatly on the surface of the floor when we set down prefab instances of it. It would stick through the floor. Since the pivot point is the point that will be at the position given to the object, if we want the bottom to be on the surface that we point our mouse at (and we do), we must make that the pivot point. Good thing we did that already! Now when we place the object, it lines up correctly every time.

© Casey Hardman 2024
C. Hardman, *Game Programming with Unity and C#*, https://doi.org/10.1007/978-1-4842-9720-9_5

Editing Prefabs

Place a few extra Skyscrapers onto the floor in the scene, and let's learn to edit a prefab so we can see all our instances change when we're done.

To edit a prefab asset, just double-click it in the Project window.

This opens a sort of fake scene in Unity, where nothing exists but an instance of the prefab. Look at the Hierarchy window, and you'll see that none of your other GameObjects are there anymore, and a bar stretches across the top of the window showing the prefab name and the little blue box icon that represents a prefab GameObject. This bar has an arrow on its left side that can be clicked to bring you out of prefab editing and back to the scene you were in before.

There's also a similar bar stretching across the top of the Scene window, which lists, from left to right, the scene environments you've been in. The one you're in now will be on the rightmost side, and the path you've traveled to get there will be on its left side, as shown in Figure 5-1.

Figure 5-1. *The top of the Scene view while editing our Skyscraper prefab*

As of right now, it looks simple: Scenes on the left, which is the normal view where you're looking at the loaded scene itself, and then the Skyscraper prefab, which is where we are now, viewing just the objects that are part of the prefab. This bar becomes more notably useful when you begin having prefabs within prefabs (it sounds scary, I know) and you start opening a prefab while viewing another prefab. The bar pretty much shows you the rabbit hole you've gone down, in proper order. At any point, you can click one of the names to switch back to that environment.

Let's change our Skyscraper here in the editing environment. The Scene window will function as it normally does, so all our transform tools will work as they did before. Do something crazy to the Skyscraper, like grab the Cube Middle and drag it high above the Cube Base. By default, the prefab will save its changes shortly after you make them. If you don't like this, uncheck the "Auto Save" checkbox all the way to the right side of the scene path (shown in Figure 5-1) that we were just talking about in the Scene window. If you do that, make sure to use Ctrl+S to save your prefab whenever you make changes.

Once you've made your change and saved the prefab, navigate out of the prefab editing environment using the top bar of the Hierarchy window (click the arrow on the left side) or the scene path in the Scene window (click "Scenes" on the left side).

Now that you can see your scene again, all the Skyscrapers will have changed to reflect the prefab.

Another way to edit prefabs is to simply make some changes on an instance of the prefab in your scene. Then, to apply those changes to the prefab, just drag and drop the instance from the Hierarchy to the asset in the Project window. This makes the asset the same as your modified instance in one simple motion.

Overriding Values

Sometimes, you want a prefab instance that behaves a little differently than the blueprint dictates – such as an enemy with more speed or an enemy that holds an axe instead of a hammer.

You can make little changes like this to an instance of a prefab, and Unity will keep track of what is different across your instances. These are called **overrides**. To describe it technically, when you override something on a prefab **instance**, any change to that something on the prefab **asset** will not reflect on the overridden instance.

For example, let's say we have a prefab "Soldier" representing some enemy soldier that we've placed many instances of across all of our scenes. But we want to put down an instance that has a bit more health than the rest, a particularly strong soldier. We go into the Inspector and increase the health of this soldier instance, and we rename it to Burly Soldier so we know it's special.

But later, we decide that all of our soldiers have too much health, and we want to decrease it a little. To do this, we change the prefab asset, decreasing its health a little. This causes every instance of the prefab to reflect those changes, making them have a little less health and saving us a lot of trouble finding them all and changing the health of each one individually.

However, since we overrode the health for our Burly Soldier, his health won't change. Unity will recognize that we overrode that value and leave it alone when we change the prefab asset.

This way, overrides are preserved when the prefab asset is changed, so that any one-off differences you make are not undone the next time you edit and save your prefab.

This applies to values in the components of the GameObjects associated with the prefab – including nested (child) GameObjects. This applies as well to the Transform component, so that position, rotation, and scale can be overridden for children of the prefab root (the master parent of the prefab). Of course, the position and rotation of the prefab root itself are considered overridden at all times, since you wouldn't expect all of your instances to share a position or rotation with the asset itself. The rotation of the root does affect how new instances will be rotated by default when you first place them into your scene, though – this can be useful, but remember that after they're placed, changing the rotation of the root in the asset won't affect the rotation of the instances anymore. As I said, the root position and rotation are always overridden (their scale, however, is not).

However, since the children use local position and rotation based off the root, their position and scale won't be considered "overridden by default." We'll go over this with an example in a bit.

But component values aren't the only things that can count as overrides. Removing components, adding components, and adding extra child GameObjects all count as overrides as well. So if you delete a component from some GameObject in your prefab instance and then later update the prefab asset, the deleted component will not be added back to the instance. Unity recognizes that you made a conscious override and preserves it. The same goes for adding an extra component: it won't be removed when you edit the prefab.

Component values that have been overridden will have bold (thicker) text for their name and value. This includes the position, rotation, and scale, since a Transform is technically a component.

Let's override one of the Skyscraper instances we have in our scene. Using the position tool (hotkey W), just grab the Cube Middle of one of the Skyscrapers and pull it up or down a good bit, so it's noticeably off from the rest of the instances. You'll notice that its Y position in the Inspector will become bold, because it's now an overridden local position. It's not in the same place as it should be according to the prefab, so it is marked as an override.

Now that one of the instances is unique, try editing the prefab to move the Cube Middle someplace new. If you moved it earlier when we first started editing the prefab, just put it back to where it should be, with its bottom touching the Cube Base. It's okay if it's not exact. Save the prefab and then return to the scene.

All but one Skyscraper should reflect the changes now. Since we overrode the local Y position of the Cube Middle for one of the instances, when that value is changed in the prefab, it is ignored by this one instance. We have given it a special value, and Unity will respect that and preserve it for us.

There's an easy way to view the overrides you have applied to a prefab instance. Select the Skyscraper instance that you have overridden the Y value for. As long as you have the root selected (the one named Skyscraper, not any of the children), you'll see some extra options in the header of the Inspector (just under the field containing the name of the GameObject). The text "Prefab" will be on the left, and to its right side, you'll have buttons "Open" and "Select," as shown in Figure 5-2.

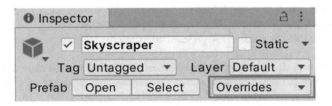

Figure 5-2. *Prefab options are listed for the Skyscraper GameObject*

"Open" will open the associated prefab asset for editing, and "Select" will select the prefab asset in the Project window (in large projects, this can be easier than fishing around for it yourself).

To the right side of these buttons is a drop-down button titled "Overrides." Clicking this button will show a hierarchy of GameObjects included in the prefab. Nested inside GameObjects, it will also show their components which have had values overridden, as well as components which have been added or removed and GameObjects which have been added.

The purpose of this list is essentially to show you all of the differences between a prefab instance and the actual prefab asset, and to allow you to **revert** those changes, which means switch back to how it is on the asset, or **apply** them, which means make the change on the asset as well, so that it's no longer an override – it's just the norm. There are also the buttons "Revert All" and "Apply All" on the bottom of the list, which, as their titles suggest, revert or apply all the overrides at once.

For the overrides of the Skyscraper we've tampered with, we should see the hierarchy showing Skyscraper, inside that (indented to the right) Cube Base, and then Cube Middle inside that; and then, inside Cube Middle, we'll see its Transform component. Clicking the individual GameObject names will show a pop-up window on the left saying "No Overrides." But clicking the Transform will cause the pop-up window to display two views of the Transform values side by side, as shown in Figure 5-3.

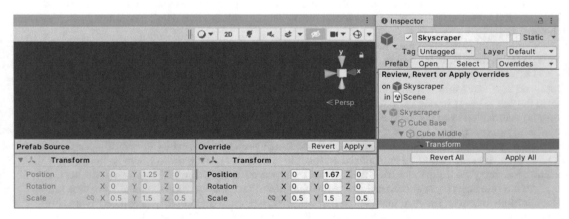

Figure 5-3. *The Overrides drop-down list, with the Transform component of Cube Middle selected. This results in the pop-up boxes stretching out on the left side*

The left side is titled "Prefab Source" and is all grayed out so we can't edit the values. It is just showing us what the values are set to on the prefab asset and does not let us make changes. The right side is titled "Override" and shows the values of the Transform component, allowing us to edit them right there if we desire. At the top-right corner of this "Override" pane, we see the buttons to revert and apply the overridden values. This is how you revert/apply for a specific component. Let's revert the change to make this Skyscraper go back to normal and stop defying the laws of physics. Just click the "Revert" button.

One final note on overrides: You can't remove a GameObject from a prefab as an override. You can add them, but you can't remove them. This is because you can't just restructure a prefab instance like this – you must **unpack** it first, which disassociates it with the prefab altogether so that it's just a bunch of normal GameObjects. This is done by an option available when right-clicking the GameObject in the Hierarchy. Or you can edit the prefab asset and delete the GameObjects, but of course, this applies to all instances. But neither of these is a satisfactory solution. Instead, to effectively remove a GameObject for a single instance, you can **disable** it with the checkbox on the left side of the name field in the Inspector header, which is essentially keeping the object around, but not running any of the functionality of its components: it won't be rendered, and it won't collide with things. This also disables all its children.

This is how you might do something like having a single instance of an enemy wield an axe instead of a hammer, as we mentioned at the start of this chapter. Disable the hammer GameObject that comes with the prefab by default, and then you can add a new axe GameObject as an override and position it where the hammer would normally be.

Nested Prefabs

Nested prefabs allow us to have prefab instances which are part of the hierarchy of other prefabs. Changes made to a nested prefab through its asset will automatically apply to instances of the prefab even if they are nested inside other prefabs.

For example, you might have a bunch of prefabs for different types of enemies – soldiers with male and female versions, ones with thick armor and ones with light armor, or ones which use different kinds of skills or magic. You have a variety of different weapons they'll wield – some use swords and others use spears or axes. Many of them will end up using the same weapon. So you make prefabs for the weapons and nest an instance of the weapon prefab inside each of the enemy prefabs.

This way, each enemy prefab has an instance of the weapon prefab inside it. If you ever want to change something about the weapon, you can change that weapon prefab, and all the enemies who use that weapon type will reflect the changes. If you had not used prefabs for the weapons, you'd just have separate instances of the weapon in each of the enemy prefabs, probably copy-pasting them from one to the other. Then if you wanted to make a change to a weapon, you'd have to go through each prefab that uses that weapon and change it individually.

You've probably noticed that, in the Hierarchy window, the icon to the left of the name of a GameObject is sometimes a blue cube and other times a gray cube. Perhaps you've figured it out already, but a blue cube means that a GameObject is the root of a prefab. A gray cube means it is not the root.

The color of the name also differs. Some have black text for their name and others blue. Blue text is for the GameObjects which are part of the prefab. Black text is for those which are not – they may be added as an override, but they'll still have black text because they aren't included in the prefab asset itself.

When you nest prefabs, you'll see blue cube icons as children of other blue cube icons. This helps you distinguish which pieces of a GameObject hierarchy are part of another prefab.

Aside from this, nested prefabs are pretty self-explanatory – prefabs within prefabs. But one notable difference is the applying of overrides made to nested prefabs.

The Overrides drop-down button in the Inspector will only show for the root of the prefab – not for nested prefabs. With an override applied to a nested prefab, you'll be offered two options when using the Overrides list to apply changes made to the prefab: one to apply the change as an override to the root prefab and another to apply the change to the nested prefab itself. The difference here is whether or not the nested prefab asset has the change applied to it. Either way, the change is going to affect the root prefab, since it contains an instance of the nested asset – the question is, do you want the nested prefab and all instances of it (nested or not) to have the change? Or do you just want the change to exist in the root prefab's instance of the nested prefab, as an override? This just depends on the situation, but it's an important distinction to make.

These two options will show whenever you click the Apply button when selecting an override to a nested prefab in the Overrides drop-down. Where before the Apply button would offer a drop-down list with only one option, it will now offer two: one to apply to the nested prefab itself and the other to apply as an override to the root prefab.

Prefab Variants

A prefab variant is a prefab asset that overrides another prefab called the **base**. It's like a copy which serves as a way to make a variation of an existing prefab. Values that haven't been overridden in the variant will be kept up to date with their settings in the prefab base.

For example, you might have variations of enemy types: a larger version of the same enemy that has more health but moves slower, or a version that wields a different sort of weapon. All the base functionality is kept in the base prefab – the model, the animations, and the scripts that provide it with its AI and logic. But in the variant, little changes are made on the component values, or a weapon is disabled and a different one is swapped into its place.

This is a useful way to keep prefabs working for you while still providing you some flexibility. You can have these variations with their overrides while still benefitting from the fact that any change to the base prefab will automatically take effect on the variants, unless the variant has overridden the value. If you had instead copy-pasted the base prefab to make the variants, any change that you wish to make to some common value across the prefab and all of the variants would have to be done individually for each variant, which is the main problem that prefabs seek to solve.

To create a prefab variant, right-click a prefab asset in the Project window, select Create, and then select Prefab Variant, an option which can only be clicked if you have right-clicked a prefab. This will create a new variant next to the base prefab in the Project and will allow you to type out a name for it. Alternatively, you can create a new variant by dragging a prefab instance from the Hierarchy to the Project, which will result in a prompt asking if you'd like to create a new, original Prefab or a variant of the existing prefab.

You can even create variants whose base is another variant, if you wish.

The icon for prefab variants in the Project and Hierarchy is a blue cube, like prefabs, but one side is decorated with stripes to indicate that it is a variant.

When using variants, it's important to note that they pretty much work like a prefab instance with overrides. Anything that is different on the variant is considered an override to the base. As such, you often don't want to apply any of their overrides, because their overrides apply to the base prefab, not the variant asset. The variant asset is simply a place to store your overridden version of the prefab. You'll override what you want – change values, add components, remove components, add GameObjects, or deactivate GameObjects, whatever you need – and save the variant asset. That's all. Applying overrides is not necessary.

For example, if you were to create a "Bulky" variant of your enemy type, edit it, increase its scale, and decrease its speed, and then go to the Overrides drop-down and apply all of the changes, you would end up switching the base prefab to be Bulky, and the variant would be the same as the base – which eliminates the purpose of having the variant at all.

Summary

In this chapter, we learned the following:

- A **prefab** is a GameObject that is saved as an **asset** by dragging it from the Hierarchy window and dropping it in the Project window.

- We place **instances** of the **prefab asset** by dragging the asset from the Project window into the Hierarchy or into the Scene.

- The prefab **asset** can be edited by double-clicking it in the Project window. Any changes made here will automatically occur on **all instances** of that prefab across all of your scenes.

- If you're creating a certain type of GameObject that you plan on copying and placing many instances of throughout your scenes (like an enemy or power-up), you should make a prefab for it and place instances of the prefab. You'll only have to edit the prefab once, and all of the instances will update. This can save you a lot of trouble.

- Any changes made to the values of components in a prefab **instance** are qualified as **overrides**. If the prefab **asset** makes a change to a field that the **instance** has overridden, the change will not occur on the instance. In other words, overridden values are preserved, allowing us to make one-off changes to specific instances that won't be undone the next time we edit the asset.

- A prefab **variant** is a prefab asset that copies from another prefab asset. A variant can be used to create a consistent different version of an existing prefab asset, such as an enemy with a different kind of weapon or with more health. Values which are not overridden are in control of the base prefab asset. Those which are overridden are in control of the variant asset.

PART II

■ ■ ■

Programming Fundamentals

CHAPTER 6

Programming Primer

Most people don't really know what programming is all about. They just know that "you have to be really smart to do it" and "it's complicated." This chapter will go over the basic concepts of programming to lay the foundation for beginners. If you're a more intermediate reader and you've already dabbled in writing code yourself, you can safely skip to the last topic in this chapter to learn how to prepare a script to write code in.

So what are we, as programmers, expected to do? What is programming, really? To put it simply, programming is writing code, and code is text that a computer knows how to read.

Programming Languages and Syntax

There are many different kinds of programming to serve different purposes, and one sort of code doesn't fit every situation. So we have **programming languages** for different purposes.

We're using the programming language C# (pronounced *C sharp*), because we want to code video games in Unity, and that is the programming language Unity expects and supports. If we instead wanted to code a web page like one you visit on the Internet, we would use HTML and CSS – HTML defines the layout and contents of a page, and CSS defines the appearance of a page. They're not at all like C#. Using them is a very different sort of experience, but one would still constitute it as programming.

We've taught computers how to read code written in different programming languages and to translate those languages into the effects we desire. But because the code we write is read by a computer, and computers are very technical things that cannot think for themselves, we must follow what we call a **syntax**.

Syntax is, simply put, what you write in the programming language and what the effect is. It's the set of rules that the language follows. What the computer expects to see is a very rigidly defined thing – albeit more so in some languages than others.

The computer knows only the syntax. It doesn't really know how to guess or assume what we mean to do. If we screw up the syntax even slightly, the computer will read our code, see something it doesn't expect, scratch its head, and tell us we're wrong. And we can't tell it "Come on, you know what I meant!" because it's just a computer.

Every programming language has its own syntax, its own rules for what you type and what it does. A lot of them are quite similar to each other. For example, learn C# and you can pick up Java with ease, because the languages share a lot of commonalities.

A lot of beginning programmers think very hard about what language they're going to learn. Maybe you spent a long time looking at your options before you decided on this book, because you weren't sure if you should learn C++ because it's "more respectable" or Python because it's "beginner-friendly."

But in truth, it's not such a big deal which language you start with. It's not so much about learning the right language as it is about learning how to program. Once you know how to program, learning a language pretty much boils down to learning a syntax. And syntax is just a set of rules and keywords you memorize. It's the easy part.

© Casey Hardman 2024
C. Hardman, *Game Programming with Unity and C#*, https://doi.org/10.1007/978-1-4842-9720-9_6

So the hardest part is learning the core principles of programming. It's made harder for beginners by the fact that they're also learning the syntax of a programming language for the first time, adding these technical and at times frustrating little rules they must follow. This is why a common piece of advice for budding programmers is to *pick a language and stick with it*. Avoid wasting time with hopping from one syntax to another, learning to use this keyword instead of that one, and you free yourself to learn the fundamentals of programming. Once you've got those down, the process of learning a new programming language becomes much easier: you're just learning the syntax rules and the common practices of that language.

Because the fundamental concepts are so important, we're going to spend a good chunk of time really exploring those concepts. But we're going to get our hands dirty and write code ourselves while we do it, and later in the book, we're going to start making example projects to put the fundamentals of programming into practice.

What Code Does

So, if programming is writing code, and code is a language that computers understand, what are we telling the computer to do with our code?

What we're learning is referred to as **object-oriented programming**, or **OOP**. We call it that because it's largely to do with data, and the computer looks at that data as "objects."

Objects are data, and data can store other data inside it.

That data has some kind of type. It can be a simple type, like a number, text (which is referred to as a string), or true-or-false value (which is referred to as a Boolean or, in C#, just bool). Or it can be a type that we, the programmer, created ourselves to resemble some more complicated piece of data.

When we declare a type ourselves, we give it a name – a descriptive one, depicting what that type is supposed to be. Let's say we're making a type called Person.

Inside it, we might store information that relates to a person – things that every person should have associated with them, like a first name, middle name, and last name, and a day, month, and year of birth. These are all data that go "inside" a Person, often called **fields** or **members**.

In a video game, a Person might also have a field of data for each piece of their equipment – their gloves, boots, breastplate, and helmet. And these fields are their own type of data: an Item data type, which stores its own fields for name, worth, how much defense it provides, and so on.

A large part of programming is organizing your data and working with it. As programmers, we must depict how to portray, for example, a single projectile fired by an enemy in our game. We must alter its position (which is just data stored inside it) to make it move through the air. Our game engine will help us with things like collisions, but we must determine what happens if it does collide with another object, to make it deal damage if it hits the player or simply break apart if it hits a wall. And then, when a player takes damage, we must code the logic that subtracts from their health and make them die if they've lost all their health.

All of these functionality-related things that make up the mechanics of a game rely on programming to get them done. In order to program them, you must ask a lot of questions about how they work and what sort of data you will need to make available within them. Does the projectile pierce through enemies (a bool, true or false)? How many enemies can it pierce through at most (a number)? How fast does it move? How far can it travel before dissipating on its own?

Strong vs. Weak Typing

Our programming language of choice, C#, is what we call a **strongly typed** programming language. This means that any object we refer to will always have a type, and we cannot change that type on the fly. We declare types ourselves or use built-in types that exist by default in our programming language. To create an object, we must specify the type we want to create, like a Person. The declaration of a Person will depict what members it stores: age, name, and so on. Each of these members has a type as well: "age" is a number, and "name" is a string.

This means that the type of an object is always known. It is clear what members it should have. If we attempt to refer to a member, like "name," it is clear that the member exists. If we attempt to refer to a member that doesn't exist on that type, we'll receive an error telling us that we're not doing something correctly. Similarly, if we try to assign the wrong type of data to a member, like assigning a number or bool to the "name" field of a Person, we'll get an error.

In this way, strongly typed languages police you about your data. You can't add or remove members for an object on the fly, because then it doesn't match the type anymore. You can't assign the wrong type of data to a member. Everything follows this structure, and if we ever stray from that structure, our code can't run anymore.

Some programming languages do not concern themselves with data types. They have basic types for numbers, strings, Booleans, and so on. More complicated types are just "objects." They store what's in them, and that's all you need to know. Want to make a Person? Just make an object and give it a first name, middle name, last name, and so on.

As you might expect, these languages are referred to as **weakly typed**. They are more flexible about how they handle data. You can assign new fields of data to existing objects on a whim. You can assign a different type of data to a field than what it normally stores and get away with it.

This can be an advantage or a disadvantage. Strongly typed languages are scarier. Many argue that they are harder for beginners to start with. They're not as approachable. Your computer is going to yell at you (figuratively) more often about things you will probably initially think are stupid and inconsequential. But these languages always call you out. They keep you consistent, and they catch errors before your code even runs. Before the code gets a chance to be performed, the compiler can tell you that it's incorrect, because it can see that you're trying to do something that breaks the code – for example, assigning the wrong type to a field or referencing a member that shouldn't exist in the given type.

These errors may otherwise have happened for a user in some niche situation you hadn't thought about, causing your game to glitch or crash. Strongly typed languages may seem unnecessarily strict, but they're just ensuring that everything is working as it should.

We're not going to get into the debate of whether strongly typed programming languages are better than weakly typed ones. They aren't better or worse, just different. Each one has advantages over the other. If you learn other programming languages in the future, you may run into these fundamental differences. The important takeaway is that every object has a type and the members of that type cannot be changed on the fly. This makes it important for us to carefully consider how we lay out our data.

File-Type Extensions

As I said before, code is text that a computer knows how to read. There's nothing special about it. A code file is just a text file, and the only way software like Unity can know that it's meant to be a code file is because we give it the correct **file-type extension**.

This is the text coming after the period at the end of the file name. It's a way for computers to identify what a file is meant to contain. If our scripts were meant to be mere text files, we'd have the extension ".txt". That's short for text.

Programming languages all have different file-type extensions. Usually, it's the name of the language – or, if that's too large, some crumpled-up rendition of the name of the language. For C#, it's ".cs", because the "#" symbol isn't valid in a file name.

That goes at the end of our code files so that Unity recognizes them as code files and treats them as such. Write some code, save it, name it anything you want, and then add ".cs" at the end, and you have written yourself a code file. Often, the software you're working with will add the file-type extensions for you, usually without even showing you them.

Scripts

Unity refers to our code files as **scripts**. We don't use Unity to actually write the code, but Unity will detect when the code changes.

Every time we change the code, Unity will know that the code has changed and will read it again to **compile** it.

Compiling, as far as we're concerned, is the computer making sense of our code and converting it to a machine-readable format. Luckily, we don't have to concern ourselves with this process.

All we really need to know is

- We change the code.

- Unity automatically notices the change and tries to make sense of our code again.

- If it fails because we're not following the rules properly, it tells us in the Unity window known as the **Console**.

The **Console** window lists compiler errors in our code.

Whenever something isn't right, an error is thrown at us, telling us what went wrong. Sometimes they're super useful and explicitly worded. Sometimes they're really vague. It just depends on the context.

Let's start writing code. That's the fun part, after all.

Go to your Project window. Right-click the Assets folder and click Create and then Folder. Name your new folder "Scripts." Right-click our new Scripts folder, then click Create again, and this time choose C# Script. Name it "MyScript". In this case, Unity automatically recognizes that it's meant to be a code file and will add the ".cs" at the end of the file without us knowing or seeing. We can tell that Unity recognizes the file as a script by the icon it displays to the left side of the file name in the Project window: the icon has "#" on it.

Before opening the file, ensure that Visual Studio Code is your default code editor for Unity. At the top left, click the Edit drop-down menu, then click Preferences. This will pop up a Unity window showing you some options for the engine. On the left side are categories you can click, and the settings available for the selected category will show on the right side. On the left, click External Tools. The first option in the section on the right will be "External Script Editor." It will have a drop-down button you can click. Click that and look for Visual Studio Code within the options.

If this option is not available, you'll have to click the "Browse…" option, which will open a prompt for you to search for the executable of Visual Studio Code on your computer. This will be wherever you installed it on your computer, so navigate there and select the executable for Visual Studio Code.

Now you should be able to close the Preferences window, then double-click the new script in the Project window to open it in Visual Studio Code.

Once our code editor opens the file, we'll see what's written in every Unity script by default. This is the basic code you need to sort of "inject" your code into the Unity engine – that is to say, to write code that runs at some point during the playing of our game.

We'll be learning more about that in the next chapters.

Summary

In this chapter, we learned the general concepts behind programming. It largely deals with organizing data and defining the functionality of the game. It's up to the programmer to implement the mechanics of a game, to make it all work.

- Code is just text that instructs a computer on what to do.

- Programming languages expect us to write our code in a **syntax** that determines what we write and what the effect is. If we fail to follow the syntax – even just a little typo or a missing symbol – we'll get errors.

- **Scripts** are text files containing our code. They're how we get our code into the Unity engine. We create them in the Project window and open them in our code editor.

- If our scripts have errors in them, Unity will show us these errors in the Console window. We won't be able to play the game until the errors are resolved.

CHAPTER 7

Code Blocks and Methods

We're about to go over some universal rules of code syntax to learn the structure of code files and to understand some fundamental terms and concepts.

Statements and Semicolons

The term **statement** refers to what is essentially a single instruction of code. Different sorts of statements exist to do different things.

A statement will end in a semicolon ";". This tells the computer where one statement ends and the next is to begin. Some languages don't use semicolons at all and instead allow the end of a line to signify the end of a statement. The advantage of using semicolons instead of line breaks is that we can make one statement span multiple lines, because the computer isn't reading until it hits a line break – it's reading until it hits a semicolon. So if a statement becomes large and unwieldy, we can format it however we want – that is, we can break it into multiple lines.

Certain statements expect a **code block** to come after them. In this case, you do not write a semicolon to end the statement.

Code Blocks

In programming, code follows an almost hierarchical structure, where some code "goes in" other code. Code can go inside that code too, like boxes within boxes within boxes.

We call them **code blocks**. In C#, they are resembled by a set of curly braces: "{" to begin the block and "}" to close the block. Anything between those two symbols is considered "in" that block of code.

In the default code of our new script, you'll see several code blocks (i.e., sets of curly braces) already declared. You'll also see a bunch of words and symbols you don't understand. That's fine. It'll make sense soon enough.

Again, statements which have a code block coming after them don't end in a semicolon. The start and end of their code block is like their semicolon: they end when their code block ends, so to speak. When a statement expects a code block after it, we refer to it as "**prompting a block**."

Code blocks are used to create a section of code that's associated with the statement that came before it. Often, this block of code only runs in certain situations. Note that when we say that code **runs**, that means it happens, or gets performed, or "does its thing."

© Casey Hardman 2024
C. Hardman, *Game Programming with Unity and C#*, https://doi.org/10.1007/978-1-4842-9720-9_7

The easiest way to describe it, in my opinion, is by giving some examples of statements that prompt a code block and what they do with the code inside that block. We're going to learn about these in greater detail later, but for now, they'll help you understand why code blocks are so widely used and important:

- The "if" statement will evaluate a condition, checking if it is true or false. The "if" statement prompts a code block after it. That code is the code which will only run if the condition evaluates to true.

- The "else" statement can be used after the code block of an "if" statement ends. The "else" statement itself prompts a block of code. That code will only run if the "if" condition evaluated to false. In other words, if the "if" code block did not run, the "else" statement provides a code block that should run instead.

- The "while" statement is a loop. It evaluates a condition, just like an "if", and prompts a block. It will evaluate the condition, and if it is true, it will run the code in the block; it then repeats, checking the condition again and running the code again if it is true, on and on until the condition is false (if the condition is never false, you'll get an infinite loop that will freeze Unity!).

- The "class" statement declares a data type (like the Person data type we were talking about before). Unlike the "if", "else", and "while" statements, the code inside a class isn't necessarily "run" on the spot. Rather, the code inside is just declaring fields (like "first name" or "last name") that the data type stores inside it. It's all just a declaration, the configuring of a template that we plan on using in different parts of our code, and the code block is used to wrap up all the code that belongs to that "class" statement.

As I said, we'll learn more about these types of statements later, and we'll write them ourselves to see how it's done. But for now, that should make it clear why we use code blocks: to create sections of code that either run only in some certain condition or that "belong to" a certain statement.

Comments

You'll notice some statements in the default script look like plain old English sentences. Notably, they are these statements:

```
// Start is called before the first frame update
[...]
// Update is called once per frame
```

These are known as **comments**. A comment is a line of code that doesn't run. It's a note that we write to document what some code does or why it does something. They're notes that the programmer writes to themselves or to other programmers who might also read their code. They're super useful, but easy to underestimate. You might think you don't need comments, but then four years later, you read the code you wrote and have no idea why you made certain decisions. Or you find that the comments you wrote are just fluffy nonsense that don't help you understand what's happening (which sucks because you have no one to blame but yourself).

Comments start with two forward slashes "//". It pretty much tells the computer "Don't read this, it's not for you." We can write whatever we want there, and the computer just ignores it. If we wrote comments without using the forward slashes, the computer would think it was meant to be code and would throw an error.

Two forward slashes are for single-line comments. They end as soon as the line breaks.

We can also make multiline comments. They start with "/*" and end with "*/". Everything between will be a comment, even including the line breaks, which lets you write a large comment across multiple lines without typing a new "//" for each line:

```
/*
This is a comment
that spans
multiple lines.
*/
```

Comments can also be used to temporarily disable code. For example, you can wrap a large chunk of code in a multiline comment to stop that code from running and then later come back and take out the "/*" and "*/" symbols to make the code run again. This is often referred to as "commenting out" the code. It's useful in some situations for testing or trying out a different approach. I myself (and I'm sure many others) will sometimes comment out a whole chunk of code to write it again with a different idea or approach.

That being said, it's bad practice to leave a bunch of commented-out code lingering in your code because you think you may need it one day. If you don't need it anymore, cut it out. If you aren't using it right now but may need it again one day, back it up somewhere else.

Methods

For now, we're going to skip over the first lines of code and focus on the ones within the first set of curly braces:

```
// Update is called once per frame
void Update()
{

}
```

This is a **method**. Some languages would call it a **function** instead, and a lot of people use the two terms interchangeably; but officially, it's called a method in C#.

Methods are a very important part of programming in C# and in many other languages too.

To put it simply, a method is a named block of code that can be referred to by name to run the code within, anywhere else in your code, any number of times. Running the code within is known as **calling** the method.

You can reuse a block of code by making it a method and then calling it all over the place. This prevents the need of copying and pasting the same code to multiple places in your project when you need to do the same chunk of code in many different places. This also means if you ever need to change the code within the method, you only need to change it in one place, rather than having to copy and paste the code in the many other places you repeated it.

It's important to note that declaring a method is just that: declaring one, not running one. If you write a method, but never actually call it, then it might as well not exist in your code at all, because it does nothing. It's never used.

So how is a method declared? What is this "void Update" method that Unity declares for us? Is it named "void," or is it named "Update"?

We'll go into much more detail on the "void" part down the road. For now, know that it's a special keyword that you'll learn about later.

The "Update" that comes after the "void" is the name of the method. The name is, of course, what we use to refer to the method when we want to call it. But this method is declared by default in a Unity script because the Unity engine itself will be calling the method.

As the comment says, "Update is called once per frame." In other words, Unity will constantly call Update for us, which means the code within the method is going to be running quite often. We aren't expected to call the method ourselves. We just let Unity do that for us.

■ **Note** If you're interested in game programming, you might know what a *frame* is already. It's a single calculation of the game logic run by the computer — a small bit of game time is played out each frame. Games are constantly updating: running their physics and other such game logic in a small increment and then rendering again to show those updates on the screen. These increments are the frames. You've likely heard the term *frames per second (FPS)* or *framerate* before. That's the number of frames, or updates, the game gets per second. Each one will inch the game forward in time by a small increment. If the frames per second is too low, the game may look slow or choppy — this happens when the computer is taking too long to run all the operations it needs to each frame. When the FPS is sufficiently high, it looks comfortable and smooth, so we can't tell that the whole experience is being brought to us in many tiny updates.

So let's finally write some code ourselves to make something happen when we play our game in Unity. If you skipped the last chapter, its last heading went over on how to create a script and open it in our code editor, so refer back there and come back when you're done.

The easiest way to get a result is to call a method ourselves, one that logs a message to the Console window. Just to prove that the Update method really is being called constantly, I'm going to give you a line of code to write and explain what it means after.

In your "MyScript" file, write this statement within the code block of the Update method (in other words, between the curly braces that come beneath the "void Update" line):

```
Debug.Log("Hurray!");
```

Then, save your script with Ctrl+S or by going to File ➤ Save in the top-left corner of your code editor.

Navigating to Unity, we'll get some progress windows popping up and churning away, depicting that Unity is compiling: chewing on the changes we made to our code and testing the code for errors again. If you don't see it, then it may have happened too fast for you to catch it (or you forgot to save the changes to the script in your code editor).

There's one more thing we need to do before we play our game to see the results. As we mentioned previously, Unity uses what we call **scripts** to get our code into the game, and scripts are components, so they can be attached to GameObjects. We wrote our code inside a script, of course – which is just a code file in our project. Now we have to add the script as a component to some GameObject in our scene.

This is essentially "creating an instance of our code." We can add the same script to hundreds of GameObjects in our scene, and each script will have its Update method called once per frame. Each one is a separate instance with its own data associated with it – although we haven't really declared any data for it yet.

Adding the script as a component is easy. Just left-click the script file in the Project window, and then drag and drop it onto a GameObject in the Hierarchy window, onto a GameObject in the Scene view, or into the Inspector of a selected GameObject.

If you don't have any GameObjects available, create anything, like a simple Cube or an empty GameObject, and add the script to it.

Once you select the GameObject, you'll see in the Inspector that it now has an instance of our script listed as one of its components, shown in Figure 7-1.

Figure 7-1. *An empty GameObject with a MyScript component added*

With that in place, click the Play button at the top of the screen. This will start our game within the Unity engine (although it isn't much of a game right now). Your Scene view will automatically switch to a Game view, which acts like the Scene, but shows the view from our Camera within the game, as the game runs.

While the game is running, all the scripts we have in the scene will get updated, so we'll see the message "Hurray!" being logged many, many times over in the Console window while the game is playing. Stop playing by pressing the same button again.

Isn't that exciting? You've written your first little line of code and gotten a result out of it in your engine.

Calling Methods

Now let's examine what we're actually doing with this Debug.Log call we've placed in Update.

This is simply a method call. We spoke about it before: a method is declared somewhere and assigned a name, and then other places in your code can call it by name to run the code inside it.

But what is Debug.Log? Is that the method name? Why's there a period in it?

The period is very important in programming. So to speak, a period "reaches into" an object, allowing you to access fields inside that object. So the method isn't named Debug.Log. It's named Log, but the method is a field inside an object called Debug. So we're referencing Debug and then "reaching into" it to reference the method Log.

Now you're probably wondering what Debug is. Maybe you don't know what "debug" even means. It's a term that programmers use a lot – it pretty much means "find and fix errors in code." To debug code is to figure out why something is going wrong and fix it.

But what is the Debug object? Where did it come from and what else can we grab from it? We've only briefly discussed this so far, but it's called a **class**. It's a concept we're going to get into more later. But for now, the easiest way to describe it is that the people who coded Unity wrote up this Debug object and gave it some useful methods and fields so that we, the consumers of the engine, can use them to help us debug our game. There are other useful features in there too, like the Debug.DrawLine method, which lets us draw a colored line in the world, from one point to the other. You might use that to visualize something happening in your code to confirm whether it's working how you expect.

But enough about that. We'll learn more about it later. Let's move on.

To call a method, you reference it (by typing its name, Log), and then you place a set of parentheses (). If you don't place parentheses, you're not calling the method. You're just referencing it – pointing at it, so to speak.

After the parentheses, we supply data in the form of a **string**. We spoke briefly about this in the last chapter. A string is a basic data type. It represents text. It's called a string because it's considered "a string of characters," where each character is a single symbol/letter/number.

A string is an elementary form of data that you'll use all the time in programming: names, descriptions for things like items or spells, dialog between characters in your game, and so on.

To write a string, we don't just type whatever text we want. Then the compiler would read it as code, and of course, it would throw an error when it fails to make any sense of what we wrote. We use a set of quotation marks "" to tell the compiler that we're writing a string. Anything between those quotation marks is the text that the string represents.

You can probably guess why we write this string where we do. You saw it already – it is the text that's being logged in the Console by the Debug.Log method call.

This is the functionality of what we call **parameters**. Parameters are named fields of data that we "pass" to the method when we call it. When a method is declared, it can declare parameters. Each one has a name and the data type it stores. A method can have any number of parameters, or it can simply have none. Within the method declaration – that is, the code block that the method runs when called – the parameters can be referenced to get their value and make some use of it.

In this case, the parameter is a string resembling what we want to log to the Console.

The purpose of parameters is to allow a method call to be configurable, so to speak. Each call can accomplish something a little different, without requiring different method declarations with different names.

For example, let's say you had an Enemy script, and you gave it a method called TakeDamage. This method makes the enemy take damage.

But how much damage?

That can be decided by a parameter. It would be a simple number value. Whenever you call the method, you're expected to give it the parameter. You can make them take 5 damage, 20 damage, or whatever you want, just by changing the value you give as the parameter when you call the method.

This allows the same TakeDamage method to be called all over your code, for different results, instead of you having to make different methods that deal different amounts of damage, which would be terrible in all sorts of ways.

Basic Data Types

We just learned about how the string data type was supplied as our parameter value. Let's go over the basic data types and what the purpose of each one is, since we'll be using them quite a lot.

The major basic data types you'll be working with as a C# programmer are **int**, **float**, **bool**, and **string**.

int and **float** are number values, but there's one extremely important distinction between them: float stores a number value that can have a fractional value (a decimal point), while int does not.

That is to say, an int can be 4 or 5, but it cannot be anything between – like 4.2 or 4.68. A float can be 4 or 5 or 4.2 or 4.68 or whatever else.

string is text, as we just covered. It must be surrounded with quotes "". You may use single quotes '' as well if you would rather, but it's important to note that a single symbol wrapped in single quotes, such as 'c' or '1', is considered a different data type: **char**, which is short for "character" – a single character. Remember, a string is "a string of chars," which pretty much means one or more characters arranged together – simply put, text.

bool is *true* or *false*. Those are the only two values a bool can hold. Type false or true and you've created a bool value. You might use this value type as a field representing whether or not a player character is currently alive, or an item can be sold at the shop, or an unlockable ability has been learned.

Returning Values with Methods

Sometimes, you want to call a method to get some piece of data back from the call, to use it in the code which called the method. Many methods are intended to be used this way. Every method must specify a return type, which is the data type that the method will return.

The keyword "void" is used to specify that a method returns nothing. Call it, and you get nothing back. It's used to do something, not to return something. The Debug.Log method we've been using is an example of this. Its purpose is just to log a message, so it need not return anything.

Methods can return basic data types (like int, float, string, bool, etc.) or data types declared by programmers. The Unity engine has many data types declared, and many of its built-in methods return instances of these data types. For example, a method which checks for collisions might not only return "true" if a collision was found and "false" if a collision was not found, but rather, a specific data type with information about the collision: where it occurred along the tested area and information about the object it collided with. It's data that we can then use to do whatever we're doing – such as to navigate around the collision or prevent an entity from moving to avoid causing a collision.

Declaring Methods

Now that we've learned how methods work, let's learn how to declare our own. We're going to start with simple methods that are pretty much useless, just to demonstrate the syntax used to declare methods – that is, what to type and why to type it.

A method declaration always starts with the return type, then followed by the method name and then a set of parentheses. As you've just learned, the "void" keyword specifies that a method returns nothing. Now you know the full syntax of the Start and Update methods:

```
void Start()
{

}
void Update()
{

}
```

They are really quite simple now that we've learned how methods work: just a basic method that doesn't return anything.

Let's declare a method that logs our message for us. We must write it in the same code block that the Update and Start methods are written in. Whether above, below, or between them, it doesn't matter to the compiler. However, it's common practice to keep all your built-in Unity methods (like Start and Update) down at the bottom, with your script-specific methods above:

```
void LogMyMessage()
{
    Debug.Log("Hurray!");
}
void Start()
{

}
void Update()
{

}
```

Now, we can change our Debug.Log call in the Update method and, instead, simply call the LogMyMessage method and supply no parameters. Remember, although we won't be giving any parameters, we still need an empty set of parentheses "()" to signify that we are *calling* the method, not just *referencing it* (or *"pointing at it"*):

```
void Update()
{
    LogMyMessage();
}
```

Now if you save the script and run your game, you should notice the "Hurray!" message is logged just as you would expect. Of course, we are pretty much needlessly complicating the process by doing this, but once again, this is for demonstration purposes. We'll make proper, clever use of methods later, once we've fully grasped the concept and worked with it.

Let's learn how to use parameters. As you've learned, when we supply parameters when *calling* the method, they go between the parentheses – so you can probably guess where we *declare* parameters for the method: in the parentheses after the method name, in its declaring line:

```
void LogMyMessage(/* parameters go here...*/)
```

Each parameter is declared first with its type and then its name. You can declare any number of them, but each one must be separated from the next by a comma. For example, let's say we wanted to declare that "TakeDamage" method we spoke of earlier. We want a parameter for the amount of damage dealt, and let's say we also want a parameter for the "penetration" stat of the damage. The damage is a float, because we allow damage to have a fractional value, and let's say the penetration is an int.

We would declare it like so:

```
void TakeDamage(float damage, int penetration)
```

Armed with this knowledge, you can probably figure how to declare our message-logging method with a parameter:

```
void LogMyMessage(string message)
```

We declare a parameter, using the type "string" and naming it "message."

■ **Note**   Always try to find a fitting name for your parameters. It's the message we'll be logging, so we name it "message." It could be funny to name it something like "porridge" or "heyThere," but a good name goes a long way in writing clean, readable code. In fact, proper naming can play a big part in making code that is clear enough to make writing comments for it redundant – code that, you could say, "comments itself."

So how do we use the parameter within the method code? You can probably guess – by referencing it or pointing at it, which is as simple as typing its name. Wherever we type the name of the parameter, we can imagine that the computer substitutes that name for the value stored in the parameter – which will be the string supplied whenever the method is called. We simply need to cut out that string we wrote and write the name instead. That means cut out the string quotes too – remember, if we left them, we'd just be logging the actual name of the parameter, "message," because the compiler will see the quotes and think "This is text, not a reference to a parameter."

We end up with this:

```
void LogMyMessage(string message)
{
    Debug.Log(message);
}
```

Now of course, we have produced an error. We need to give the parameter when we call the LogMyMessage method, since we cut the parameter out earlier. If you save the code now and navigate to the Unity editor, you'll see an error in the Console explaining the terrible mistake we've made – such a heinous crime, in fact, that our program falls apart and we can't even play the game anymore until we fix the error. Such is the life of a programmer.

But the fix is easy. Just change the Update method, again, and supply a string as the "message" parameter in our call to LogMyMessage:

```
void Update()
{
    LogMyMessage("Hurray for parameters!");
}
```

Operators

Wherever we are expected to supply data in our code – for example, as a parameter in a method – we can use what we call **operators** to perform equations. Operators are symbols, like a plus "+" or minus "-", which combine two data pieces and return them in some modified state. The most obvious example would be simple math equations: adding, subtracting, multiplying, or dividing numbers.

A very important operator is "=". Often called the **assignment operator**, it can be used to assign a new value to some named piece of data. For example, we can reassign the value of our parameter "message" to something else if we want to, by typing the name "message" and then using the "=" operator and then typing a new string value to assign:

```
void LogMyMessage(string message)
{
    message = "Something else.";
    Debug.Log(message);
}
```

This directly modifies the value of "message" so that when we log the message with Debug.Log, it is "Something else." instead of the value that was given in the parameter call (essentially making the parameter useless, for demonstration purposes).

Different data types can be operated on in different ways. For example, a string can't be divided, subtracted, or multiplied – but it can be added to another string with the "+" symbol, essentially gluing the left-side string to the right-side string and returning them as one. For example, we could prefix the message we were logging by typing out a string and then adding the value of "message" to it with a "+" operator:

```
void LogMyMessage(string message)
{
    Debug.Log("A message is being logged: " + message);
}
```

If we wanted, we could instead modify the "message" value to prefix it and then log it afterward, using a mix of both the "=" operator and the "+" operator. Take note that we are referencing the value of "message" while assigning a new value to "message" itself – of course, the old value is what we're getting from the reference:

```
void LogMyMessage(string message)
{
    message = "A message is being logged: " + message;
    Debug.Log(message);
}
```

The operators for common mathematics are

+	Addition
-	Subtraction
*	Multiplication
/	Division

Many operators can be used in a single equation, and we can also use sets of parentheses "()" to change the order of operators occurring. As you may already know, if no parentheses are present in an equation, division and multiplication will always happen first, from left to right; afterward, addition and subtraction will occur.

As an example, this equation

$$A + B * C$$

will naturally flow like this

$$A + (B * C)$$

because the "*" and "/" operators will always occur first, in a left-to-right order, and then the "+" and "–" operators will occur after – once again, in a left-to-right order. However, we could write a set of parentheses around "A + B" to change the order of operators:

$$(A + B) * C$$

By grouping the "A + B" portion of the equation into its own set of parentheses, we have changed it so that the "*" operates second, on the result of "A + B", instead of first, on "B" alone.

Summary

In this chapter, we've learned some extremely important fundamentals:

- **Code blocks** are represented by a set of curly braces, between which the contained code should go: { ... }

- **Comments** are ignored by the compiler, letting us write notes about our code. Two forward slashes "//" makes a single-line comment, while "/*" and "*/" make a multiline comment.

- **Methods**, also called **functions**, are named blocks of code that can be **called** in other places to run the code there. They can declare **parameters**, which are values that must be supplied when the function is called. They can also **return** a value, which causes the method call to give a value back when it is called.

- **Operators** are symbols that go between two values to operate on them and return a new value, such as adding (+ operator) or multiplying (* operator) two numbers, or adding two strings together.

Next, we'll learn how to incorporate some logic into our code.

CHAPTER 8

Conditions

We're about to learn how to use the bool (true or false) data type to check conditions – in other words, to run code only if some value evaluates to true.

The "if" Block

The "if" block is a means of evaluating a condition and, if that condition is true, running the code inside the "if" block. The code is somewhat self-explanatory: we type the keyword "if", then a set of parentheses () in which we type the condition to test, and then a code block {} to run if the condition is true:

```
if (/* Conditions go here */)
{
    //This code only runs if the condition is true.
}
```

A condition is simply some value (often called an **expression**) which results in an instance of the type bool – as we've established, the bool type can only store true or false as its value.

Let's exhibit conditions with an example a bit more interactive than our previous ones. We're going to check for the user clicking a button, using a built-in Unity method, and log something when the user clicks the button.

The method we'll be using is Input.GetKeyDown. This is a method which checks if the user has begun pressing down a key at just this moment. If so, it returns true. If not, it returns false. An alternate version of this method, called Input.GetKey, checks not if the key was *just* pressed down, but if the key is currently being *held* down. They both take a single parameter, which specifies which key we want to check. We can check any key on your average keyboard: letters, numbers, function keys (like F1, F2, etc.), whatever we want.

To effectively use a method like this, we need to call it from the Update method. As we've said before, the Update method is constantly called. To put it more specifically, it's called once per frame – so once every time our game logic is being run by the computer to keep the game moving forward in time.

Some games limit framerate to a certain cap, like 60 frames per second (roughly 0.016 seconds between each frame). It won't go higher than that, even if it could. Other games, particularly newer ones, do not use this tactic and simply run the code as fast as the computer can run it. For a game like ours, with nothing rendering to the screen and no real game logic being calculated each frame, even a low-end computer should be able to run many frames per second. As soon as an update occurs after the user presses the key, the Input.GetKeyDown function will return true – right there in that next Update call. Until then, it'll be returning false, likely hundreds of times per second.

© Casey Hardman 2024
C. Hardman, *Game Programming with Unity and C#*, https://doi.org/10.1007/978-1-4842-9720-9_8

Let's give it a whirl. Write this code for your Update method:

```
void Update()
{
    if (Input.GetKeyDown("c"))
    {
        Debug.Log("C key was pressed.");
    }
}
```

Save the code and go play the changes. Press the C key on your keyboard, and you should see the message logged in the Console window. It'll be logged once each time you press the C key.

Note that there's a Collapse feature to the Console window that can be toggled with the button visible in the top-left corner of the Console window. Clicking the Collapse button will turn it on or off. While it is on, all identical messages are "collapsed" into a single entry in the Console, with a number on the right side of the entry denoting how many times that exact message has been logged. If this is on, you may think that the message is only logging once, when you first press C, but if you take a closer look, you'll notice the number is going up by 1 per press. Toggle the Collapse feature off, and you'll see all the individual entries instead.

Collapse can be useful to turn on if you happen to get in a situation where lots and lots of the same messages are being logged, flooding the Console window and making it difficult to read individual messages.

Anyway, back to the "if" block: the condition coming after the "if" keyword is just an **expression** (a value, so to speak) which results in a bool type – true or false. We're providing this in a very simple way: by calling a method which returns a bool.

It's worth mentioning that you can shorten the "if" we wrote to make the code a little smaller if you want. Whenever you have an "if" with just one line of code inside it (one statement, ending with a semicolon), you can simply remove the curly braces. The "if" corresponds to the next statement coming after it; then it automatically ends immediately after that statement:

```
if (Input.GetKeyDown("c"))
    Debug.Log("C key was pressed.");
```

If you ever want to add more statements to an "if" declared this way, you'll have to go and add the curly braces.

If you're doing it this way, you should always make sure to indent the statement coming after the "if", as we have in the preceding code. It'll still work if you don't, but the indention makes it visually obvious that the statement is associated with the "if". If you use the same indention for the "if" and its contained statement, any other programmers who must look at it will probably come after you with torches and pitchforks. I know I would.

Overloads

In C#, we can declare different "versions" of the same method, but with different parameters. These methods are called **overloads**. Their purpose is to offer varying means of calling the same method. The Input. GetKeyDown method has two overloads – two ways of being called. They do the same thing and have the same name but take a different type for their parameter. The first one takes a string, which should contain the character of the key to check for. The second one takes a custom data type called **KeyCode**, declared by Unity, which we'll learn about in a second. We can supply either data type when we give our parameter, and it will work and run quite the same way.

Overloads are often used to provide more specific versions of functions containing extra parameters to further customize how the function works or versions which use a different data type or even return a different data type. A common example would be math-related methods, which often have an overload that works with the "int" data type and one that works with "float" instead. One overload will return int and/or take int parameters, while another returns float and/or takes float parameters.

Enums

The KeyCode data type is what we call an **enum**. An enum is a simple sort of object for the most part, although they have some advanced features that we won't get into just yet. They are essentially a set of names that correspond to number values. Rather than looking at these number values as meaningless numbers, we look at them by their names to make things much more readable. A common basic example of when you might use an enum is to resemble a season. We could use an int and say that 0 is spring, 1 is summer, 2 is fall, and 3 is winter. Or we can declare an enum called Season, which can be one of four values: Season.Spring, Season.Summer, Season.Fall, or Season.Winter.

Declaring such an enum is pretty simple:

```
//We start with the 'enum' keyword, then provide the name 'Season':
enum Season
{
    Spring, //Inside, we place a list of possible values.
    Summer, //These values are comma-separated.
    Fall,
    Winter //The last value should not have a comma.
}
```

The KeyCode enum has many more options than our example, but serves the same purpose: rather than assigning a number code to each key and having to refer to some chart to see which number to use for which key, we use an enum and type out the actual name of the key. Internally, the computer converts the name to a number and deals with it like that. But we get to see what we actually mean, not some meaningless number. Rather than, for example, the "A" key being 0 and "B" being 1, we simply type KeyCode.A and KeyCode.B.

KeyCode contains a value for each key you might find on a keyboard, from letters to numbers to arrow keys and symbols.

This is a somewhat cleaner means of supplying a key to an input function. If the KeyCode you type compiles with no errors, then you're good. All the options you can choose are clearly defined. With a string, however, there's the danger of passing an invalid string to it. For example, we could type "page up", but accidentally put two spaces separating "page" and "up". If we typed the name incorrectly with the KeyCode, our code would throw an error leading us right to the problem. But if we mistype the string, either it will fail quietly and always return false (a very undesirable outcome when trying to debug) or it will throw an error only at runtime when the code is reached, depending upon how the method is implemented.

Let's switch our usage of the Input.GetKeyDown function to use KeyCode. Just replace the "c" string parameter with KeyCode.C:

```
void Update()
{
    if (Input.GetKeyDown(KeyCode.C))
    {
        Debug.Log("C key was pressed.");
    }
}
```

Save and play, and the changes shouldn't even be noticeable. Everything should behave just as it did before.

Enums work well in many situations like this, where one might otherwise think to use some number code or a handwritten string. Usually, it's in situations where various options or settings are available and a value is expected to be one of those things. Some game-related examples would be the class or profession of a character (warrior, archer, cleric) or the type of an item (armor, weapon, consumable, material).

The "else" Block

Now that we've learned how to use an "if" block, let's take a look at a related block, the "else". You might be able to guess what it does. It's a way to provide a block of code that will run in the case where the "if" condition returns false, not true. It's code to run instead of the "if" block code.

An "else" block is declared simply by typing the "else" keyword after the closing curly brace "}" of an "if" block. Then, you write a block for the contents of the "else" block.

To demonstrate, let's change our Input method call from GetKeyDown to GetKey. Once again, the only difference is that GetKey will return true so long as the key is held, while GetKeyDown will return true once on the frame the key was first pressed and will not return true again until the key is released and then pressed again.

So let's log a message when C is held and a different one when it is not held – notice that, since our code blocks have only one statement in them, we omit the curly braces for style points, as we established earlier:

```
void Update()
{
    if (Input.GetKey(KeyCode.C))
        Debug.Log("C is held");
    else
        Debug.Log("C is released");
}
```

Of course, with the rate at which Update is called (likely hundreds of times per second), you'll see lots and lots of messages appearing in your Console, all the time. That's expected. The important part is that the message changes when we hold C.

The "else if" Block

If you want to check for a different condition to run some other code if the last "if" returned false, you can use an "else if" block. It's just an "else" block, except it has its own condition attached to it as well. We might use it to check if a different key is being pressed:

```
void Update()
{
    if (Input.GetKey(KeyCode.C))
        Debug.Log("C is held");
    else if (Input.GetKey(KeyCode.D))
        Debug.Log("D is held");
    else
        Debug.Log("C and D are both released");
}
```

In this case, we check first if C is held, and log a message if it is. If it's not held, we then check if D is held, and log a message if it is. Otherwise, if neither is held, we log a different message.

Notice that we can still use the "else" afterward. We can put as many "else if" blocks between the first "if" and the "else" as we want. And, of course, you don't need to have an "else" at the end – you can omit it if you don't need it.

When you chain many "else if" blocks together, remember that as soon as one of the conditions passes, any "else if" blocks below won't have their condition checked at all.

The first "if" or "else if" that evaluates to true will run its code block, and after that, all the rest in the same chain are ignored. That means if you hold down both C and D, you won't get both "C is held" and "D is held" messages being logged at once. You'll only get "C is held" messages, because it's topmost in the chain of conditions – as soon as it evaluates to true, the rest of the chain is jumped over and ignored.

Operators for Conditions

As we said, the condition we're providing after an "if" is just a value – an expression, as we call them. They're no more than an equation that results in a bool value, true or false. It can simply be "true" or "false". Or it can be a method that returns a bool, like Input.GetKeyDown, among many others.

But this also means we can use **operators** to form more complicated conditions. Remember, an operator is a symbol which takes some value on its left and some value on its right and operates on both values, returning some new value as a result. There are a handful of operators which return bool values – to ask if one value is greater than another or equal to another and so on. Let's review these operators.

Equality Operators

The "==" operator (two equals symbols, not one) simply asks, "Is the value on the left equal to the value on the right?" It's not just one "=" because that's the assignment operator, which we used before to assign a new value to an existing object. To check equality, we use "==".

■ **Note**   Sometimes, particularly intricate Boolean expressions can get your head swimming. If all this true-false talk is tripping you up, try thinking of "true" as answering "yes" and "false" as answering "no," and the if statement is asking "should I run my code block?"

An easy example is to compare some numbers. If the numbers are equal, "true" is returned. If the numbers are not equal, "false" is returned. A condition of "5 == 5" will always return true. Of course, that's somewhat useless – you're much more likely to, for example, check if your player is at maximum health: "currentHealth == maxHealth" would return true if they are and false if they are not.

You can compare strings too. They must be exactly equal, or false will be returned, even if a single letter is capitalized in one and not in the other or a single space is missing.

You can even compare bools too, which can result in some unnecessary fluffing of already functional code. An example is that some coders will add an unnecessary "== true" after a bool value in their "if" block. We could've done this ourselves:

```
if (Input.GetKeyDown(KeyCode.C) == true)
```

This is redundant because we're already getting a bool from the method call. It's already going to make the condition pass if it returns true. The operator isn't changing that. However, we could check if the key was **not** pressed down, essentially "inverting the condition," by using "== false":

```
if (Input.GetKeyDown(KeyCode.C) == false)
```

If the key was pressed, the method returns "true", which means the condition evaluates to "true == false". Of course, this means the operator will return "false" – the value "true" is not equal to "false". We are left with the result of that operator, "false", so the "if" does not pass and the code inside does not happen.

If the key was not pressed, the method returns "false", which means the condition evaluates to "false == false". Now, since the value "false" is indeed equal to "false", the operator will return "true". Since it returns "true", the "if" passes and the code runs.

There's also an operator which does the opposite of "==". The "!=" operator, sometimes called the "inequality operator" (I just call it "false equals" in my head), will return true only if the two given values are *not* equal. You can do the same thing in different ways by using one operator over the other – these two are the same:

```
if (Input.GetKeyDown(KeyCode.C) == false)
if (Input.GetKeyDown(KeyCode.C) != true)
```

In one case, we return true only if the left-hand value is equal to false. In another, we return true only if the left-hand value is not equal to true – which is just a roundabout way of doing the same thing. Both "if" blocks will only occur if the key was not pressed on that frame.

There's yet another way to flip things around. The exclamation mark can be used before a bool value to flip it – if it's true, it becomes false, and if it's false, it becomes true. We can place an exclamation mark "!" before the method call to flip the value it returns (I just read the exclamation mark as "false" in my head).

So, for example, if you want to check that a key is not currently held down this frame, you can do it either of these ways:

```
if (Input.GetKey(KeyCode.C) == false)
if (!Input.GetKey(KeyCode.C))
```

In the first case, we simply use the equality operator "==" to check if the value is false. In the second case, we insert a sneaky exclamation mark before the method call to flip the value it returns. If the key was not held, the method call would return false; then we have "!false" which flips the value to true, and the condition passes.

Greater Than and Less Than

The ">" and "<" operators check if one value is higher or lower than another, respectively. The ">" (greater than) returns true if the value at its left is greater (higher) than the value at its right and false if it is not. The "<" (less than) returns true if the value at its left is less (lower) than the value at its right and false if it is not.

These two operators have counterparts: ">=", greater than or equal to, and "<=", less than or equal to. They simply do the same thing but will also return "true" if both values are equal, just like the "==" operator.

Or

The "||" operator is often just called the "or" operator. Some languages even use a keyword "or" instead of the symbols. You probably never use this symbol – it's uncommonly seen in normal text. It's called a vertical bar. It almost looks like a lowercase L, but it's not. On a standard QWERTY keyboard, it's made with the key above Enter (the backslash) while holding Shift.

You'll use this operator quite a lot. Technically speaking, it takes a bool on its left and right sides and returns true if one or the other is true. In other words, if either one of the conditions is true, it will return true. If both are false, it will return false. To sum it up, it just means "or". You can use it to chain several different conditions together. For example, if you have a KeyCode enum stored in a parameter "key", you might check if it's one of several different keys:

```
if (key == KeyCode.A || key == KeyCode.B || key == KeyCode.C)
```

Now we're mixing operators. We're using the "==" operator to see if the "key" value is equal to a certain KeyCode value. This operator will give us a bool, so we can use it as a left-hand and right-hand value to the "||" operator, just as it expects.

If it looks confusing, you can separate the functionality with extra parentheses (although that would be somewhat redundant):

```
if ( (key == KeyCode.A) || (key == KeyCode.B) || (key == KeyCode.C) )
```

This makes it more noticeable how the "||" operators will be acting on the results of the "==" operators. The "==" will all occur first, then the "||" get their turn and operate on the results.

And

The "&&" operator (two ampersands) resembles "and". It takes a bool on its left and right sides and only returns true if both of those bools are true. If either one is false, it returns false instead. This makes it useful for just throwing multiple conditions into a single "if" instead of making separate, nested "if" blocks for each one.

A simple example of its use would be to check if a number is within a minimum and maximum range:

```
if (value >= 3 && value <= 6)
```

This checks if the given value (which should be a float or int) is between 3 and 6. To read it out: If "value" is greater than or equal to 3 and "value" is less than or equal to 6.

To put this in a final example that's more practical and game-related, we could check if our health is between 50% and 75% of our maximum health:

```
if (health >= (maxHealth * .5f) && health <= (maxHealth * .75f))
```

In this example, we're placing a lowercase "f" after the number values of 0.5 and 0.75. This is just telling the compiler that we want them to be float values. Remember, an int has no decimal point, while a float does. You'll have to write that little "f" after any number value, so long as it's not intended to be an int.

Summary

In this chapter, we learned further important fundamentals about bool operators and checking for conditions:

- How to use an "if" to run a block of code only if an expression evaluates to true.

- How to chain "else if" and "else" blocks with an "if" block. Remember, no more than one block in the chain will ever run at a time!

- An "enum" is a simple collection of names that can be used to identify a set of options instead of using number codes, which give no useful context, or strings, which are prone to mistyping errors that the compiler won't catch for us.

- How to use the Input.GetKey and Input.GetKeyDown methods with the built-in KeyCode enum to test if a key is being held down (GetKey) or was just pressed on this frame (GetKeyDown).

- How to use various operators like +, -, || (or), && (and), ==, and !=.

CHAPTER 9

Working with Objects

Remember when we talked about how programming is largely concerned with organizing and manipulating data? We interact with data as **objects**. A single piece of data is called an **object**, and an object might have other objects stored inside it – as we described in our previous examples, a data type resembling a "Person" might have a first name, last name, date of birth, and so on. We've already dealt with some basic objects: bool, int, float, and string are all objects as well. Now let's learn about creating our own objects and dealing with other, less basic types of data.

Classes

A **class** is a type of object. Classes are how we might depict things like "Person" or "Item" as we described before. They're the syntax we use to say "we plan on using this data type, and it stores these members" – where the **members** are other data inside it (sometimes also called **fields**). The class depicts what sorts of objects are stored inside it, what names we use to refer to them, and what type each one is. We declare classes to serve as something of a template for the creation of objects: declare a class, and elsewhere in your code, create instances of it. Each instance stores the same members but is its own unique set of those members – a copy of the base template, so to speak. So when we declare a class, we aren't creating an object on the spot. We're just defining a type of object.

To declare a class, you use the "class" keyword followed by the class name and then prompt a block:

```
class Person
{
}
```

Classes can only be declared within certain kinds of blocks. You can't declare a class within a method, for example.

Looking at our code again, you may notice that all the code we've been writing has been inside a class block this whole time – including our Update and Start methods:

```
public class MyScript : MonoBehaviour
{
    //etc.
}
```

There's some extra syntax there – the "public" keyword and the " : MonoBehaviour" bit at the end. We'll learn more about that later.

© Casey Hardman 2024
C. Hardman, *Game Programming with Unity and C#*, https://doi.org/10.1007/978-1-4842-9720-9_9

For now, let's write a simple class resembling an item in a game. We'll declare it (i.e., write the class code) inside the "MyScript" class code block we just mentioned, and we'll cut out all the code we wrote inside our Update and Start methods. You should end up with this:

```
public class MyScript : MonoBehaviour
{
    class Item
    {
    }
    // Start is called before the first frame update
    void Start()
    {
    }
    // Update is called once per frame
    void Update()
    {
    }
}
```

Now we have an Item class. We could create instances of it, but they won't store anything yet, because the code block coming after the "class Item" line is empty, so they'll just be empty objects.

Variables

A **variable** is a named member which stores an object. Variables always have a type, depicting what kind of object they store. This type can be one of the basic types we've already used (int, bool, etc.) as well as any other class – for example, our Item class could store another Item inside it, as a variable, or even instances of classes the Unity engine provides for us.

Let's add some variables to our Item declaration, and then we'll dig into the syntax:

```
class Item
{
    string name = "Unnamed Item";
    int worth = 1;
    bool canBeSold = true;
}
```

Variables are declared as "[type] [name] = [value];"
In the preceding example, we've declared three variables:

- A string named "name" with the value "Unnamed Item"

- An int named "worth" with the value 1

- A bool named "canBeSold" with the value "true"

You can declare a variable without the "= [value]" portion – for example, we could have just written "bool canBeSold;" – if you do this, the value will be initialized to a default value. For int and float, this means 0; for strings, it's the value **null**, which is what you get when an object is expected but one was never assigned; for bool, it's always false by default.

These variables are considered **instance variables**. They exist on each instance of the class.

But we can also create variables in other code blocks. In this case, they're called **local variables**. They're declared the same way, but they're not attached to any sort of object. We can just reference them by name when we want. However, they only exist within the block of code they were declared inside and, of course, below the variable declaration itself (not above it). For example, if we declare a local variable inside our Update method, that variable only exists in the Update method code block and in any blocks nested therein. This is why we call them local – they exist only in their local block, the one they were declared in.

Let's exhibit the creation of an instance of our class. To play around with this, we'll write our code in the "void Start()" method declared in our script by default. It's similar to the Update method that we talked about before. It's a method that the Unity engine will automatically call for us. Update is called once every frame, but Start is called just once when the script first initializes. For a script that is part of the scene, that means it will be called right when the scene is first loaded in (in our case, that's right when we start playing). If we were creating a GameObject on the fly, its scripts would have their Start called right as the GameObject is created, before any Update calls go through.

This gives us an easy way to run our code for testing, without having to check for input or run the code every frame (possibly hundreds of times per second).

We'll start by writing the following code **inside our Start method**:

```
Item item = new Item();
```

This is a **variable declaration**: first, you'll notice the type is "Item", which is the type we declared ourselves. We name it "item". This is a common naming convention – the names of types and methods will have a capitalized first letter (like Item), while the names of variables will have a lowercase first letter, and if they're more than one word, then any words after the first will have a capital first letter to make them readable (as in "canBeSold"), which is known as "camel case."

We then assign a value to the variable with "=", after which we see the "new" keyword, followed by "Item()" which is much like calling a class like it's a method. This gets us an instance of the class and is known as a **constructor call**.

A **constructor** is pretty much exactly like a method, but it's used to return an instance of a class. In this case, we're calling the default constructor – we didn't declare it ourselves. Later, we'll declare a constructor that has parameters (just like a method) for the variables in the class, which lets us assign the variables when the class is created. But let's get into that later – for now, let's demonstrate some interaction with our instance.

Accessing Class Members

After the local variable is declared and we've called the constructor with the "new Item()" syntax, we can reference the variable by its name, "item", and, as we exhibited before, use a period to "reach into" the object and access its data. Of course, in this case, the data inside it would be those variables we declared in the class block: name, worth, and canBeSold.

We can assign values to the members here by accessing them and using the "=" operator. Let's assign some values to our new variable:

```
void Start()
{
    Item item = new Item();
    item.name = "Goblin Tooth";
    item.worth = 4;
    item.canBeSold = true;
}
```

First, we declare the local variable and create the instance; then, we have three separate statements, each one assigning a value to one of the variables inside the item. We reference those variables by using the period " . " to "reach into" the Item instance and access the data stored inside. Of course, these variables are declared in the Item class, and if we tried to access a name that isn't declared in the class, it would result in an error preventing us from playing the game. And, as we went over earlier, since C# is a *strongly typed* language, it won't allow us to, for example, assign a string value to "worth", because it expects an int. It'll throw an error in that case too.

And speaking of errors, it looks like we've got some waiting for us now. If you've written the preceding code, saved, and navigated to Unity, you'll notice the Console window is showing three errors. This leads to the next concept of object-oriented programming that we must address: **access modifiers**.

An **access modifier** is a keyword you write before a nonlocal variable declaration. There are three main options: **public**, **protected**, and **private**. They determine whether a member, such as the three variables we declared in the Item class, can be accessed from outside the class itself.

- **public** means that the member can be freely accessed from outside the class block.

- **protected** means that the member can be accessed only from within the class block or by classes which "inherit" the class – we'll get into that concept a few chapters down the road, though, so don't worry about it too much for now.

- **private** means the member can only be accessed inside the class block itself.

We didn't provide an access modifier at all when we declared our three variables. When you don't provide an access modifier, it always defaults to private.

This is the cause of our error: we can't access the variables from outside the class block itself because they're private, but we're trying to.

The fix is simple. Put the keyword "public" before each variable declaration in the Item class, so it looks like this:

```
class Item
{
    public string name = "Unnamed Item";
    public int worth = 1;
    public bool canBeSold = true;
}
```

Save your code and the errors should go away.

Now let's use those values in a Debug.Log call – just to see something happening and make sure the values are what we expect them to be.

In our Start method, add the following line – it must be below the variable declaration and the assigning of the values:

```
Debug.Log("This " + item.name + " is worth " + item.worth + " golden coins!");
```

Here, we're chaining many "+" operators together to add referenced values together into one string. In the end, we'll expect to have a string saying "This Goblin Tooth is worth 4 golden coins!"

You may have noticed we're mixing types here. The "item.name" is a string, so that makes sense – a string can be added to a string. But "item.worth" is an int, yet we're trying to add it to the string. This works just as you'd expect it to – the value of the int is added as number characters to the string, and the resulting string is returned. Some base types can quietly convert to other types like this.

So save and play – here's a quick recap of **what your Start method should look like now**:

```
void Start()
{
    Item item = new Item();
    item.name = "Goblin Tooth";
    item.worth = 4;
    item.canBeSold = true;

    Debug.Log("This " + item.name + " is worth " + item.worth + " golden coins!");
}
```

You should get a message in the Console window just as you would expect.

Instance Methods

Methods can go inside classes. When you do this, you've declared an **instance method**. They're folded up inside the class itself, so that means you must reference an instance of a class, reach into it with a " . ", and then call the method by name.

Because the method is attached to an instance of a class like this, it can seamlessly access any of the variables that belong to the class. Inside the instance method, you can type "name" or "worth" or "canBeSold" to reference the corresponding variables of the class instance.

Let's move our Debug.Log call into an instance method. First, we'll declare the method in the Item class block. Methods have access modifiers too. We haven't used them yet, but now that we're declaring a method inside a class, we need to make sure we designate it as "public" so we can access it from outside the class later. It returns "void" (nothing), it will be named LogInfo, and it has no parameters, so an empty set of parentheses "()" after the name:

```
class Item
{
    public string name = "Unnamed Item";
    public int worth = 1;
    public bool canBeSold = true;

    public void LogInfo()
    {
        Debug.Log("This " + name + " is worth " + worth + " golden coins!");
    }
}
```

Now you'll notice that we've typed the same Debug.Log message, except this time, we've taken out the "item." before the "name" and "worth" references. Just like we talked about earlier, since the method is inside the class block, it must be called through an Item instance, and thus, the method has access to all the members of the Item by default. And by "members" I don't just mean the variables – if we declared other methods inside the class, we could reference them just by their name as well, and since we're inside the class block, we could reference them even if they were private or protected.

Of course, this won't change anything when we play until we actually call the method instead of running the same old Debug.Log line we had before. Replace your old Debug.Log line in the Start method with this:

```
tem.LogInfo();
```

Save and run the game. You should see quite the same message as before. You might think, "Well, what was the point of all this, then?" After all, haven't we just written more code than we had to and accomplished the same result? Instead of the Debug.Log line in the Start method, we now have a different line, and we declared the method in the class itself!

Well, there's a little rule of programming called "**Don't Repeat Yourself**," or "DRY." The main point of this is that we now have the method and can call it whenever we need to do the same thing again. Say we wanted to log the same information for a different item, somewhere else in our code, and we never made our instance method. We just copy-paste the Debug.Log call over and we're done, right? But what if we want to change what the message logs? Now we have two instances of the same code to change. What if we'd copy-pasted it 20 times already? We've created a bunch of extra work for ourselves.

There could be a great benefit to having a single place for the code. By creating a method for it, we've made sure that it exists in one place only, even if it's called from many other places, and so if we ever want to change it, we need only change it once. This is one of the reasons why we say Don't Repeat Yourself. If you find yourself copy-pasting code all the time, you could probably be doing something in a more efficient and clean way, and you might be setting yourself up for heartache somewhere down the road.

As well as this, it splits the code up into relevant portions. The code which logs item-related information is kept neatly folded inside the Item class itself, not inside our code which implements the class. The implementing code simply reaches into "item" and calls a method – no parameters necessary.

Let's expand on this method and get a little more functionality into it. After all, you've learned enough by now to code a method that's more than just one line, haven't you?

We're going to make the method log something different based on whether the item "canBeSold". We do this with a single "if" and "else" block. Remember, since "canBeSold" is a bool, we can just type "if (canBeSold)" with no need for an "== true" operator:

```
public void LogInfo()
{
    if (canBeSold)
        Debug.Log("This " + name + " can be sold for " + worth + " golden coins!");
    else
        Debug.Log("This " + name + " cannot be sold.");
}
```

Since the "if" and "else" are both followed by a single statement only, we don't need to write curly braces "{}" for their code blocks, as we established before. Now, the message that's logged will be different based on whether the item can be sold. If it can't be sold, there's no need to tell the user what it's worth, right?

Now, save the code and try it out. The message should be a little different now, since we changed the text in the strings. To make sure our condition is working as we expect, you can also change the "true" to "false" in the Start method when we set "item.canBeSold" and then run the code again. The message should change as expected.

Declaring Constructors

We discussed what constructors are earlier. They're much like methods, but they're called to generate an instance of a class. When the instance is created, the code in the declared constructor is run on that instance before the created instance gets returned. When calling a constructor (making an instance of a class), you pretty much call the class by its name, as if it were a method, and you must have the "new" keyword come before it.

It's a good practice to use constructors to set up new instances of your class. Typically, a constructor will have a parameter for each variable in the class you expect to be set with each instance – whatever custom fields might require a different value each time the class is created. In our case, the three variables we declared ought to be parameters in a constructor – it's silly to use three separate statements to provide the values of variables that we're going to set every time anyway, right? Not only that, but constructors make it obvious to you, and anyone else using your code, which values are meant to be assigned when an instance of a class is created. They are orderly, and they set a standard for the usage of a class.

Constructors are declared inside the class block itself, usually below variables, but above methods. They are as simple as "[access modifier] [class name]([parameters]) {...}". The access modifier we desire is "public". Private constructors can only be used from within the class itself – there are some cases where this is handy, but this is not one of them, so we need to make sure we type "public" because if we don't, "private" will be defaulted.

This is how our constructor will look – written within the code block of "class Item":

```
public Item(string name, int worth, bool canBeSold)
{
    this.name = name;
    this.worth = worth;
    this.canBeSold = canBeSold;
}
```

Before we get into the statements within, let's review the declaration itself. Start with the access modifier "public" and then the name of the class, "Item". Think of it like declaring a method that doesn't have a name, just the access modifier and then the return type – after all, constructors always return the type of the class itself, since they're used to create an instance of it. Then we do the same set of parentheses "()" we're used to, with parameter declarations just as we declared for our methods.

Now, what are these three statements beginning with "this."? It's simple – they're assigning the values of the parameters to the values of the variables in the class instance.

When we made instance methods just a little bit ago, we exhibited that you can simply type the name of a class variable to reference that variable. This is the same within a constructor. The class instance already exists, and the code is running on it immediately after. So within this constructor, if we type "name", we get the value of "name" for the class instance that's being created by the constructor. All the variables for this instance already exist.

But since the parameters are named the exact same thing as the variables themselves, "name" also refers to the parameter. We can't just type "name = name;" and expect the computer to know what we're talking about. That creates ambiguity that the computer cannot solve on its own – the compiler doesn't make guesses like this. It needs us to clear the situation up. This is because the parameters are part of the constructor declaration, which is the block the code is operating from; the variables, however, are one block up the hierarchy, and thus, they get overridden by the parameter names.

Simply put, the most recently declared names are taking precedence over (sometimes called "shadowing") the class variable names. This means if we type "name = name;" we're assigning the parameter value to itself, not to the variable instance.

So to avoid this confusion, we use "this", which is a keyword that always refers to the instance that the code is running for. Inside our constructor, "this" is the class instance being created. Inside our instance method, "this" would be the instance whose method is being called.

By referencing "this" first, we take the ambiguity out of the situation – the computer no longer sees it and says "Wait, what?" It sees that we mean to say "set the value of the class instance variable 'name' to the value of the parameter 'name.'"

The "this" keyword can be used in instance methods as well as constructors, if you ever need a means of referencing the instance itself. A very common use case for it is to avoid name conflicts as we've just demonstrated.

Another solution to these name conflicts would be to simply not name the parameters the exact same thing as the class variables. For example, we could put an underscore before each parameter name and take the "this." out:

```
public Item(string _name, int _worth, bool _canBeSold)
{
    name = _name;
    worth = _worth;
    canBeSold = _canBeSold;
}
```

But this is frowned upon. The former way (using "this.") is the norm, because it's clear, concise, and obvious. The parameters are being applied directly to the variables themselves, so why name them anything else?

Now that you've added the constructor to the Item class, it should look like this:

```
class Item
{
    public string name = "Unnamed Item";
    public int worth = 1;
    public bool canBeSold = true;

    public Item(string name, int worth, bool canBeSold)
    {
        this.name = name;
        this.worth = worth;
        this.canBeSold = canBeSold;
    }
    public void LogInfo()
    {
        if (canBeSold)
            Debug.Log("This " + name + " can be sold for " + worth + " golden coins!");
        else
            Debug.Log("This " + name + " cannot be sold.");
    }
}
```

Using the Constructor

Now that we've declared our constructor, saving the code and checking Unity will result in an error in the Console window.

This is because a class with no constructors declared will have a single, default constructor automatically provided, which takes no parameters and returns an instance of the class with all its variables at their default settings (the ones given in the variable declarations). But once you've declared your own constructor, this default constructor will no longer exist for the class. There is now only one way to declare the class, and it takes three parameters, but we're still calling the constructor with no parameters at all in our Start method.

So navigate back to this code in your Start method:

```
Item item = new Item();
item.name = "Goblin Tooth";
item.worth = 4;
item.canBeSold = true;
```

This is where our error occurs. We're trying to make an Item without giving any parameters to the constructor. You can probably guess how we'll go about changing this to call the constructor instead. Replace the code with this:

```
Item item = new Item("Goblin Tooth", 4, true);
```

We've turned our repetitive four lines of code into one clean line. The parameters are provided in the constructor call, just like with our methods, and of course, we must follow the same order that the parameters were declared in the constructor: "name" first, then "worth", and then "canBeSold".

All the constructor code will be executed before the next line of code after we declare our "item" variable, so we know all the fields are assigned before the instance is returned to us. Everything is set up and ready for the instance to be used in a neat and consistent way.

Now if we create Item instances in a hundred different places in our game code, we can just change one block of code – the constructor declaration – if we ever need to change how items are set up when they are created.

Static Members

One last thing we'll cover about classes is the idea of **static members**. They're pretty much the opposite of the instanced members we've been working with in this chapter.

Instanced variables, like the variables we declared for our Item class, exist as separate pieces of data on each Item instance we create.

An instanced method, like the LogInfo method, operates through an instance of the Item class. You must reach into an Item instance to call the LogInfo method. Since it's running through an instance of the Item, it can work with the instanced variables, as our method does to log the name and worth of the item.

Static variables, however, exist as one instance for the entire class. From outside the class, you must reach into the name of the class itself, like "Item", to access its static members. Only if they're public, though – if they are private or protected, they cannot be accessed from outside the class at all.

Static methods work in the same way, and since they can be called simply by reaching into the class name, this means the method cannot access instanced members since there is no specific instance tied to the call. For example, if we made our Item.LogInfo method into a static method instead, it would throw compiler errors because the LogInfo method is referencing the "name", "worth", and "canBeSold" instanced variables within a static method, where no instance will be tied to the method call.

Let's demonstrate. An easy example would be to count how many instances of the Item class are created.

First, with your other Item variables, declare a static variable to count the number of instances of Item:

```
public static int NumberOfInstances = 0;
```

This is the same as a normal variable declaration, just with "static" coming after the access modifier.

Next, in the Item constructor, add a line to add 1 to the instance count with the "+=" operator:

```
NumberOfInstances += 1;
```

Now we have a static variable that increases by 1 whenever we use the Item constructor (in other words, whenever a new Item is created). Since it's static, it's attached to the Item class itself, not separately to each of its instances. Each instance can access the variable within the class, and since it's declared as public, we can access it outside the class (e.g., in our Start method) as "Item.NumberOfInstances". However, the variable holds the same value for each instance, and if any instance changes the value, it changes for all of them. Think of it like each instance "pointing at" one value.

To make use of the variable, we could declare a static method to log the number of instances. Add this within the Item class:

```
public static void LogInstanceCount()
{
    Debug.Log("Number of Item instances is: " + NumberOfInstances);
}
```

We're declaring the method as public and static just like the variable. It returns void (nothing) and simply logs a message telling us how many instances there are.

Again, note that you only need the "Item." before the variable if you wanted to access it outside of the Item class. Inside the class, it acts the same as instance variables. Try moving that Debug.Log call to the Start method, and notice that you'll get an error if you don't change it to "Item.NumberOfInstances" instead.

Also, remember, within that static method, any attempt at accessing an instanced member will result in compiler errors. We can't call LogInfo or use our name, worth, or canBeSold variables because the static method isn't tied to any particular instance of Item, and those variables exist on every instance, not on the class itself.

Let's update our Start method to demonstrate calling the method. To demonstrate the count going up after we create our first Item, we'll call it once before the item is created and once again after:

```
void Start()
{
    Item.LogInstanceCount();
    Item item = new Item("Goblin Tooth", 4, true);
    Item.LogInstanceCount();
}
```

As you can see, we're calling the static method through a reference to the actual type name itself, "Item", with an uppercase "I". We aren't referencing the instance we're storing in our local variable, which is "item" with a lowercase "i". You can't reach into an instance to access its static members. You must go through the class name itself.

If you test this updated code, you should see two messages:

Number of Item instances is: 0

Number of Item instances is: 1

This demonstrates the NumberOfInstances going up when we create the new Item.

Now that you understand this distinction, you might realize we've been calling a static method many times already in our examples: Debug.Log. "Debug" is just a class, and "Log" is a public static method declared inside it. Thus, we can access Debug.Log whenever we want.

This is how many of the built-in methods are exposed to us, including the Input.GetKey and Input.GetKeyDown methods we called in the previous chapter.

Summary

In this chapter, we learned that a **class** provides a template for a type of object. We add **members** like variables and methods to the class definition. Every instance of the class will have those members. Instances of classes are made by calling a constructor using the "new" keyword. We can declare our own constructors for classes to provide a consistent means of initializing new instances and giving values for their variables.

We also learned the distinction between **instanced variables** (those within a class) and **local variables**, which are declared in the body of a method (among other things). Local variables are created on the fly and cannot be accessed again once their containing code block ends (e.g., a method or an "if" block).

Another important thing to remember is that methods declared within a class are instanced, meaning you must call the method through a reference to an instance of the class (like with "item.LogInfo()"). Within that method, you can access other members of the class, like its variables, directly by name. If you instead mark the method with the "static" keyword, it is accessed through the class name directly, not through an instance.

CHAPTER 10

Working with Scripts

Now that you've learned about the basics of objects, let's learn about scripts. I should warn you – we're getting dangerously close to coding our first game.

Scripts are components for our code files. They get our code into the game. We've worked with a script already (MyScript) just to get our code running, but we haven't explored them thoroughly yet.

When it comes down to it, they're objects. A script is a code file that declares a class. The class acts as a component, allowing us to attach it to GameObjects just as we might attach cameras, lights, colliders, mesh renderers, and whatever else.

But rather than creating instances of scripts with constructors and the "new" keyword as we did with our own class, we use the Unity editor to create instances by adding script components to GameObjects. If we want to create instances of the script through code, we use built-in Unity methods for that too. Since they're components, they must be attached to some GameObject in order to exist.

As we've already demonstrated, we can declare event methods like Update and Start in our scripts, giving us a means of running code at certain queues in-game. There are other events as well – some you might never use and some we'll be using in our example projects.

Scripts are meant to serve as a piece of functionality that can be added to a GameObject. It can be as complex as all your player logic or as simple as a script that constantly rotates an object.

Often, that little piece of functionality requires variables to work. Just like with a class, we can declare instance variables for our scripts, so that every instance of the script has this data "inside it." But with scripts, since they act as components, their variables can be exposed to us in the Inspector, allowing us to edit variable values on a per-instance basis. A script that constantly rotates an object might have a vector variable (an X, Y, and Z value) that depicts how much it rotates per second. With this exposed in the Inspector, we can use the same script to achieve different things across different GameObjects. Some could rotate faster than others, or some could rotate on one axis instead of the other.

Not only that, but we can even change the values of script variables through the Inspector while playing our game. When we quit playing, the values are reverted to their original setting. This makes it easy to test different settings for variables – for example, physics-related settings like how high a player jumps or how fast they fall – without losing your old settings.

Let's make the simple script we mentioned that rotates a GameObject by some constant amount. It doesn't take many lines of code, and it'll give us a taste for working with scripts.

With the Project tab selected, click the plus-shaped button just beneath the Project tab and create a C# Script, as shown in Figure 10-1.

© Casey Hardman 2024

C. Hardman, *Game Programming with Unity and C#*, https://doi.org/10.1007/978-1-4842-9720-9_10

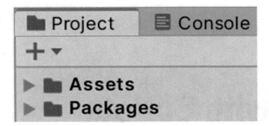

Figure 10-1. *The "+" button at the top-left corner of the Project window, just underneath the window tab*

Name it SimpleRotation. Open the script, and you'll be met with the base script code, as we've already seen once before. Let's go over it top to bottom this time, now that you're getting savvy with code.

Usings and Namespaces

This should be the first thing you see at the top of your script file:

```
using System.Collections;
using System.Collections.Generic;
using UnityEngine;
```

These are **usings**. They tell the compiler what other code we're going to use in this file. We start them with the "using" keyword, followed by a reference to what is known as a **namespace**.

A **namespace** is a simple, named block of code that contains other definitions inside it. In a sense, they're like folders for your computer. A folder can store files inside it, as well as other folders. A namespace can store definitions inside it, such as classes, as well as other namespaces.

The purpose of a namespace is to separate a relevant chunk of code from other scripts that won't be using it.

You can reach into a namespace to reference other namespaces inside it, as well as other classes inside it. It's much like grabbing members out of an object. You just use the period. If we declare something inside a namespace, we must access it through the namespace, typing out the namespace name, then a period, and then the definition (e.g., a class) that we want to reference. But this can be tedious. That's why we have usings.

When we include a using statement in our file, we're pointing to a namespace and saying "Give me everything in that one." This lets us directly reference classes inside the namespace without "reaching into" the namespace to get them.

So a using statement will always point at a namespace, and it lets us directly reference all the definitions declared inside that namespace. They're for convenience. They shorten how much stuff we have to type.

The namespaces we're pointing to are part of the base frameworks provided to us by default.

System.Collections and System.Collections.Generic are namespaces holding classes that can be used to store "collections" of other objects. We aren't going to actually use them, but they're included by default in a new script because they're commonly used.

UnityEngine is a namespace containing most of the core definitions you'll be interacting with when coding your game in Unity, so of course, it only makes sense that it would be included by default as well.

UnityEngine includes things like the classes that define major components. You've already heard about some of these: Transform, Camera, Light, Mesh Renderer, and Mesh Filter are some examples. Of course, there's also a class for a GameObject.

So to sum it up, if we did not have the "using UnityEngine;" line at the start of our script, we would have to type UnityEngine.GameObject or UnityEngine.Transform (and so on) to refer to these classes. But since we have the using, we can just type GameObject or Transform.

While we aren't actually going to use anything in the other two namespaces, it's not going to hurt anything to leave the usings be.

Script Class

Moving on down the file, we have the class definition:

```
public class SimpleRotation : MonoBehaviour
```

The class is automatically named the same thing as our script file. This is important. You actually won't be able to attach the script to a GameObject as a component if you don't name the file and the class the same thing! So remember, if you ever want to rename one of your scripts, rename both the script file in the Project window, as well as the script class name declared here.

This extra bit at the end is what we call class inheritance. We'll learn how that works in the next chapter, but just know that the " : MonoBehaviour" part is what makes the class a script that can be added as a component, not just a normal class. It's an odd name, but just think of it as "script" whenever you see it.

The code block inside the class will be familiar from our experience with MyScript. We have some comments. If you recall, those are the lines that start with "//", which are ignored by the compiler and serve as little notes for us to read. We also have a "void Start()" method and a "void Update()" method, each with an empty code block after. We learned about these before: Update is called once per frame, while Start is called just once at the start of the game.

Let's start with declaring variables for our script. We're going to use a new type of data that we haven't worked with yet. It's called Vector3. It's a single object that stores three floats: X, Y, and Z. We've seen this before. The position, rotation, and scale of our Transforms are all represented as instances of Vector3 because they all have an X, Y, and Z value. This is just the first time we're dealing with the data type in our code.

We're going to use a Vector3 to represent how much we want to rotate our Transform per second, on each axis. As you may recall, each of the three axes (X, Y, and Z) will tilt the object in different ways.

Declaring variables for a script is always done inside the script class (SimpleRotation) code block. You can put them anywhere, but pretty much everyone agrees that your variables should be kept at the top, above all your methods. When a coder (including yourself) goes to look for a variable declaration, they're going to look for it up at the top, not mixed in arbitrarily with the methods.

You're an expert now, so you should know how to declare a variable yourself. We'll make this one public, of type Vector3, named "rotationPerSecond":

```
public Vector3 rotationPerSecond;
```

While we're at it, let's remove the Start method. We won't be using it, so we don't need to declare it. But we will be using Update in a bit, so don't remove it.

It's important that the variable is public. Protected and private variables are not visible in the Inspector, so we won't be able to customize the value for each individual script if we don't make the variable public.

Now save your code. In your Unity editor, find some GameObject you want to rotate. It can be one of the Skyscrapers we made earlier, if you still have those around, or you can just add a plane or a cube to the scene. It just has to be something you can see.

Add the SimpleRotation script to the GameObject. In case you've forgotten, you can do this by dragging and dropping the script file from the Project to the desired GameObject in the Hierarchy, in the Scene view, or in the Inspector while the GameObject is selected. You can also select the GameObject, go to the

Inspector, and click the "Add Component" button displayed beneath all the GameObject's components. This will pull down a little menu you can use to navigate to your SimpleRotation script, or simply type the script name into the search bar to find it and click it.

Once the script is added, you'll see our variable listed inside it as an editable field in the Inspector, as shown in Figure 10-2.

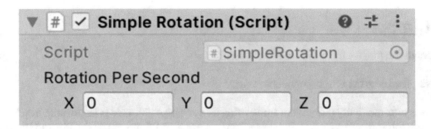

Figure 10-2. *An instance of the SimpleRotation script component showing in the Inspector*

It shows the name, all prettied up with extra spaces and proper capitalization so it reads "Rotation Per Second." Beneath (or beside it, if your Inspector is wide enough), it shows three number fields, one for each axis.

If you don't see the field, make sure you declared the variable as public, and make sure it's inside the script class code block (the code block after "class SimpleRotation"). And, of course, make sure you saved the script file in your code editor since you added the variable declaration!

Rotating a Transform

Now, having the variable is great, but we still need to use it to rotate our object. Good news – we only need one line of code to do this, placed in our Update method. With the "rotationPerSecond" variable we declared earlier, we'll add this line of code to our Update method:

```
transform.Rotate(rotationPerSecond * Time.deltaTime);
```

You'll recall that the Transform component of a GameObject is what handles its position, rotation, and scale, among other things. It should only make sense that we must go through the Transform to rotate the object, right?

And since our class is a script, we automatically get access to certain members that all scripts have. One of those is "transform" – note the first letter is lowercase. "Transform" is the class type, and "transform" is our member. It's a reference to the Transform component of the GameObject that the script is attached to.

That little bit in the class declaration pointing to "MonoBehaviour" is what technically gives us access to this member – it's the part that makes it a script, not just any old class. It's known as inheritance. We'll be learning more about it in the next chapter. For now, just know that our script class has automatic access to these useful little members that all scripts have. Another such member is "gameObject", a reference to the GameObject the script is attached to.

So we use "transform" to refer to the Transform component. Luckily, Unity provides us with this convenient "Rotate" instance method in the Transform class to rotate it. We reach in with a " . " and reference that method. The method has several overloads, but the one we're using takes just one parameter of type Vector3. It rotates the Transform by the values of the given Vector3. Since rotation is an X, Y, and Z value, it only makes sense that it expects a Vector3, not a single float.

By now, your script should have this code in it:

```
using System.Collections;
using System.Collections.Generic;
using UnityEngine;

public class SimpleRotation : MonoBehaviour
{
    public Vector3 rotationPerSecond;

    // Update is called once per frame
    void Update()
    {
        transform.Rotate(rotationPerSecond * Time.deltaTime);
    }
}
```

Make sure you save your changes in the code editor, and then go back to Unity. Remember, we don't initialize the "rotationPerSecond" to any default value, so it's automatically going to be (0, 0, 0) on all new instances of the script. This means it won't rotate at all. Select the GameObject you added the script to earlier and make sure you set its rotationPerSecond to something that's not (0, 0, 0) in the Inspector. You can use negative or positive values. Set it to whatever you want. A value of 360 will be one full circle per second, to give you a frame of reference.

Now play the game, and you'll see your rotation in effect. Congratulations. You did that. Don't worry, we'll be doing more fun stuff in no time, like implementing actual player movement.

You can also play with the value while the game is running, as we mentioned earlier. Go ahead and change the rotationPerSecond while the game is playing. Raise or lower it on any of the axes, and it should respond immediately. Once you stop playing, the value will go back to what it was when you started.

Frames and Seconds

You'll notice we're doing a little bit of math on the rotationPerSecond when we supply it as a parameter to the Rotate call. We have a "*" operator, which is for multiplication, followed by "Time.deltaTime", which is a float. You can probably guess that multiplying a Vector3 by a float is going to multiply each axis of the vector by the float. So what we're effectively getting is (x * Time.deltaTime, y * Time.deltaTime, z * Time.deltaTime), just in a lot fewer words. But what is this Time.deltaTime float supposed to resemble?

Remember that Update happens once per frame. And your game is running at some odd number of frames per second that could change on a dime. It's probably happening hundreds of times per second, since we barely have anything going on in our scene that would slow down your computer. But during the course of playing a game, the framerate might raise and lower based on the situation. It's not reliable.

We named our variable "rotationPerSecond" for a reason. It's not rotation per frame. If we just pass rotationPerSecond for the parameter as is, we'll rotate a whole lot more than we want to. We'll be rotating by the amount we want per second, but we'll be doing it hundreds of times per second (you should try it, it looks humorous). To change it from "per frame" to "per second" is actually somewhat simple.

"Time" is a UnityEngine built-in class for useful static variables and methods, and "deltaTime" is one of those. It's a static float that's constantly updated and simply stores the time, in seconds, since the last frame occurred. This is often a tiny little fraction. If we're running at 100 frames per second, it'll be a mere 0.01. We use this as a multiplier for our rotationPerSecond to go from "per frame" to "per second".

Think about it. Let's simplify it and say we're running at a measly two frames per second. That means half a second per frame, right? So Time.deltaTime will be at 0.5 on each Update call. Multiply something by 0.5 and you get half. This means we get half the rotationPerSecond per call. If our rotation is 50 per second on all axes, we get 25 per frame. This is 50 in two frames. At two frames per second, that's rotating at 50 per second. This means we did just what we were looking to do.

This concept is used when we move objects as well, to move them by units per second, not per frame. It's as simple as multiplying by Time.deltaTime.

If you're interested, let's dive into some context for this method of doing things (as opposed to moving by an amount per frame) to help you understand why we do things this way.

This is what you'd call **framerate independence**. In a framerate independent game, a low framerate will make the game very choppy, giving the user an unsatisfying experience – however, it won't cause the game to appear to be in slow motion. Each update will move objects based on the time that has passed, due to the way we use the "delta time."

On the other hand, in a framerate dependent game, the values given are per frame, not per second. You would expect a given "target framerate," like 30 or 60 per second, and then cap the framerate at this amount, not allowing it to run faster than the target amount. You then measure the speed and timing of things in your game as "per frame," keeping in mind what that target framerate is and expecting it to always be met exactly. If the framerate is lower than the target value, it makes the game appear to run in slow motion, since everything is operating per frame, making the actual time between frames not a factor.

This is a much more common practice with games that are targeted for game consoles due to the fact that they know exactly which console they're targeting, so they know the hardware inside that console and what it is capable of handling, allowing them to design around it.

PC games, on the other hand, expect to deal with a range of hardware running their game, so depending on a specific framerate can isolate players with weaker hardware, who are unable to reach the target framerate, or frustrate players with hardware that could be running the game much smoother, but are stuck at 30 or 60 frames per second.

Since Unity can build games for PC as well as game consoles, this system of "per second" values allows us to work with one measurement that operates the same way on any platform.

Attributes

An attribute is something like an instance of a class that gets attached to code definitions. It sounds odd, but it's somewhat like a way for programmers to introduce metadata into their code. A programmer might declare attributes to specify certain things about a definition. We then attach attribute instances to definitions we declare, like classes, variables, methods, and so on. Other code will then read these attributes and do something with them.

A good example can be found in some of the attributes that the UnityEngine namespace provides us. For example, there is an attribute called HideInInspector, which we can attach to a variable to – you guessed it – hide it from the Inspector. You can use this to hide a variable while keeping it public so that other scripts can access the variable through a reference. Sometimes, you want public variables in your script, but you don't want them to be tampered with in the Inspector (or simply don't want them clogging up your Inspector).

To apply an attribute to a definition, you'll type the attribute name in a set of square braces "[]" before the definition.

For example purposes, let's hide our rotationPerSecond member by adding the attribute:

```
[HideInInspector] public Vector3 rotationPerSecond;
```

The definition is the same, but we have the square braces "[]" and the attribute name declared before the variable. Save the code and head back to Unity. Select your GameObject with the SimpleRotation script on it, and you'll notice the rotationPerSecond has disappeared in the Inspector.

You can write multiple attributes for a single definition. Each one must be surrounded by its own set of square braces "[]". You can also put a line break between attributes and the definition, if you want to spread the definition out so it's a little more readable:

```
[HideInInspector]
public Vector3 rotationPerSecond;
```

If you had multiple attributes, you could even devote an entire line to each attribute, if you wanted.

But we don't want this attribute on our rotationPerSecond member, since we need to edit it in the Inspector. That was just for demonstration. You can go ahead and delete the attribute.

Let's demonstrate another attribute that can come in handy: Header. This is an attribute that you attach to a variable to cause a bold header with the text of your choice to show above it in the Inspector. This can be useful for visually separating different groups of variables to tidy up your Inspector. For example, a script representing your player character might have separate headers for variables relating to movement, jumping, and attacking.

This header takes a parameter, which is a string for the header text. Declaring attributes with parameters looks much like a method call or a constructor call. Instead of just typing the name of the attribute, we add a set of parentheses "()" with the string value inside it:

```
[Header("My Variables")]
public Vector3 rotationPerSecond;
```

Save and check the Inspector again, and you should see your bold title "My Variables" above the rotationPerSecond variable, as shown in Figure 10-3.

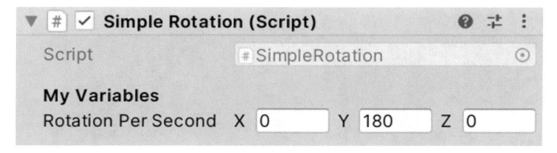

Figure 10-3. *SimpleRotation script instance shown in the Inspector, with our "My Variables" Header attribute displaying as a bold title above the variable field*

If you put the Header attribute on a variable that's not showing in the Inspector, such as a variable with the "[HideInInspector]" attribute or a private variable, you won't see the header at all.

These two simple attributes can be useful in keeping the Inspector for your scripts tidy.

Summary

In this chapter, we learned how to attach our code files to GameObjects as script components, and how to code our scripts so we can customize each instance by exposing variables in the Inspector.

- Public variables declared in a script class can have their value viewed and edited in the Inspector. You can edit the values while playing the game to test out different settings, but those changes won't stick around after you stop playing the game.

- The class declared in the script file must be named the same thing as the script file. If the names don't match, you won't be able to attach the script as a component to a GameObject.

- Scripts naturally have access to a "transform" member pointing to the Transform of the GameObject the script is attached to.

- Attributes are declared with a set of square braces "[]". Unity declares some built-in attributes that we can apply to variables for things like hiding a variable from the Inspector or applying a bold text header above a variable for organizational purposes.

■ ■ ■

CHAPTER 11

Inheritance

A major staple of object-oriented programming is the concept of inheritance. Inheritance is when types of data (such as classes) adopt fields – such as variables and methods – from another data type.

Say you have two classes that both share nearly all the same fields, but one has an extra field or an extra method that the other does not have. Coding each one separately is tedious. They behave in the same way for the most part. If you want to change something that both classes have, you need to make the change twice and make sure it's consistent. It becomes even more of a problem if you have many classes that share most of their functionality.

Inheritance is the solution to this. You can create a **base class** holding the functionality which both classes are meant to share, all in one place. Then, other classes **inherit** from the base class to automatically share its variables and methods without having to rewrite them. Everything stays declared in one place, keeping the functionality consistent across all the inheriting classes.

Inheritance in Action: RPG Items

A classic example of inheritance is the concept of items in a roleplaying game (RPG). Every item has certain fields:

- An int for its **worth**, which is how many golden coins it is worth in the shop
- A bool depicting whether it **canBeSold** at a shop
- A string for the item **name**

As well as any other fields you might intend to use in your game, like perhaps a description and a weight value to determine how hard it is for the player to lug the item around in their backpack.

But then we have more specific types of items. For now, let's say we have armor that goes in certain equipment slots and weapons that go in other equipment slots.

To implement this, we use inheritance. A **base class** stores the members that all items have. It resembles any sort of item, so we just call it **Item**. Now we can create classes that inherit from Item but have more particular uses.

Let's say every piece of equipment, whether it's a piece of armor or a weapon, has a durability value that wears down as the equipment is used. Armor loses durability as you take damage while wearing it, and weapons lose durability as you whack enemies with them.

We create an inheriting class called **Equipment**. Since it inherits Item, it has all those fields we give to the Item class, like name and description and so on, but we also give it an int for current durability and another for maximum durability. The current durability will go down by a point every so many hits a piece of armor takes or a weapon gives. The equipment breaks when the current durability hits 0. Repairing it will raise the current durability back to the maximum durability so we can start wearing it down again.

© Casey Hardman 2024
C. Hardman, *Game Programming with Unity and C#*, https://doi.org/10.1007/978-1-4842-9720-9_11

Now we make a class **Weapon** which inherits Equipment, adding fields like minimum and maximum damage, how fast the weapon attacks, and what kind of weapon it is (an enum with options like axe, sword, hammer, knife, a particularly sharp stone, and so on).

We have a separate class named **Armor**, which inherits from Equipment as well. We add a field for how much defense the armor provides. We'll also need an enum for the type – boots, belt, gloves, chest, or helmet – which we use to dictate which equipment slot the armor is allowed in.

If we wanted to also have a **Consumable** class for items that can be consumed, like drinking a potion or eating some food, we could have another class that inherits directly from Item. Ultimately, we end up with a hierarchy of classes looking like this, where classes that are indented further to the right are inheriting from the upper class:

```
Item
    Equipment
        Armor
        Weapon
    Consumable
```

Let's get the terminology down. **Lower types**, or **subclasses**, are **more specific** than their **upper type**, or **superclass**. Item is the upper type, and more specific versions of it, like Consumable or Equipment, are lower types of it. Yet more specific versions of Equipment are Weapon and Armor. This creates a hierarchy of classes, becoming more and more particular as we go down through the subclasses.

Declaring Our Classes

We can use the Item class we already declared as our base class. Up until now, we've had it nested inside our good old MyScript class, which means other scripts won't be able to access the Item class. You should do this when the nested class is **only** going to be used by the class it's nested inside. For a class resembling an Item, it really should be declared in its own script file, called "Item", so that it can be accessed across your whole project.

Since we're just using this Item class for example purposes, we'll keep it where it is, nested in the MyScript class, for convenience. We'll also cut out any of the old code we had lying around, giving us a fresh start with no constructor and no methods:

```
public class MyScript:MonoBehaviour
{
    class Item
    {
        public string name = "Unnamed Item";
        public int worth = 1;
        public bool canBeSold = true;
    }
}
```

This is our base class – the least specific kind of item. We declare our variables that all items have, and we give them default values. Later, we'll be giving them constructors, so the default values shouldn't be necessary because they should always be set by a constructor, but it won't hurt to have them anyway.

Let's declare the class for **Equipment** – which will serve as the upper type for Weapon and Armor. We'll put it in the same code block that Item is nested in, just under the Item class. Of course, this means it's not a child of Item, but it's a sibling – they're both nested in the same block:

```
public class MyScript:MonoBehaviour
{
    class Item
    {
        public string name = "Unnamed Item";
        public int worth = 1;
        public bool canBeSold = true;
    }
    class Equipment:Item
    {
        public int currentDurability = 100;
        public int maxDurability = 100;
    }
}
```

Notice the syntax is pretty much the same as any other class declaration, except that after "class Equipment" we have the colon ":" to designate that our class will inherit another; then we provide the name of the class we want to inherit from, which is "Item". That little part of the declaration is all we need to make Equipment inherit the members of Item.

Next, let's declare **Armor**. While we're at it, let's exhibit some of what we learned previously and declare an enum called **ArmorType**, which differentiates between the different kinds of armor (gloves, helmet, etc.). Place both of these definitions **within the MyScript code block, just under the Equipment class**:

```
enum ArmorType
{
    Helmet,
    Chest,
    Gloves,
    Belt,
    Boots
}
class Armor:Equipment
{
    public ArmorType type = ArmorType.Helmet;
    public int defense = 1;
}
```

The enum declaration is pretty self-explanatory, and we've already gone over that previously.

The Armor class inherits from Equipment, which in turn inherits from Item. This creates a chain. Ultimately, Armor inherits all the variables declared in Item, as well as those declared in Equipment. It adds its own members, one of which stores an instance of the ArmorType enum, which we default to Helmet, and an int for the defense rating of the armor, which we default to 1.

Now we can declare our **Weapon** class. Again, put the code **within the MyScript code block, beneath the Armor class**:

```
enum WeaponType
{
    Sword,
    Axe,
    Hammer
}
```

```
class Weapon:Equipment
{
    public WeaponType type = WeaponType.Sword;
    public int minDamage = 1;
    public int maxDamage = 2;
    public float attackTime = .6f;
}
```

This is the same deal as the Armor class. We declare a WeaponType enum with some basic weapon types in it. We then declare the Weapon class, which inherits Equipment and adds some of its own members: the weapon type, its minimum and maximum damage per hit, and the time it takes to perform a single attack with the weapon.

Constructor Chaining

Now we need to add constructors to all these classes so we can neatly create instances that apply the proper values to all these members we've set up. You can probably imagine how painful it can be to declare a unique constructor applying the members for each class, considering each of our lower types will need to have the same code to apply values held in the upper types. We'd have to declare parameters and apply their values for each member declared in Item, like worth and name, in every single lower type as well.

Luckily, we have a tool to make this easier, called **constructor chaining**. The constructors of lower types can "chain" into the upper type constructor, which can in turn chain into its next upper type, and so on. This chaining is pretty much just calling the upper constructor and supplying the parameters on the spot, right in the declaration of the constructor.

Think about it like this: every constructor must declare the parameters of all its upper types, but that doesn't mean we have to apply them all ourselves when we already have these upper constructors that could do it for us. So every constructor will declare all the necessary parameters, including the ones for members of its upper types. But any parameters that are not specific to that lower type will simply be "passed up" the constructor chain, letting the upper constructors handle their assignment. For example, Equipment will "pass up" the members declared in Item, letting Item apply them with its own constructor.

Let's see it in action. First, let's write our Item constructor. **Write this code within the Item class code block**:

```
public Item(string name, int worth, bool canBeSold)
{
    this.name = name;
    this.worth = worth;
    this.canBeSold = canBeSold;
}
```

This is your average constructor definition, as we learned about before. Because the parameters are named exactly the same as the members we declared in Item, we use "this." before the member name when applying the value, as discussed in the last chapter. Aside from that, all we're doing is just assigning the parameter values to the Item variables.

Now, let's declare the Equipment constructor. Of course, it goes **in the Equipment class, beneath the variables**:

```
public Equipment(string name, int worth, bool canBeSold, int maxDurability)
:base(name, worth, canBeSold)
{
    //Apply max durability:
    this.maxDurability = maxDurability;

    //Make current durability match max durability:
    currentDurability = maxDurability;
}
```

Now things are getting bulkier. The first thing you'll probably notice is the **":base"** coming after our parameter list. This is where the constructor chaining occurs. The keyword "base" refers to the upper class, the one that we are inheriting from – in this case, it's Item. We then have a set of parentheses afterward, which is pretty much equivalent to calling the upper constructor – the constructor of the base class Item.

When we call the upper constructor, we pass in all the first parameters that this constructor declares, which are all the same as those declared in the upper constructor. These are the parameters that are not specific to Equipment. They belong to Item, so we give them to the Item constructor. We already declared that constructor to apply all those values earlier, after all – and as programmers, we'd hate to repeat ourselves.

We also declare our own extra parameter in this constructor, **"maxDurability"**. This parameter is for a member that's specific to Equipment, so we don't pass it into the Item constructor. Item doesn't concern itself with durability. We use this parameter in the body of our constructor, to apply the value.

You'll notice we only have "maxDurability". We didn't make a parameter for "currentDurability". We apply the "maxDurability" parameter value first ("this.maxDurability = maxDurability"), and then we simply set our "currentDurability" to the given "maxDurability" value so the weapon starts out with maximum durability by default. Remember, "currentDurability" can be accessed simply by typing its name because it's an instanced member of the class that our code is nested inside. And since we don't have a parameter named "currentDurability" in the constructor, we don't need to type "this." before it.

Now we can take it a step further, adding another link to our chain. Let's make a chaining constructor for Armor. Again, place the constructor **just beneath the variables in the Armor class**:

```
public Armor(string name, int worth, bool canBeSold, int maxDurability,
ArmorType type, int defense)
:base(name, worth, canBeSold, maxDurability)
{
    this.type = type;
    this.defense = defense;
}
```

This is the same concept as before. We have all the same parameters in the same order as the upper types provide them. We can just copy-paste those over. We then chain the constructor to pass all those parameters up the hierarchy. This time, since Equipment is involved, we also add "maxDurability" to the base constructor call. We have extra parameters for the two members associated with Armor (type and defense), and we apply them in the constructor body.

To give you an overview of the way the parameters of each constructor are passed up the chain, here's a look at each constructor, with the new parameters in bold:

public Item(**string name, int worth, bool canBeSold**)
-   public Equipment(string name, int worth, bool canBeSold, **int maxDurability**)
-   -   public Armor(string name, int worth, bool canBeSold, int maxDurability, **ArmorType type, int defense**)
-   -   public Weapon(string name, int worth, bool canBeSold, int maxDurability, **WeaponType type, int minDamage, int maxDamage, float attackTime**)

Any parameters which are being "passed up the chain" to be handled by the upper type's constructor will be in normal text, while those which are handled by that specific constructor are bold. The indention also shows how the classes inherit from each other.

Now the assigning of "currentDurability" is automatically handled for Armor and Weapon, since we're just delegating the parameters up the chain to the Equipment constructor and letting it handle that for us. If we weren't chaining our constructors, we'd have to copy-paste all this code around, making a messy situation that's dangerously easy to become inconsistent if we ever need to make a change.

Moving on, let's declare a **Weapon** constructor. You could probably do this one yourself at this point:

```
public Weapon(string name, int worth, bool canBeSold, int maxDurability, WeaponType type,
int minDamage, int maxDamage, float attackTime)

:base(name, worth, canBeSold, maxDurability)
{
    this.type = type;
    this.minDamage = minDamage;
    this.maxDamage = maxDamage;
    this.attackTime = attackTime;
}
```

You get the gist – our constructor declares parameters for our Item members, then our Equipment (which is just the "maxDurability"), and then its own unique members. And again, we chain the constructor, just as we did with Armor, to pass up the parameters that aren't specific to Weapon.

Okay, that's the last of it. Now we have all our constructors and data set up for Item, Equipment, Armor, and Weapon.

Subtypes and Casting

When dealing with classes that inherit from each other, we often need to refer to them by an upper type when storing them, and then figure out what lower type they are on the spot and react accordingly.

For example, it's fine for us to store our player's equipped armor as Armor references and their weapon as a Weapon reference. Those are the only types we would allow the player to equip in their armor and weapon slots. But what about managing the player's inventory? In that case, we would want to use the base class, Item, to store each individual item in the player's inventory, because the player can pick up any type of item, right?

Inheritance helps us with this. If we have a variable of type Item, it can store any of the lower classes (or subtypes) as a reference. Thus, the player's inventory can store all of the items inside it as the Item type, but those items could be any subtype of Item, like Weapon or Armor, without causing any compiler errors. The thing is, since we're looking at them as an Item, we can only get the Item-specific members like "name", "worth", and so on. Trying to get members from a lower type would throw an error.

This is where the **typecast** comes into play. If you wanted to access members of a lower type like Weapon or Armor, you must first typecast the reference to the expected type.

A typecast is how we tell the compiler what we expect a type to be. It can then look at a reference to some generic type, like Item, as a more specific type, like Weapon.

Take the following code, where we create a Weapon. We provide some generic values for its parameters, defining it as a Rusty Axe. Most importantly, though, we store it in a local variable of type Item, not Weapon:

```
void Start()
{
    Item item = new Weapon("Rusty Axe", 4, true, 40, WeaponType.Axe, 4, 9, .6f);
}
```

> ■ **Note** We've briefly touched on this before, but in case you've forgotten, we're writing that "f" at the end of the last parameter value (".6f") to tell the compiler that the value is meant to be a float. At the end of this chapter, I'll explain why we need to do that in a little more detail.

This variable declaration demonstrates what we were just learning about. The reason we can store a Weapon in an Item variable is because Weapon is a lower type of Item. A Weapon is more specific, but can still be summed up as an Item because it has all the same members, even if it has some extra ones tacked on as well. This wouldn't be allowed the other way around – we can't store an instance of Item or Equipment in a variable of type Weapon or Armor, for example.

This is because when we reference a Weapon or Armor instance, we expect them to have all the members associated with those types. If they're instead storing a less specific type, that's just inviting unsavory errors. This is why our compiler won't let us do it in the first place. Part of the reason we use strongly typed languages is to enforce these rules upon us, to keep our code good and clean and to stop us from doing things we probably shouldn't even be doing in the first place.

Now that we've stored our Weapon instance as an Item reference, let's try getting it back to a Weapon reference and see what happens. We'll add a line of code declaring a local variable of type Weapon, and we'll assign the Item value to this variable:

```
void Start()
{
    Item item = new Weapon("Rusty Axe", 4, true, 40, WeaponType.Axe, 4, 9, .6f);

    Weapon weapon = item;
}
```

We **know** there is a Weapon stored in the "item" variable, so this should work – but if you save and check Unity, you'll see an error saying this:

> *Cannot implicitly convert type 'MyScript.Item' to 'MyScript.Weapon.' An explicit conversion exists (are you missing a cast?)*

What we're trying to do here is mentioned in the error message: implicitly converting a type.

Converting types can be done **implicitly** or **explicitly**.

The difference is simply in whether we, as the programmer, have manually ordered the conversion. In this case, we haven't used any special syntax to tell the compiler "I want to convert this type to that other type." So that makes this an **implicit** conversion, because if it's going to happen, it's going to happen without us necessarily telling it to.

These errors sort of act as guards set up to prevent us from accidentally, unknowingly doing type conversions that maybe shouldn't be done in the first place. The compiler doesn't know if that Item stores a Weapon. We may know because we just declared it, but compilers aren't in the habit of making assumptions, even when the context is just one line of code above the error.

We must make an **explicit** conversion by casting the type. This is an on-the-spot conversion that happens at runtime (meaning while the game is playing). We have to write special syntax to make this happen, which is why it's considered explicit – we know we're doing it. We specifically asked for it to happen, rather than it just happening on its own.

There are two ways to make this conversion. They each do the same thing but behave a little differently in the case where the types aren't actually compatible as we're expecting them to be.

The first way is to write the name of the type you want to cast to, wrapped in a set of parentheses, right before the "item" reference:

```
Weapon weapon = (Weapon)item;
```

This method **will result in an error** at runtime (meaning, while the game is playing) if the types aren't compatible – that is to say, if "item" is not actually storing a Weapon or a subtype of Weapon when this code occurs, an error will be thrown. Otherwise, it typecasts "item" to a Weapon.

The second method is with the **"as" operator**:

```
Weapon weapon = item as Weapon;
```

This method **will not** throw an exception if the types aren't compatible. Instead, it simply returns null, which is the equivalent of a reference that points at nothing. If it succeeds, it returns the type we expect, which is Weapon.

Of course, a failure in this case will usually result in an error afterward anyway, because you're likely going to go ahead and use the "weapon" variable as if it's actually storing a weapon. You'll reach in and try to grab some data from it or run a method in it, and since it's null, an error will be generated – just a different kind of error.

Type Checking

In the test cases we've dealt with so far, it's obvious to us what types we're dealing with, so we don't really have to worry about errors. But often, you'll first need to verify whether the type of a reference is actually what you think it is before you interact with it.

Say you've got a reference to an Item. For the sake of explanation without getting into a whole other set of problems, let's just assume we have an Item reference spat at us by some code that manages our player's inventory, and we need to check what lower type it is to determine what sort of functionality it should have.

There are several ways of doing this. Assuming we have a variable or parameter "item" of type Item, how do we check if it's a Weapon or Armor?

One method is with the **"is" operator**. This takes some value on its left-hand side and a direct reference to a type on its right-hand side. If the value is either exactly the same as the type or is a lower (more specific) type of it, the operator returns true. Otherwise, it returns false:

```
if (item is Weapon)
    Debug.Log("Item is a weapon.");

else if (item is Armor)
    Debug.Log("Item is an armor piece.");

else if (item is Equipment)
    Debug.Log("Item is some kind of equipment, but not Armor or Weapon.");
```

In this example, we log one message depending on whether the "item" is a Weapon or Armor, and if it's neither, but is a piece of equipment, we have a generic message to log instead. If it's not Equipment, nothing will be logged at all.

Another method to check if the Item reference is a more specific type would be to use the "as" operator we demonstrated earlier to assign the item to a new variable of that more specific type and then simply do an "if" to test if the result is null. If it was null, then we know the item is not that type. If it was not null, the item was that type, or a subtype of it:

```
Weapon weapon = item as Weapon;
if (weapon == null)
{
    //Cast failed, 'item' is not a Weapon instance
}
else
{
    //Cast succeeded, we can proceed to use 'weapon' reference
}
```

Sometimes, you might want to check if the instance is exactly the type you're comparing it with. In this case, the code looks a little less explanatory compared to our other examples. You call the instance method **"GetType"** on your object to get a reference to its exact type. You can compare that type with the "==" operator to another to see if they exactly match. But when referring directly to a type like this, you can't just write the name of the type. You must also wrap the type name between the parentheses of **"typeof(…)"**, as shown in the following example:

```
if (item.GetType() == typeof(Equipment))
    Debug.Log("Item type is exactly Equipment.");
```

When we declared "item", we assigned a Weapon instance to it. Since we're checking to see if the item is exactly Equipment, this will return false and the message won't be logged, because while the Weapon is technically Equipment in that it's a more specific, lower type, it's not *exactly* Equipment.

Using these three methods, you can cover pretty much any situation you might come across where you need to check a type.

Virtual Methods

One final aspect of inheritance is the concept of **virtual methods**. We're going to work with them later, during our second example project, so we'll learn all about the syntax and usage of them then. However, since we're on the topic of inheritance, let's learn about the theory behind them – what they are and what their purpose is.

You can mark methods as **virtual**, which means that they can be **overridden** by lower types so that the lower type can tack on its own functionality or even completely overwrite the upper type's functionality.

An example of the purpose of this might be if we had a few extra classes for item types. Let's say we had classes **"Consumable:Item"** and **"Food:Consumable"**.

The Consumable class is meant to represent things like potions or other such items that can be "used" to consume them on the spot for some effect. It has a virtual method declared inside it called **Use**. This method takes a "target" parameter pointing at a specific entity in the game – a player or an NPC. When the player or an NPC uses a potion, they call Use and provide a reference to themselves as the target. The virtual method will determine what happens to the target.

We can then make some classes like **"HealthPotion:Consumable"** and **"ManaPotion:Consumable"**. We override the virtual method Use, declaring a new version of it in each of these classes. Using the supplied "target" parameter, each implementation of the virtual method can do its own thing. The health potion will restore the target entity's health, and the mana potion will restore their mana. They each provide their own definition of Use.

We could then make a **"Food:Consumable"** which overrides Use to simply decrease the target's hunger value by the "tastiness" of the food, which would be a member variable specific to the Food class.

Then, given a reference to a Consumable, we can simply call Use on any target, without concerning ourselves with what exact lower type the consumable is. The correct method override will be used automatically – the food will sate hunger, and the potions will restore health or mana based on their type.

This can be a powerful feature, allowing inheriting classes to provide their own responses to given events, or their own ways to implement a feature they share in common.

Number Value Types

I promised I'd explain what the "f" means when it's placed at the end of a number value, like ".6f". It's known as a **suffix**.

A suffix can be tacked onto the end of number values to denote what value type we want the number to be stored as. So far, we've learned of **int** and **float**, but there are a variety of different types which have differing limitations on how high or low a number they can store. Other number types exist which either store a larger range of numbers but take up more memory or store a lower range and take up less memory.

For example, an **sbyte** is a much smaller int. Where int can store a value over 2 billion at the highest (and negative 2 billion at the lowest), an sbyte can store no lower than -128 and no higher than 127. As a result, an sbyte takes up less space on the computer, but it's not going to be able to store a high enough value in many situations.

There are also **unsigned** versions of data types. Unsigned means they can't store a negative value (their lowest value is 0), but as a result, they can store twice as high a positive value. For example, the "s" in "sbyte" means "signed." An unsigned version of the same type is just **byte**. It stores a value between 0 and 255. There's also an unsigned version of int: **uint**. It can go over 4 billion, but still can't go under 0.

Some of these types have a suffix you can use to easily write a number out as that type, like "f" to make a float. Some don't, and you have to use an explicit conversion to make them a certain type, for example, "(byte)120" to make a byte instead of an int.

By default, a value with no fraction will be an int, unless it stores a value outside the range of an int, in which case it goes up to the next largest type that can store the value.

On the other hand, a value with a fraction will store a **double**, which is twice as large as a float, but generally more accurate with its fraction value. If a parameter expects a float value, but we pass in a number like 0.6, we're really giving it a double. That will give us an error, so we tack that "f" suffix on the end to make it a float instead, fixing the error.

For most purposes, int and float will serve you perfectly well, and pretty much all of the built-in methods in the Unity engine will expect one of those two for number values. Unity's built-in methods use floats for values with a decimal point, so you'll be seeing that little "f" after numbers quite often.

This is another good example of type conversions, and how they can be implicit or explicit. Why doesn't a double just implicitly (automatically) convert itself to a float whenever it's given where a float is expected? Why are we forced to type this "f" after our numbers?

The answer is simple: because a double stores more information than a float. If we convert from double to float, we lose decimal places – information is lost that could be important to our program. Thus, an implicit conversion won't happen – we have to explicitly agree to make the conversion. The same goes for converting from a float to an int: the decimal value of the float would have to be thrown away to store the value in an int, so the conversion won't happen without our explicit permission.

However, if we were to assign something like a byte – as mentioned, that's a number from 0 to 255 – to an int, the conversion will be implicit. It'll just happen, without us having to type anything extra. This is because an int can store all the information of a byte without losing any, so the conversion doesn't have any chance of throwing away data we may not have intended to dispose of.

As I said, in Unity, we'll pretty much exclusively be dealing with int and float as number types. However, should you ever need to use another value, Table 11-1 gives a rundown of the values for integer types and their suffix, if any (some types don't have a suffix).

Table 11-1. *Integer value data types and their associated suffixes*

Data Type	Value Range	Suffix
sbyte	–128 to 127	--
byte	0 to 255	--
short	–32,768 to 32,767	--
ushort	0 to 65,535	--
int	–2,147,483,648 to 2,147,483,647	--
uint	0 to 4,294,967,295	U
long	–9,223,372,036,854,775,808 to –9,223,372,036,854,775,807	L
ulong	0 to 18,446,744,073,709,551,615	UL

On top of that, there are three different value types we can use for number values with a decimal – also known as "floating point" values (which is where the name "float" comes from):

- **"float"** uses the **"f"** or **"F"** suffix.

- **"double"** is the default when no suffix is used, although you can also use **"d"** or **"D"**.

- **"decimal"** uses the **"m"** or **"M"** suffix.

Doubles are called double because they're double the size of a float. A decimal doubles the size yet again, making them four times the size of a float.

To make a somewhat complicated topic short and sweet, floating point values are not totally accurate all the time, particularly when storing high values in them. You might set their value to something, then later get the value back with the fraction slightly different, off by just a tiny bit. Data types which are larger than float can store larger values and remain more accurate throughout. Again, float will likely serve you just fine in most situations you'll encounter working with Unity. The only times you may encounter problems would be when storing very high values.

Summary

You've now been primed on the fundamental concept of inheritance. It's a somewhat vast topic, and there are some pieces we haven't covered yet, but you hardly need to know all the intricacies of inheritance to be able to code some simple games, and as you grow as a programmer, you'll learn more.

As we continue, we'll exercise these concepts bit by bit and grow more comfortable with them, learning to use them to avoid repeating our code by sharing the functionality that's common between our classes.

Here are some things to keep in mind:

- A **lower type**, or **subtype**, is a type that **inherits** from an **upper type**. For example, our Armor type is a lower type which inherits from its upper type, Equipment.

- Lower types share all the same members, such as variables and methods, as their upper type. The lower type can then declare additional members unique to itself. This means the lower type is **more specific** than the upper type.

- **Constructor chaining** allows our lower types to "pass up" the parameters that their constructor shares with their upper types, allowing the constructor of the upper type to handle them instead.

- A variable or parameter whose type is that of an upper type is allowed to store an object that matches any of its lower types. For example, our Item class can store a Weapon or Armor instance without any errors.

CHAPTER 12

Debugging

We touched on debugging in the first chapter. Now that you've learned the basics of programming, we'll see how the debugging features of a code editor actually work and how to use them to find problems in your code. If you've opted to use a code editor that doesn't support debugging with Unity, you won't be able to follow along on your own computer, but you'll still learn how these features work and why you might use them. I'll be using Microsoft Visual Studio Community 2019 for this chapter, but the basic features of debugging are usually quite similar regardless of the editor you're using, so things will probably look and behave roughly the same way if you're using a different editor, like JetBrains Rider.

Debugging is a fancy feature of code editors that allows us to mark any line of code as a **breakpoint**, causing the game to pause when we reach that line of code. Once the game is paused, we can hop over to our code editor and see the values of our variables, frozen in time, and even play out one line of code at a time while keeping the game paused.

This can be immensely useful when our code isn't doing what we intend it to do and we want to figure out why. It's especially useful when dealing with subtle errors that can't really be visually studied, such as in situations where you're just modifying data that you have no way of viewing. A common alternative approach would be to start calling "Debug.Log" to give yourself a view of data that might not be what you expect it to be. This can be sufficient in some situations, but is often quite tedious.

With debugging, we can just drop a breakpoint at the problem area, and when that code is reached, the game pauses and we can view the values of all of our variables. For example, if we break during an Update call for a script, we can view instance variables for that script itself (ones declared in the script class) as well as local variables declared within the Update method. We can then continue through the execution of the program one line of code at a time, even going inside the calls of other methods to watch their execution one line at a time.

Setting Up the Debugger

If you haven't started up Visual Studio yet, you can do so through the Unity editor by hitting the Assets menu button at the top of the window, then clicking "Open C# Project" near the bottom of the drop-down menu. If you installed Visual Studio with Unity through the Hub, this should automatically start it.

In Visual Studio, you should see a button at the top that says "Attach to Unity" as shown in Figure 12-1.

Figure 12-1. *The Attach to Unity button at the top of the window in Visual Studio, shown with a red outline*

© Casey Hardman 2024
C. Hardman, *Game Programming with Unity and C#*, https://doi.org/10.1007/978-1-4842-9720-9_12

Before debugging in Unity, you have to hit this button. It tells Visual Studio to start listening to your Unity editor.

Breakpoints

Before we start debugging, let's learn how to place a breakpoint to stop our program when a certain line of code is about to run. Otherwise, attaching the debugger to Unity won't actually do anything.

One way is to click the empty space at the left side of the line of code you want to break on, to the left of the line number. You can also press F9 to create a breakpoint at the line of code that your text cursor is currently placed – just click anywhere on the text of a line of code that you want to stop on, then press F9, and a breakpoint will be made there.

Once you've set a breakpoint, a red dot will appear at the left side of the line of code. You can click the dot again or press F9 again to remove the breakpoint.

Let's do a quick example to demonstrate debugging features. Create a new script named "DebuggingTest" and add an instance of it to a GameObject in your scene. We won't be paying attention to the GameObject or anything in the scene, so it doesn't really matter what you put it on.

We don't need the Update event, so you can delete that, but we will use the Start event to declare a local variable and then change its value three times. This is how your script class should look:

```
public class DebuggingTest : MonoBehaviour
{
    // Start is called before the first frame update
    void Start()
    {
        int a = 5;
        a += 5;
        a *= 2;
        a = 0;
    }
}
```

This code isn't doing anything, really. We're just aimlessly changing the value so we can see it happen one line at a time with the debugger, for the purpose of example.

Add a breakpoint to the "int a = 5;" line, which should make it look like Figure 12-2: a red circle is shown at the left side of the line number, and the line of code itself has a red highlight.

Figure 12-2. *A breakpoint is added to the line of code, symbolized by the red circle at its left side*

Now, make sure you've got the DebuggingTest script added to an instance of a GameObject in your scene, click the **"Attach to Unity"** button in Visual Studio, then go to the Unity editor and hit the **play** button to start your game.

The Start method call of our DebuggingTest script instance will immediately occur, and that breakpoint will cause the game to be suspended in the Unity editor. Heading back to Visual Studio, the line that we placed our breakpoint on will be highlighted, signifying that the execution of the code has reached that point and is now paused. The line of code will run next, but not until we tell it to. The Unity editor will be frozen, waiting for us to tell it to start again through Visual Studio. Until then, our game is paused.

At the bottom of Visual Studio, the "Locals" window shows us all of the variables that are available to us in this context – that is, in the block of code that the breakpoint has stopped us on. Here, you can see the "a" variable we declared, and you can see the value of it is 0, as shown in Figure 12-3.

Figure 12-3. *The Locals window in Visual Studio after our breakpoint has activated*

It also shows **"this"**, which is the keyword we can use to reference the class that's running the method. Since "this" is a script and has many members inside it to view, it has a little arrow at its side, signifying that it can be "unfolded" to view its contents. Clicking that arrow will show you the other members of the script, although there's not much to see there. If you were working with complex data types, you could unfold them and search through their members this way.

What we're focused on is our "a" variable, though. Notice that its value is 0. This is because the breakpoint will suspend the program **before its line of code runs**, not after, so our "int a = 5;" has not assigned the value of 5 to the variable yet.

Now that the program is suspended by a breakpoint, the "Attach to Unity" button will become a "Continue" button. Pressing this will unpause the game and continue debugging, meaning the game will pause once again when the next breakpoint is reached. For us, that means it won't pause again, since we only have the one breakpoint in our Start method.

To the right side of the "Continue" button, you'll notice some other options, shown in Figure 12-4.

Figure 12-4. *Debugging options in Visual Studio*

From left to right, the buttons are as follows:

- **Stop Debugging** (hotkey Shift+F5) – This button ends the debugging process. Your game will keep playing in Unity, but it won't pause at breakpoints anymore.

- **Restart** (hotkey Ctrl+Shift+F5) – This restarts the debugger, but does not restart your game in the Unity editor. For Unity, this button isn't very useful. In general, you'll probably instead want to stop debugging, stop playing the game in the Unity editor, and then Attach to Unity and start your game again, rather than clicking this button.

- **Show Next Statement** (hotkey Alt+Numpad *) – This button will move your view to the next statement that will be run. It can be useful if you're viewing different script files while debugging, and want to quickly get back to the current breakpoint.

- **Step Into** (hotkey F11) – This is for when you are paused at a line of code that contains any method calls (if not, it works just like Step Over). The program will "step into" that method instead and suspend again at the first line of code within that method.

- **Step Over** (hotkey F10) – This runs the current line of code and then pauses execution again. The term "step over" comes from the fact that it won't bring you into any method calls in the current line, like Step Into does. It just runs the code and moves on to the next line. It may sound like it means to "step over" the line of code by not running it, but that's not true.

- **Step Out** (hotkey Shift+F11) – This executes whatever is left of the current method and then suspends again. If you accidentally step into a method when you didn't mean to, you can use this to hop back out.

These controls can be very useful in certain circumstances. Sometimes you want to see how a method ends up returning what it does, in which case you can step into it and watch it execute one line at a time. After, you'll be brought back to the original line of code that called the method. If multiple methods are called throughout a line of code, you can step into each one individually, one after the other, as they are executed. You might do this, for example, if your breakpoint was on a line of code that called a method, but also called many other methods to return values for the parameters of that method:

```
SomeMethod(A() + B(), C(), D());
```

In that case, you could step first into A, then B, then C, then D, and then finally the "SomeMethod" call.

But enough chatter about the theory of it all: we have a breakpoint, so let's watch it in action. After you have attached to Unity and started your game, you'll be paused on that first line of code, where we declare our variable.

Click Step Over once. The highlighted line of code will move forward to the next line. In the Locals section, you should see the value of "a" update to become 5.

Now, we're paused before the "a += 5;" line. Click Step Over again to run that line, and you can see the value of "a" update to become 10. Run "a *= 2" and the 10 becomes 20. You get the point.

Once we run out of code in our Start method to run, Step Over will begin to take you to the next natural line of code to run. This might not even be your own code – it could end up taking you to some engine code. It's best to let your breakpoints lead you to the places you want to check out, then Continue once you're finished; otherwise, you never know where you'll end up.

As a final note, notice that none of the controls actually skip code. The code will still be executed – the controls simply dictate how much of it to execute before stopping again.

Using Unity's Documentation

Debugging is a means of finding out what the cause of a problem is on your own. A large part of being a programmer is problem-solving: you have to figure out what's going wrong or how to go about doing something. While we're on that topic, let's learn a little bit about how to find helpful resources as a programmer.

I can tell you how to do this and that throughout the course of this book, and you can learn a lot, but eventually, you'll have to strike out on your own and figure out how to do something yourself. And that's what can make or break a programmer. A large part of your learning is probably going to come when you start programming your own stuff, when you're learning what to do as you go, putting the pieces together to achieve something. You want to eventually make your own games, right?

When faced with a challenge to overcome, you need information on what you're dealing with. Any decent search engine will often return Unity's official documentation as one of the first results. Just search for "unity" followed by the class name or component type you want to learn more about, like Light or Rigidbody.

Unity separates its documentation into two forms – the **Manual** and the **Scripting API** (API is short for application programming interface):

- The **Manual** documentation is more of an instructional page describing how a component works and how one might use it, usually with images and examples. It is aimed at teaching a new concept to the reader.

- The **Scripting API** is technical documentation specifically for programmers. It describes classes and their members, such as variables, properties, and methods. You can navigate to a page devoted to any of these individual fields, which will give further information – notably, a description of the field's purpose, but also important information like what type a variable stores, what type a method returns, the types and names of parameters that a method expects, all of the overloads of a method and how they differ from each other, and so on. It is aimed at programmers looking for information about Unity's built-in types and methods and usually provides code samples of how to use and interact with individual members or types.

The latter form of documentation is commonly found in various programming environments. If you ever stray away from Unity and into a different game engine, there will likely be API documentation with a similar structure and layout, showing you types and their members. For example, Microsoft – the company behind the C# programming language – maintains similar documentation for the many built-in types offered with the language.

For example, want to learn how to save and read from files on the user's computer? That sort of stuff is in the "System.IO" namespace. Search for it, and you'll probably get the official Microsoft documentation as one of the first results. There you can find the classes and methods you'll use to get the job done, including descriptions and code samples. If you don't have someone to tell you where to find the relevant classes, just search for a more general term, like "how to read from a text file in C#". Follow the trail until you know what to write!

Good API documentation like this can make a huge difference on your experience with coding in an environment. You might hit a point where you don't really want to read a tutorial on how to use a component – you just want descriptions of the types you'll be working with and the fields they store. With proper documentation, you can get this with a simple search and be on your way.

Becoming comfortable finding information on your own this way can be a huge help in allowing you to solve problems and make stuff work on your own.

Summary

In this chapter, we learned how to run our debugger and work with its controls. While it may seem redundant right now, a debugger can be a lifesaver, allowing you to look at the process your code is taking one line at a time as it executes. Being able to read the values of variables at each step in the code can do much more to illuminate a problem than "Debug.Log" calls. You also learned how Unity's documentation is organized and how you might go about finding information for yourself whenever you're working on something outside the scope of this book.

PART III

Obstacle Course

CHAPTER 13

■ ■ ■

Obstacle Course Design and Outline

Now that you've been introduced to the basics of the Unity engine and the fundamentals of programming, we're going to develop our first example project. You might not feel totally confident with all the things we've learned so far. Maybe some things have slipped through the cracks. That's okay. More and more of it will stick around as you put the concepts to use.

Before you get too excited, note that the example projects we develop won't have flashy graphics and audio. We're focusing on the code that runs them, not on making or importing art and audio assets. This way, you can focus on your own domain until you've got it down. Once you've finished this book, you can branch out depending on what your goals are. A lot of independent game developers will learn to do a little of everything, but you could also find assets on the Internet – some are even free – and use those to give yourself more time to spend mastering programming. Or you could just pair up with some like-minded individuals who want to make a game with you and have them work on the art and audio for you.

Developing a game can be a daunting task. A lot of moving parts and pieces go into the creation of a game. Things may change while you're developing a project and putting those parts together – something may have seemed like a good idea only for you to find out it kind of sucks once you've seen it in action. It happens, but it's no excuse to go in blind.

There's a fine line between planning too little and too much, and you might never get it totally right. You might plan for all sorts of stuff that never comes about because it turns out to not be feasible – you can't implement it or you run out of time or any other number of excuses. Some developers just don't plan much at all and let the pieces fall in place. You'll find your middle ground with time.

But before we dive in, we're going to do a little bit of planning. It'll make it easier to get things how we want it the first time, so we don't find ourselves doubling back and redoing things.

Gameplay Overview

Let's go over how the game will play. It will use an overhead camera, pointing down at the player character. The player will move with the WASD keys or the arrow keys, and press Space while holding a movement key to perform a quick dash in that direction. The dash has a short cooldown before it can be used again, but otherwise has no cost to performing it.

The game levels will be blocked out with cubes for walls, colored differently than the floor to distinguish them. The player will collide with these walls on touch, confining them to the playing space we've set up.

© Casey Hardman 2024
C. Hardman, *Game Programming with Unity and C#*, https://doi.org/10.1007/978-1-4842-9720-9_13

The objective of the game is to avoid touching obstacles within that playing space. Each level has a starting point where the player begins and a goal to reach at the end, which is just a simple, circular podium. Dying at the hands of the obstacles will respawn the player at the beginning of the level until they reach the end (or give up and quit out of frustration).

Obstacles will include

- **Patrolling hazards**, which move from one point to the next in a series of points, return to the original point when finished, and then repeat. We will set the points up ourselves, individually, for each patrolling hazard we place in a Scene. As hazards, they kill the player on touch.

- **Projectiles**, which are fired by obstacles, traveling in a straight line until they hit a wall. They are also hazards that will kill the player on touch.

- **Wandering hazards**, which are confined to a single rectangular area, occasionally choosing a new random point to go to. Upon choosing a new point, they gradually rotate to face that point and then begin moving toward it. The rotation before moving is to give the player a moment to react before the hazard starts its movement.

- **Spike traps**, which periodically raise a circle of hazardous spikes and then lower them down again. The player must cross when the spikes are down.

The main menu will allow the player to select which level they want to play on. They can cycle through the levels to load them and view them from overhead. When ready, they click a button to begin playing the level.

From within a level, the player can press Escape to bring up an in-game menu, which allows them to return to the main menu if they do not wish to play the level anymore.

At first, we'll implement the important stuff. Game developers often focus first on the core mechanics, which will determine whether the game is fun or a dud. We hardly need any proper menus and level selection if the game isn't fun at the core, right?

We'll keep it confined to one scene while we implement these core mechanics, like the player movement, the obstacles, and the player dying and respawning.

We'll worry about proper level selection and whatnot after we get our major features functioning.

Technical Overview

To prepare for our project, we should outline what we expect to have to implement and consider how these things will be implemented in our engine. With experience, this becomes easier, but even if you're a beginner, it doesn't hurt to at least try to figure out the general idea behind implementing each feature before you start on any of them. While going over everything, you might spot things you hadn't thought about yet or flaws in the way you thought you might do something. Having a high-level overview of the whole project going through your head at once can be useful in that way.

Player Controls

The player will be represented by a cube with another little cube on the top, colored differently and pointing along their local forward direction (otherwise, you won't be able to tell which way they're facing). This is shown in Figure 13-1.

Figure 13-1. *The player, facing toward the camera. The blue arrow gizmo at the bottom shows the local forward axis of the player*

The Player script will be on the root GameObject, which we'll base off an empty GameObject. This will hold separate GameObjects for the cubes that visually represent the player. When we rotate the player to face toward their last movement direction, we only rotate the cubes, not the root player GameObject.

This way, we can make the camera a child of the player so it moves with them, and since the root itself isn't rotating, the camera won't rotate with it – which would be very awkward, unintended, and jarring. We want the camera to stay in the same position relative to the model, even when the model rotates.

We'll have a Player script that handles all the player-related functionality. Primarily, this means movement and dodging.

The movement will be done either with WASD keys or the arrow keys, since some users prefer one over the other. We'll put a little bit of momentum to it. The player will take a bit to reach full speed and to lose full speed. We won't go too crazy with this, though, as we risk making the player too slippery. We want to keep things pretty accurate to avoid frustrating accidents because our character was skidding around when we wanted them to stop, but we still want a little bit of springiness so the movement doesn't look or feel too jerky.

Dodging will be done by pressing space, providing a fast lunge in the direction the player is facing. It'll be over quick, but during that time, the normal movement won't be calculated so that only the dodge velocity goes through. You'll have to be moving in any direction when you press space; otherwise, the dodge won't activate.

Death and Respawn

When the player dies, we'll wait a short duration and then return (or "respawn") them at the start of the level. While they're dead, we don't want to let them move around, so we'll disable the Player script until the respawn has finished. Disabling scripts is a useful feature, so this will be an important thing to learn about.

Levels

All we really need to shape a level is just a plane underneath the player acting as the floor with its own unique color, and then we'll place raised blocks and size them however we need to block out the "walls" of the level. When the player moves, they'll collide with the walls, stopping them from leaving the play area. The game will be viewed from above with an orthographic camera, which is a camera that doesn't use perspective – sort of like viewing the world in a 2D way. This way, you don't really see the walls as raised, but rather, they just look like a different color among the rest. We won't see the sides of walls (since there's no perspective), and we won't have shadows or lighting. You'll see how this works once we get to that point, so don't worry if it sounds confusing right now.

This is a somewhat hacky way of designing levels, but first and foremost, it'll be functional and quick to produce. If we were making a game we planned on publishing, we'd be dealing with art assets and designing our levels in some other way, but we aren't focused on such things.

To allow the player to win the level, we'll have a Goal script that detects when the player walks (or slides, I should say) over it, returning them to the level selection screen when they do.

Level Selection

Each level will have its own scene dedicated to it. The main scene will be loaded by default when the user starts the game, and this main scene will have our menu code in it. Our menu will allow the player to cycle through levels, which will load in the scene for the desired level so we can preview it. When we load in a new scene, the last one will be cleaned up and removed for us automatically.

Each level scene will have a preview camera in it, which we'll position over the level to give the player a preview of its entirety.

Once we begin playing a level, we'll switch to the player camera and disable the preview camera.

Obstacles

We went over a similar concept for our obstacles in an early chapter, when we were first learning about components. We'll make these scripts:

- **Hazard**, which makes a GameObject "kill" the player on touch
- **Wanderer**, which gives a GameObject the erratic "wandering" movement we described
- **Patroller**, which lets us set up a path for a GameObject to repeatedly move along
- **Shooting**, which makes a GameObject periodically fire projectiles
- **SpikeTrap**, which makes a hazardous GameObject rapidly spring outward and then lower harmlessly back into its spot, waiting to raise again after a specified wait duration

By mixing these scripts on GameObjects, we can implement all the obstacles we desire.

Project Setup

Let's get a new Unity project ready for this game. Open Unity Hub and create a new project with the "New project" button in the top-right corner. We've been here before, so you might remember the window that pops up. Select the 3D template, name your project ObstacleCourse, and save it to whichever folder you want, as shown in Figure 13-2.

Figure 13-2. *Creating our "ObstacleCourse" project using the default 3D template in the Unity Hub*

In your Project window, navigate to the Assets folder, where you'll see there's already a folder named Scenes inside it. In the Assets folder, add three new folders to give the Scenes folder some company: Materials, Prefabs, and Scripts.

While we're at it, let's rename the default SampleScene asset (located in your Assets/Scenes folder) to "main". This can be done by right-clicking the asset in the Project and then selecting "Rename". After confirming the rename, Unity might pop up a window asking you if you'd like to reload the scene. Go ahead and do that.

The scene will have a Directional Light and a Main Camera in it by default. We can leave those be, but we also want to add a basic floor for the player to stand on.

- Using the top-left menus, select GameObject ➤ 3D Object ➤ Plane.

- Select the Plane in the Hierarchy if it isn't already selected, and navigate to the Inspector.

- Name it "Floor".

- If it is not already, set the Transform position to (0, 0, 0) to ensure that it is centered at the world origin.

- To make it large enough that we shouldn't have to worry about running out of space, set its scale to (1000, 1, 1000).

Your Project view should look like Figure 13-3 when you're done.

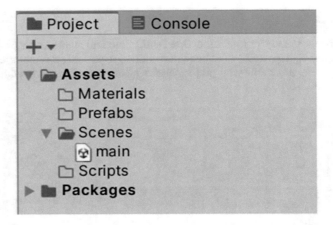

Figure 13-3. Our Project window once we've added our folders and renamed the scene

Summary

We've established how our project is expected to play: a simple top-down obstacle course where the player moves around with the WASD keys and avoids dangerous obstacles while attempting to navigate to the end of the level. Knowing what we expect of our game, we can start implementing the pieces one at a time.

CHAPTER 14

■ ■ ■

Player Movement

With our new project in place, let's start coding our player's movement. We're going to get a little fancy with it to exercise our programming skills and learn about some new methods.

As we mentioned in the last chapter, we want movement to be fluid – not jerky, but not slippery, either. A little bit of time to build to the maximum speed will make it less of a sudden jerk when the player begins moving. Likewise, we want some time to lose speed after you stop holding down the movement keys. It won't be much, because a game like this requires tight control of the character, so we definitely don't want the player feeling like they're skidding around.

We've talked about these concepts along the way to this point, so you should remember some of what I'm about to say.

We'll handle the player's movement velocity frame by frame. The velocity is a Vector3 (a type that stores X, Y, and Z values) that depicts the change in position the player will be constantly experiencing from their movement. We use units per second as our measurement. For example, if velocity is (15, 0, 12), then the player will be moving right at 15 units per second and forward at 12 units per second. They won't be moving on the Y axis at all for this game, because the player has no up or down movement – just forward, back, right, and left. When playing the game, you might think to describe the Z axis as "up and down," because that's the direction it will take your character on the screen, but it's actually forward and back in world space.

Remember, the camera is positioned overhead, pointing down at the player, so if the player were to actually go directly up in world space, they'd be going toward the camera. Thus, we won't be using the Y axis in our velocity. The player will remain on flat ground throughout, and they'll never have anything but 0 for their Y velocity, because that would only move them toward or away from the camera.

To move the player with the sort of smoothness we're after, we'll be increasing or decreasing the velocity based on the player's input, and we'll constantly move them by that velocity (per second). The WASD and arrow keys will both work for movement, so the player can use whichever they prefer. While holding the keys, the velocity will change gradually to produce the desired movement.

While the player is moving, we'll point their model in the direction their velocity is taking them. To visualize this, the player is given a simple model made of a few cubes, one of which pokes out along the player's local forward axis. This makes it obvious which direction the model is facing. It may not be fancy or pretty, but it gets the job done and lets us focus on the code.

Player Setup

Let's set up our player GameObject. We'll be staying in the same "main" scene for now, using it as a playground of sorts to develop and test whatever we're working on at the moment.

The hierarchy will look as pictured in Figure 14-1 – we'll walk through the process of creating each GameObject in a bit. We made the Floor in the last chapter: it's just a Plane positioned at (0, 0, 0) with a scale of (1000, 1, 1000), which will serve as the floor for our whole game.

© Casey Hardman 2024

C. Hardman, *Game Programming with Unity and C#*, https://doi.org/10.1007/978-1-4842-9720-9_14

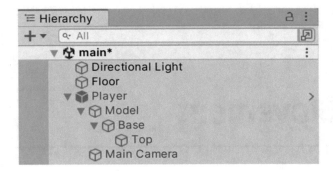

Figure 14-1. *The Hierarchy window once we've finished setting up our player*

The base GameObject named "Player" is the Transform that we'll actually move. Of course, this means the children will move with it. But we don't rotate this Transform, because it holds our camera. Remember that children will act as if they are physically attached to their parent, so if we spin that base Player GameObject around, the camera will swivel around with it. This will be very jarring and disorienting for the player.

To avoid this, we create an empty GameObject named Model and place it inside the Player. This is the "model holder." It's just there to store all of our model-related GameObjects. Our script will reference this Transform and rotate it to face the movement direction. This way, the base GameObject (which holds the camera) is never rotated. Only the model is.

The model holder simply has two cubes inside it, one named Base and one named Top.

Here's what you'll do to create the Player and all of its children:

- Create an empty GameObject (Ctrl+Shift+N on Windows or Cmd+Shift+N on Mac) and name it "Player".

- Create an empty child of this GameObject (while selecting the Player, Alt+Shift+N on Windows or Opt+Shift+N on Mac) and name it "Model". Ensure that its local position is (0, 0, 0) so that it's positioned exactly on the Player.

- Create a cube that's a child of Model by right-clicking Model in the Hierarchy and selecting 3D Object ➤ Cube. Name this cube "Base". Set its local position to (0, 2.5, 0) and set its scale to (1.4, 5, 1.4). This is local scale, but all of its parents have a scale of 1, so it's equivalent to world scale. The local Y position is half the Y scale, to keep the bottom of the cube at the pivot point instead of the center (the pivot point being the position of the Player GameObject).

- Create a second cube, this time a child of Base. Name it "Top" and set its position to (0, .5, .5) and its scale to (.33, .1, .7).

- The Main Camera GameObject should already be present in the scene. If not, create one with GameObject ➤ Camera and rename it to "Main Camera". Drag the camera onto the Player GameObject, making it a direct child of the player root (not the Model!). For now, we'll give it a local position of (0, 24, -5) and rotation of (70, 0, 0) to put it a good way over the player's head, back a little bit, and tilted down. Figure 14-2 shows how the camera Transform should look in the Inspector.

- Create a prefab for the Player by dragging the Player GameObject from the Hierarchy window to the Prefabs folder in the Project window.

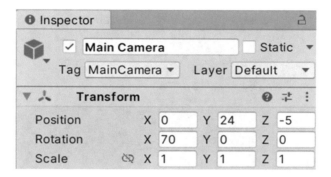

Figure 14-2. *The Transform component of our Main Camera in the Inspector*

At this point, you should now have a Hierarchy window looking like Figure 14-1 from earlier.

The Top cube will poke out along the forward axis of the player (the facing direction). This way, we always know where the player is pointing.

Materials and Colors

Now we want to color the cubes, each one a different color so the Top stands out from the Base. To do this, we use **materials**. A material is a built-in Unity asset that stores information about how a mesh (or a 2D image) should be rendered. Most notably, they allow you to apply **textures** to meshes. **Textures** are pretty much normal 2D images that are stretched over and wrapped around a mesh (3D object). This is how we turn objects from flat surfaces that render only a single color to things like rock, tree bark, tile floors, plaster walls, and so on. Some games use pictures of real things; others use stylized drawings.

Materials have many different settings, but they relate mostly to integrating art assets into your game project. As I've said before, we're not really going to dig into that over the course of this book. We'll use materials simply to apply color to our solid objects, which is one of the most basic ways to use a material.

In the Project view, right-click the Materials folder and select Create ➤ Material. Create a material named Player Base and another one named Player Top. With either one of the new materials selected, the Inspector will show a somewhat daunting list of fields we can edit for the material. Luckily, we only need one little control. Near the top, just beneath the bold text "Main Maps," there's a swatch of color to the right side of the word "Albedo" (see outlined section of Figure 14-3), with an eyedropper icon beside it.

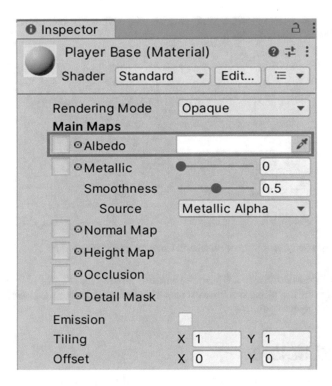

Figure 14-3. *The Inspector with our Player Base material selected. The "Albedo" color field is highlighted*

This is a color field for the material. By default, it's a shade of white. The rectangle of color to the right side of the "Albedo" text is the color that the material is currently set to use. Click that white rectangle to pop up a color window that lets us change the color, shown in Figure 14-4. You can also click the eyedropper and then click a color anywhere on your screen to select that color.

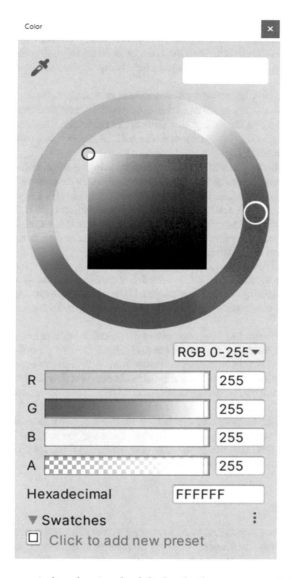

Figure 14-4. *The color pop-up window showing the default color for a new material*

Let's learn how computers look at color. It's a concept that will likely come up often for a game developer, even if you're just programming. Don't worry, it's not too complicated.

The top half of the color pop-up window is an interactive wheel with a square in the middle. Click the wheel to change the hue of the color. Click within the square to change how vibrant and bright the color is.

The bottom half of the window lets you set number values directly. The first three fields will resemble individual **components** of the color, showing a single letter on the left side, a colorful bar to the right of it, and then a little box with a number in it. The number is the value of that color component. The letter is short for a word that depicts what the component controls. The bar is a visual representation of how raising or lowering that component value will change the color. You can click within the bar to change the color component individually. You can also just edit the number directly, if you're savvy like that.

So what are the color components? It depends on the **color model** you're using. There are two main models that computers use to depict a color: **RGB** (red, green, blue) and **HSV** (hue, saturation, value). Each model resembles a color in a different way, but they can both be easily converted to and from the other. You can change the color model with the little drop-down field beneath the color wheel, which by default is set to RGB (0–255).

The **HSV** model tends to be a little easier to understand and predict. **Hue** is the color – red, green, blue, purple, cyan, yellow, and so on. It is a value from 0 to 360, which corresponds to an angle on the color wheel. **Saturation** is a value from 0 to 100, depicting how vibrant the color is. A lower value will make it turn closer and closer to a gray shade. **Value** is the brightness of the color. A lower value will shift the color closer to black. It also ranges from 0 to 100.

The **RGB** model stores the amount of red, green, and blue in the color, either ranging from 0 to 255 or, alternatively, from 0 to 1 (using fractional values). All shades of color can be obtained by mixing the correct proportion of these three primary colors. For example, black is no color (0, 0, 0), white is the maximum amount of each color (255, 255, 255), and yellow is a mix of red and green (255, 255, 0). Colors which use a more even mix of all three components will appear less saturated; colors which use high values in one or two components will be more vibrant, the sort of shade you might see in toys or fancy sports cars. Colors which use a low amount in all components will be darker.

That covers the first three fields, but what about the fourth field, with the letter **"A"** beside it?

This is **alpha**. It's there regardless of the color model. It determines transparency and ranges from 0 to 100. Changing it won't do anything because our material itself doesn't support transparency, but just so you know, a low alpha makes the color more transparent (see-through), and a high alpha makes it more solid (also called opaque).

Finally, the bottom field is the **hexadecimal value** of the color. Sometimes shortened to hex value, this is a way to describe a color in a single string of letters and numbers. Change this field, and you'll change all of the color components at once. It is, however, less user-friendly and pretty much looks like an arbitrary slur of characters. It's an easy way for me to give you a short code that you can easily type into the hex value field to get the same colors I'm using (if you want), though, so I'll use it to describe colors to you whenever I'm making materials.

I've chosen a dark blue for the base and a pale blue for the top. You can exhibit some creativity and choose your own colors if you like, but if you want to have it chosen for you, the hex value for the base is 7CBAD0, and for the top, it's B6DAF5. Just type those codes into the Hexadecimal field in the color window for either material, and you'll get the same color.

Applying Materials

Now that you have your materials, you just need to apply them to the correct cube GameObjects. Technically, this is done through the Mesh Renderer component in the Inspector, but it's easiest to just click and drag the material asset from the Project window to the desired GameObject in the Hierarchy or Scene window, which will apply the material to the Mesh Renderer automatically. Just make sure you apply the Base to the larger cube and the Top to the little cube on the top.

If you'd like, you can also create a new material and apply it to your Floor plane to give a new color to the floor. I'm going to give mine a color with a hex value of C3D7C4, making it a slightly minty grayish-green.

And at that, we have our player hierarchy set up, and we even have a colored model. Let's press on and start doing some coding.

Declaring Our Variables

To begin coding our movement, we'll need a script that we have attached to the Player. Right-click the Scripts folder in the Project window and navigate to Create ➤ C# Script and name it Player. Place an instance of the script as a component on the root GameObject, the one named Player, by dragging the script from the Project window to the Player in the Hierarchy window.

Now, open up your new Player script by double-clicking it in the Project window. If this doesn't bring up your code editor, you probably need to set the editor by navigating through the top bar to Edit ➤ Preferences ➤ External Tools and setting the External Script Editor field.

The first thing we'll do is declare some variables that we'll be using to handle the movement of the player. They'll go right at the top of the class declaration for our script:

```csharp
public class Player : MonoBehaviour
{
    //References
    [Header("References")]
    public Transform trans;
    public Transform modelTrans;
    public CharacterController characterController;

    //Movement
    [Header("Movement")]
    [Tooltip("Units moved per second at maximum speed.")]
    public float movespeed = 24;

    [Tooltip("Time, in seconds, to reach maximum speed.")]
    public float timeToMaxSpeed = .26f;

    private float VelocityGainPerSecond { get { return movespeed / timeToMaxSpeed; } }

    [Tooltip("Time, in seconds, to go from maximum speed to stationary.")]
    public float timeToLoseMaxSpeed = .2f;

    private float VelocityLossPerSecond { get { return movespeed / timeToLoseMaxSpeed; } }

    [Tooltip("Multiplier for momentum when attempting to move in a direction opposite the
    current traveling direction (e.g. trying to move right when already moving left).")]
    public float reverseMomentumMultiplier = 2.2f;

    private Vector3 movementVelocity = Vector3.zero;
}
```

You've pretty much seen everything we're doing here already at some point in the previous chapters, except for the declarations **"VelocityGainPerSecond"** and **"VelocityLossPerSecond"**. These are *properties*, a concept we haven't discussed yet. They probably look a little confusing to you right now, but we'll clear that up in a bit.

The first thing we do is declare references to other components that we plan on using. When you declare a variable of a component type (like Transform), you can set the value of the variable through the Inspector, so we don't have to write code to find the component we want. We just set the references once in the Inspector, and then we can use them anywhere in our code. We use the Header attribute on the first reference, **"trans"**, to put a bold title above the references in the Inspector, keeping them in their own little section at the top of the script.

We have a "trans" variable to point to the player Transform, which we do for performance reasons – it's slightly faster for a script to hold its own reference to its own Transform instead of using the built-in member "transform" each time. We also have a reference to our model holder transform, **"modelTrans"**, and a reference to a component we haven't used yet, called a **"CharacterController"**. This is how we'll be moving our character – we'll add that component and learn about it later in this chapter.

Moving down, we have a comment **"//Movement"** and a new header to separate a different set of variables, these ones pertaining to movement. We also use the **Tooltip** attribute with each variable, which gives us a way to provide a description for our variables. These are neat because they'll show up in the Unity editor when you hold your mouse over a variable field in the Inspector. Not only do they act something like comments for your code, but they'll also help document the purpose of your variables within the engine. If you're programming for a team of game developers, this can be useful to help guide non-coders on how to use the scripts you write.

The tooltips offer some insight on what each variable is for, but let's go over them in one place:

- **movespeed** is the maximum speed at which the player is capable of moving per second.

- **timeToMaxSpeed** is the time taken, in seconds, to build up to the maximum speed.

- **timeToLoseMaxSpeed** is the time taken, in seconds, to go from the maximum speed to stationary when you stop holding down the movement keys entirely.

- **reverseMomentumMultiplier** is used to make it easier for the player to stop traveling in one direction and begin traveling in the opposite direction at a moment's notice. While working against existing velocity (e.g., if the player begins holding the right arrow, but they were already traveling left), the velocity that we gain is multiplied by this value. So if we want to gain speed twice as fast when working against existing velocity, we would set this to 2. If we want to gain speed 50% faster, we'd set it to 1.5. Conversely, we could make it harder to reverse momentum by making the value lower than 1.0, although we don't plan on doing that. The goal of this is to make the movement feel tighter and easier to control for the player.

These are the movement-related variables we expose in the Inspector. These ones can be changed to alter the player's movement dynamics if we ever see fit. Once we've got some obstacles and game mechanics in place to give us a frame of reference, we may want to change the values a bit.

Lastly, movementVelocity is a private variable of type Vector3, which is a data type exposed by the Unity engine to resemble a vector of three axes: the X, Y, and Z values. As we've learned already, vectors can resemble various things, from a rotation angle (each axis is between 0 and 360) to a position to a scale. We use it to represent the current ongoing velocity of the player, measured in units per second. The values will range from movespeed to negative movespeed on the X and Z axes. The Y value should never be changed.

Properties

"VelocityGainPerSecond" and **"VelocityLossPerSecond"** are two examples of our first usage of **properties**. We've declared them as simple means of "folding up" a common math operation to a more understandable name, so we can just point to that name instead of typing out the math operation every time we want to use it. Remember, Don't Repeat Yourself!

Properties can be looked at as something of a cross between variables and methods. They are declared much like variables, but they prompt a block of code instead of ending with a semicolon, and they don't get a default value assigned to them. When referring to them and setting them, they are treated like variables: you can get their value, and you can set it.

But when declaring them, you define what gets returned when their value is referenced and/or what happens when their value is set. This is where they behave something like a method. Within the code block of a property, you can declare what we call a **getter** and a **setter**. Simply enough, they are declared with the **get** or **set** keyword, respectively, followed by a code block.

The **getter** is a block of code that is run whenever the property is referenced. Just like methods, it must return a value with the "return" keyword.

The **setter** is a block of code that is run whenever the property is being set to a new value. It does not return a value. Within the setter block, you can access the value being assigned to the variable by typing "value".

A property can declare a getter, a setter, or both. If only one is declared, you can only perform that operation on the property. That is to say, you can't get the value of a property that doesn't declare a getter, just as you can't set the value if it doesn't declare a setter. In our case, we aren't declaring a setter. We don't plan on setting the value for either of these properties, since we're just using them to give us a shortcut to a common math operation. So we just declare a "get" block and put a single line of code in it that returns the result of the math operation.

It might look a little confusing because of the way it's formatted. As we've depicted before, C# doesn't really pay attention to line breaks and indention. It isn't part of the syntax. When the code is read by the computer, it's not really using line breaks and indention to know when statements and code blocks end. Rather, it's paying attention to curly braces and semicolons. It doesn't care if we throw a bunch of line breaks in the middle of a statement, so long as we end that statement with a semicolon like we're supposed to (and don't break up any names with spaces, tabs, or line breaks, of course). We just use line breaks and indention in specific ways to create a consistent and readable standard for code – not because the syntax is forcing us to.

These rules can be stretched and broken at times. We've done that with our property declarations. Since they're just a single, simple line of code in a "get" block, we don't space them out as you would normally space out a property. We declare it all in one line for brevity's sake.

Normally, you might format it like this:

```
private float VelocityGainPerSecond
{
    get
    {
        return movespeed / timeToMaxSpeed;
    }
}
```

You can do it this way if you prefer. Some people might even insist that you space it all out like this, because it's "the proper way." But I think it's less clunky on one line, so I do it like that. If I had a setter as well, or if my getter had more than one line of code in it, I would absolutely spread it out like that last example, but this is a good example of when it's not a big deal to forsake the "rules" of code formatting if you're more comfortable with the result, especially if you're working on a personal project.

Tracking the Velocity

Now we know what sort of variables are available to us in our script, so let's start working on the per-frame update logic that makes the movement actually happen. Most of this logic is about handling the "movementVelocity" variable – that's the bread and butter, because it depicts how much we move every second.

Before we start typing away in the Update method, one practice you might want to develop is the act of separating different chunks of Update logic into smaller methods.

For example, to neatly separate the movement logic from any other logic we may be running in the Update method somewhere down the road, we can just declare a method "private void Movement()", write all our movement logic there, and then call that method in Update.

This can be an organizational lifesaver if you ever have a particularly complicated script. Your code editor will help you out by letting you fold up individual blocks of code, so you can easily hide away the code you don't need to see.

This is what it'll look like, before we throw down any of the actual movement logic. All of this is nested in the script class block, of course, down **below the variables** we just declared:

```
private void Movement()
{
    //...movement code goes here.
}
private void Update()
{
    Movement();
}
```

We declare Movement as a simple, private method with nothing to return. We then call it in Update. If we implement something new in the Player script later, we can do the same thing, keeping the new set of logic in its own space as well.

Now let's start filling the Movement method with code. Keep in mind, all of this code is running every frame, so it'll be running in small but very frequent increments, constantly. And of course, any value that we expect to be applied "per second" must be multiplied by "Time.deltaTime" as we did before.

First, we'll use a nested series of "if" and "else" blocks to alter the "movementVelocity" based on the player input as well as the current state of the "movementVelocity" (to allow us to apply the "reverseMomentumMultiplier" when working against existing velocity). After that, we'll check if there is currently any "movementVelocity" on this frame and, if so, use it to move the player.

Let's get to it. We'll start with the Z axis to implement forward and backward movement and go over it piece by piece. First, we'll detect the W key or the up arrow key to handle forward velocity. To cap the velocity so that it never goes over "movespeed" in either direction, we use simple math methods "Mathf.Min" and "Mathf.Max". Each method lets us pass two float parameters into it and will return the lowest (Mathf.Min) or highest (Mathf.Max) of the two. Pretty basic, right?

This is a common way to cap a value while increasing or lowering it. It's a cleaner, shorter alternative to adding to the value and then checking if it's higher than the maximum to set it back down to the maximum if it is. We just have one line of code that uses "Mathf.Min" or "Mathf.Max" to set the value. Instead of increasing or decreasing the value, we set it to the result of the Min or Max call. Here is an example of increasing a value this way:

```
value = Mathf.Min(maximumValue, value + addedAmount);
```

In this example, we set **"value"** to the result of the Min method. The Min method is given two parameters and will return the lowest of the two. The first one is the maximum amount we want "value" to be capped at. The second is the current state of "value" plus whatever amount we want to add to it. If the result of adding to "value" is lower than that maximum amount, then the result is returned. But if the result goes over the maximum value, we'll always get the "maximumValue" instead. Beautiful, isn't it?

A similar concept can be used when subtracting:

```
value = Mathf.Max(minimumValue, value - addedAmount);
```

120

Here, we use "Mathf.Max" instead, and we subtract instead of adding. In this case, if the result of subtracting from "value" is higher than the minimum value, we will get the result. If the result goes under the minimum value, we'll get the "minimumValue" instead.

To sum it up,

- Use **Min when adding** to cap at a **maximum amount**

- Use **Max when subtracting** to cap at a **minimum amount**

Putting the pieces together, we handle forward movement like this:

```
//If W or the up arrow key is held:
if (Input.GetKey(KeyCode.W) || Input.GetKey(KeyCode.UpArrow))
{
    if (movementVelocity.z >= 0) //If we're already moving forward
        //Increase Z velocity by VelocityGainPerSecond, but don't go higher than
        'movespeed':
        movementVelocity.z = Mathf.Min(movespeed, movementVelocity.z + VelocityGainPerSecond
        * Time.deltaTime);

    else //Else if we're moving back
        //Increase Z velocity by VelocityGainPerSecond, using the reverseMomentumMultiplier,
        but don't raise higher than 0:
        movementVelocity.z = Mathf.Min(0, movementVelocity.z + VelocityGainPerSecond *
        reverseMomentumMultiplier * Time.deltaTime);
}
```

This may look a bit scary at first, but let's break down what's happening. Keep in mind that "velocity.z" will be negative if the player is moving backward and positive if the player is moving forward. Since our camera is above the player, looking down at them, "forward" is going to go up on our screen, and "backward" is going to go down on our screen.

If "velocity.z" is "movespeed", then the player is moving at full speed forward. If "velocity.z" is "-movespeed" (negative movespeed), then the player is moving at full speed backward.

The process goes like this, in plain English:

- If either the W key or the up arrow key is held

- ...and the player currently has forward (positive) momentum or no momentum at all, then add to the forward momentum, but never let it go higher than "movespeed".

- ...else if the player currently has backward (negative) momentum, increase and use the "reverseMomentumMultiplier". Since the velocity is negative, we don't allow it to go over 0. This way, as soon as we hit 0 velocity, we stop using the "reverseMomentumMultiplier".

Understand this, and you'll be fine for the rest of this chapter. Whenever we change the velocity, we change it using this concept of Min and Max to cleanly cap the value while we assign it.

The amount we're adding to the velocity to increase it is making use of one of the properties we declared earlier: "VelocityGainPerSecond". Let's take a look at the amount we're adding in seclusion (when not reversing momentum):

```
movementVelocity.z + VelocityGainPerSecond * Time.deltaTime
```

This is fairly straightforward. Thanks to the property, it practically describes itself in plain English: start with Z velocity that we currently have, and add the velocity gain per second. Since it's "per second," it has to be multiplied by "Time.deltaTime", as we learned before. Another thing we previously learned: The multiplication operator "*" will take precedence over a "+" or "-" operator. This means it's always calculated first, with whatever is on its left and right sides, and then the "+" or "-" will be calculated with the result of that. So we know that "VelocityGainPerSecond" alone is being multiplied by "Time.deltaTime", not the result of "movementVelocity.z" + "VelocityGainPerSecond".

If you want this to be visually clear, you can use parentheses to separate them yourself. Some might argue that it's not necessary, since it does the same thing, but if it makes it easier for you to read and understand, then go for it:

```
movementVelocity.z + (VelocityGainPerSecond * Time.deltaTime)
```

Moving on, when we're reversing momentum, we have this:

```
movementVelocity.z + VelocityGainPerSecond * reverseMomentumMultiplier * Time.deltaTime
```

It's the same thing, but we throw the "*" operator in there to apply the "reverseMomentumMultiplier". You probably know that the order in which we multiply things doesn't count for anything. We could switch the position of any of those latter three references however we want, and the result is the same.

And with that, you've learned pretty much all of the concepts you need to learn to understand how this velocity-handling system operates. There are no surprises left – just little variances on what we've already done.

Moving on, we can now see how backward movement looks. This code will go immediately **after the "if" code block** that we just wrote (the one that checks for W or the up arrow key being pressed):

```
//If S or the down arrow key is held:
else if (Input.GetKey(KeyCode.S) || Input.GetKey(KeyCode.DownArrow))
{
    //If we're already moving forward
    if (movementVelocity.z > 0)
        movementVelocity.z = Mathf.Max(0, movementVelocity.z - VelocityGainPerSecond *
        reverseMomentumMultiplier * Time.deltaTime);
    //If we're moving back or not moving at all
    else
        movementVelocity.z = Mathf.Max(-movespeed, movementVelocity.z -
        VelocityGainPerSecond * Time.deltaTime);
}
```

This is pretty much a copy-and-paste of the forward movement, but with certain little changes made. Notice that it starts by checking for the S or down arrow key, but this time with an "else if", not a normal "if". This is to ensure that if both the up and down movement keys are held, only one of them (the up key) will have priority instead of both happening at the same time.

As well as this, we now use Max instead of Min, because we're subtracting the velocity now.

Let's put it to plain English again:

- If either the S key or the down arrow key is held

- ...and the player currently has forward (positive) momentum, then decrease the forward momentum while applying "reverseMomentumMultiplier", but never let it go lower than 0.

- ...else if the player currently has backward (negative) momentum or no momentum at all, decrease the momentum, but never let it go lower than "-movespeed".

This leaves one final condition we need to account for: the loss of velocity when neither the forward nor backward key is held. If we don't implement this, the player will just keep going after releasing the movement keys. That's definitely not what we want.

We'll put an "else" after the "else if" that checks if the back key is held, which means this "else" block will occur whenever neither forward nor back is being held. If momentum is positive, we decrease it and cap at 0. If it's negative, we increase it and, again, cap at 0. If it's exactly 0, we don't do anything:

```
else //If neither forward nor back is being held
{
    //We must bring the Z velocity back to 0 over time.
    if (movementVelocity.z > 0) //If we're moving forward,
        //Decrease Z velocity by VelocityLossPerSecond, but don't go any lower than 0:
        movementVelocity.z = Mathf.Max(0, movementVelocity.z - VelocityLossPerSecond * Time.
        deltaTime);

    else //If we're moving backward,
        //Increase Z velocity (back towards 0) by VelocityLossPerSecond, but don't go any
        higher than 0:
        movementVelocity.z = Mathf.Min(0, movementVelocity.z + VelocityLossPerSecond * Time.
        deltaTime);
}
```

This leaves us with nothing to do but copy over these principles and apply them to right/left instead of forward/back. To write this code, we can recycle most of what we've already written. We'll copy and paste the code that handles forward/back movement (everything in the Movement method so far) and then change the hotkeys to A/D and the left/right arrows. We'll also change any reference to the Z axis to instead reference the X axis and edit the comments to keep them accurate.

Be diligent with this! If you accidentally leave a ".z" instead of a ".x" somewhere, you'll be in for some unexpected behavior:

```
//If D or the right arrow key is held:
if (Input.GetKey(KeyCode.D) || Input.GetKey(KeyCode.RightArrow))
{
    //If we're already moving right,
    if (movementVelocity.x >= 0)
        //Increase X velocity by VelocityGainPerSecond, but don't go higher than
        'movespeed':
        movementVelocity.x = Mathf.Min(movespeed, movementVelocity.x + VelocityGainPerSecond
        * Time.deltaTime);

    else //If we're moving left,
        //Increase x velocity by VelocityGainPerSecond, using the reverseMomentumMultiplier,
        but don't raise higher than 0:
        movementVelocity.x = Mathf.Min(0, movementVelocity.x + VelocityGainPerSecond *
        reverseMomentumMultiplier * Time.deltaTime);
}
//If A or the left arrow key is held:
else if (Input.GetKey(KeyCode.A) || Input.GetKey(KeyCode.LeftArrow))
{
```

```
    //If we're already moving right
    if (movementVelocity.x > 0)
        movementVelocity.x = Mathf.Max(0, movementVelocity.x - VelocityGainPerSecond *
        reverseMomentumMultiplier * Time.deltaTime);

    else //If we're moving left or not moving at all
        movementVelocity.x = Mathf.Max(-movespeed, movementVelocity.x -
        VelocityGainPerSecond * Time.deltaTime);
}
else //If neither right nor left are being held
{
    //We must bring the X velocity back to 0 over time.
    //If we're moving right,
    if (movementVelocity.x > 0)
        //Decrease X velocity by VelocityLossPerSecond, but don't go any lower than 0:
        movementVelocity.x = Mathf.Max(0, movementVelocity.x - VelocityLossPerSecond * Time.
        deltaTime);
    //Else if we're moving left,
    else
        //Increase X velocity (back towards 0) by VelocityLossPerSecond, but don't go any
        higher than 0:
        movementVelocity.x = Mathf.Min(0, movementVelocity.x + VelocityLossPerSecond * Time.
        deltaTime);
}
```

Applying the Movement

This leaves us with nothing left but applying the movement velocity so the player actually moves. To do this, we'll use the **CharacterController**. This is a built-in Unity component designed to provide movement and collision detection for a character. If we just moved the player by setting their Transform position, it wouldn't detect collisions (the player would pass through everything). But moving them with a CharacterController component will cause them to bump into and slide against solid objects in their path – assuming those objects have a collider component attached. Whenever you create basic shapes like cubes, spheres, etc. through the GameObject menu, they will automatically have a collider of the correct type to cover their shape.

First, let's set up the CharacterController component on the Player GameObject (the same one with the Player script component attached to it).

Add a CharacterController by selecting the Player in the Hierarchy, then navigating to the bottom of the Inspector window, and clicking the Add Component button. This will bring up a little drop-down box. Now you can navigate to the CharacterController by clicking Physics and then CharacterController. Alternatively, you can search for a component type by name in this same drop-down box: type "character controller" into the search bar and press Enter or click the CharacterController listing when it shows.

The CharacterController uses a capsule shape to test for collisions. This is represented in the Scene window as a wireframe set of green lines. That's how big the player is perceived to be with the current settings of the Controller.

Locate the Center, Radius, and Height members of the CharacterController in the Inspector. For our purposes, we want a **Center** of $(0, 2.5, 0)$, a **Radius** of 1, and a **Height** of 5. This makes the collider mostly cover the Player, with a bit of overhang on the sides so we retain a little bit of personal space. The rest of the settings can be left as is. When you're done, the CharacterController should look like Figure 14-5 in the Inspector.

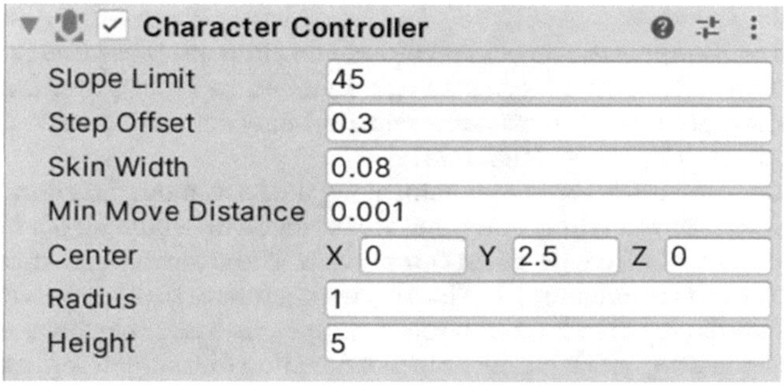

Figure 14-5. *The CharacterController component of the Player is shown in the Inspector*

With that set up, we can now set the reference to the CharacterController variable that we declared in our Player script.

Applying references to components in the editor like this can be done in various ways:

- **In the Inspector**, click the little circle icon at the right side of the "characterController" field in the Player script. This opens a pop-up window that lets you select any GameObjects in the Scene that have a CharacterController attached. Click one to set the value.

- **In the Inspector**, left-click and drag the bold text "Character Controller" that makes up the header of the component. You can then drop it onto the variable field in the Player script to set the reference.

- **In the Hierarchy**, left-click and drag the Player GameObject itself into the Inspector and drop it on the variable field in the Player script. Unity will recognize that the field wants a CharacterController reference and find that component on the GameObject you're dragging.

Any way will work, and some are more convenient than others at times.

Once the field is set, it will show the name of the GameObject who owns the CharacterController, and after it, it will specify "(Character Controller)" to note the actual Component type that's stored.

While we're at it, we'll also need to set the reference to "trans" and "modelTrans", which should be listed just above the CharacterController field that we just set.

This works the same way. You can drag the Transform component of the player directly onto the "trans" field using the Transform header in the Inspector, and then drag the Model GameObject from the Hierarchy onto the field in the Inspector.

Now we can head back to our code and apply the movement. At the bottom of the Movement method, beneath all of the code that handles the input and movement velocity, add this bit:

```
//If the player is moving in either direction (left/right or up/down):
if (movementVelocity.x != 0 || movementVelocity.z != 0)
{
    //Applying the movement velocity:
    characterController.Move(movementVelocity * Time.deltaTime);
    //Keeping the model holder rotated towards the last movement direction:
    modelTrans.rotation = Quaternion.Slerp(modelTrans.rotation, Quaternion.
    LookRotation(movementVelocity), .18F);
}
```

This starts out pretty simple. We check if the X and Z axes have movement: if X is not 0 or (the "||" operator) if Z is not 0. If so, we apply the movement by reaching into our "characterController" reference and calling its method **Move**. This method takes a single argument: a Vector3 for the movement desired on this frame. That's the whole point of our movement velocity, but of course, our movement velocity is "per second," so we must multiply it by "Time.deltaTime".

Beneath this, we rotate the model holder to point along the movement direction. This involves working with rotations, something we haven't done much yet, so it comes with a little bit of unfamiliar territory.

Unity represents rotations with a type called **Quaternion**. These are mathematically somewhat complicated (they even *sound* intimidating), but luckily, we don't have to mess with that math. Mostly, you just call built-in methods when working with rotations like this. Just know that a single instance of Quaternion represents a rotation, which is pretty much a direction that something can point toward, or an angle at which something can be tilted. In the Inspector, we look at it as a Vector3, where each value is between 0 and 360, because that's a more user-friendly way of looking at it. But internally, Unity represents rotations as Quaternions.

The built-in methods we're using here are **"Quaternion.Slerp"** and **"Quaternion.LookRotation"**.

Slerp is a term you'll hear somewhat often in game development, particularly when dealing with vectors and rotation. It is short for "spherical linear interpolation." To put it simply, it's a method that takes three arguments:

- The rotation we start with (a Quaternion)

- The rotation we want to end with (also a Quaternion)

- A float for how fast we want to get there

The float is a multiplier, between 0 and 1, and pretty much means "What fraction of the way to the desired rotation will we be going on this frame?" So if it's set to 0, we'll go nowhere at all; if it's set to 1, we'll get there immediately. But if it's set to something like 0.18, we'll get 18% of the way there.

If you look at how we use this method, you'll see how this generates a smooth change. In each frame, we set the rotation of our Model Holder, calling the Slerp method to do so. Each call to the Slerp method takes the current rotation as the start and the same target rotation as the end. So we'll rotate 18% of the way to the desired rotation on the first frame, then another 18% of what remains on the next frame, and so on. In each frame, the difference between the current rotation and the target rotation becomes smaller and smaller. This generates a comfortable sort of "spring effect" where at first, the rotation is snappier and more pronounced, but as the difference becomes smaller, the rotation smoothly comes to a stop. This will make it look somewhat more visually appealing than rotating by a flat amount each frame, and it also makes spinning around 180 degrees quick and snappy instead of taking longer than a quarter-turn.

To get the desired rotation (the second parameter in the Slerp call), we call **"Quaternion. LookRotation"**. This is a method that takes a Vector3 parameter and returns back a rotation (Quaternion) pointing forward along whatever direction that vector is heading.

To sum up the whole line of code, we pass in "movementVelocity" to a "Quaternion.LookRotation" call to get a Quaternion pointing us forward along the direction our velocity is currently taking us. We use Slerp to take our rotation toward that one by 0.18× the difference per frame.

If we didn't want a smooth effect, we could do this instead:

```
modelTrans.rotation = Quaternion.LookRotation(movementVelocity);
```

That will directly set the model rotation to jerk our player to face along the movement direction immediately. It won't look terrible, but it will be jerky – particularly when going from a standstill to flip in the opposite direction.

With that said, we've implemented our movement. It looks nice and it feels nice. At last, we could now play our game and see it in action. Make sure your Player script is saved since the last changes you've made, make sure you've correctly set those variables under the References header in your Player script, and then you'll probably want to drop some cubes or spheres down into the scene around your player. Otherwise, it'll be hard to even tell the movement is happening, since you'd just be moving on a huge, empty floor.

You should be able to move your player around with either the WASD keys or the arrow keys. The camera should stay in a fixed position above the player, moving with them as they go (but remaining in the same local position). The player model will smoothly rotate to point along the current movement direction.

Summary

In this chapter, we gave our player the ability to move. We learned how to create and apply basic materials to add some color to our GameObjects, how to use the "Mathf.Max" and "Mathf.Min" methods to cap values as we raise or decrease them, and how to handle our player's velocity per frame so they gradually pick up and lose speed based on their input with the WASD or arrow keys. We also exercised some foresight in how we wanted our GameObjects to be set up in the Hierarchy to make sure our model rotated separately from the rest of the Player. This keeps the camera in the same location even as the player model turns to point along the movement direction. Some other key points to remember are as follows:

- A **property** is much like a variable, but it defines code blocks for exactly what happens when we **get** or **set** the variable.

- When **adding** to a number value, use **Min** to cap the resulting value below a maximum amount.

- When **subtracting** from a number value, use **Max** to cap the resulting value above a minimum amount.

- The **Slerp** method can be used to smoothly move one value toward another by a fraction of the difference between those two values.

- A **Quaternion** is a data type that resembles a rotation. The "Transform.rotation" member is a Quaternion that resembles a Transform's current facing direction.

- The **Quaternion.LookRotation** method takes a Vector3 as its parameter and returns a Quaternion rotation to point a Transform toward the direction that vector travels.

CHAPTER 15

■ ■ ■

Death and Respawning

In this chapter, we'll be implementing a bare-bones system to allow us to "kill" our player (don't worry, it's very nonviolent) and send them back to the spawn point.

We'll set the spawn point when the game first starts, so that wherever we place the player in the scene, that's where they'll respawn. We won't be doing anything flashy for now. When the player dies, their model will disappear, and the Player script will be disabled to keep it from updating. After a few seconds of wait (to punish them for failing), we'll move them back to the spawn point and enable them again.

To start, we'll declare these variables in the **Player script** class, underneath the movement-related variables we declared in the last chapter:

```
//Death and Respawning
[Header("Death and Respawning")]
[Tooltip("How long after the player's death, in seconds, before they are respawned?")]
public float respawnWaitTime = 2f;

private bool dead = false;

private Vector3 spawnPoint;
```

Since these variables relate to a different system, we'll start them with a new Header attribute to keep our Inspector looking tidy. We declare a float that we can edit in the Inspector if we want to, depicting how long the player must wait before they are revived.

We also declare two private variables for our own uses, which we don't need to be setting in the Inspector:

- **dead**, a bool depicting whether the player is alive (false) or dead (true) at the time
- **spawnPoint**, a Vector3 for the location at which the player will respawn

Real quick, let's write our Start method to set that "spawnPoint" variable to the player's position when the game first begins. It's just one line of code in the method:

```
private void Start()
{
    spawnPoint = trans.position;
}
```

That's pretty self-explanatory: as soon as the script is first enabled, we set "spawnPoint" to the Player's "Transform.position". After this, we won't be changing the spawn point.

Enabling and Disabling

We've touched on the concepts of enabling and disabling scripts and GameObjects in the first part of the book, but now we're going to put it to use, so let's dig a little deeper into how it all works. In Unity, both GameObjects and individual scripts can be effectively "turned off." We use slightly different terms for each: a GameObject is either **active** or **inactive**, while a script is either **enabled** or **disabled**.

When a GameObject is active, all of its components will run and update. We can deactivate a GameObject by selecting the GameObject and unchecking the box just left of the GameObject name at the head of the Inspector (see Figure 15-1).

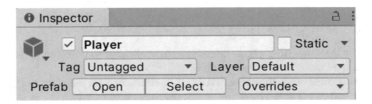

Figure 15-1. *The head of the Inspector showing the Player GameObject. The checkbox to the left side of the Player name can be unchecked to deactivate the GameObject*

Deactivating a GameObject stops all of its components from running. That includes renderers, collision detection and other physics-related components, lights, cameras, and so on. It also means all of the children of that GameObject won't be active, either. Deactivated GameObjects will have gray text for their name in the Hierarchy to make it obvious that they're not active. Since the children of an inactive GameObject are also deactivated, their names will be gray as well (see Figure 15-2).

Figure 15-2. *An inactive GameObject beside an active GameObject in the Hierarchy*

This goes for components too, and that includes script components. Each component which supports enabling/disabling will have a checkbox beside its header in the Inspector (see Figure 15-3).

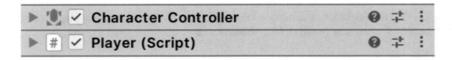

Figure 15-3. *Folded Player script component and CharacterController component in the Inspector. The checkbox to the left of the component name can be unchecked to disable the component*

Components are enabled by default, but we could disable them in the editor if we only want them to begin operating at some later point in the game, when our code enables them.

Some components and scripts won't have this checkbox because they don't have any consistent logic that can be turned on or off on a moment's notice. For example, your scripts won't have the checkbox if they don't declare any of the built-in Unity events, like Start or Update.

As mentioned, deactivating a GameObject will deactivate all of its children too. But each GameObject has its own, individual state depicting whether it is active or disabled. Even if a GameObject is active in and of itself, it could still effectively be disabled because any of its parents are inactive.

Unity retains the state of each individual GameObject, but its "actual state" is dependent upon the state of its parents as well. This means if you have a child that's deactivated, and then you deactivate and later enable its parent, the child remains deactivated – it stores its own state.

Unity also gives us the ability to make this distinction ourselves in our code. With a reference to a GameObject, we have two separate bool variables we can access to check the GameObject state:

- **GameObject.activeInHierarchy** is the GameObject's current, effective state, which will be false (inactive) if any of its parents are inactive and true (active) if its parents are active and the GameObject itself is active.

- **GameObject.activeSelf** is the GameObject's individual state. Even if this is true, the GameObject could still be inactive because any of its parents are inactive. To put it simply, this state is only used if all parents are active; if any of the parents are not active, this is ignored, and the GameObject will be inactive regardless.

Technically, these are properties, like those math properties we made for movement in the last chapter. They only allow us to get them, not to set them. To set the active state of a GameObject, you need to call a method: **GameObject.SetActive**. This method takes one parameter, a bool depicting whether the GameObject should be made active (true) or inactive (false).

While we're on the topic of enabling and disabling, let's talk about one final nuance: the **Awake** built-in event. Just like **Start**, it is called as soon as the script is first initialized, but with a few little differences:

- When a scene first loads in, all Awake calls will always happen **before** any Start calls happen. If one script should always be initialized before another, you would use Awake on that script and Start on the other.

- Awake will happen as soon as the script is initialized, whether the script is enabled or not. On the other hand, Start will happen on the first frame that the script is enabled.

- Regardless, if the GameObject that the script is attached to is inactive when the scene first loads in, **neither** Start nor Awake will be called until the **first frame** that the GameObject is active. This applies as well to creating instances of prefabs through code: any inactive GameObjects in the prefab will not have their Start or Awake called when they are first created – only when the GameObject is first activated.

You generally want to use Start if you don't need Awake. If you use Start by default with all your scripts, then you have the option of using Awake to easily make a script initialize before the others if you need to sometime down the road.

This is why you'll see us using Start pretty much exclusively – however, the distinction between Start and Awake is nice to know about if you ever get into some edge case where you want Awake instead!

Death Method

Now we have our spawn point. Let's make a method that kills the player when it's called. We'll make it public, and we'll have it return nothing (void):

```
public void Die()
{
    if (!dead)
    {
        dead = true;
```

```
        Invoke("Respawn", respawnWaitTime);
        movementVelocity = Vector3.zero;
        enabled = false;
        characterController.enabled = false;
        modelTrans.gameObject.SetActive(false);
    }
}
```

First, we make sure we avoid an awkward case where the Die method somehow gets called when the player is already dead, with a simple "if" that checks if we're alive before proceeding. Remember, the "!" flips the value of a bool, so what we're really asking is "are we *not* dead?"

We then immediately set "dead" to true, since we plan on being very dead by the end of this method. We use a new concept, **Invoke**, which we haven't used yet before.

Invoking methods is a means of calling a method after a given wait period. First, we give a string for the name of the method we want to call: "Respawn". Then, we give it a float for the number of seconds we want to wait before the method should be called.

We haven't declared this Respawn method yet, but we will after. It's important that the names are exactly the same. Even if you just mess up the capitalization, for example, by naming the method "respawn" instead of "Respawn", it won't be called. Unity will, however, log a message in the Console for you if it fails to invoke the method, to let you know why it's not working.

When you invoke a method, you can't pass any parameters into that method. It only follows that the method must also be declared with no parameters as well. If it has parameters, the invoke will fail.

After the Invoke call, we want to make sure the player loses all of their momentum when they die, so they don't have any left when they respawn later. The movement velocity is reset to (0, 0, 0) using a bit of shorthand: **"Vector3.zero"**. It's just a slightly shorter way to type "new Vector3(0,0,0)". It does the same thing. Technically, "Vector3.zero" is just a static property in the Vector3 type. It has a getter, but no setter, and always returns a "new Vector3(0,0,0)".

Then we set "enabled" to false. This is an instance variable that every component type has, depicting whether or not the component is enabled. Scripts are components too. Set it to false, and your script stops running. It's as easy as that. This doesn't interrupt the code that's currently running, it just prevents built-in events like Update from occurring until the script is re-enabled. Our invoked method will still happen even though the script is disabled.

We do the same for the CharacterController. Since this is the component that's catching collisions for the player, if we don't deactivate it, the player will still be there as far as physics are concerned, so they'll still be touched by anything that might pass by.

Finally, to deactivate the model to stop it from showing, we have to call the "GameObject.SetActive" method we talked about earlier. We go through the "modelTrans" to access its GameObject. Remember, a Transform is just a more specific version of a Component, and all Components (including scripts) have a ".gameObject" member pointing to the GameObject that they're attached to. Using this, we don't need to declare a separate reference to the model GameObject.

Respawn Method

The Respawn method is already being invoked, so now we just need to declare it. It will set "dead" back to false, place the player back at the spawn point, and enable the script, CharacterController, and model again. This reverts the player back to a normal, functioning state, ready to try the level again:

```
public void Respawn()
{
    dead = false;
    trans.position = spawnPoint;
    enabled = true;
```

```
    characterController.enabled = true;
    modelTrans.gameObject.SetActive(true);
}
```

That pretty much does it for our simple death-and-respawn system. Now, when a hazard touches the player, all we need is a reference to the Player script, through which we can call the public method Die. We'll handle that in the next chapter, but to test if the method works beforehand, we can throw down some simple, temporary code that lets us kill the player on the spot with a hotkey. Since you're an expert programmer now, you can write this up in no time, right? Just write this code in the Update method:

```
if (Input.GetKeyDown(KeyCode.T))
    Die();
```

Save, run the game, move away from the initial point, and press **"T"**. Your character should vanish, and since we deactivate the model instead of the root Player GameObject, our camera doesn't get deactivated with it. After the wait time, which is two seconds by default (you can adjust it in the Inspector if you want), you should pop back up at the spawn point and be able to move around again.

One final measure we could take would be to reset the player's rotation to the same angle it was when they first spawned in as the game began, so they don't respawn at the angle they were facing when they died. This won't be hard at all.

Beneath your "spawnPoint" variable, declare this variable:

```
private Quaternion spawnRotation;
```

Set that variable to the "modelTrans.rotation" **in your Start method**:

```
spawnRotation = modelTrans.rotation;
```

This marks down the rotation of our model when the game first begins. Now we can just apply the rotation to the "modelTrans" somewhere **in the Respawn method**:

```
modelTrans.rotation = spawnRotation;
```

Now, if you ever want the player to spawn at a particular rotation, you can rotate their Model GameObject to point that way, and it'll stick throughout the game. You can vary this for each level, if you ever need to, so that the player faces toward the direction you expect them to go when they start your level and/or when they respawn.

Once again, the reason we're dealing only with the Model instead of the root when it comes to rotation is because the camera is a child of the root, so if we ever rotate the root, the camera pivots around it, which changes the direction the camera faces. Since all of our movement is in world directions, none of it is going to change to match the new camera rotation.

You can try this for yourself, if you want to see what I mean in action. Apply some Y rotation to the Transform of the root Player GameObject in the Inspector – 90 degrees, let's say. Then play, and try moving around. The W or up arrow key will now take you to the left side of your screen, and the S or down arrow key will now take you to the right side of your screen. It's no fun, right?

Just switch that Y rotation back to 0 when you're done playing, and everything will go back to normal.

Summary

In this chapter, we set up our player's death and respawning. Now we'll have a method to call to "kill" the player when we're coding our hazardous obstacles in the next chapter. Some key points to remember are as follows:

- Deactivating a GameObject will stop all of its attached components from doing whatever it is they do. As well, all child GameObjects will be considered inactive.

- You can deactivate a GameObject by selecting it and unchecking the box to the left of its name in the Inspector header.

- **Awake()** and **Start()** are both built-in events you can declare in a script to run the code within as soon as the script is loaded and ready, one time only for each script instance.

- All **Awake** calls will occur **before** any **Start** calls – however, both must wait for the first frame that their GameObject is active before they can occur, regardless of whether or not the script is enabled.

- **Awake** calls will occur even if the script is disabled. The script might be disabled by default in the Scene, or it could be disabled within a prefab, which means it will still be disabled when an instance of the prefab is created. Either way, the Awake calls are still going to go off as soon as possible.

- **Start** calls will not occur on a disabled script. They will wait until the script first becomes active before they are called.

- The **Invoke** method can be used to call a function by name on the script after a given wait duration.

CHAPTER 16

■ ■ ■

Basic Hazards

Now that our player can be killed, let's start coding up some villainy to kill them. We'll make a generic script called Hazard that makes a GameObject kill the player on touch. We'll use this to create dangerous projectiles and an obstacle type that periodically fires them.

Collision Detection

Before we make a script that reacts to a touch, we'll need to dive into collision detection to understand how Unity deals with such things. There are three major concepts that relate: colliders, Rigidbodies, and layers.

Colliders are components that, when added to a GameObject, give it an invisible shape that will interact with other colliders. There are various types of colliders that provide different shapes: spheres, boxes, capsules, and even a mesh collider that can add collisions to a complex mesh shape.

You'll notice that the physical objects we've created thus far, like the floor we created under the player (a plane) and the cubes that make up the player model, all have collider components of some sort on them. A plane will have a Mesh Collider, and a cube will have a Box Collider.

I didn't mention it before to avoid treading this ground too early, but we don't actually need any colliders on our player model itself. We already have the CharacterController providing collisions for the whole Player object. So you can go ahead and remove the Box Collider components from the Base and Top GameObjects that make up the player model, just to tidy them up. You can do this by clicking the three vertical dots at the top right of the component listing in the Inspector and then clicking "Remove Component," shown in Figure 16-1.

Figure 16-1. *After clicking the three dots in the top-right corner of a component header in the Inspector, the "Remove Component" option can be selected*

A collider can be marked as a **trigger collider** via a checkbox field in the Inspector. Trigger colliders don't act as physical objects, allowing other objects to pass through them – however, they still send certain event messages to attached script components, which lets us use them to detect when an object enters an area or gets near a switch or something to that effect.

© Casey Hardman 2024
C. Hardman, *Game Programming with Unity and C#*, https://doi.org/10.1007/978-1-4842-9720-9_16

A **Rigidbody** is a component that adds physical behavior to a GameObject. When a Rigidbody is attached to a GameObject, it is realistically affected by collisions – for example, it will be pushed and rotated by other objects hitting it or pressing against it. It also adds gravity to the object and enables you to add force (motion) and torque (twisting and rotating) to the object through scripting.

To enable collisions, a Rigidbody still needs a collider – that's what defines its shape in the physics engine. An object with a Rigidbody but no collider can have gravity and can have forces applied to it, but it will pass through other objects.

If you're using a Rigidbody like this, you would not directly move or rotate the Transform through your code. Rather, you'd add force and torque to it through a reference to the Rigidbody component. Interfering with the Rigidbody by changing the Transform directly could cause unwanted results, since the Unity engine is simulating the physics itself and doesn't account for any sudden movements you cause to the Transform.

Nothing in this game is going to require such realistic physics control. What we'll be doing to move things like projectiles, where we directly move the Transform, is known as **kinematic movement**.

Rigidbodies can be marked as **kinematic** through the "Is Kinematic" field in the Inspector. This will override these behaviors that move and twist the object. If you want to have finer control over an object, like a player character, you would mark it as kinematic. If it's kinematic, you'll apply movement to it through the Transform, but it will still trigger collisions in other objects.

The general rules of thumb are as follows:

- If it moves, use a Rigidbody. If it remains still, don't use a Rigidbody.

- If it moves by script or animations, make the Rigidbody **kinematic**. If it moves like a normal, physical object with forces and torque, don't make it kinematic.

- If you need scripts to respond to collisions between two GameObjects, at least one of those GameObjects needs to have a Rigidbody attached.

For our Player GameObject, we don't have a Rigidbody attached. This is because we're using a CharacterController to move our Player, and the CharacterController acts as a Rigidbody.

Layers are another concept that can influence collisions. Every GameObject is part of a single layer. You can see a GameObject's layer in the header of the Inspector, with the text "Layer" beside a drop-down field. The layer "Default" is automatically assigned to new GameObjects, so all of ours will have this layer. A GameObject has to be part of a layer. There are some setup in Unity by default, which you'll see if you click the Layer drop-down for any GameObject (see Figure 16-2).

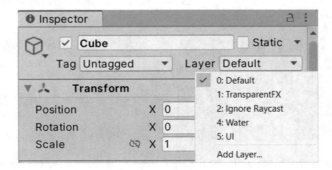

Figure 16-2. *The Layer drop-down button for a generic Cube GameObject in the Inspector. The button has been clicked, which expands the list to show available layers. Clicking a layer will assign it to the GameObject*

You can also create your own layers and name them whatever you like. To do this, go from the Layer drop-down menu of any GameObject and click the "Add Layer..." button at the bottom of the list (visible in Figure 16-2).

The Inspector will change to show a list of all layers, as pictured in Figure 16-3.

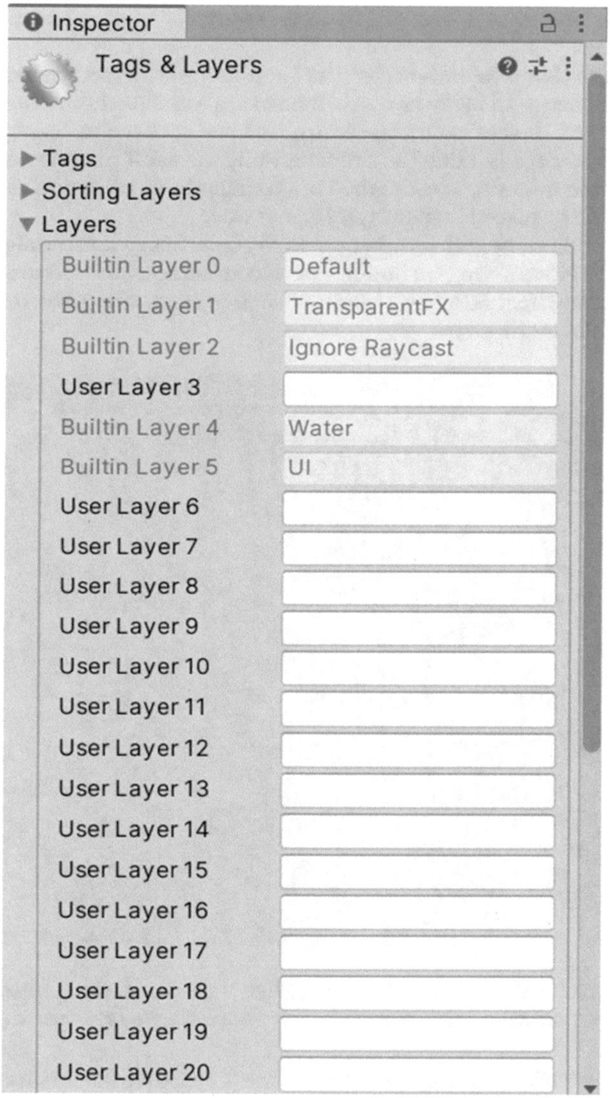

Figure 16-3. The Inspector "Tags & Layers" view, showing fields for each layer

There are a total of 32 slots you can use for layers. By default, layers 0, 1, 2, 4, and 5 are layers that you cannot rename. The rest are all for us, the game developer. We can type a name into any of these slots to make the layer available for assigning to a GameObject.

You're probably wondering what the point of them is. The two major purposes are rendering and collisions. You can make cameras only render GameObjects of certain layers, and you can make certain layers only collide with certain other layers. For example, you could selectively hide GameObjects from the player camera, or distinguish between friend and foe so that the player is not hurt by friendly attacks or projectiles, or make player characters on the same team pass through each other but collide with enemies.

Let's declare layers for our project so that we can have fine-tuned control over which objects will be colliding with each other.

Name layer 3 "Player" and layer 6 "Hazard." It's as easy as typing the names into the fields shown in Figure 16-3.

Now select your Player GameObject and click the Layer drop-down (shown before in Figure 16-2) in the Inspector again. You'll notice all of the layers we named are now showing in the drop-down list – all you have to do is assign a name to "create" a new layer. Go ahead and click the "3: Player" layer to assign it. When you change the layer of a GameObject that has children, Unity will ask if you want to change the layer of the children as well. That's what we want, so select the "Yes, change children" option, and all of the children of our Player GameObject will be placed in the Player layer as well.

As of now, all layers will collide with all other layers. We can change that through the Edit ➤ Project Settings window. Click the Physics entry on the left side of your screen, and if necessary, scroll down to the bottom of the contents on the right side of the window. You'll see something like a staircase of upside-down checkboxes, as shown in Figure 16-4.

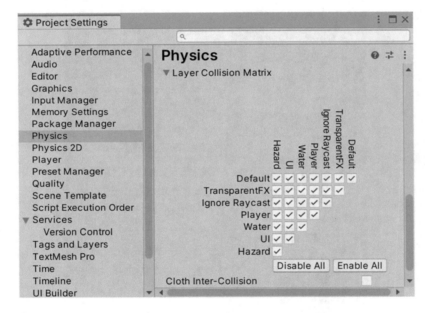

Figure 16-4. *The Project Settings window, showing the Physics section. At the bottom, the Layer Collision Matrix field is unfolded to show an array of checkboxes corresponding to layer names*

If you don't see it, the field is probably folded. Click the "Layer Collision Matrix" text at the bottom to unfold it so the checkboxes show.

This "collision matrix" depicts which layers are able to touch each other. There are layer names on the left side and on the top side of all these checkboxes, and where those layer names cross, that is the layer combination that the checkbox is associated with. Easier yet, if you place your mouse over any of the checkboxes, it will display the two layers associated with it – for example, "Default/Player" or "Hazard/ Player." If the box is checked, these layers can collide with each other. If it is unchecked, the layers will pass through each other. You can even make a layer unable to collide with objects of the same layer, if you want.

This can be useful to ensure that the hazards don't touch anything they don't need to touch. We only need them touching the player; we may also want them to hit walls and the floor. Generally, the Default layer can be used for environmental objects, so we'll plan to leave our floor and walls in the Default layer and enable collisions between Hazard and Player and Hazard and Default. As far as we're concerned, we don't want the Hazards colliding with anything else. We can even disable their collisions with themselves, so that traveling projectiles don't touch each other. To set it up like this, the matrix should look as pictured in Figure 16-5.

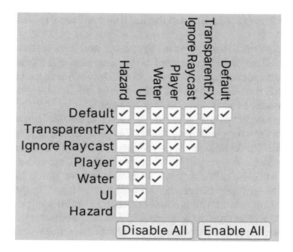

Figure 16-5. *The Layer Collision Matrix field after we've set our Hazards to only collide with Default and Player layers*

Hazard Script

Let's get to creating our Hazard script. This will make a GameObject kill the player on the spot when they touch. The collision will be handled by Unity, and we'll set up our collider to make the shape we want our hazard to use. Our code just has to define what happens when the collision occurs.

There are built-in script event methods for this. The one we'll be using is **OnTriggerEnter**. It occurs once when a trigger collider of ours first hits another collider. It won't occur again unless the object stops touching our collider and then touches it again. It takes a single parameter, of type **Collider**, which will be given by the Unity engine when it calls the event. This parameter points to the other Collider that we touched, so we name it **"other"**.

Create a script named "Hazard" and fill it with this code (leave the "using" lines at the top alone):

```
public class Hazard : MonoBehaviour
{
    private void OnTriggerEnter(Collider other)
    {
        if (other.gameObject.layer == 3)
        {
            Player player = other.GetComponent<Player>();

            if (player != null)
                player.Die();

        }
    }
}
```

Here we see the OnTriggerEnter event in action, declared as a private method with that "other" parameter of type Collider, which is a type resembling any kind of collider component. We use the "other" parameter to grab the associated "gameObject" member that the Collider is attached to, and through it, we can check the layer. All in all, this leaves us with **"other.gameObject.layer"** which is an int variable that depicts the number of the layer, as we saw them in the Inspector earlier: 0 is Default, 3 is our Player layer, and 6 is our Hazard layer.

We check if the layer is 3, to make sure we've hit the player, and if so, we use a new method, **GetComponent**, to check for a Player script attached to the same GameObject as the collider we've touched. This method searches for a component of a given type on the GameObject, and if it finds one, it returns it as a **Component** type, which is the base type for all components (such as Camera, Light, Transform, and so on). If it cannot find a component of the given type, it returns null.

We create a local variable named **"player"** and store the result of the GetComponent call there. Then, we check to see if we actually found the component we're asking to get by asking if "player" is not ("!=" operator) null. If so, we call the Die method that we declared in the last chapter, which handles the death and respawn for us.

The GetComponent method can be accessed through any other Component reference. In this case, we use the Collider "other". It can also be called through a GameObject reference. Both methods do the same thing – the Component version just operates on the GameObject that the Component instance is attached to.

The <...> part of our GetComponent call is a new concept for us. To put it loosely, it is the concept of **generics** – a feature of C# that allows types to be passed around as parameters to classes and methods, among other things, by listing the types between angle brackets (the < and > symbols).

The GetComponent method declares a **generic type parameter** that specifies which type of component we want to get. Within the GetComponent method, this parameter can be referenced as though it was an actual type, allowing some pretty cool and powerful behavior to be defined. Rather than returning some specific type, the GetComponent method returns the generic type it is given when called.

This means the return type effectively changes on the spot to whatever type we pass in when we call the method. You can't do that with a normal parameter. This allows us to call **GetComponent<Player>** and receive a reference to a Player instead of a reference to a Component. This way, we don't have to make a typecast to apply the reference to our new local variable, and the GetComponent call already knows what subtype of Component we're asking it to get for us – it's right there in the generic type parameter.

If we didn't have generic type parameters, we'd have to specify the type of component we wanted to get through a normal parameter, and we'd get a Component returned to us instead. As a less specific class, the Component instance can't be stored in a Player reference, and we'd get an error. We'd have to fix it with a typecast. Ultimately, the generic type parameter just makes things cleaner and easier for us.

Generics are a somewhat complicated topic, so I could definitely say more about them here, but luckily, you don't need to be well-versed in the inner workings of generics to simply use them in method calls. That's a path you can go down at a later time.

That does it for the Hazard script. Let's test it real quick by creating a stationary Hazard that we can touch with the player:

- Create a Sphere. Set its scale to (3, 3, 3). Place it somewhere near the player, either by dragging it with the position handle (hotkey W) or by copying the player X and Z positions into the Sphere position in the Inspector, then adding some to one of them so it's not right on top of the player. Set its Y position to 1.5 to make sure it's resting on the floor neatly.

- Set the Sphere's layer to **Hazard** in the Inspector.

- Check the **Is Trigger** field of the Sphere Collider component in the Inspector. It won't receive OnTriggerEnter calls if it isn't marked as a trigger collider.

- Attach a Hazard script component to the sphere.

Now play the game and run your Player into the Sphere. It should kill the player on contact. Since our "Player.Die" method also invokes the Respawn method, your player should pop back into existence at the spawn point shortly after.

You can delete the Sphere after you've finished playing around with it. Or, if you'd like to keep it around as a stationary hazard (maybe give it a green material and imagine it's a very prickly bush or something), you could make a prefab out of it instead by dragging and dropping it from the Hierarchy window into the Prefabs folder in your Project window.

Projectile Script

With the ability to make something kill the player on touch, we're one step closer to making an obstacle that fires deadly projectiles. Let's work on the projectiles themselves next and create a Projectile script that provides forward movement. When we get around to it, we'll make our Shooting script, which will spawn the projectiles and point their forward axis in the direction they should be traveling. Knowing that, all we need to do is make the projectile move forward until it reaches its maximum range.

We'll create a "Projectile" script and declare some variables:

```
[Header("References")]
public Transform trans;

[Header("Stats")]
[Tooltip("How many units the projectile will move forward per second.")]
public float speed = 34;

[Tooltip("The distance the projectile will travel before it comes to a stop.")]
public float range = 70;

private Vector3 spawnPoint;
```

The Tooltip attributes describe the purpose of each variable, so read over those if it's unclear. These also show in the Unity editor if you mouse over the variable fields in the Inspector. We use the same "trans" reference, since it should be a little bit faster than referencing "transform" itself (plus it's a bit easier to type). The "spawnPoint" will be set in Start, to memorize where the projectile was when it spawned:

```
void Start()
{
    spawnPoint = trans.position;
}
```

We'll use "spawnPoint" and "range" to make sure it doesn't travel further than it should, **in the Update method**:

```
void Update()
{
    //Move the projectile along its local Z axis (forward):
    trans.Translate(0, 0, speed * Time.deltaTime, Space.Self);

    //Destroy the projectile if it has traveled to or past its range:
    if (Vector3.Distance(trans.position, spawnPoint) >= range)
        Destroy(gameObject);
}
```

This time, since we're not using a CharacterController like we were when we moved our Player, we instead use the **Translate** method to move the Transform. This method has various overloads that allow slightly different parameter inputs, but the one we've chosen is using three float values for the X, Y, and Z movement we want and an **enum Space** which determines whether the Transform should be moved in world or local coordinates. This enum only has two options: **"Space.World"** and **"Space.Self"** ("self" meaning "local").

This fourth parameter has a *default value* of "Space.World". This means if you want, you can omit the parameter entirely, and it will assume its default value and run just fine. However, since we want to rotate the projectile however we like and have it always go along its own forward axis, that means we want local movement instead, so we need to specify the parameter.

After applying the movement, we use another new method, **"Vector3.Distance"**. This takes two Vector3 instances and returns the distance between them as a float. We check if the distance between the position of the projectile and the spawn point has exceeded the "range" variable. If so, we destroy the GameObject that the Projectile script is attached to, with a method Destroy, available through any Unity object.

Now let's create a projectile prefab. We'll set it up in the scene and then drag and drop it to the Project to make the prefab asset.

It'll be pretty simple:

- Create a Sphere named **"Projectile"**. Set its layer to **Hazard**.

- Set its Transform scale to (2, 2, 2).

- Check the **Is Trigger** box in its collider.

- Add the Hazard and Projectile scripts. Set the "trans" reference for the Projectile script to reference its own Transform.

- Add a Rigidbody component using the "Add Component" button at the bottom of the Inspector. Check the **Is Kinematic** box. You can uncheck the **Use Gravity** box if you want, but gravity won't apply to a kinematic Rigidbody anyway.

- Create a new Material named "Projectile" in your Project view. Using the "Albedo" field in the Inspector to set the material color, I've picked a slightly off-red color with a hex value of EE3C3C, although you can pick a different color if you'd like.

- Drag the new material from the Project window onto the Projectile in the Scene or Hierarchy window.

- Now we're done, so make a prefab for the Projectile GameObject by dragging it from the Hierarchy to the Assets ➤ Prefabs folder in the Project.

If everything is set up correctly, your Projectile should look like Figure 16-6 in the Inspector.

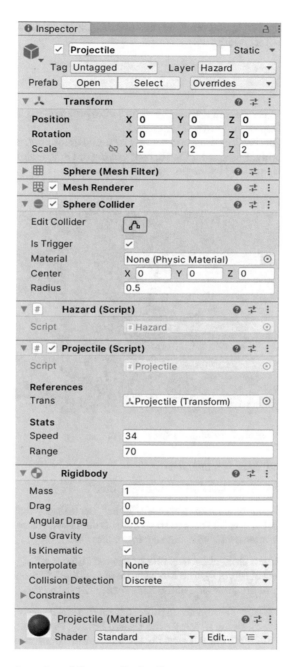

Figure 16-6. *The Inspector view of our fully setup Projectile*

If you want, you can give it a test and position the projectile somewhere in your scene, play the game, and watch it move. You can even try to get in front of it with the player to see the Hazard script in action again, if you're so inclined.

Once you're done playing with it, you can safely remove the projectile instance from the scene, assuming you made a prefab of it already.

Shooting Script

Now we'll create a "shooter" obstacle and a Shooting script to fire projectiles. This will give us our first example of spawning GameObjects on the fly through code.

Let's build the GameObject. We're going to use a very minimal amount of creativity to make this one. We'll use a cube for its base and a cylinder for the "barrel" poking out of it, making a crude little cannon. It should look something like Figure 16-7 by the time you're done with it.

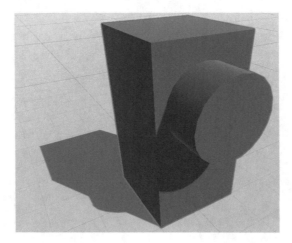

Figure 16-7. *The final appearance of our Shooter GameObject*

Here's how you'll go about putting it together:

- Create an empty GameObject and name it **"Shooter"**.

- Create a cube as a child of Shooter. Name it **"Base"**. Set its local position to (0, 2, 0) and its local scale to (2, 4, 2). You can leave the collider on it as is, so that if we ever bump into the shooter itself, we'll slide against it like a wall.

- Create a cylinder as a child of Base. Name it **"Barrel"**. Give it a local position of (0, .2, .7), a local rotation of (90, 0, 0), and a local scale of (.8, .2, .4). It should now be a short cylinder poking out the front side of the Base cube, near to the top.

- Create an empty GameObject with no initial parent (GameObject ➤ Create Empty from the top toolbar). Name it **"Projectile Spawn Point"**. Drag it onto the Barrel in the Hierarchy to make it a child. Leave the local scale and rotation as is. Set its local position to (0, 1.5, 0) to put it a little bit in front of the barrel.

- If you want, make a Material named Shooter and apply it to your Base and Barrel. I've colored mine purple, with a hex value of A669BE.

- Create a prefab out of the Shooter GameObject by dragging it from the Hierarchy to the Prefabs folder in the Project.

The Spawn Point will be an invisible GameObject used for its position and rotation. We'll spawn new projectiles there and rotate them to point in the same direction. The reason we made the Projectile Spawn Point with no parent and then dragged it onto a parent after, instead of right-clicking our Base or Barrel and creating it as a child immediately, is to keep it from being rotated or scaled according to its parent. If we made it as a child of the Barrel, it would be affected by the Barrel scale and rotation and wouldn't face forward along the world direction by default.

Let's get to it. Make a script named "Shooting" and open it up.

This one's pretty short, and you're an expert at this process now, so here it goes – this will be the contents of the script (minus the usings at the top):

```
public class Shooting : MonoBehaviour
{
    [Header("References")]
    public Transform spawnPoint;
    public GameObject projectilePrefab;

    [Header("Stats")]
    [Tooltip("Time, in seconds, between the firing of each projectile.")]
    public float fireRate = 1;

    private float lastFireTime = 0;

    //Unity events:
    void Update()
    {
        //If the current game time has surpassed the time we last fired, plus the rate
        of fire:
        if (Time.time >= lastFireTime + fireRate)
        {
            //Spawn a projectile and mark the time we did it:
            lastFireTime = Time.time;
            Instantiate(projectilePrefab, spawnPoint.position, spawnPoint.rotation);
        }
    }
}
```

We have a reference to the Spawn Point Transform and to the GameObject of the Projectile prefab. We set these in the Inspector, as always.

We also have a public **"fireRate"** variable and a float which stores the current game time at which a projectile was last fired. To implement the wait time between each shot, we use the **"Time.time"** variable, which gives the time, in seconds, since the game began. It starts at 0 and counts up over the course of the game being played. To see if it's time to spawn a new projectile yet, we just need to check if the current time ("Time.time") is greater than the "Time.time" at which we last fired (**"lastFireTime"**), plus the seconds between each firing (**"rateOfFire"**). In order for this to make any sense, we have to also reset the "lastFireTime" to the current "Time.time" again every time we fire a projectile.

To spawn a prefab on the fly, we use the built-in method **Instantiate**. It takes three parameters: a pointer to the thing we want to create, a Vector3 for the initial position we want it to have, and a Quaternion for the initial rotation we want it to have. We'll point to the projectile prefab and use the position and rotation of the Spawn Point to neatly align the projectiles with the barrel.

That's it! We can save the script and attach it to the base Shooter GameObject. Set the script's reference to Spawn Point by dragging it from the Hierarchy to the field in the Inspector. The projectile prefab can be dragged from the Project window onto its respective field in the Shooter script.

Now you can play and test the results. If you've set the Shooter up as described, it will keep spawning projectiles at the Spawn Point position, firing them off along its forward direction, toward where the so-called barrel points. Watching from your Scene window, you can travel out with the projectiles to see that they're disappearing once they reach the end of their range. If your Shooter is not positioned at the correct vertical location, just set the root "Shooter" GameObject Y position to 0 (assuming your Floor is at a Y of 0 as it should be), or delete it and drag and drop a new prefab instance down, which should snap to the correct Y location automatically since we made its pivot point at the bottom.

Summary

This chapter implemented the basic system for hazards that kill our player on touch, as well as our first obstacle type, a stationary Shooter that fires projectiles periodically. Some things to remember are as follows:

- A **Rigidbody** can be added to a GameObject to provide realistic physics simulation for that GameObject, including gravity and forces that push, twist, and turn the GameObject.

- A Rigidbody that is marked as **kinematic** will not be controlled by the physics system. If you're going to directly move a Transform, its Rigidbody should be kinematic; otherwise, your influences on the Transform position will cause unpredictable disruptions to the natural physics performed by the Unity engine.

- For collision-related events to be sent on scripts, one of the colliding entities must have a Rigidbody attached, even if it's a kinematic one.

- The CharacterController counts as a kinematic Rigidbody. You don't need a Rigidbody attached to a GameObject that already has a CharacterController.

- Every GameObject is part of one **layer**. Layers can be used to determine which objects collide with each other and which do not.

- The **OnTriggerEnter** built-in event is called when a trigger collider first detects a collision with another collider.

- The **"Transform.Translate"** method is used to move a Transform by a given X, Y, and Z amount. Whether the movement occurs in world or local space can be specified using the fourth parameter.

- The **Destroy** method is available from within scripts and can be used to destroy a given GameObject, removing it from the game world entirely.

- The **Instantiate** method is also available from within scripts. It can be used to create a new instance of a prefab, with the desired initial position and rotation as parameters.

CHAPTER 17

Walls and Goals

Now that we have some obstacles taking shape and our player movement working nicely, we can start thinking about setting up levels and a win condition for them: touching a goal object.

To block out our levels, we'll use simple cubes based off a prefab, with variations on their scale and position to stretch them out however we need to make our level. It might look a bit shoddy, but again, we're focused on learning to program and piece together our games first and foremost.

Walls

Create a cube and name it **"Wall"**. Make a material, also named "Wall", apply whatever color you like, and throw it on there. I'm using a dark, grayish blue with a hex value of 687D89. We'll leave the collider as is. It won't be a trigger, because we want it to be physical and block the player. It doesn't need a Rigidbody because it doesn't move.

We'll give it a Y scale of 10 and position it so the bottom is touching the floor. When we set up our "Floor" plane at the start of the project, we made sure to position it at (0, 0, 0). This means the floor has a Y position of 0, so you can perfectly touch the bottom of the wall to the floor by setting the wall Y position to half of its Y scale (5).

All in all, the Y scale won't affect how the walls look too much in our game, so leaving them at 10 should do the trick – we don't want them so high they might touch the camera, after all.

I'd recommend never changing the Y scale of individual walls, to keep them all uniformly flat on top. It just looks nicer, and having varying heights might cause trouble down the road.

Now we can make a prefab out of this wall. Going forward, we'll make sure all the walls we add to any of our levels are instances of this prefab. Yes, it was easy to make, but if we make new ones each time or make a separate one for each level and copy-paste it, we won't be able to make a change to all of them at once if we should ever need to.

To shape a level and confine the player within it, we can copy-paste (Ctrl+C, Ctrl+V) or duplicate (Ctrl+D) instances of this prefab and change their position, rotation, and X/Z scale however we like, letting them overlap and stick together.

Whenever we start making a new level (we'll make each one in a separate scene), we just throw a wall prefab instance down, reposition its Y correctly (its pivot point is at the center, so it won't line up to the floor correctly when we place it), and then just copy-paste that to make more instances on a dime.

The rect tool (hotkey T) can be particularly useful in quickly sizing a block like this. Just make sure you set the Tool Handle Rotation control (hotkey X) to Local, not Global, so that when working with rotated walls, the rect tool matches the rotation of the selected wall. Figure 17-1 shows the location of the Tool Handle Rotation button up at the right side of the transform tools in the toolbar.

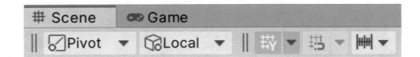

Figure 17-1. *The Tool Handle Rotation, just under the Scene window tab, shown in the Local setting*

You can then drag the edges or corners of the walls to pull them, allowing you to easily stretch and shrink the walls. Remember, the rect tool will adjust how it resizes your cube based on the angle at which your Scene window camera is facing it. Get above the level, looking down at it like your player might be, for ideal results.

An easy way to get to a view like this is to use the little orientation gizmo in the top-right corner of the Scene window (see Figure 17-2).

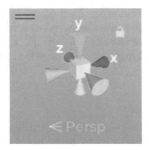

Figure 17-2. *The orientation gizmo, located in the top-right corner of the Scene window*

We went over this gizmo early on, but let's observe it again since it can be particularly useful to us now.

You can click the gray cube at the center of the gizmo to switch between Perspective and Isometric camera modes. The current setting is displayed in text beneath the gizmo (Persp or Iso). Just click that cube to toggle between the two settings. Isometric mode makes everything look "more 2D," so to speak, while Perspective mode looks more standard, with field of view stretching objects as they near the edges of the screen. Isometric mode can make it easier to line objects up accurately.

The gizmo also shows little cones pointing off the central cube. Three of these cones are color-coded by their axis (red, green, and blue) and labeled for the X, Y, and Z axes. Any of the cones can be clicked to spin the camera around to view the world from straight on at that angle: top, bottom, left, right, and so on, depending upon which cone you clicked. If you click the green cone, you get a view from the top of the world, letting you get a bird's-eye view of the level as you edit it.

Try switching to Iso mode, hitting that green cone, selecting your Player in the Hierarchy, and then pressing F to hone your view in on the player. Scroll back some with your mouse wheel to get a higher-up view, and then try selecting a wall and using the rect tool (T) to drag its sides and corners around. This should make blocking out walls for your level convenient. From here, you can easily move your camera around the level by middle-clicking and dragging the mouse, or by pressing Q to switch to the hand tool, then left-clicking and dragging the mouse. You can also easily toggle full screen for your Scene window (or any currently focused Unity window) with Shift+Space.

As we develop more functionality and hazards for our game, you can play with your own level designs and get creative with it.

Goals

Alright, let's make a simple Goal script to define a means of winning the level. This is going to be much like a Hazard: detect a touch from the Player and run some code when it happens.

Let's make a layer to use for our goals first. We covered this in the last chapter when we made our Player and Hazard goals, so you ought to know how to add another user layer. If not, check back with the last chapter.

Add a layer named **"Goal"** to the **User Layer 7**, just beneath our Hazard goal. Then go to the collision detection matrix in Edit ➤ Project Settings, under the Physics section, and make the Goal only collide with the Player.

Now, let's create the GameObject for our Goal:

- Create an empty GameObject named **"Goal"**.

- Add a cylinder child to the Goal GameObject and scale it to (4, 0.1, 4), making it like a thin disc. Give it a (0, .1, 0) local position. Check the **"Is Trigger"** field in its collider. That's important – it will act as a physical collider if you forget this, so the player will sort of just walk on it without any effect.

- If you want, make a material named "Goal" and apply it to the cylinder to give it some color. I'm using a bright green (it's the color of success in video games, after all), with a hex value of 2CFF28.

- Apply the Goal layer to the root Goal GameObject. This should also provide a pop-up window asking to apply the layer to all children as well. Select "Yes, change children."

- Give the root Goal GameObject a **kinematic** Rigidbody. There may not be a collider attached to the Goal itself, but the Rigidbody will use the child cylinder's collider without any further setup on our part.

By the end, it should look something like Figure 17-3. The collider sticks up past the cylinder a little, but that won't hurt anything.

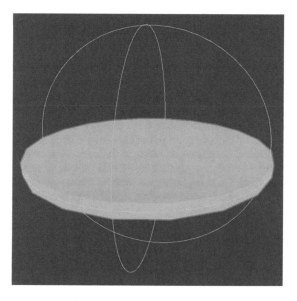

Figure 17-3. *Our Goal GameObject, with the shape of its collider visible as green lines arcing over and beneath it*

Now, create a Goal script in your Scripts folder in the Project window. Attach an instance of the new script to the Goal root GameObject.

While we're at it, make a prefab out of the Goal GameObject by dragging it from the Hierarchy to the Prefabs folder in your Project window.

The Goal script will be pretty short: when the player touches the Goal, we'll load the "main" scene again. We haven't gotten there yet, but eventually, each level is going to be in its own scene, and the "main" scene will be the menu that the user sees when they start the game, allowing them to select a level to play on. For now, we'll just send them over there again when they win. It's not much of a rewarding experience, but it's the journey that counts, right?

To do this, we need to add a new "using" statement at the top of our script file, up there with the rest of them. You've probably paid little attention to these since their first mention. To recap, they exist to tell the compiler what other "namespaces" (tidy containers for related code definitions) we want to use in this script file.

We need a particular namespace that allows us to run a method to change the current scene in-game. Add this "using" anywhere in there with the rest, up **at the top of the Goal script**:

```
using UnityEngine.SceneManagement;
```

Now, we can delete the default Start and Update methods and add our **OnTriggerEnter** method – the same built-in event we used with our Hazard scripts in the last chapter. When the Goal script detects a touch by anything in the Player layer, we'll count that as a victory and load the main scene again. Here's how your Goal script should look (minus the usings):

```
public class Goal : MonoBehaviour
{
    void OnTriggerEnter(Collider other)
    {
        //If the other is in the Player layer
        if (other.gameObject.layer == 3)
            SceneManager.LoadScene("main");
    }
}
```

We've seen most of this before: we detect a touch from our trigger collider and make sure the other GameObject is the player (layer 3), and if so, we run this method to load a scene by its name, "main". If you never actually named the scene "main", either do that now in the Project window (right-click the scene and click Rename), or just write whatever name your scene uses in the string we pass to the LoadScene method call (but use the exact same capitalization, and make extra sure you don't mistype it).

This method can be customized with an extra parameter to specify that we want to load the scene "additively," which means the loaded scene gets mixed in with the current one and none of the GameObjects of our current scene get lost. But if you don't specify this, it loads the new scene in by replacing the existing scene entirely (including the Player). For now, we're just loading the same scene in again, so it will just reset everything back to its original state. This is what we want, and it'll still be what we want when we get our main menu working, so everything is in order.

We're not done just yet, though. Before we can load a scene in-game, that scene has to be added to our **Build Settings**. Let's learn what that means.

Build Settings for Scenes

If we ever want to turn our game into a program that we can send to users to play without the use of the Unity editor, we need to **build** the project. This copies our Unity project into a set of files that can run the game independently of the editor – for example, as an executable (.exe) file. But first we need to add any scenes we're using to the **Build Settings**. If the scenes aren't in the Build Settings, they don't get "put in the build" and can't be loaded in-game. We may be able to open them and play them in the Unity editor, but if we want to load them through a script, they must be added to the build.

The Build Settings (see Figure 17-4) are accessed by heading to File ➤ Build Settings or with the hotkey Ctrl+Shift+B (Cmd+Shift+B on Mac).

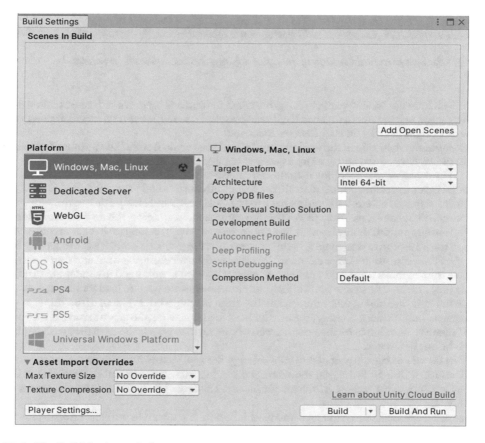

Figure 17-4. *The Build Settings window*

This is where you can find your target platform, which should be "Windows, Mac, Linux" by default. On the right, we have relevant options specifying how the project would be built, such as the specific target platform (Windows, Mac, or Linux, although you'll need to have installed the appropriate build modules in the Unity Hub to see all these options). To the left, there's a listing of other platforms available to target. You can switch the target platform here. That's how you would target things like WebGL (to let your game run in a web browser) or even game consoles. We won't dive into those topics right now, though.

We're focused on the top portion of the window, the **"Scenes In Build"** section. Right now, it's just an empty rectangle. At the bottom-right corner, we can click the button "Add Open Scenes" to put our currently opened "main" scene into that list, as pictured in Figure 17-5.

Figure 17-5. *The Scenes In Build section of the Build Settings window, after we have added our main scene to the list*

This will include the "main" scene in the game when the game is built. We only need to do it this one time, and the scene will remain in that list. If we want to delete a scene, we can select it and press Delete on our keyboard, or right-click it and click Remove Selection.

All the way at the right side of the entry for our "main" scene, you'll see a little number 0. This is the scene **build index**. It starts at 0 and goes up as we add scenes. If we had other scenes in here, we could reorder them by dragging and dropping with the left mouse button.

The build index is another means of loading a scene with the method we used in our Goal script. Now that our "main" scene is in here, we could go back to our Goal script and change the "main" string to use the build index instead, meaning we'd just pass a 0 as the parameter. In our case, it'll do the same thing.

But the most important thing about adding the scene to the build settings is to ensure that it actually makes it into the build and to designate it as the first scene in the project, so that it's the first thing that loads when you start the game. In the Unity editor, we just load whichever scene we want and don't worry about this, but if we were to make a finished product and send it to players, we'd need to send them to the correct scene when they first load the game up. Similarly, any level scenes we want to load for the player will have to be added to the build settings to make them available when playing a built version of the game.

The scene at build index 0 is always the one that will load first when the game is run from a build. Since our "main" scene is intended to be the home screen where the user selects the level they wish to play, we want that to be our first scene.

Now that the main scene is part of the build settings, the goal should function just as expected. Go ahead and test it out. Touching the goal should reset the scene back to its original state, reloading all the GameObjects within. It might cause a little bit of a hiccup. That's expected – loading in new scenes can come with a short wait.

If it doesn't work, make sure your goal and its child cylinder are both in the Goal layer, the root Goal GameObject has a Goal script and a kinematic Rigidbody, and the child cylinder's collider has the **Is Trigger** box checked. Also, remember to keep your Goal at a Y position of 0 to line it up with the floor vertically.

Summary

This chapter taught us how to set up walls for our level and how to edit them conveniently with the rect tool. We've coded our Goal script and set up a prefab for a consistent Goal GameObject which will take the player back to the "main" scene when they touch the goal. Some points to remember are as follows:

- To access the class required to load a scene, include a "**using UnityEngine. SceneManagement;**" line at the very top of the script file.

- If you want to load a scene in-game, it must be added to the build in the **Build Settings** window.

- In the list of scenes added to the build, each scene is assigned its own **build index**, a number based on the scene's order in the list.

- To perform a scene load, call the **"SceneManager.LoadScene"** method. You can use a string for the name of the scene to load or an int for the scene build index.

CHAPTER 18

Patrolling Hazards

Now that the game is shaping up more, it's in need of some greater obstacle variety. In this chapter, we'll implement "Patrollers," and along the way, we'll get hands-on experience with a heap of important, powerful concepts.

Patrollers are objects that we set up with a series of points they'll travel along. They move from one point to the next, starting at the first point and going down the list. Once they reach the last point, they double back to the first point again and then repeat the process. We can set the points up however we want and use however many points we want. If we want an obstacle to travel in a simple line back and forth, we can just use two points: one at one end of the line and another at the opposite end. Alternatively, we could have them run along a series of points that lead them down a more complicated path.

Resembling a Patrol Point

The first challenge we'll need to face is managing the patrol points. How are we going to resemble each patrol point and access it in our Patroller script?

The only data we really need for patrol points is a position – that's all they really are, right? So we could expose Vector3 instances in the Inspector and manually type in the position of each patrol point. But that's not very convenient.

Instead, we can use empty GameObjects in the Scene to resemble patrol points. This way, we can position them using the transform tools and view them in the Scene window to know where they actually are. Then, we can set references to each patrol point Transform and grab its ".position".

If we'd used Vector3s, we wouldn't really be able to visualize where a point is. We'd have to make a GameObject, put it where we want, and then copy its position value into a field in our Patroller script. And if we're doing that, why not just use empty GameObjects as the points instead?

The next challenge we face is how we'd go about referencing all of these patrol point Transforms in our Patroller script. We might think to declare a bunch of variables, one for each patrol point. We'd name them "patrolPoint1", "patrolPoint2", and so on. We'd set them as references to patrol point Transforms in the Inspector. We could declare, say, ten of them, because we don't think we'll ever need more than ten. Any points that aren't set (meaning the value is null) would be ignored, so we'd double back to point 1 as soon as we reach the last point that isn't null.

But that's kind of awful. Not only is it a pain to code the logic for switching from one point to the next, it's simply not doing all we want it to do. It's limiting us to however many points we're willing to spend the time creating variables for, and it requires that we set a reference to each point.

This is where **arrays** come into play.

© Casey Hardman 2024
C. Hardman, *Game Programming with Unity and C#*, https://doi.org/10.1007/978-1-4842-9720-9_18

Arrays

Arrays are a means of storing a collection of a certain data type in a single object. An instance of an array is given a **type** (such as Transform) and a **length**. The length is the number of items that the array stores.

Say we create an array of type Transform, with a length of 20. We now have a single object that stores 20 separate Transform references, all of which are initially set to null.

But how do we access individual items within the array?

This is known as **indexing**. Each item in the array corresponds to an index – an integer value, like an ID that can be used to point to a specific "slot" in the array. The index of the first item will be 0. The next item will be 1 and then the next 2, going all of the way up to 19 in an array with a length of 20 (since it starts at 0, not 1, the last index will always be 1 point less than the length).

To declare an array, you declare it like a normal variable, but after the type, you put an empty set of square braces []:

```
public Transform[] arrayOfTransforms;
public Vector3[] arrayOfPoints;
```

To create an instance of an array, it's much like calling a constructor to create an instance of a class as you normally would. The difference is that we use square braces [] instead of parentheses () after the type name. Within those square braces, we put a single parameter, which is the number of entries the array will store. This parameter resembles the array length. It can be accessed at any time through the ".Length" member:

```
//Create an array storing 5 Transforms:
Transform[] arrayOfTransforms = new Transform[5];

//Log the length:
Debug.Log(arrayOfTransforms.Length); //This will log the number 5
```

In the preceding code, we've declared an array storing up to five Transforms. The first has an index of 0, and the rest have indexes of 1, 2, 3, and 4. Notice that the **last index** is equal to **Length - 1**, not Length. Again, that's due to the index starting at 0 instead of 1. This is a very important thing to remember when dealing with indexes!

To access the Transforms through the array, we reference the array and then type an **indexer**, which is a square brace set [] with an integer value inside it. That integer value is the index of the item we want to grab out of the array. For example:

```
Transform first = arrayOfTransforms[0];
Transform last = arrayOfTransforms[4];
```

Often when working with arrays, we don't just pass in literal values like 0 or 4 as our index. It kind of eliminates the purpose of arrays.

What we can do is keep an integer **"currentPointIndex"** variable in our Patroller and use that to keep track of the index of the point we're currently traveling toward.

When we reach the point, we increase "currentPointIndex" by 1 and then use it as an index to grab the next point in the array.

If you ever try to grab from an array using an index that's **too high** for the size of the array or is a **negative value**, an error will be thrown. It doesn't just double back to the beginning automatically for us, so we have to account for that ourselves.

Luckily, that's not so hard. Whenever we're ready to switch to the next point, we simply check if the "currentPointIndex" is already the last index in the array, which is equal to "array.Length - 1". If so, we set the "currentPointIndex" back to 0. If not, we just increase it by 1.

This creates a neat loop through the items of the array, and it works no matter how many items we store in the array.

Setting Up Patrol Points

Let's figure out how we plan on setting up references to our patrol points before we begin coding anything.

Arrays can be *serialized* just like other data types (so long as they store a type that also supports serialization). If you'll recall, a value being serialized means it shows up in the Inspector so that we can view and edit it.

When an array is serialized, you can set its length to whatever you want, and Unity will give you a field for each item (index) in the array. We could then drag and drop the Transforms of our patrol points into those fields to set the array up manually. It would look something like this in the Inspector, shown in Figure 18-1.

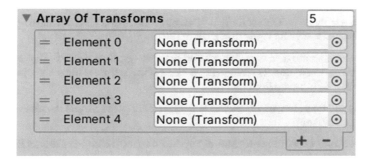

Figure 18-1. *A view of a serialized array of Transforms in the Inspector. We've set the length to 5 manually. None of the references have been set yet, showing as "None" (equivalent to null)*

But we're not chumps, so we won't be doing that. Dragging and dropping patrol points into this array to set up the Patroller will be somewhat tedious, so we'll be setting the references through code instead.

We want to automate this part of our workflow so it's easier for us to set up Patrollers. It may be *slightly* less performant as a result. Finding the patrol points at runtime is always going to be slower than just setting up the references directly in the Scene, when the game isn't playing. But the performance hit shouldn't be noticeable anyway, particularly for a game with such a small scope. Sometimes it's worth it to implement a simple feature like this to make the game easier to develop. If you're too hard on yourself just to make the game run as fast as possible, you might end up never releasing the game in the first place because developing it drove you crazy!

So what do we have to do to set up these patrol points and grab the references to them in our code?

In order to find all of the patrol points associated with a single Patroller instance through code, we'll be grabbing all of the children of the GameObject with the Patroller script attached. So all of the empty GameObjects we use to resemble patrol points will have to be children of the Patroller they belong to. This keeps them neatly tucked inside the Patroller they belong to in the Hierarchy, so it's a win-win.

But we don't want them to move or spin with the Patroller, so we'll just unparent them as soon as we find them and set up our references. That way, they stay put in the scene even as the Patroller moves and rotates. It would be anarchy if we forgot this step. The Patroller would keep moving toward a point that stays a fixed distance away from it, so it'd never reach the first point at all.

We need to distinguish patrol points from other children that aren't meant to be patrol points. We're simply going to use the GameObject name to do that. We'll name them all "Patrol Point" followed by a set of parentheses with the patrol point index within it, such as "(0)" for the first point and "(1)" for the next.

Our code is going to use that index value to properly order the patrol points in an array, so it's important that we always get it right.

Luckily for us, Unity will automatically do this sort of numbering for us when we copy-paste GameObjects.

Try it yourself. Create a Cube in the scene, and with Ctrl+C and Ctrl+V, copy and paste it a few times. You'll notice that Unity automatically renames the new cubes, adding a "(1)" after the first copy you create and then a "(2)" after the next, and so on.

We'll use this to our advantage to make it easier to plop down a bunch of patrol points. We can just name the first patrol point "Patrol Point (0)", and then whenever we copy and paste it, Unity will increase the index value for us. We'll still have to manually change the numbers if we ever want to add or remove a patrol point in the middle of the sequence, though. We'll just have to suck it up and deal with that.

Let's set up the GameObject for a Patroller so we can see this in action.

We'll use a system similar to that of the Player. A base, empty GameObject aligned with the floor (a Y position value of 0) will hold all the other GameObjects. We'll have a model within, which we'll be rotating instead of the base GameObject:

- Create an empty GameObject named **"Patroller"**. Position it somewhere by your Player and make sure its Y position stays at 0.

- Create a Cube, name it **"Model Base"**, and make it a child of the Patroller. Set its local position to (0, 1.5, 0) and its scale to (3, 3, 3). As always, the 1.5 local Y position keeps the bottom touching the floor nicely.

- Since this will be a Hazard, check the **Is Trigger** field of the Model Base's Box Collider component.

- Create a second cube, name it **"Model Top"**, and make it a child of Model Base. Set its local position to (0, .5, .5) and its local scale to (.2, .2, .7). This will stick out at the top and front of the model, much like with the player, to give us better indication of where it's pointing. We'll also delete its Box Collider component so the player isn't killed by this little protruding piece.

- Set the layer of the Patroller to **Hazard**, and when Unity pops up a box asking to change the layer of children, agree.

- Give the root Patroller GameObject a Rigidbody component, and make it kinematic by checking the **Is Kinematic** box.

- Add a Hazard script component to the root Patroller GameObject. It will automatically use the box collider present in its child, the Model Base, to detect collisions that kill the player.

- You can create a new material for the model if you want. I'll use the same color for the Patrollers as well as the wanderers we'll be making later, so I'm giving the material a more generic name: **"Mobile Hazard"**. I'll color it a dark pink, with a hex value of EF7796. I'll apply that material to both the Model Base and Model Top cubes.

The model will look something like shown in Figure 18-2.

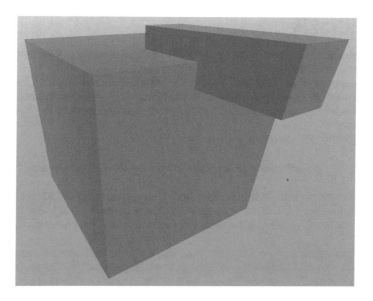

Figure 18-2. *Our Patroller model*

Now, let's set up patrol points so we'll have them ready when we start testing the code that detects them. Just create an empty GameObject that's a child of the Patroller with Alt+Shift+N (Option+Shift+N for Mac users) or GameObject ➤ Create Empty Child while selecting the Patroller. As we discussed, name it exactly **"Patrol Point (0)"**. That'll be the first point. Leave it right where the Patroller GameObject is, with a local position of (0, 0, 0). That way, the Patroller will always double back on its initial Scene position. This will be convenient for us, since we can just drop a new Patroller where we want it, then copy and paste the first point, move it where we want, and expect the Patroller to go back to where it started when it's done.

Since we've got this set up nicely for how we'll want to use it when creating new Patrollers, let's **make a prefab of the Patroller now**, before we muck it up for testing purposes.

After making the prefab, copy and paste the Patrol Point and position the new one at the next position you want the Patroller to run to. The index in the name should go up by 1 point automatically, becoming "Patrol Point (1)". If you want, keep doing that until you've mapped out a path you're satisfied with (or just leave it at two points for a straight line). Remember, after reaching the last point (the patrol point with the highest index number), the Patroller will go back to "Patrol Point (0)" and do it all again.

If you've created four patrol points, your Hierarchy should look something like Figure 18-3.

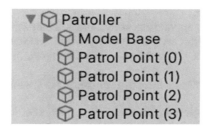

Figure 18-3. *The hierarchy of our Patroller GameObject after we've created four patrol points*

Detecting Patrol Points

Now we can start coding the Patroller. Create a script called **Patroller** and attach an instance of that new script to the root "Patroller" GameObject.

Before we implement anything else, let's do the part that relates to arrays: set up the patrol points. We're going to handle a couple of different firsts here, so bear with me – they're important concepts.

We'll declare an array of Transforms called "patrolPoints", nested directly in the Patroller script:

```
private Transform[] patrolPoints;
```

You'll notice it's private, which makes it not show in the Inspector, since we won't be setting it up that way.

Now we need to set the array up in the Start method. We're going to split this functionality up a little bit to keep things neat-looking. We'll do so by declaring a private method for us to use in our Start method. This private method will get all children of the Patroller and return only the ones with a name that starts with "Patrol Point (".

To do this, we'll be exploring some new concepts. First, we'll use the built-in method **GetComponents InChildren<T>**, which you can call from a GameObject or a Component. The **<T>** part means that it takes a single generic type parameter, as we saw before with the GetComponent<T> method that we used in our Hazard script. It works much the same way: it's simply asking us what type of component we want to look for. It'll search all child GameObjects of the GameObject we call the method from and return an array storing all instances that it found of the given component type within the children.

Since every GameObject has a Transform that can't be removed from it, we can call **GetComponentsI nChildren<Transform>** on our root Patroller GameObject to get a Transform for each child within it. Then, we can easily grab a reference to the GameObject of each child, since Transforms (like all Component types) have a ".gameObject" member pointing to the GameObject that the Transform belongs to. Thus, finding all of the Transforms is just as well as finding all of the GameObjects.

Then we need to go over each item in that array and select only the ones with the correct name (the patrol points).

This is where we need a **List** and a **loop**.

The List is our first example of a class that takes a generic type. Technically, it should be List<T> since it takes one generic type parameter.

A list is an array that's generally a bit less performant, but has less of the limitations that arrays have.

Arrays have to be created with a length. You must abide by that length from that point on. You'll have "Length" items in the array, no more and no less. You can set items to null if you don't need them, but they'll still be there in the array.

A List doesn't need to be created with a length in mind, and it allows you to add and remove items on the fly. This is perfect for us. We have no idea how many patrol points there will be at first, so we very well can't create an array to store them in.

Aside from that difference, Lists operate like arrays. You still index them with a set of square braces [] to grab the items within. They'll still throw an error if you try to grab an index that doesn't exist.

We're going to create a List, fill it with just the patrol point Transforms, and then return that List in this private method.

The loop is what we use to go through all of the Transforms in the initial array so we can add only the patrol points to the List.

We'll get to that in a second, but let's finally declare this method and get ready to add our loop. You know how generics work for methods, but this is the first time you'll see them for class types:

```
private List<Transform> GetUnsortedPatrolPoints()
{
    //Get the Transform of each child in the Patroller:
```

```
Transform[] children = gameObject.GetComponentsInChildren<Transform>();

//Declare a local List storing Transforms:
List<Transform> points = new List<Transform>();
}
```

Here, we declare a private method called **GetUnsortedPatrolPoints**. The return type is a List. When supplying a generic class as a type, you need to write out the <T> part as well and replace the T with the type you're returning. That's how the compiler knows what sort of object should be stored in the List. This way it knows that when we call this method, we'll get a List of Transforms returned to us.

Within the method, we use the **GetComponentsInChildren** method, as we talked about earlier. All we have to supply is the generic type parameter, which is **<Transform>**. We create a local variable called "children" to store this resulting array of Transforms.

Then, we declare a new local **List<Transform>** to store just the points in. This line looks somewhat redundant: List<Transform> comes first to signify the variable type, and then shortly after, we're typing it out again to construct a new instance.

There's a little "syntax sugar" you can use to avoid this, if it hurts your eyes so badly. The "var" keyword can replace the variable type, which makes the compiler simply figure out what the type is meant to be itself. In this situation, it's easy to do so: we're assigning a value to the variable immediately after, and that value is obviously going to be a List<Transform>, right?

```
var points = new List<Transform>();
```

When I say "syntax sugar," I mean that this is purely in the syntax: it's not changing the functionality of our variable at all. It still stores a List<Transform> and only that. It's just that we're telling the compiler we're too lazy to type the name out ourselves and asking it to figure it out for us.

The "for" Loop

Now we're set up to do our **loop**. Simply put, a **loop** is a block of code that can run multiple times. There are different kinds of loops for different purposes, but the one we're using is a **for loop**.

Let's look at a simple example that's not exactly what we need, but it shows a basic use of the for loop:

```
for (int i = 0; i < 5; i++)
{
}
```

First, we give the "for" keyword and then a set of parentheses (). Within the parentheses, we have three separate tiny statements, all declared on the same line, but each one still separated by a semicolon ";" like they normally are.

The first statement is the **initializer**. It's a variable declaration that occurs at the start of the loop. We declare an int named **"i"**. This variable is initialized when the loop begins and only exists within the code block of the loop. You can't access it outside of the loop.

The second statement is the **condition**. We've written **"i < 5"**. This is just a bool expression – something that returns true or false.

The third statement is the **iterator** which is just **"i++"**. This is a slightly shorter way of typing "i += 1". You can use the "++" operator after any number value to add 1 to it. You can also use "--" (two minus signs) to decrease it by 1.

So what is this loop doing?

First, the initializer code runs one time at the start of the loop, declaring the variable.

Then, this recurring process happens any number of times:

- The **condition** is evaluated (i < 5).

- If the condition is true, the code inside the block is run, then the **iterator** is run (i++), and then this process repeats – back to the condition again.

- If the condition is false, break out of the loop (meaning the loop ends).

In the example, this means the code in the block runs five times. After each iteration of the loop, the variable "i" increases by 1. Once "i" becomes 5, the condition is no longer true, so the loop stops iterating.

When the loop finishes, the code beneath it will continue running as normal.

At any point within the loop, we can access "i" to get its current value.

You might be able to guess how we can apply that to our current problem.

We want to loop over every item in the "children" array of Transforms, operating once on each item. We'll use the "i" variable to refer to the current item in the loop – the index we want to grab from the array. It starts at 0 and goes up by 1 each iteration, which is perfect to go through each item in the array.

To ensure that we operate on each index in the array, we just need to know how many items are in the array, to make sure the loop stops as soon as we hit that last index (otherwise, we'll get an error at runtime for trying to access a nonexistent index). To do that, we use the **"children.Length"** value in the condition:

```
for (int i = 0; i < children.Length; i++)
{
    ...
}
```

This is the standard way to iterate over every item in an array or list and perform some action on each of those items individually. To get the item, we just use "i" as the index: **"children[i]"**.

Now, what are we doing to each item in our loop?

What we need to do is check if the GameObject name starts with **"Patrol Point ("** and, if so, add it to the "points" List we made earlier.

This is how our method looks once we've added our for loop:

```
private List<Transform> GetUnsortedPatrolPoints()
{
    //Get the Transform of each child in the Patroller:
    Transform[] children = gameObject.GetComponentsInChildren<Transform>();

    //Declare a local List storing Transforms:
    var points = new List<Transform>();

    //Loop through the child Transforms:
    for (int i = 0; i < children.Length; i++)
    {
        //Check if the child's name starts with "Patrol Point (":
        if (children[i].gameObject.name.StartsWith("Patrol Point ("))
        {
            //If so, add it to the 'points' List:
            points.Add(children[i]);
        }
    }

    //Return the point List:
    return points;
}
```

Within the loop, we use "children[i]" to get the current child Transform in the loop. We reach into that and access the ".gameObject" and then reach further to access its name. This is a string, which has a handy instance method called **StartsWith**, which simply returns true if the string starts with the given string parameter.

If so, we reference our "points" List and call its instance method **Add**. This takes one parameter, which is the item to add to the List. The item will be added to the end of the List (meaning it has the highest index).

We wouldn't want to forget to actually return the list when we're done, so we add that "return points;" statement to the bottom.

At last, we've made our GetUnsortedPatrolPoints method. Now we just have to put it to use.

Sorting Patrol Points

We have a method to get an unsorted List of patrol points. Now we need to get that list and, once again, employ a for loop. Iterating over each patrol point, we'll isolate the index out of the patrol point name, convert it to an integer, and store the patrol point by that index in our "patrolPoints" array.

Remember, our main goal is to set up "patrolPoints", the array we declared in the script to store the properly sorted array of patrol points. When we get all the children of the Patroller, they'll be sorted as they are in the Hierarchy, so we can't be sure they'll be correctly ordered from the first patrol point to the last. That's why we sort them into our array by index, not by their order in the Hierarchy.

So let's declare that Start method and see what it looks like:

```
void Start()
{
    //Get an unsorted list of patrol points:
    List<Transform> points = GetUnsortedPatrolPoints();

    //Only continue if we found at least 1 patrol point:
    if (points.Count > 0)
    {
        //Prepare our array of patrol points:
        patrolPoints = new Transform[points.Count];

        //Loop through all patrol points:
        for (int i = 0; i < points.Count; i++)
        {
            //Quick reference to the current point:
            Transform point = points[i];
            //Isolate just the patrol point number within the name:

            string indexSubstring = point.gameObject.name.Substring(14, point.gameObject.
            name.Length - 15);

            //Set a reference in our script patrolPoints array:
            patrolPoints[int.Parse(indexSubstring)] = point;

            //Unparent each patrol point so it doesn't move with us:
            point.SetParent(null);

            //Hide patrol points in the Hierarchy:
            point.gameObject.hideFlags = HideFlags.HideInHierarchy;
        }
```

```
        //Start patrolling at the first point in the array:
        SetCurrentPatrolPoint(0);
    }
}
```

First, we use the "var" keyword again in our declaration of a local variable **"points"** storing the result of calling that private method we just wrote. Just like that, we'll have all of our Patrol Point GameObjects stored in a List<Transform>.

Pressing on, we see our first use of the **"List<T>.Count"** member. This is equivalent to the ".Length" member of an array, but for a List, it's called Count and resembles the number of items currently stored in the List. It's just a little naming quirk you'll have to get used to.

Using this Count member, we declare an "if" that ensures there's at least one item in the list before we press on.

Now that we have "points.Count" to tell us how many patrol points there are in total, we can pass that as the length of the "patrolPoints" array.

This initializes the array with just the right amount of items: one for each patrol point in the list. They're all null at first, but we're about to set each one in the for loop we declare next.

The loop iterates over each point in "points", using "points.Count" as the total number of iterations to perform.

This time, we do a common operation at the start of the loop code block:

```
//Quick reference to the current point:
Transform point = points[i];
```

This creates a local variable storing the current point we're iterating on. Now, instead of typing "points[i]" to refer to the current point, we just type "point".

Grabbing an item from a collection (like a List or array) takes a little longer than referencing an existing variable, so if you're going to access an item more than a few times in your loop, it'll most likely be faster to store it in a local variable instead. Not only that, it's also just a little easier to type, which is especially true if you were reaching into a bunch of different objects to get to the array you're looping over.

The next section involves a new concept regarding the manipulation of strings:

```
//Isolate just the patrol point number within the name:
string indexSubstring = point.gameObject.name.Substring(14, point.gameObject.name.
Length - 15);
```

To understand how this works, let's learn a little more about strings. We touched on them early on, but let's get a refresher now that we're actually working closely with them.

Strings are just collections of **characters**, where each character is a single letter, number, or symbol in the string. Technically, these characters are resembled as the **"char"** data type.

Strings actually function something like an array or a list, in that you can index them to grab a specific character from them. And just like an array, their index starts at 0 for the first character and then goes up by 1 per character. They even have a ".Length" member you can use to get the total number of characters in the string.

The **Substring** method takes a **start index** and a **count**, both integers. It returns a piece of the string (a substring, so to speak). It starts at the start index (believe it or not) and returns a new string containing "count" characters from that point of the string and onward.

To put it simply, it'll return a piece of the string, starting at "startIndex" and ending at "startIndex + count". This does not affect the original string – it returns a new string.

Our goal is simply to get a new string containing only the characters between the "(" and the ")" in the Patrol Point name. If you count out the characters in "Patrol Point (" , you'll see there are 14 characters. Count again, but start at 0, because that's how indexes work, and you'll count up to 13 and land right at the "(" character, making it the character at index 13. So just go one character higher (14), and we'll start at the character immediately after the "(".

The second parameter in our Substring, the count, is the number of characters we want to get. We need a string with just the numbers of the index in it – it can't include the ")" at the end or anything else. We need to be precise.

We know how many characters are in the "Patrol Point (" part (14), and we expect there to be a ")" at the end. What we can't know is whether the number between those parentheses is one digit, or two, or heaven forbid, three or more.

But we can get the length of the string with the ".Length" member, and we know we're starting at index 14 (one character past the "("). Thus, we can simply get the number of characters in the string, minus the "Patrol Point (" and the ")". Thus, we get the Length, minus 15.

This gives exactly the index portion of the string.

For example, let's say we had "Patrol Point (26)" as our string. There are 14 characters in "Patrol Point (", and remember, string indexes start at 0, just like arrays, so index 14 is the character "2". Starting there, if we just got 1 character, we'd only get the 2. But the Length of this string is 17, minus 15, which is 2 characters, which gives us the "26" exactly. If we had a three-digit number (never mind that that would be a very complicated patrolling path), the Length increases by 1, giving us one more character, and so on.

Okay, moving on, we see why we needed this data in the first place:

```
//Set a reference in our script patrolPoints array:
patrolPoints[int.Parse(indexSubstring)] = point;
```

We assign the patrol point to our array of patrol points using the indexer "[...]". Since the indexer expects an int, not a string, we convert the string by using the static method **"int.Parse"** which takes a string and converts it to an integer.

If the string has any non-number characters in it, an error will be thrown. That's why we had to be all picky about how we created the substring.

With that, we've found the correct index to place the point in the "patrolPoints" array, ensuring everything is ordered how it should be.

Next, we have this bit:

```
//Unparent each patrol point so it doesn't move with us:
point.SetParent(null);

//Hide patrol points in the Hierarchy:
point.gameObject.hideFlags = HideFlags.HideInHierarchy;
```

The first line is somewhat self-explanatory. We call the **SetParent** method of the point (remember, the point is a Transform). This takes one parameter, the Transform we want to set the parent to. We pass in null, which means "no parent at all." This makes sure the patrol points don't move with the Patroller when it moves.

The next line is another new concept.

Unity uses this enum **HideFlags** to let us specify certain little things about the destruction and visibility of objects. It can hide scripts from the Inspector so they don't show at all. It can also hide GameObjects from the Hierarchy, which is what we're asking it to do here: we set the "hideFlags" member of each point GameObject to **HideInHierarchy**, which does just as the name suggests – makes the GameObject no longer show up in the Hierarchy.

This is just to clean things up for us while we're playing. Since the patrol points are no longer parented to their respective Patrollers in-game, they'll all be spread about in the Hierarchy when we're playing. This can make it somewhat cluttered (particularly if we had lots of different Patrollers in the same scene), so we fix that by hiding them.

As always, Unity will revert everything back to the way it was once we stop playing, so all of our patrol points will be visible in the Hierarchy again.

The final line is the calling of a method that we're going to declare in a bit:

```
//Start patrolling at the first point in the array:
SetCurrentPatrolPoint(0);
```

It does just what it says. It sets our current patrol point – the one the Patroller will be moving toward – to the first one in the "patrolPoints" array. Like I said, we'll be declaring that in a bit.

And that's that! It took learning a few new concepts, but our patrol points should be setting themselves up properly in-game – however, since we haven't made the Patroller move yet, and we haven't declared the SetCurrentPatrolPoint method, we won't be able to compile and see the fruits of our hard work yet.

Moving the Patroller

Let's move back up to the top of the script to declare the variables we'll be needing to handle moving the Patroller. So far, the only variable we have is the "patrolPoints" variable. Head back up there, and write this code **directly above the existing "patrolPoints" variable**:

```
//Consts:
private const float rotationSlerpAmount = .68f;

[Header("References")]
public Transform trans;
public Transform modelHolder;

[Header("Stats")]
public float movespeed = 30;

//Private variables:
private int currentPointIndex;
private Transform currentPoint;
```

The very first variable declaration is another new concept.

It's called a **"const"**. It's short for **constant**. Shortly put, it means "a variable that can't be changed."

It's declared just like a normal variable, but you throw that "const" keyword before the type name. This marks the variable as constant. You have to assign a value to it right there when you declare it, and if you ever try to reassign its value somewhere else in your code, a compiler error will prevent you.

This is used to ensure that a variable that shouldn't be changed won't be changed. This way, you can assign a name to some value you're planning on using within your code, and if you ever need to change it, you can do so in one place. However, it makes it clear that the value is not meant to change within the code.

We'll see the purpose of this const variable later, when we start rotating the Patroller to face the direction of movement. For now, let's move on.

You know about the references, since we've done them a few times. The first one points to our own Transform – slightly faster than using ".transform" – and the second one will point to the model Transform. That's so we can rotate just the model, not the root GameObject, just like we do with the player.

We then have the movespeed, which is self-explanatory (units moved per second), and then some private variables:

- **currentPointIndex** is an int resembling the index in the "patrolPoints" array that gets the point we're currently moving toward.

- **currentPoint** is a reference to the Transform of the patrol point we're currently moving toward.

We're holding a reference to "currentPoint" to ensure we only need to grab the point we're heading toward from our "patrolPoints" array once whenever we change to a new point. We could get it from the array every time we move toward the point in the Update method by using "currentPointIndex":

```
patrolPoints[currentPointIndex]
```

However, indexing the array to get the point instead of just storing it when we first switch to a new point is more costly.

Before we start moving, let's declare that method we called earlier. It's a simple, two-line method that sets those two private variables we just talked about. It just ensures that we Don't Repeat Ourselves when assigning our current point.

Declare this method **just above your Start method:**

```
private void SetCurrentPatrolPoint(int index)
{
    currentPointIndex = index;
    currentPoint = patrolPoints[index];
}
```

Simple enough, right? It just takes an index as a parameter and uses that to set our current index, as well as to grab the point from the array and assign it to the "currentPoint" variable.

Now for movement. This will go in our "void Update()" method, where the real magic happens:

```
void Update()
{
    //Only operate if we have a currentPoint:
    if (currentPoint != null)
    {
        //Move root GameObject towards the current point:
        trans.position = Vector3.MoveTowards(trans.position, currentPoint.position,
        movespeed * Time.deltaTime);

        //If we're on top of the point already, change the current point:
        if (trans.position == currentPoint.position)
        {
            //If we're at the last patrol point...:
            if (currentPointIndex >= patrolPoints.Length - 1)
            {
                //...we'll switch to the first patrol point (double back):
                SetCurrentPatrolPoint(0);
            }
            else //Else if we're not at the last patrol point
                SetCurrentPatrolPoint(currentPointIndex + 1); //Go to the index after the
                current.
        }
        //Else if we're not on the point yet, rotate the model towards it:
        else
        {
            //Calculate look rotation:
            Quaternion lookRotation = Quaternion.LookRotation((currentPoint.position -
            trans.position).normalized);

            //Slerp towards look rotation:
```

```
        modelHolder.rotation = Quaternion.Slerp(modelHolder.rotation, lookRotation,
        rotationSlerpAmount);
    }
  }
}
```

First, assuming we have a currentPoint, we move the root Transform toward the point, using the method **"Vector3.MoveTowards"**. This takes three arguments: a Vector3 for the position being moved, a Vector3 for the position to move toward, and a float for the distance to move. It moves the first vector toward the second by that float amount and returns the result. If the movement amount is enough to overshoot the target point, it'll just return the target point instead – it won't go past it. That way, we won't have any awkward situations where the Patroller shoots on past its patrol point.

After performing the movement, we do an "if" asking if our position is equal to the point position – in other words, if we've already reached the point. We know the MoveTowards method will return exactly the "currentPoint.position" once we reach it and won't overshoot that point, so we can safely compare the positions this way.

If we have reached the point, we then check whether our current point index is equal to or greater than the length of the "patrolPoints" array – minus 1, to account for the indexes starting at 0. In other words, we're asking "Are we at the last point?" If so, we call our SetCurrentPatrolPoint method to set the patrol point to the first patrol point by giving it the index 0.

Otherwise, if we're not at the last point, we call the same method, but pass the "currentPointIndex + 1" to use the next patrol point in the array.

If we have not yet reached the point, we'll just rotate our model toward it. We do this with much the same method as we used to rotate the Player model, Slerping the current model rotation toward the rotation required to look at the point. We use that const variable we declared earlier, "rotationSlerpAmount".

The main difference here is the equation we use to get our LookRotation. This is vector stuff, and we aren't going to get too deeply vested in it during this first example project. We'll have more room to play with directions and whatnot in later chapters. For now, just know that when trying to get a direction to point from a Vector "**from**" to a Vector "**to**", you simply do this:

```
(to - from).normalized
```

In our case, "to" is the current point, and "from" is our position: we want the direction **from** our position **to** the position of the point, so we end up with this:

```
(currentPoint.position - trans.position).normalized
```

As we've demonstrated before, **"Quaternion.LookRotation"** converts this to a Quaternion pointing along that given direction.

What's happening here is that we're doing a "-" operator on two Vector3 instances within a set of parentheses. The parentheses contain the Vector3 that this operator returns, and then we can directly reach into the resulting Vector3 to access the **"normalized"** member. As I said, we'll go into more detail on what a *normalized* vector is down the road, when we're working closely with 3D movement systems. For now, just remember that this "(to - from).normalized" equation is your go-to when you need a direction going from one point to another.

But anyway – it's been an arduous journey, but we should finally be able to see our Patroller in action. Make sure you've saved in your code editor and added the Patroller script to your Patroller (on the root GameObject), and make sure you've set up your references. As always, "trans" should point at the Transform of the Patroller itself. "Model Holder" should point at the Model Base within the Patroller.

With at least two patrol points, named "Patrol Point (0)" and "Patrol Point (1)", you should now be able to play and see it in action. The points find themselves on Start, the Patroller begins moving, and it properly rotates the model to face the current point while moving toward it.

Remember, in order for your Patroller to kill the player on touch, the Patroller needs to have a **kinematic** Rigidbody, the Model Base cube needs to have its collider **Is Trigger** checkbox checked, and the Patroller and all its children need to be in the **Hazard** layer (well, the patrol points don't really need to be in the Hazard layer, but you get the point).

Now that you've got the Patroller script all set up, make sure you update your Prefab to match. Since we didn't have the Patroller script attached when we first made our prefab, you can make use of the prefab overrides drop-down in the Inspector, as we discussed back in Chapter 5. Select the Patroller script, click the Overrides drop-down (just under the Layer), select the Patroller script, and then click Apply, as shown in Figure 18-4.

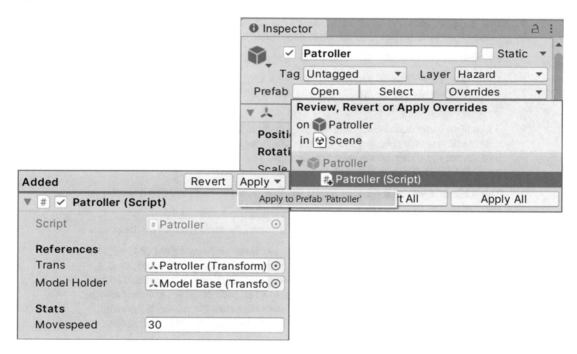

Figure 18-4. *The Overrides drop-down is used to apply our script override to the prefab*

Specifically applying the Patroller script override, rather than selecting Apply All, will ensure that if you've got extra patrol point children added to your Patroller instance, they won't be added to the prefab as well, so you can start with a clean Patroller when placing instances of the prefab.

Summary

This chapter taught us some pretty handy tricks and went over a lot of new and very important concepts. We implemented a new type of obstacle and learned how to work with arrays and the "for" loop. We also worked with generic methods and classes (resembled by the angle brackets "<>") a little more. Some things to remember are as follows:

- An **array** stores many instances of a specific data type in a single value. We'll refer to one of these instances as an **"item"** in the array.

- To access a specific item within an array, square braces [] are used. This is called an **indexer**. Within the square braces, we provide an integer for the **index** of the item we want to access. The index is a number value used to represent an item in the array.

- The "**.Length**" member of an array returns the number of items stored in the array. This cannot be changed after the array is created.

- The first index in an array is always 0. The last index is the Length of the array minus 1.

- Serialized arrays will show in the Inspector, allowing you to set their length and assign a value to each member. Public variables will always be serialized by default, but private variables will not.

- A **List** is an array that does not have a fixed Length. With a List, you may add and remove items on the fly, and the ".Length" member is replaced with "**.Count**", which returns not the maximum number of elements that can be stored, but rather, the number of items currently stored.

- The "**GameObject.hideFlags**" member can be set to hide a GameObject from the Hierarchy.

- In general, a **loop** is a block of code that can run multiple times based on the situation.

- A **for loop** is a block of code that commonly **declares an iterator variable** to store an integer value and then repeatedly runs the code in its code block and, each time, performs some operation on the iterator – usually either increasing it by 1 or decreasing it by 1. You'll see and use the for loop all over the place and for various purposes, but its most common use is to iterate over each item in an array and perform some code on each item inside it, using the iterator as the item index.

- The "**GameObject.GetComponentsInChildren<T>**" method takes a single generic type parameter (the "T") and can be called to return an array of type T. This array stores references to all instances of components of type T found in children of the GameObject that the method was called from.

- To get all GameObjects that are a child of a given GameObject, you can just get the Transforms of all children with a call to GetComponentsInChildren<Transform>() and then use the "Transform.gameObject" member to grab a reference to the GameObject that each returned Transform belongs to.

- The **Substring** method can be called when reaching into a string to return only a portion of the text contained in the string. It takes two parameters: the index of the character to start at and the number of characters afterward to include in the returned string.

- A variable that is declared with the "**const**" keyword is a variable that cannot be changed from whatever value it is initially assigned.

CHAPTER 19

Wandering Hazards

In this chapter, we'll implement an obstacle type that we'll call Wanderer. They'll look like the Patrollers we implemented in the last chapter, but instead of moving along a set of points repeatedly, they'll be confined to a rectangular region, and they'll periodically wander over to a new point inside that region. We can put multiple Wanderers in the same region, and they'll all act separately, finding a new place to move to every so often. We'll use a little bit of random number generation to make them wait some amount of time between a minimum and maximum number of seconds before moving again, which we can configure in the Inspector.

To avoid sudden movement that kills the player in frustrating ways, we'll make the wanderers turn to point in the direction they're going to travel next, wait a little, and then move. This gives the player a little time to react.

Wander Regions

The Wanderer script will be used to create obstacles that are confined to a box, randomly selecting a new point to run to within that box. When they select a new point, we call it **retargeting**. Every time they retarget, they turn to face that new point, wait a certain duration, and then begin moving toward it. Once they reach it, they just stand there and wait for their next retargeting.

As always, they'll use the Hazard script to kill the player on touch.

First of all, we need to define the boxes they're confined to.

We'll create a script to resemble one of these boxes, called a wander region. Go ahead and make a new script named **WanderRegion**, and while you're at it, make a **Wanderer** script, too. The Wanderer is the script that goes on the obstacle itself, the thing that moves and acts as a hazard.

Open up the WanderRegion first, and let's get started on it.

The WanderRegion does two things:

- Defines a rectangular space that Wanderers will attach themselves to, providing them with a method to get a random point within that space.

- Contains all Wanderer obstacles as its children. On Start, it finds all of these children and gives them a reference to itself (the region). The Wanderers will use this reference to get a new point whenever they need to retarget.

In order to visualize this region, as well as to know its size so we can find a point within it, we'll use a flat cube. We won't give it a collider – it will just be a colored cube, almost like a plate on the ground, that lets the player know the bounds of the wander region. This way, they know when they're in danger.

Let's set this up first:

- Create a new empty GameObject and name it **"Wander Region"**. Keep its Y position at 0 at all times.

- Add a Cube as a child of the Wander Region, and name it **"Region"**. Set its scale to (25, .2, 25), and as always, keep it nicely positioned on the floor by setting its local Y position to 0.1 (half of its scale).

- Set the local X and Z position of the Region to 0.

- In the Inspector, remove the Box Collider component from the Region. Do so by right-clicking its header (where it says Box Collider) and clicking "Remove Component".

- I'll create a material named "Wander Region", with a dark green color using the hex value 6C9179, and apply it to the Region cube.

Now we have a cube that's colored a bit differently than the floor. Since it doesn't have a collider, anything that passes over it will phase through it. It's just there to indicate the region, and we'll also be using its local scale to find random points within the region.

By the end, your Wander Region should look something like Figure 19-1. Nothing much to see, right?

Figure 19-1. *Our Wander Region*

Let's get to the code – place this within the WanderRegion script class:

```
[Header("References")]
public Transform region;

public Vector3 GetRandomPointWithin()
{
    float x = transform.position.x + Random.Range(region.localScale.x * -.5f, region.
    localScale.x * .5f);
    float z = transform.position.z + Random.Range(region.localScale.z * -.5f, region.
    localScale.z * .5f);
    return new Vector3(x, 0, z);
}

void Awake()
{
```

```
    //Get all the Wanderer scripts in our children:
    var wanderers = gameObject.GetComponentsInChildren<Wanderer>();

    //Loop through the Wanderers:
    for (int i = 0; i < wanderers.Length; i++)
    {
        //Set their .region reference to 'this' script instance:
        wanderers[i].region = this;
    }
}
```

We start with the familiar "References" header, and only one measly little variable: a reference to the Transform of our Region cube.

Then, we declare our **GetRandomPointWithin** method. This will be called by the Wanderers. It uses random number generation to grab a point somewhere within the box.

The method we use to generate a random number is called **"Random.Range"**.

It's pretty simple: give it a minimum value and a maximum value. It returns some random value between the two.

We reference the Transform of our Region cube and use the **".localScale"** member, which will return what we see in the Inspector when viewing our Region's scale. This is the size of the area inside which we wish to contain our Wanderers. Since the Region is centered on the Wanderer, we use a random value between negative half the scale and positive half the scale, and we increment our own position by that. This gives us a point anywhere within the Region cube.

We only care about the X and Z axes because the Wanderers should remain at a Y position of 0 throughout the game (just like almost everything else). That's why, when we return the point, we make a new Vector3 and pass the X and Z values, but give a value of 0 for the Y.

One note on this: it doesn't support rotating our Regions. If you rotate the Region, the Wanderer will still go to random points in a rectangle centered around the Wanderer Region. There are ways around this, but to avoid complicating things too much, we won't get into them. Just remember to keep your Regions at (0, 0, 0) rotation; otherwise, your Wanderers are going to be walking outside the box sometimes.

Moving on to the Awake event, we've just learned about arrays and the **GetComponentsInChildren** method in the last chapter, so the Start method we've written is pretty familiar. As you'll recall, the "this" keyword can be used to refer to the object instance that the code is running from – in this case, the WanderRegion instance. So all we're really doing is finding all of the Wanderers that are children of the Region by referencing their Wanderer script, looping through those script instances, and giving each one a reference to this WanderRegion.

We haven't actually declared that ".region" variable in our Wanderer script yet, so we'll get a compiler error regarding this. That's okay. We'll declare it in a little bit.

We're doing this in "void Awake()" because, as we learned before, Awake occurs before Start. This way, we can expect that our Wanderers will already have their ".region" set when their own Start method is called. This is because we're going to be telling our Wanderers to set a new target right in their Start method, as you'll see in the following texts.

Now that we've got our WanderRegion script set up, this would be a good time to put it on the Wander Region GameObject, set its reference to the Region, then create a prefab for it, so we can always drop a fresh Wander Region into our scene whenever we like.

Wanderer Setup

Before we write the script for it, let's set up the Wanderer GameObject.

The Wanderer will have a very similar hierarchy to the Patroller. We'll use the same model, too. Follow these steps to set up your Wanderer:

- Create an empty GameObject named **"Wanderer"**.

- Attach a Hazard script and a kinematic Rigidbody.

- Copy-paste the Model Base and its child, Model Top, from the Patroller we made in the last chapter. Make the Model Base a child of the Wanderer and set its local position to (0, 1.5, 0). Leave the scale as it is. If you deleted your Patroller, just drop an instance of the prefab down in your scene and copy the Model Base from it.

- The Model Base should have **Is Trigger** checked on its Box Collider component already, but if not, make sure to do that.

- Make sure the Wanderer and all of its children are in the **Hazard** layer.

The Wanderer needs to be a child of the Wander Region it belongs to as well, so don't forget to drop it in there.

Wanderer Script

We've put it off long enough – it's time to tackle the script resembling a wandering obstacle.

Let's detail how they'll behave as far as the programming is concerned.

At any given moment, a Wanderer will either be Idle, Rotating, or Moving:

- While **Idle**, they just stand there and wait.

- While **Rotating**, they're not moving, but are turning toward the next position they've targeted. After they finish turning, they wait a certain extra amount of time to give the player time to react to the final rotation. Then, they begin Moving.

- While **Moving**, they travel toward the point (which they will now be directly facing) until they reach it, where they stop and become Idle again.

We've worked with enums before, like **KeyCode** for input detection, **"Space.Local"** in our Translate method for our Projectile script, and **HideFlags** to hide our patrol points in the last chapter. Now, we're going to declare our own and use it to handle our state, giving it those three states we listed earlier.

This is a common practice to handle objects that need to toggle in and out of different "modes" that designate different behavior. In our Update method, we'll use the current value of "state" to determine what the Wanderer should be doing at any given moment.

Let's get started and declare our variables in the **Wanderer** script class**:**

```
private enum State
{
    Idle,
    Rotating,
    Moving
}

private State state = State.Idle;
```

```
[HideInInspector] public WanderRegion region;

[Header("References")]
public Transform trans;
public Transform modelTrans;

[Header("Stats")]
public float movespeed = 18;

[Tooltip("Minimum wait time before retargeting again.")]
public float minRetargetInterval = 4.4f;

[Tooltip("Maximum wait time before retargeting again.")]
public float maxRetargetInterval = 6.2f;

[Tooltip("Time in seconds taken to rotate after targeting, before moving begins.")]
public float rotationTime = .6f;

[Tooltip("Time in seconds after rotation finishes before movement starts.")]
public float postRotationWaitTime = .3f;

private Vector3 currentTarget; //Position we're currently targeting
private Quaternion initialRotation; //Our rotation when we first retargeted
private Quaternion targetRotation; //The rotation we're aiming to reach
private float rotationStartTime; //Time.time at which we started rotating
```

As you can see, we declare our enum with the **"enum"** keyword, the name, and then a code block containing a simple, comma-separated list of each entry in the enum. The last entry doesn't need a comma at the end.

Because **State** is a private enum declared inside the script class, we can only access it from this script class. Thus, there's no need to name it "WandererState" or anything more specific – we know this class is the only one that will be using it.

After the enum, and a variable to store an instance of the enum, we declare that **"region"** variable that our WanderRegion is already trying to reference. This means, at last, we can be rid of the compiler error telling us the variable doesn't exist.

We need this variable to be public so that the WanderRegion can set it for us, but we also don't want it to be set through the Inspector – the whole point of detecting them in the WanderRegion script is to avoid the need for this. Thus, we use the **HideInInspector** attribute that we briefly learned about in Chapter 10. This does just what it says: it makes it so we can have public variables that aren't serialized (you'll recall that a *serialized* variable is shown and made editable in the Inspector). This way, we can ensure that we never see that field in the Inspector and set it ourselves, forgetting that our WanderRegion will set it for us.

At this point, "trans", "modelTrans", and "movespeed" ought to be pretty self-explanatory.

The retarget interval is defined as a float for the minimum and another for the maximum. We'll use **"Random.Range"** to get a time between the two and **Invoke** a retargeting to happen in that amount of time.

The rotation time will be used to measure just the period of rotating toward the target point.

The **"postRotationWaitTime"** is the time it takes to start moving after the rotation finishes. So once a retargeting begins, it takes the sum of both these values before the obstacle actually moves.

The private variables are pretty much explained in their comments, and we'll go into further detail once we get to using them. Each one of these variables is set again whenever a retargeting occurs; they're all storing data that we'll need to properly perform a retargeting.

Handling the State

The rest is going to be a bit of fun. We're going to use method invoking and the changing of our states to create a sort of recurring loop between idle, rotating, and moving.

First, let's declare some methods **in the Wanderer script**, just beneath our variables:

```
void Retarget()
{
    //Set our current target to a new random point in the region:
    currentTarget = region.GetRandomPointWithin();

    //Mark our initial rotation:
    initialRotation = modelTrans.rotation;

    //Mark the rotation required to look at the target:
    targetRotation = Quaternion.LookRotation((currentTarget - trans.position).normalized);

    //Start rotating:
    state = State.Rotating;
    rotationStartTime = Time.time;

    //Begin moving again 'postRotationWaitTime' seconds after rotation ends:
    Invoke("BeginMoving", rotationTime + postRotationWaitTime);
}

void BeginMoving()
{
    //Make double sure that we're facing the targetRotation:
    modelTrans.rotation = targetRotation;

    //Set state to Moving:
    state = State.Moving;
}
```

Here, we declare a **Retarget** method to handle the assigning of a new target. Inside, we call that method we declared in the WanderRegion script to get a new random point, assigning it to our private variable **"currentTarget"**. We save our current rotation and use the same **"(to – from).normalized"** formula that we saw in the last chapter to get the direction from the current position to the target position, plugging that into the handy "Quaternion.LookRotation" method to convert it from a Vector3 direction to a Quaternion rotation. That will be our target rotation, which we'll reach over the course of the **"rotationTime"**.

To initiate rotation, we mark the time that it began, and we set our state to Rotating. Now that our state is Rotating, we won't be moving anymore; we'll be standing still, turning toward the next point (which we'll implement next).

After, we invoke the method we declared just below this one, called **BeginMoving**. It will occur once the "rotationTime" and the "postRotationWaitTime" have both elapsed.

The BeginMoving method is just a few lines of code: set the state to Moving and ensure we're pointing exactly at the target rotation, just to be safe in choppy situations where there's a lot of time between frames.

With that in place, we just need to make sure that we initiate the process **in our Start() method**. We just need to call Retarget():

```
void Start()
{
    //On start, call Retarget() immediately.
    Retarget();
}
```

Reacting to the State

Now we just need the frame-by-frame logic that moves or rotates the Wanderer based on the current value of "state". For that, we'll need an Update method:

```
void Update()
{
    if (state == State.Moving)
    {
        //Move towards the target by the delta:
        trans.position = Vector3.MoveTowards(trans.position, currentTarget, movespeed *
        Time.deltaTime);

        //Become idle and invoke the next Retarget once we hit the point:
        if (trans.position == currentTarget)
        {
            state = State.Idle;
            Invoke("Retarget",Random.Range(minRetargetInterval, maxRetargetInterval));
        }
    }
    else if (state == State.Rotating)
    {
        //Measure the time we've spent rotating so far, in seconds:
        float timeSpentRotating = Time.time - rotationStartTime;

        //Rotate from initialRotation towards targetRotation:
        modelTrans.rotation = Quaternion.Slerp(initialRotation, targetRotation,
        timeSpentRotating / rotationTime);
    }
}
```

With you being an expert programmer now, the movement is old news. We did the same thing with patrollers in the previous chapter: use **"Vector3.MoveTowards"** to move the root Transform (first parameter) toward the target point (second parameter) by "movespeed" per second (third parameter).

After, we make sure to stop moving once we reach the point by becoming Idle – again, MoveTowards won't overshoot the point, but we might as well save ourselves some unnecessary calculation and stop calling it when we know we're already there. Also, we use this moment to invoke the Retarget method again. We use "Random.Range" to get a random time within the retarget interval.

The rotation of the model is where things get a bit different – notably, we're using Slerp in a different way than we have before.

As you'll recall, Slerp takes one rotation and moves it toward another by a fraction of the difference between the two and returns the result.

Some examples are as follows:

- If that fraction is 0, there's no change, so we simply get the first rotation returned back as is.

- If the fraction is 0.5, a rotation halfway between the two is returned.

- Make it 1, and the rotation is moved all the way to the target, so we simply get the target rotation (second parameter) returned back as is.

Up until now, we've only used this by passing in the **current** rotation of some Transform as the first rotation and Slerping it toward a target rotation to get a smoother rotation than just using a flat value of rotation per second, or snapping the rotation without any transition.

But that's not the only way to do it. We're making a game here, and we want to implement this mechanic in a way that makes it more fun. We're making the wanderers rotate toward their target to ensure that the player sees them do it so they can react to the rotation and get out of the way. So we want it to take a certain amount of time for the rotation to finish, consistently. The method we've used up until now doesn't really do that.

To counter this, we'll use the same two rotations every time we call the Slerp method and keep applying the result to the Transform. Before, we Slerped the current rotation toward the target rotation. In every frame, the current rotation got closer to the target rotation, so that over time, the amount that we actually rotated became smaller and smaller. Now, we've instead marked the initial rotation of the wanderers when they began the turn, and we're going to Slerp that initial rotation toward the target rotation.

The tricky part is figuring out what fraction we pass in as the third parameter. We've already set up the variables required to do this earlier. We know how long we want it to take to make the turn ("rotationTime") and the time at which the turn began ("rotationStartTime").

So we want the fraction we give to the Slerp to start at 0 when we first begin turning and then raise to 1 over the turn duration. In other words, start at the initial rotation, and change to the target rotation over the duration.

We do this by grabbing the "time spent rotating so far." This is just "current time - begin time." For example, if we began at 16.2 and the current time is 16.6, that's 16.6 - 16.2 = 0.4 seconds spent rotating so far.

Then, we just need to turn that into a fraction (a value between 0 and 1) of the total time we want it to take.

Whenever you have to ask "What fraction of the value Y is the value X?", you just do "X / Y". In a more understandable example, let's say we're coding an RPG and we want to know what percentage of their maximum health our player character is at.

To get this, you'd just do "currentHealth / maxHealth". This is a fraction, so a value between 0 and 1, but you can easily turn it to a percentage by multiplying it by 100 and then tacking a % sign on the end.

We're doing much the same thing here. We're dividing the "rotation time so far" by the "total rotation time desired," thus converting it to a value that starts at 0 and raises to 1 over the rotationTime.

And that covers it all – we should have operational Wanderers now. All we have to do is set up the script.

Attach the **Wanderer** script to the root Wanderer GameObject, set its "trans" like we always do, and set the "modelTrans" to that of the Model Base.

Ensure that the Wanderer is a child of a Wander Region with a big enough box to play around in, hit Play, and watch it go.

As always, don't forget to **make a prefab of your Wanderer** so you can place more in the future.

Summary

This chapter put another new obstacle into motion. We learned some basic random number generation, as well as a new way to utilize the "Quaternion.Slerp" method. We also got to make our own enum.

- The **"Random.Range"** method takes two int or float parameters and returns a random value between the two. **If you're passing two int values as parameters**, note that the second parameter, the maximum value, is *exclusive* – it will never be returned. Just add 1 to it if this isn't what you want.

- When you need to determine the time that has passed since a certain event occurred, you can set a float variable to "Time.time" when the event first occurs. Afterward, use "Time.time - floatVariable" to get the time, in seconds, since the event occurred.

- To calculate what fraction the float "X" is of the float "Y", just divide "X / Y". This will return 0.5 if X is half of Y, or 0.75 if it is 75% of Y, and so on.

CHAPTER 20

Dashing

To give the player a bit more interesting movement, we're going to implement an option for them to quickly "dash" in the direction they're moving – or, more specifically, in the direction they have held down with the movement keys. If they're holding W and D, they'll dash diagonally forward and right, for example.

When dashing, the player will stop moving by normal means, giving control to the dash movement instead. Once they finish dashing, we'll revert control back to the normal movement, and we'll set the movement velocity to full power in the direction they were dashing. This way, they'll continue moving in the dash direction after it finishes, instead of coming to an instant stop. If they're not holding any movement keys anymore, the momentum will fade away smoothly as it always does.

Dashing Variables

Let's set up our variables to begin implementing the dash. Write these variables **beneath your existing variables in the Player script**:

```
//Dashing
[Header("Dashing")]
[Tooltip("Total number of units traveled when performing a dash.")]
public float dashDistance = 17;
[Tooltip("Time taken to perform a dash, in seconds.")]
public float dashTime = .15f;

[Tooltip("Time after dashing finishes before it can be performed again.")]
public float dashCooldown = 1.8f;

private bool CanDashNow
{
    get
    {
        return Time.time > dashBeginTime + dashTime + dashCooldown;
    }
}

private bool IsDashing
{
    get
    {
        return Time.time < dashBeginTime + dashTime;
    }
}
```

```
private Vector3 dashDirection;
private float dashBeginTime = Mathf.NegativeInfinity;
```

As you can see, the only variables we actually need to expose in the Inspector are the dash distance, dash time, and dash cooldown. The dash will travel in the movement direction by **"dashDistance"** units over **"dashTime"** seconds. After we finish, we can't dash again for **"dashCooldown"** seconds.

Beneath our public variables, we have a few useful properties to break down the math into plain language:

- **CanDashNow** is how we determine if our dash is on cooldown. Whenever we dash, we set the private **"dashBeginTime"** float to the current **"Time.time"**. In order to check if we're able to dash now, we just check if the current **"Time.time"** is higher than the time we began dashing, plus the dash cooldown time, and we throw in the dash time itself as well, so the cooldown doesn't start until the dash is finished.

- **IsDashing** returns true if we're currently dashing and false if not. This is done by checking if the current "Time.time" is less than the "Time.time" when the dash began, plus the dash time itself. Once the "Time.time" goes past that, we stop dashing automatically, because this property stops returning true. This means all we have to do to start dashing is just set the dash begin time. This is a nice, elegant way to handle it, as opposed to declaring a bool variable that we have to set to true or false as our dash begins and ends.

Then we have the **"dashDirection"** – the direction we're currently dashing in, which we set again whenever a dash begins – and the aforementioned **"dashBeginTime"** which is set to **"Mathf. NegativeInfinity"** by default. This is a built-in shortcut to get the very lowest number we could possibly get.

This is just a safety measure: if we merely set the "dashBeginTime" to 0 at the start of the game, then we would technically be performing a dash as soon as the game begins. By setting the begin time to a very low value, we ensure that even if we (for some reason) have an extremely long-lasting dash, we won't be dashing right when the game starts.

In reality, we could probably get away with something like -5 (negative five), because when would we ever have a dash that lasts five seconds or longer? But hey, better safe than sorry, and now you know this static variable exists in the Mathf class. It also has a positive counterpart, **"Mathf.Infinity"**, if you ever need an infinitely high number.

As for the dash direction, this will be set to 0, 1, or -1 on its X and Z axes. When we move, we'll multiply the movement per second by this direction. For example, if we held only the D or right arrow key, the "dashDirection" would be (1, 0, 0). Multiplying that by a float value is just a simple way to apply the movement only to the appropriate axis: the other two axes are 0 and, thus, no movement occurs.

If we held D and W, we'd get (1, 0, 1) instead, applying movement also to the Z axis, and so on for all the different directions one can move with the WASD/arrow keys.

Dashing Method

The Dashing method will be much like our Movement method. It will handle all of the dashing-related logic, keeping it tucked away in a separate private method that gets called in our Update method. We'll declare it just below the Movement method we made before.

The logic will be fairly simple:

- If we are not dashing, we'll check if the space key is pressed. If so...

- Figure out the dash direction by checking which movement keys are held. If no movement key is being held, we don't perform the dash at all. If at least one key is held, we perform the dash.

- If we are dashing, we'll simply move along the dash direction using the CharacterController, just like when we move normally. Since the "IsDashing" property will automatically start returning false as soon as the dash time is up, we don't have to worry about bringing the dash to an end.

Let's get to the code. Remember, this is going to be called in our Update method. Place this Dashing method **just beneath the Movement method in the Player script**:

```
private void Dashing()
{
    //If we aren't dashing right now:
    if (!IsDashing)
    {
        //If dash is not on cooldown, and the space key is pressed:
        if (CanDashNow && Input.GetKey(KeyCode.Space))
        {
            //Find the direction we're holding with the movement keys:
            Vector3 movementDir = Vector3.zero;

            //If holding W or up arrow, set z to 1:
            if (Input.GetKey(KeyCode.W) || Input.GetKey(KeyCode.UpArrow))
                movementDir.z = 1;

            //Else if holding S or down arrow, set z to -1:
            else if (Input.GetKey(KeyCode.S) || Input.GetKey(KeyCode.DownArrow))
                movementDir.z = -1;

            //If holding D or right arrow, set x to 1:
            if (Input.GetKey(KeyCode.D) || Input.GetKey(KeyCode.RightArrow))
                movementDir.x = 1;

            //Else if holding A or left arrow, set x to -1:
            else if (Input.GetKey(KeyCode.A) || Input.GetKey(KeyCode.LeftArrow))
                movementDir.x = -1;

            //If at least one movement key was held:
            if (movementDir.x != 0 || movementDir.z != 0)
            {
                //Start dashing:
                dashDirection = movementDir;
                dashBeginTime = Time.time;
                movementVelocity = dashDirection * movespeed;
                modelTrans.forward = dashDirection;
            }
        }
    }
    else //If we are dashing
    {
        characterController.Move(dashDirection.normalized * (dashDistance / dashTime) *
        Time.deltaTime);
    }
}
```

Most of this is probably pretty self-explanatory, since you're an expert now and you've dealt with much of it already. Let's go over it and I'll point out the oddities that you might be confused by.

We declare a Vector3 and set its X and Z values based on the movement keys currently held down. We then only proceed to perform the dash if at least one movement key was held. This is all occurring in our "ifs" that ensure the player can dash now (and just pressed Space to attempt a dash).

We then initiate the dash by setting the direction (the same as the movement direction we just pieced together) and marking the time that the dash began. Now that the begin time is set, "IsDashing" will start returning true, up until the point the dash ends because "Time.time" is higher than the begin time plus the dash time.

Next, we set the movement velocity. This is not what makes us move, it's just to ensure that once our dash ends, we don't immediately come to a stop. We keep moving in the direction we dashed and can continue if we hold our movement keys, or if we aren't holding any movement keys, we'll come to a stop gradually like we normally do when moving. This keeps things smooth.

The next line "modelTrans.forward = dashDirection;" is a new concept. The **".forward"** property is a Transform member that allows us to get or set the forward-facing direction of the Transform. When setting, we pass it a Vector3 direction and it instantly turns the Transform so that its front side (its positive Z axis) faces that direction.

Similar variants exist for **".right"** and **".up"** to set the right-side facing and the top-side facing of a Transform. Conversely, if you wanted to point the bottom, back, or left side along a specific direction, you'd simply set the ".up", ".forward", or ".right", but flip the direction you're applying to the value by multiplying it by -1. That is to say, if you wanted to point the left side along a direction, all you have to do is point the right side at the opposite direction, right? That's why there are only members for forward, right, and up.

We also have our "else" that moves our CharacterController, much like with our normal movement. In order to achieve the desired distance, we need to move by the "dashDistance" divided over the "dashTime" and, as always, multiply by "Time.deltaTime" to ensure that it happens per second.

What may be confusing here is the usage of that **".normalized"** member. We've seen it before, like when getting a direction from one point to another point. Simply put (don't worry, we'll put it less simply in later chapters), normalizing a vector is "turning it into a direction." It's ensuring that, when you multiply a Vector3 (that you intend to use as a direction) by some float value (like "movespeed * Time.deltaTime", for example), you're getting 1 unit of distance per 1 point you multiply it by, and no more.

For example, if you dash directly in one direction, like right, you'll have a **Vector3(1,0,0)** as your direction. If you dash diagonally right and up, you'll instead have **Vector3(1,0,1)**. When you multiply the vector by the movement, you're moving in both directions at once, which actually gives you more distance than you would get if you just went in one direction.

Normalizing the vector simply ensures that you get the same distance from a diagonal dash as you would from a dash that only moves along a single axis (straight up, down, left, or right).

Again, we'll be getting into the nitty-gritty details of working with vectors in our final example project, where the specifics are directly applicable, so don't fret too much if you have more questions about this.

Final Touches

We need only make a few more changes to fully implement dashing.

First, we need to go to our **"private void Movement()"** method and wrap all of that movement code in an "if (!IsDashing)" block:

```
//Only move if we aren't dashing:
if (!IsDashing)
{
    //...the rest of the movement code goes here
}
```

This prevents any of the movement logic from occurring while a dash performs.

We also need to add the Dashing method call in Update, so that the Update method looks like this:

```
void Update()
{
    Movement();

    Dashing();
}
```

You'd be surprised how easy it is to forget this step, test the code, and wonder why nothing is happening!

One final bit of robustness we'll add is to ensure that dashing always ends as soon as we die. That way, if we've set up our game to have a very low respawn wait time and a long-lasting dash, the dash won't continue after we respawn.

Add this line anywhere within the **"if (!dead)"** block of your **"public void Die()"** method:

```
dashBeginTime = Mathf.NegativeInfinity;
```

Again, we set it to "Mathf.NegativeInfinity" instead of 0 just to be extra safe.

That should do us. You can now test your dashing in-game: just hold any movement keys down (at least one key is necessary) and press Space.

If you want, you can play with the dash distance and time in the Inspector until you like the way they feel. Remember our code that moves the CharacterController while dashing? The actual amount moved per second while dashing was "dashDistance / dashTime". So if you're playing with the time and distance and want to compare the dash speed to your movespeed to ensure your dashes are sufficiently quicker than normal movement, just use that calculation.

Summary

This chapter gave our player an extra tool to use in avoiding obstacles – a quick dash. Our player's movement for this project is now at its final stage, with no more features to add.

We also learned how the Transform facing direction properties ".up", ".right", and ".forward" can be used to turn a certain side of the Transform toward a direction.

CHAPTER 21

Designing Levels

In some of the first chapters, we talked about mixing the functionality of components and scripts to form different kinds of obstacles. Well, now we finally have a game that can put some of those concepts to use. Let's see how we can use our existing scripts to make some unique types of hazards, and while we're at it, let's consider how to use prefabs to give our game a consistent design for our players.

We'll also learn how to make new levels and prepare them for the next chapter, where we make a level selection menu to allow the player to choose which level they'd like to play from the main scene.

We'll make a separate scene for each level and position a camera in each one that views the level from above as a sort of "sneak peek" when choosing levels. In the next chapter, we'll make the menus and handle the activation of the Player and the removal of this "sneak peek" camera so we don't have two cameras in our scene.

Mixing Components

We have a Hazard component to make something kill the player on touch, a Shooting script to periodically fire projectiles, and the Wanderer and WanderRegion scripts.

Let's consider a few types of hazards we could build off of what we already have. This can give us some "compound hazards" that add more fun options for us when we're designing levels.

Four-Way Shooters

Right now, our Shooters only fire in a single direction. Let's make a new type that fires in four directions at once: one barrel at each side of the base cube.

- Drop an instance of the Shooter prefab into your Hierarchy. Rename it to **"Four-way Shooter"**. We're going to reuse the Shooter to make it easier to build our Four-way Shooter.

- Right-click the Four-way Shooter in the Hierarchy, select **Prefab**, and then select **Unpack**. This disassociates the instance of the Shooter with the prefab, making it and its children just a normal GameObject in the scene. Now we can construct our Four-way Shooter using the basic Shooter, without any attachment to the existing Shooter prefab.

- Remove the Shooting script component from the Four-way Shooter.

- Add a Shooting script to the Barrel child instead. Set its Spawn Point to the Barrel's child Spawn Point Transform, and don't forget to set the Projectile Prefab reference, too – drag the Projectile prefab from the Project window onto the field.

- Now we have a separate Shooting script for the barrel itself. Copy and paste the Barrel, and set the new Barrel's local Z position from 0.7 to -0.7, placing it at the opposite side of the Shooter from the first barrel.

- Notice the Spawn Point that is referenced by this new Barrel's Shooting script is pointing to its own child Spawn Point, not the old one. Unity has automatically set it up for us. However, to make sure its Spawn Point forward axis is pointing along the correct direction, we'll have to flip this new Barrel around by setting its **Y rotation** to **180**.

- Create a new empty GameObject, make it a child of the Four-way Shooter, and set its local position and rotation to (0, 0, 0). Leave the scale alone.

- Copy and paste both Barrel instances, make them children of the new GameObject we just made, and then set that new GameObject's local Y rotation to 90. This will spin it so the third and fourth Barrel copies will be at the unoccupied sides of the cube.

- Now you can make the third and fourth Barrels be children of the Base again, then delete that empty GameObject. We were just using it for convenient rotation.

- Don't forget to **make a prefab** for the Four-way Shooter!

This leaves us with a Shooter with a barrel at each of its sides, all of which have their own Shooting script that all fire at the same times (shown in Figure 21-1). Just remember, if you want to adjust the rate of fire, select all four Barrels at once before setting it; otherwise, they'll get out of sync!

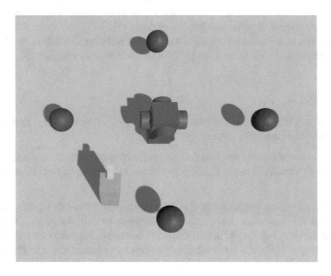

Figure 21-1. *Our Four-way Shooter fires projectiles while our player stands nearby*

Spinning Blades

When we were first learning the fundamentals of coding, we made a simple script that rotated its Transform constantly. Let's make that script again and use it to provide constant rotation to a new type of hazard, a hovering "blade" that constantly spins, acting as a hazard.

Now that you've come this far, this script is easy. Let's name it **ConstantRotation** this time:

```
public class ConstantRotation : MonoBehaviour
{
    public Transform trans;
    public Vector3 rotationPerSecond;

    void Update()
    {
        trans.Rotate(rotationPerSecond * Time.deltaTime);
    }
}
```

It simply applies a rotation per second to the referenced Transform, which should be set to the Transform that the script is attached to.

Now let's make a spinning blade:

- Create an empty GameObject named **"Spinning Blade"**.

- Add a child Cube, set its scale to (4, .5, .5), and set its local position to (0, 2.5, 0) so it hovers above the ground when the root is positioned directly on the ground (as it will be when we place a prefab instance).

- Check the **Is Trigger** checkbox of the Cube's Box Collider.

- Copy and paste the Cube and set its local Y rotation to 90, giving us two cubes making a plus shape.

- Give the Spinning Blade a **kinematic** Rigidbody, a **Hazard** script, and a **ConstantRotation** script with its "trans" set to the Spinning Blade's Transform. Set the rotation per second of the ConstantRotation script to give it some Y rotation, which will cause the blades to twirl. I'm giving mine 460 so it rotates a little more than a full circle per second.

- Set the Spinning Blade layer to **Hazard**.

- I'll give the cubes of my Spinning Blade the same MobileHazard material we applied to the Patrollers and Wanderers.

- Make a prefab for the Spinning Blade.

Now we have a more deadly looking, plus-shaped hazard that spins and kills on touch. Yes, I know the "blades" look rather blunt to be called blades, but using your imagination is key here.

Blade Carousels

Let's make more interesting use of our spinning blades: a simple hazard that contains these spinning blades as children positioned at consistent points and then itself rotates constantly to cause those blades to "orbit" around it like a deadly carousel. With just one more usage of our ConstantRotation script, we can make a whole new obstacle.

I'm going to make this central spinning object be a tall cylinder. We can think of it like a magic totem that's spinning the blades around it.

This will be no trouble at all.

- Make an empty GameObject named **"Carousel"**. Set its Y position to 0 and give it a **ConstantRotation** script component with a rotation per second of (0, 150, 0). Don't forget to set the reference to the Carousel Transform.

- Add a Cylinder child with a scale of (2, 3, 2) and a local position of (0, 3, 0). We use an equal Y position and scale because, if you'll recall, cylinders (unlike cubes) are twice as tall as their Y scale.

- I'm going to make a new material named Carousel with a pale purple color using a hex value of C16BE0, which I'll apply to this cylinder.

- Add four instances of the Spinning Blade prefab as children of the Carousel, and set their local positions to (-10, 0, 0), (10, 0, 0), (0, 0, 10), and (0, 0, -10), arranging them all at equal distances around the Carousel, as shown in Figure 21-2.

- As always, don't forget to make a prefab out of your Carousel.

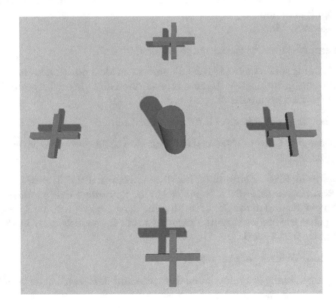

Figure 21-2. *A Carousel with its Spinning Blade instances at its top, right, bottom, and left sides*

This gives us four spinning blades that spin in a circle around the Carousel. The cylinder at the center won't kill the player on touch, but will block their movement. Of course, you can tweak the rotation speed, if you'd like.

Note that this is an instance of *nested prefabs*, which we learned about when we first learned of prefabs. The Spinning Blade has its own prefab, and instances of that prefab are nested in the Carousel prefab. This means if you edit the Spinning Blade prefab, such as to make it spin faster or slower, it will change all instances of the Spinning Blade, whether they are alone in the scene (e.g., as stationary hazards) or part of a Carousel.

Prefabs and Variants

Now that we have all these types of hazards to design levels with, you ought to consider how you'll go about making little tweaks in the balance as you go along. We discussed the purpose of prefabs and their variants early on. This is one of those moments where you'll want to give them some thought – it might save you some heartache down the road.

We can always perform overrides on prefab instances to make, for example, very fast patrollers, shooters that fire more or less often, or fire projectiles that move faster or slower or are bigger or smaller.

However, if at any point you need to make a change, you'll end up with scattered overrides across various instances and scenes.

A smarter alternative might be to make prefab variants for the slightly different versions of your obstacles. If you stick to this, you can have consistent variations across your levels that the player will recognize. Make a fast and slow variant for the projectile prefab. Make a slow, large patroller variant. Make a quick, tiny wanderer variant.

This not only regulates your game design to make it easier for the player to predict and adapt to situations, but it gives you a clean setup that can be changed across all your levels just by tweaking the prefabs and/or their variants. If you overrode 50 different shooter instances across 15 different levels, you couldn't change them all at once if you ever decided to make the player move a little faster or slower and found that your shooters now needed to be tweaked in comparison.

Part of the fun of making games is playing with the numbers and tweaking things until they're just right, so I'm not going to tell you how to design the game yourself. I will, however, teach you how to create a simple variant of a Shooter that fires faster than the normal prefab.

A prefab variant is created by right-clicking a prefab asset in the Project window, unfolding the "Create" menu, and then selecting "Prefab Variant," as shown in Figure 21-3.

Figure 21-3. *The right-click context menu leading us to create a prefab variant for our Shooter prefab*

This will create a new asset acting as a variant to the Shooter prefab, and you can type whatever name you want for it. Let's name it "Shooter (Fast)". If you're going to have variants for many of your obstacle prefabs, you may want to consider ways to ensure that your assets remain tidy. For example, by naming it "Shooter (Fast)" instead of "Fast Shooter", we ensure that the variant remains next to the original Shooter in the Project view – since the names are sorted alphabetically, we want a name that's similar enough to the base prefab to keep both assets sorted together. If you'd rather, you could also put all prefabs and variants for each type of obstacle in a dedicated folder, such as "Shooters" or "Patrollers".

The variant works like a prefab, so you can open it by double-clicking it in the Project view if you need to make edits to child GameObjects. We just need to change how frequently our shooter fires, so we can just select the "Shooter (Fast)" in the Project and use the Inspector to change its Fire Rate to a lower value, like 0.5.

After that, you can drag and drop the "Shooter (Fast)" into the Scene and test it out. If you want visual indication of which shooters are faster, you can use a separate material for them. Remember to open up the variant asset and apply the material to it there, rather than applying it only to the instance you've placed in the scene.

You don't have to stop there if you don't want to. Here are some ideas on further ways to use variants:

- Projectiles that move faster or slower and are larger or smaller. You can then create Shooter variants that use different types of projectiles, so not only does the Shooter rate of fire change, but also the speed and size of the Projectile they fire.

- Wanderers that are smaller, but retarget more frequently, move quicker and don't take as long to start moving after retargeting.

- Larger or smaller Patrollers with varying movespeed.

- Shooters that spin in circles with a ConstantRotation script. The same could be done with Four-way Shooters.

Making Levels

I'm not going to try to guide you through the creation of a full level and all of its obstacles, because that would be a lot of tedious work for you, and it probably wouldn't be very fun for you to spend time re-creating my idea of a level anyway. You have the tools to make your own levels now, so I'll leave you to it. Instead, I'll give you some tips on how to start, and we'll start thinking about what needs to go in each level to make the whole process come together.

Let's go over the specifics of how to make a new scene and prepare it to act as a level. Make a new scene with Ctrl+N (Cmd+N for Mac users), or navigate to File in the top-left corner of Unity and select New Scene. In the window that pops up, the "Basic (Built-in)" scene template will be chosen. Just press Enter or click the "Create" button in the bottom right of the window. This will give us a new scene with a basic Directional Light and a Main Camera.

Once you've made the new scene, use the Hierarchy to select and delete the Main Camera that comes with it by default.

First, a level should always have

- A Plane positioned at the world origin (0, 0, 0) and scaled on the X and Z axes so it's large enough to cover the whole screen at all times. Just go crazy and give it 1000 scale on both axes if you want. And don't forget to apply your **Floor** material to it. If you want, you could also make a prefab out of your Floor to take a few steps out of this process.

- A **Goal** prefab instance somewhere the player can reach it. What's a level you can't win, after all? If you never made a prefab out of your Goal, you can go back to your "main" scene and make one real quick. If you've deleted your Goal and never made a prefab, you'll have to re-create it (look over Chapter 17 again).

- A **Directional Light** to make sure there's a global source of light for the scene. We've just been using the default light that comes with a new scene, but you can change the settings of the Light component in the Inspector for the Directional Light if you want to play around with it. The most notable settings would be the color of the light (a pale yellow by default, to somewhat mimic the sun) and the intensity value, which determines how brightly the light shines.

- A **Player** prefab instance at the location you want the player to spawn. You can start it out at position (0, 0, 0) and move it if you ever find a need to.

If you notice strange lighting in your new scene compared to your old scene, use the top toolbar to navigate to Window ➤ Rendering ➤ Lighting, then click "Generate Lighting" at the bottom-right corner of the window that pops up, shown in Figure 21-4.

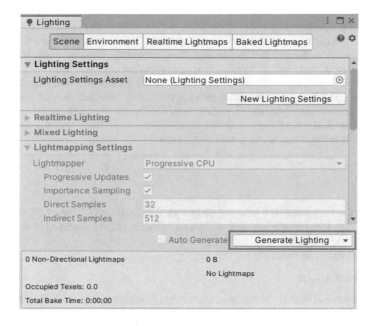

Figure 21-4. *The Lighting window with the Generate Lighting button outlined in red*

Adding Walls

With that sorted, you can place an instance of your Wall prefab down to begin blocking out the level so the player can't just go wherever they want. Once you place it, move it up so its bottom is aligned with the floor correctly. As always, do this by setting its Y position to half of its Y scale.

So you don't have to fix the Y position every time you want a new wall, just copy-paste that wall from here on out. If you want to keep your walls out of the way in the Hierarchy, consider making them all children of an empty GameObject named "Walls", which is positioned at (0, 0, 0) and simply acts as a parent so you can fold up the children in the Hierarchy to hide them. You could use a similar method with all of your obstacles, if you'd like to keep them tucked away as well.

As we mentioned before, the rect transform tool (hotkey T) can be quite useful for moving and sizing your walls. The tool will work best in this situation when viewing the walls from above. Remember, you can use the gizmo in the top-right corner of the Scene view to quickly assume a top-down view on the level – just click the green cone.

As you add walls, you can fill the space you block out with obstacles. Use your imagination and come up with some trials for the player, and rejoice at the sight of all that we've learned starting to come together!

Level View Camera

Next, we're going to make a means of previewing the level before playing it. This will be done with a simple Camera GameObject. We'll set it up to view the level from whatever vantage point we agree with for our preview. In the following chapter, we'll make use of this camera when the player is viewing the level before deciding if they want to play it or not – this camera will be their vantage point of the obstacles in the level.

If you didn't earlier, delete the preexisting camera in the scene and make a new one. Rename it to "Level View Camera" (without the quotes). Make sure you get the name exactly right (capitalization, too), because we're going to be finding it by name with our code later, and remember how picky strings are!

To easily position the camera how you like, just move your Scene camera to view the level from a nice angle by holding right-click and using the WASD keys. Then, select the Camera in the Hierarchy and, using the top menu, select GameObject ➤ Align With View, or use the hotkey Ctrl+Shift+F (Cmd+Shift+F on Mac). This will place the Level View Camera right where your Scene view camera is currently positioned and point it in the same direction. This beats dragging and rotating the camera around with the transform tools.

Once you've got these basic necessities set up in your level scene, you can save the scene. If you'd like, you could save this scene as a level template, and then whenever you'd like to make a new level, you can skip the setup by just copy-pasting the scene in your Project view.

Summary

This chapter made some new hazards by mixing scripts we'd already written and gave some advice on how to keep consistent with our hazards by using prefabs and variants. We also learned how to make new levels that are properly set up.

Every level should have the following:

- A plane for the floor

- A camera named "Level View Camera" positioned where you want the level to be previewed from

- A Directional Light (the default one will do)

- A Player prefab instance where you want the player to start the level

- A Goal prefab instance wherever you like

In the next chapter, we'll set up the flow from one scene to another so we can preview levels and properly implement menus that let the player get to all of the different levels we make. If you're having fun designing levels, don't let all this talk about progress stop you, though – knock yourself out. You can always play any level you want through Unity simply by opening the scene and hitting the play button.

CHAPTER 22

Menus and UI

Unity has three systems to provide UI for your games, called IMGUI, uGUI, and UI Toolkit. These systems have their advantages and use cases, which we'll go over briefly in this chapter. We'll then properly implement the scene flow for our game, so that we can have multiple level scenes that are all accessible through the "main" scene that opens when the game first plays. We'll provide buttons that will give the name of the scene and, when clicked, will load that scene.

UI Solutions

Let's discuss Unity's three UI solutions and why you might pick one over the other.

Immediate Mode GUI (IMGUI)

This is what we'll be using in this project, the obstacle course. It is scripted through C# and is the oldest available form of UI in Unity. It can get quick-and-dirty UI done easily if you're a programmer, but it's generally not optimal for your user-facing, end product UI. It's far from gorgeous, and customizing its appearance is a bit tedious.

It stands for **Immediate Mode GUI**, a name that stems from the fact that your scripts are drawing the GUI immediately, constantly, in every single call of the Unity event "OnGUI". IMGUI is also the default system used when creating tools that extend the Unity editor: you can use it to create custom Inspectors for your scripts and custom Windows within the Unity editor.

Because IMGUI allows us to run some simple code to quickly get some buttons on our screen that can be clicked, we'll be learning how to use it for this project. It's handy for quick solutions in GUI to allow you to test features. It may not look pretty, but in the early stages of development, we often don't care about that so much.

In our next example project, we'll use Unity UI (uGUI) to make less rudimentary and more visually acceptable UI.

Unity UI (uGUI)

This is the product of a newer solution for UI in Unity, designed to operate through GameObjects and their components in your scene – as opposed to IMGUI, which draws the UI through method calls in your C# scripts. It also supports 3D UI – in other words, you can place 3D UI elements within your scenes to create UI that appears to be in your game world, such as if you wanted to have an interactive computer screen or "holographic" screen in your game.

© Casey Hardman 2024
C. Hardman, *Game Programming with Unity and C#*, https://doi.org/10.1007/978-1-4842-9720-9_22

Since it works with the ever-present GameObject and component system, uGUI also integrates well with UI that needs to use Inspector references to MonoBehaviours (C# script components).

UI Toolkit

This is the newest solution for UI in Unity. It operates much like existing technologies that you would use when creating websites, such as HTML, CSS, and JavaScript. It is intended to be the go-to UI system that would be used in new projects going forward, but it currently lacks some features that uGUI provides, like 3D in-game UI. It is the system that is currently undergoing further development and improvements, whereas the other two are considered stable and unlikely to change or improve (aside from possible bug fixes).

We won't be learning about how to use UI Toolkit during this book due to its complexity and the fact that we can more conveniently get done all we need with the other UI systems. It introduces a new coding language to present the visuals used by the UI, but this language is rather different from C# (and quite a lot to chew if you're already learning how to code games with C#).

Scene Flow

Before we get to coding our UI, let's examine a quick overview of how the loading of scenes is expected to flow for our game by the time we're done with this.

The first scene in our build settings – the one that loads first – will be the main menu scene. We won't have anything in this scene but a basic camera and an empty GameObject with a script that handles the main menu GUI.

This script will be called **LevelSelectUI**. It will call a little built-in method to instruct Unity that its GameObject should not be destroyed when a new scene is loaded. This way, the LevelSelectUI script can keep running after a level scene is opened.

Each level will have a scene all to itself. They'll be numbered by their index in the build settings, and they'll only show in the menu once we've added them to the build settings.

An instance of the Player prefab will be in each level scene, but the Player script will be disabled by default by unchecking the box beside its name in the Inspector, as we learned before. As well as this, the Camera GameObject inside the Player will be inactive – not just the Camera component, but the whole GameObject.

You can make this change through the Player prefab:

- First, make sure you've updated the Player prefab in your level scene with any overrides you want to keep around, but haven't applied yet. For example, if you've tweaked the Player movespeed, dash time, dash speed, etc., then you'll want to apply those overrides so they match across all levels. Do this by selecting the Player in your Hierarchy, then clicking the Overrides drop-down in the header of the Inspector, and selecting Apply All, or by selecting specific overrides you want and applying them individually.

- Now open the Player prefab by double-clicking it in the Project window.

- Select the camera GameObject and make it inactive by default with the checkbox to the left side of its name in the Inspector.

- Select the Player GameObject, find its Player script in the Inspector, and disable the script by default with the checkbox to the left side of the script component header.

Now any level scenes you've created will update to have the player at the initial state we desire.

Each level scene will have a camera named "Level View Camera" in it, as we described in the previous chapter. This camera will be enabled by default, so when the LevelSelectUI loads the scene, we see the preview of the level, not the player's view of the level (since we disabled the player camera). The player model will show in the level, but since the Player script is disabled, we won't be able to move or act.

As long as we're not in the main scene, our UI script will draw us a button we can click to play the game.

Once that button is clicked, we disable the Level View Camera, enable the Player script, and activate the player's camera. Now the level is being played officially. We don't need the UI anymore, so we destroy the GameObject holding the LevelSelectUI script.

When the player wins the level or uses the escape menu to quit (we'll implement that in the next chapter), they'll be brought back to the main scene again. Since we'll be loading the main scene again, the same GameObject with the LevelSelectUI script on it will be there waiting for us again, so we can select our next level to play.

To set this up, we'll start by cleaning any excess stuff out of the "main" scene we've had around since the start. If you've made something of a level in that scene already and don't want to lose it, follow these steps:

- Rename the "main" scene in the Project window, for example, to something like "Level 1".

- Create a new scene with File ➤ New Scene or Ctrl+N and select the **"Basic (Built-in)"** template when prompted.

- Save the new scene (Ctrl+S) in your Scenes folder, naming it **"main"**.

Otherwise, if you just have a bunch of junk lying around for testing and you don't mind getting rid of it, make sure you've made a prefab out of anything important and applied any important overrides to existing prefabs, then delete it all away.

Now create a script named **LevelSelectUI**, create a new empty GameObject named "Level Selection" in the scene, and attach an instance of the new script to it.

You should have a Main Camera GameObject in your scene by default, but if you don't have one, make a basic camera with GameObject ➤ Camera. We'll need a camera in our scene for our GUI to render correctly.

Now go to your Build Settings (File ➤ Build Settings) and make sure the "main" scene is at build index 0 and any levels you've created are beneath it, as shown in Figure 22-1.

Figure 22-1. *The Build Settings with our main scene located at build index 0 (listed on the right side), with a few level scenes beneath it*

One final step you can take is to stop the camera in the main scene from drawing anything but solid color. In the Inspector for the Camera component, change the **Clear Flags** field – the first one listed for the component – from Skybox to **Solid Color**. The field directly beneath it, a color field titled **Background**, can be changed to whatever you like. The camera will draw that color in the background instead of drawing the default view of the sky. I'll set mine to a dark gray-blue with a hex value of 2D3644.

Level Selection Script

The first thing to do for our LevelSelectUI script is to make sure it doesn't get destroyed when we load a new scene. We need it to stick around to continue showing UI after we load levels to preview them.

This is a simple method call away. Change your Start method in the **LevelSelectUI** script to this:

```
void Start()
{
    //Make sure this object persists when the scene changes:
    DontDestroyOnLoad(gameObject);
}
```

That's all we need to do to handle that. Now when we load into a new scene in-game, this object will stick around in the newly loaded scene. This also means that if we load the scene this object originated from, we'll end up with two copies of it. That's why, later, we'll destroy it when the player decides on a level to play: we don't want it sticking around past that point.

Now, let's get into the UI code.

To use IMGUI, we declare the built-in event **OnGUI**. This method is called whenever a new GUI event happens. These GUI events are a range of different things: the mouse moving, mouse buttons being pressed, or keys being pressed. Most often, the event that triggers an OnGUI call is simply a "Repaint" event that happens every frame to update and draw the GUI.

The only time we can call GUI methods is within the OnGUI method.

These GUI methods can be accessed through two objects: **GUI** and **GUILayout**. They both have mostly the same functionality – the same static methods going by the same names. The difference is that GUI requires that we specify a position on the screen and a width and height of each thing we want to draw, while GUILayout automatically lays itself out, determining the position and size of GUI elements on its own unless we override it.

Positioning elements on a screen with code can be a bit of a pain. We'll be doing it a little when we code our main menu in the next chapter, but for the most part, since we're making placeholder GUI anyway, we'll let the system lay it out for us to save some development time.

First, make sure **LevelSelectUI** has this using statement at the top of the script file:

```
using UnityEngine.SceneManagement;
```

We used this before to reload the scene when we made our Goal script. It gives us access to the **SceneManager** object, which we'll use when loading in new scenes.

Then declare some variables at the top of our LevelSelectUI script class:

```
//Build index of the currently loaded scene.
private int currentScene = 0;

//Current scene's level view camera, if any.
private GameObject levelViewCamera;

//Current ongoing scene loading operation, if any.
private AsyncOperation currentLoadOperation;
```

The current scene build index (the number associated with it in the Build Settings) will be tracked so we can display the level number that we're currently viewing to the user in a text label with the GUI. It starts at 0, because that's what we expect the main menu UI to be. When we load a new scene, we'll update this index to match it.

We'll also store a reference to the level view camera of the current scene, which will initially be null for the main scene, but will be set when we load a new scene.

The last variable is of a type we haven't used yet. An **AsyncOperation** resembles an ongoing operation that occurs **asynchronously** – meaning it happens while the game continues to play.

An activity that's particularly laborious on the computer processor will cause the whole program to freeze until it finishes. This often makes for an unpleasant experience. In this situation, we can run the operation gradually in the background, devoting only part of the processing power to it. This is what **asynchronous** means. The opposite, **synchronous**, is the standard way code runs: the processor will perform one activity at a time. If you call a method with a very intensive loop inside it, that single method call may make the program freeze until the processing is complete.

Loading scenes can cause a noticeable hiccup – it's a somewhat demanding task. This is why there's a way to load them asynchronously. But we often need to react when the scene finishes loading, so we need some way to track the progress of the operation. To handle this, the method that loads a scene asynchronously will return to us an instance of AsyncOperation. We can use this instance to check if the operation has finished yet. We'll do so to know when we should try to find our level view camera.

Let's get to the code that shows our basic GUI and allows us to load in new scenes, using the **OnGUI** method we learned about before. Place this code in your **LevelSelectUI** script class:

```
void OnGUI()
{
    GUILayout.Label("OBSTACLE COURSE");

    //If this isn't the main menu:
    if (currentScene != 0)
    {
        GUILayout.Label("Currently viewing Level " + currentScene);

        //Show a PLAY button:
        if (GUILayout.Button("PLAY"))
        {
            //If the button is clicked, start playing the level:
            PlayCurrentLevel();
        }
    }
    else //If this is the main menu
        GUILayout.Label("Select a level to preview it.");

    //Starting at scene build index 1, loop through the remaining scene indexes:
    for (int i = 1; i < SceneManager.sceneCountInBuildSettings; i++)
    {
        //Show a button with text "Level [level number]"
        if (GUILayout.Button("Level " + i))
        {
            //If that button is clicked, and we aren't already waiting for a scene to load:
            if (currentLoadOperation == null)
            {
                //Start loading the level asynchronously:
                currentLoadOperation = SceneManager.LoadSceneAsync(i);
                //Set the current scene:
                currentScene = i;
            }
        }
    }
}
```

Since this is the OnGUI method, we can call **GUILayout** methods within it. Each one doesn't bother us about where on the screen we want the results to be drawn. It just moves them down as it goes, each one drawing underneath the last.

The first GUI method we see is a call to **"GUILayout.Label"**. A Label is simply a means of drawing some text on the screen. We draw the title of our game, "OBSTACLE COURSE".

We then react to the "currentScene" variable to display something different based on whether we're in the main menu or if we're already previewing a level.

The main menu is index 0, so anything that's not index 0 will be a level we're previewing.

If we're previewing a level, we show a Label telling the user which level they're viewing.

We then use a call to **"GUILayout.Button"**, wrapped in an "if" statement.

This method call not only shows a button on the screen, but returns true if it was clicked on this event or false if it was not. Anything within that "if" block will be the code we want to run if the button is clicked. In our case, we run a method we'll be declaring in a moment: **PlayCurrentLevel**.

If we're not previewing a level, we must be at the main menu. We show a different Label instructing the user to click a level below.

We then draw buttons to choose between the levels below. We'll do a "for" loop, starting at index 1 this time instead of 0. This loop will go over all of the levels in the build settings, except for the one at index 0 (the main menu). To get the number of scenes in the build settings, we go through SceneManager to reference the **".sceneCountInBuildSettings"** member.

For each level scene, we draw a button with the text "Level" plus the level number written on it.

If one of these buttons is clicked, and so long as we haven't already started loading a scene, we begin loading the scene at the current index ("i") with **"SceneManager.LoadSceneAsync"**. In our Goal script, we load the level synchronously, which is done with the method **LoadScene**. This time, we want to do it asynchronously, so we call **LoadSceneAsync** instead.

As we established before, it returns an AsyncOperation, which we apply to our "currentLoadOperation" variable to keep it around so we can check it later, allowing us to know when the scene is finished loading.

Once we determine that the scene has loaded, we'll null out this variable so we can once again load a new level. Until that happens, our "if" checking that it is null prevents the user from loading a different scene while one is still processing, since the variable will no longer be null as soon as one of the level buttons is clicked.

Now we need some per-frame logic to detect when that operation finishes so we can do some setup.

We'll do this with an Update method:

```
void Update()
{
    //If we have a current load operation and it's done:
    if (currentLoadOperation != null && currentLoadOperation.isDone)
    {
        //Null out the load operation:
        currentLoadOperation = null;

        //Find the level view camera in the scene:
        levelViewCamera = GameObject.Find("Level View Camera");

        //Log an error if we couldn't find the camera:
        if (levelViewCamera == null)
            Debug.LogError("No level view camera was found in the scene!");
    }
}
```

The AsyncOperation **".isDone"** member is a bool that we can use to check if it's finished or not. So long as we have a "currentLoadOperation", we'll check if it's done yet. We check if it's null before checking if it's done because if it were null and we tried to grab the ".isDone" member, we'd get a runtime error.

Once it's done, we set it to null again and use the "GameObject.Find" method to try to get a level view camera in the newly loaded scene.

"GameObject.Find" takes a string for a GameObject name and searches the scene for it. If it finds it, it returns it. Otherwise, it just returns null. One thing to note about this method is that it won't find GameObjects that are inactive.

If we did fail to find a level view camera, we will throw an error with **"Debug.LogError"**, which is like "Debug.Log", except that it shows up as a shiny red error in the Console instead of a neutral message. This will alert us if we ever forgot to add the camera.

Now all we need to do is determine what happens when the player clicks the Play button.

We already wrote the method call, so let's declare the method itself, just below the variables at the top of the **LevelSelectUI** script class:

```
private void PlayCurrentLevel()
{
    //Deactivate the level view camera:
    levelViewCamera.SetActive(false);

    //Try to find the Player GameObject:
    var playerGobj = GameObject.Find("Player");

    //Throw an error if we couldn't find it:
    if (playerGobj == null)
        Debug.LogError("Couldn't find a Player in the level!");

    else //If we did find the player:
    {
        //Get the Player script attached and enable it:
        var playerScript = playerGobj.GetComponent<Player>();
        playerScript.enabled = true;

        //Through the player script, access the camera GameObject and activate it:
        playerScript.cam.SetActive(true);

        //Destroy self; we'll come back when the main scene is loaded again:
        Destroy(this.gameObject);
    }
}
```

First, we deactivate the level view camera so it doesn't render anymore. We don't want two cameras trying to render at the same time.

Then we try to find the Player by name. There should be one in every level; if there isn't, we log an error. If there is, we grab the Player script component from it using GetComponent<T>, storing it in a local variable. We enable the Player script, which you'll recall, we've made disabled by default in the prefab.

We then reach through the Player script to access the **"cam"** member – which we'll need to declare because we haven't yet. Let's do that now, since our code will throw an error until we do. With the rest of the reference variables **at the beginning of the Player script class**, add this variable:

```
public GameObject cam;
```

With that line added to the Player, your code shouldn't throw any errors.

This "cam" variable will be a pointer to the player's Camera GameObject. It'll be inactive by default, so we can't use "GameObject.Find" to get it. We'll just rely on a reference in the Player script, since we need to grab the script anyway to enable it. We still need to set the reference to the camera, though, so make sure you open the Player prefab through the Project and **assign the reference** to the Player Camera there to apply it across all of your Player instances.

Anyway, after we've activated the camera, the only thing left to do is to bid farewell to the GameObject holding the LevelSelectUI script by destroying it. Remember, if we don't do this, then it will still be drawing the GUI and it will still be persisting after the main scene is reloaded, leaving us with two separate instances of it, both drawing at the same time.

With this in effect, the system should now be fully contained. Starting in the "main" scene, play the game and you'll see the GUI in the top-left corner, as shown in Figure 22-2. Of course, it's not particularly fancy, and it's just a little thing up there, but it functions.

Figure 22-2. *The main scene GUI, before any levels have been loaded. Here, we have two level scenes added to the Build Settings, providing us with buttons for Level 1 and Level 2*

If you click a level button, the level should load in. If you've set up the level correctly, the Level View Camera should be active by default, while the player's camera is not. This means we see the level at first through the Level View Camera.

With a level loaded, the GUI will adapt to show a Play button. Clicking this will deactivate the level view camera, enable the player camera, and set the player into action, allowing us to control it.

Step on a Goal in the level, and you'll find yourself transported back to the main menu, where you can go through the same process again to play another level.

Summary

This chapter gives us some additional robustness for the game and shows how you can get some quick-and-dirty GUI into your game using IMGUI. We've given the player a menu they can use to select which level they wish to play, and we return them to this menu when they reach the goal of a level. We also switch the Player script off by default and provide a preview of the level, giving control to the Player script only after the user has clicked a Play button.

Now all we need is some means of returning to the main menu from within the game, without having to reach the goal. We'll handle that in the next chapter.

Some things to remember are as follows:

- To make a GameObject stick around even when we load a new scene in-game, call the **DontDestroyOnLoad** method and pass the GameObject as a parameter.

- **OnGUI** is a built-in event where we can call certain methods to draw GUI to the screen.

- **GUI** and **GUILayout** are two classes with static methods in them that we can call within OnGUI. They're mostly the same methods, but **GUI** methods must have their position and size specified in their parameters, while **GUILayout** methods will automatically position and size themselves.

- An **asynchronous** operation is one that occurs in the background, sometimes taking many frames to finish. A **synchronous** operation is one that occurs all at once, which can cause a drop in framerate (or even temporarily freeze the game) if the operation is particularly intensive to run.

- **"SceneManager.LoadSceneAsync"** loads a scene asynchronously, returning an **AsyncOperation** instance when it is called.

- The **AsyncOperation** has an "**isDone**" bool property that can be used to check if the scene has finished loading (true) or not (false).

- **"SceneManager.sceneCountInBuildSettings"** returns the number of scenes that have been added to the build in the Build Settings.

- The **"GameObject.Find"** method takes a string and attempts to find a GameObject with that name. If it finds one, it will return it. If not, it returns null. It will not find inactive GameObjects.

- For one of our levels to work properly, it should have a Camera in it named Level View Camera. If the name isn't exact, the "GameObject.Find" call won't be able to find it.

CHAPTER 23

In-Game Pause Menu

Now we need some means of getting back to the main menu from within the game. We'll add this in the form of a menu that the player can open by pressing the Esc key. It also wouldn't hurt for that menu to pause the game while it's up and unpause when we close it.

Freezing Time

Everything in our game is based on time. We use "Time.deltaTime" to measure the distance something will move in a frame. We use "Time.time" to measure how long it's been since something happened. We use Invokes to time the player's respawning and the Wanderer retargeting.

This can all be manipulated with the **"Time.timeScale"** member.

It's a multiplier for how much time passes. It can be changed on a dime to make time pass slower, faster, or not at all.

By default, it's set to 1. If we wanted to make time pass at half speed, for example, we'd set it to 0.5. If we wanted time to pass twice as fast, we'd set it to 2. If we want to freeze time, we set it to 0.

The "timeScale" properly adjusts the timing of invoked methods, the "Time.deltaTime" variable, and the "Time.time" variable – which is great for us, because it means it just works with all of our existing features out of the box.

This means all we have to do to freeze time is this single line of code:

```
Time.timeScale = 0;
```

But we want to do it through a pause menu that's toggled with the Escape key.

This pause menu will be simple, like the level selection menu we made in the last chapter, but it will show in the middle of the screen and have two options: one to resume the game and another to quit to the main menu.

To make sure it's only operable when the level has begun playing (not when we're still previewing), we'll go ahead and implement it on the Player script class. Since the Player script is disabled until the game begins playing, we won't be able to open the pause menu when we're still in the level select menu.

First, declare a bool **"paused"** on the **Player** script, **beneath the existing variables**:

```
private bool paused = false;
```

© Casey Hardman 2024
C. Hardman, *Game Programming with Unity and C#*, https://doi.org/10.1007/978-1-4842-9720-9_23

Then, declare a Pausing method, like our Movement and Dashing methods, and drop it in there beneath the Player's **Respawn** method:

```
private void Pausing()
{
    if (Input.GetKeyDown(KeyCode.Escape))
    {
        //Toggle pause status:
        paused = !paused;

        //If we're now paused, set timeScale to 0:
        if (paused)
            Time.timeScale = 0;
        //Otherwise if we're no longer paused, revert timeScale to 1:
        else

            Time.timeScale = 1;
    }
}
```

First, it's flipping the bool value of our "paused" variable, making it the opposite of its current value. Then, based on what it is now set to, we set the time scale: 0 when paused, 1 when unpaused.

We'll call that in our Update method, and we'll also only run the Movement and Dashing logic if the game is not currently paused – change the Player's **Update** method to this:

```
void Update()
{
    if (!paused)
    {
        Movement();
        Dashing();
    }
    Pausing();
}
```

Now we won't be able to detect input for dashes or movement when the game is still paused.

This will give us the pausing functionality, but no visual indication of it. We'll need an **OnGUI** method for the menu.

To handle the displaying of the box in the middle of the screen, we'll use a **"GUILayout.BeginArea"** call. This method lets us give it a **Rect**, which is short for rectangle, to define a box on the screen that we want to place GUILayout elements within.

It works somewhat intuitively. We call "GUILayout.BeginArea", passing in the Rect we want to use as our area on the screen to contain the elements in. Then we run any GUILayout methods we want to put in the area – buttons, labels, whatever. Once we're finished, we call "GUILayout.EndArea" to break out of the area.

The part that's a bit tricky is creating the Rect to define the space on the screen that the area should take up.

A Rect constructor takes four values: an **X**, a **Y**, a **width**, and a **height**.

The X and Y work much like they do in world space units in our game, only they're resembling the 2D space of our screen now – and rather than working with the concept of units, each point is just 1 pixel of our screen. A pixel is one tiny colored dot that makes up your computer monitor. Most modern monitors are over a thousand pixels wide and tall.

Another notable difference is that a value of (0, 0) is not the center of the screen – it's the top-left corner. An **increase** in X goes toward the **right** edge of the screen, and an **increase** in Y goes toward the **bottom** edge of the screen.

Luckily for us, there's an easy way to measure the width and height of our screen in pixels: the **"Screen. width"** and **"Screen.height"** static variables.

Cut those values in half, and we get the center of the screen: (Screen.width ∗ .5f, Screen.height ∗ .5f).

But the X and Y position of our Rect isn't the center of the area we're defining. That would make this too easy. Rather, it's the top-left corner of the area. That's generally how things work in 2D space – particularly with the legacy GUI systems: the pivot point, so to speak, is at the top-left corner.

Let's declare the OnGUI method and see how we get around this problem – put this code in the **Player** script, **beneath** the **Update** method:

```
void OnGUI()
{
    if (paused)
    {
        float boxWidth = Screen.width * .4f;
        float boxHeight = Screen.height * .4f;

        GUILayout.BeginArea(new Rect(
            (Screen.width * .5f) - (boxWidth * .5f),
            (Screen.height * .5f) - (boxHeight * .5f),
            boxWidth,
            boxHeight));

        if (GUILayout.Button("RESUME GAME", GUILayout.Height(boxHeight * .5f)))
        {
            paused = false;
            Time.timeScale = 1;
        }

        if (GUILayout.Button("RETURN TO MAIN MENU", GUILayout.Height(boxHeight * .5f)))
        {
            Time.timeScale = 1;
            SceneManager.LoadScene(0);
        }
        GUILayout.EndArea();
    }
}
```

I've spaced out each individual parameter in the "new Rect" to separate them and make it easier to read. Remember, this doesn't affect the method call. It's just a formatting thing.

Again, the parameters for our new Rect, in order from top to bottom, are X, Y, width, and height.

Before we start the area, we declare some shorthand local variables for the width and height of the box we want our area to resemble, which we set to 40% of the screen width and height. Then, we use those variables when constructing our Rect to begin our GUILayout area.

For the X and Y, we start at the center of the screen (width or height multiplied in half). But since it's the top-left corner of the box that we'll be placing at the center of the screen, it won't look centered correctly if we just do that. We need to shift it to the left by half of the box width and up by half of the box height. That's why we subtract half of the box width/height from the X/Y values, respectively – remember, increasing X goes to the right, and increasing Y goes down, so we need the opposite.

After that, we can call our **"GUILayout.Button"** methods and then make sure we call **"GUILayout. EndArea"** to break the custom area we began earlier.

In those button methods, we have an extra parameter. The **"GUILayout.Height(…)"** calls coming after the button text are a way to customize a GUILayout method to have a manually defined height. Rather than letting the system determine the height on its own, we take control of it by supplying this option.

A similar option exists for **"GUILayout.Width"**, among others, but we don't have any need for that: the buttons will size themselves to the width of their containing area automatically.

In our "GUILayout.Height" options, we specify that the height should be half of our "boxHeight", so that the two buttons together take up the full height.

When the resume button is clicked, we unpause the game and revert the "timeScale" to 1 again so time flows as normal.

When the return button is clicked, we load the main scene (index 0) and also make sure we reset the flow of time, since that variable won't reset itself when the scene reloads.

Finally, remember that in order to access the **SceneManager**, we'll need to make sure the script has the correct using statement at the top:

```
using UnityEngine.SceneManagement;
```

And with that, we should now be able to play the game through the main scene, navigate to a level, click Play, and test our new pause menu.

Pressing Escape will bring the menu up, as shown in Figure 23-1.

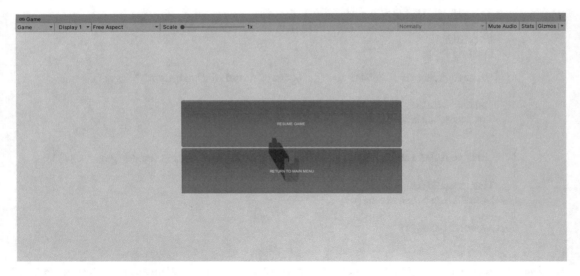

Figure 23-1. *The in-game pause menu is shown with the player character visible behind the menu buttons*

Returning to the main menu resets the process neatly, landing us back in the main scene where we can use the menu to go to a level again.

Summary

We've added one final component to our scene flow and menus: the option for the player to quit a level after they've started playing it with a menu opened by pressing the Esc key. This doubles as a pause feature by freezing time when the menu is open.

Some key points to remember are as follows:

- **"Time.timeScale"** is the multiplier for how much time actually passes in-game per second of real time. We can set it to change the rate that time flows: 0.5 is half as fast as normal, 2 is twice as fast, 0 freezes time, and so on.

- A **Rect** is a basic data type that resembles a rectangle: an X and Y position resembling the top-left corner of the rectangle and a width and height for the rectangle size.

- **"GUILayout.BeginArea"** is a method that starts a GUILayout area in a given rectangle of the screen, represented by a **Rect**. You call **BeginArea** and then any GUILayout methods you want to be part of the area, and then when you're done, you call **"GUILayout.EndArea"**.

- Most GUILayout methods that draw some element to the screen can be supplied options at the end of the call. We used **"GUILayout.Height"** to specify the height we wanted our buttons to use rather than allowing the layout system to figure it out on its own.

CHAPTER 24

■ ■ ■

Spike Traps

The final obstacle we'll implement will be a spike trap. It will teach you a new concept and give you more practice with the concepts we learned in previous chapters, like Slerping over time, working with state, and Invoking methods to time transitions in the state.

Our spike trap will be a thin, square "plate" laid out on the floor which has lots of little "spikes" sticking out of it. For simplicity's sake, we'll make the whole thing out of cubes. When the trap activates, the spikes quickly raise, poking up out of the plate. They'll remain raised for a moment and then slowly lower back down.

While the spikes are raising, the trap is a Hazard, killing the player if they're standing over it. But when the spikes are raised or in the process of lowering back down, they act merely as a normal, physical collider that blocks the player from passing by, without actually killing them on touch.

Once the spikes finish lowering back down, the player can safely walk over the trap again. To accomplish this, we'll be using two separate Box Colliders on two separate GameObjects: one for the Hazard collider and one for the harmless collider. We'll activate and deactivate them as we go, based on the state of the trap.

Designing the Trap

Before we get into the little details on how we'll implement the trap in code, let's build it in our scene. Once we're done, your trap will look like Figure 24-1.

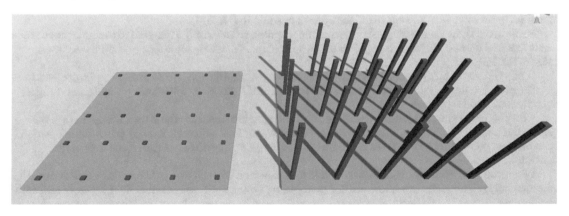

Figure 24-1. *A fully lowered Spike Trap (left) next to a fully raised Spike Trap (right)*

© Casey Hardman 2024
C. Hardman, *Game Programming with Unity and C#*, https://doi.org/10.1007/978-1-4842-9720-9_24

You can make the trap in any of your level scenes. Just move your camera off to a clear place where other stuff won't get in your way, and let's begin.

- Create an empty GameObject named **"Spike Trap"**.

- Add a Cube child to the Spike Trap and name it **"Plate"**. Set its scale to (9, .2, 9) and its local position to (0, .1, 0), giving us a thin, square plate, much like our Wander Region.

- Remove the Box Collider component on the Plate.

- Normally, you would have a model for the spikes, probably holding all of them in one mesh so a single GameObject could be used for all of the spikes at once. But we aren't creating our own meshes or artwork, so we'll use a separate GameObject for each individual spike.

- Right-click the Spike Trap and add a new empty GameObject child named **"Spikes"**. This will be the master parent for all of our individual spikes. It should be at local position (0, 0, 0).

- We'll use some tricks to distribute our spikes evenly across the surface of the plate without hand-placing each one. First, we'll need a single Spike instance that we can copy-paste around. Add a Cube as a child to the Spikes GameObject. Name it **"Spike"** and set its scale to (.2, 1, .2).

- To align the bottoms of the spikes with the Spikes GameObject, set their **Y position** to **0.5**. This is important. The bottom of each spike must be lined up with the Spikes GameObject – no higher or lower! A local Y position of 0.5 will do exactly that. The height is left at 1 to allow us to handle it through code – you'll see how we manage this when we get to that point.

Now we're at a crossroads. Do we copy-paste our spikes and drag them around with the transform tools willy-nilly with no concern for their placement, or do we try to make them neatly lined up and pretty?

If you prefer a sloppier trap (it might look a bit more gnarly and brutal that way), you could make a bunch of spikes and just move their X and Z positions around within the trap to fill it in a messy way.

But our trap, pictured in Figure 24-1, is made with some special tricks that distribute the spikes evenly without painstakingly dragging them into precise positions.

First, let's position this first spike in one of the corners. We'll put it at the top-left corner, with a little bit of margin between it and the edge of the trap. Set its position to **(-4, .5, 4)**.

Second, we know we're going to be making more spikes, so let's apply a material to the spike now. Make a new material named "Spikes" and apply it to the Spike cube. I'm giving mine a deep red color with a hex value of D33B51.

While we're at it, let's go ahead and give the Plate cube a material as well. So the spikes don't blend in with the plate too much, I'll make a new material for it named Spike Trap with a pale orange color using a hex value of F0A593.

Now you have one spike ready to be duplicated and spread across the whole trap. It's up there in the corner, but not right at the edge of the corner, since that would look a bit odd. To copy-paste it and position each one an even distance away from the last without doing it by hand, we can use a little trick in the Inspector.

When you type a number value into a field in the Inspector, you can do math equations, and Unity will automatically calculate the result for you. For example, try typing 5+5 into a number field, like a Transform's position. As soon as you press Enter or lose focus on the field by pressing Tab or clicking somewhere else, Unity will replace the equation with the result: 10.

We can use this to simply add to or subtract from one of the position axes of a Spike. Copy and paste the Spike instance and edit its X position field to add "+2" at the end. That is, leave whatever position value is currently in the field, and append the math at the end – if the field is -4, set it to "-4+2". The result will be calculated and adjusted precisely, without the need for us to drag the spike with the mouse and try to get them all evenly spaced.

Do this until you run out of space to place more spikes. You should have a row of five spikes, stretching from the left side of the trap to the right side, as shown in Figure 24-2.

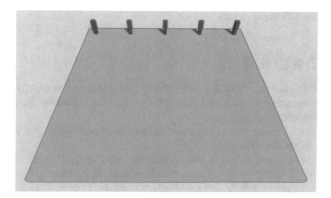

Figure 24-2. *The Spike Trap so far, with just one row of spikes*

Now, all we have to do is select all five of those spikes in the Hierarchy, then copy and paste them, and with all five of the newly pasted spikes still selected, perform the same trick, this time subtracting 2 from their Z position each time to push them down by 2 units. Then, copy and paste that row, and subtract 2 from the Z again, and so on until the whole spike trap is filled with spikes, giving us 5 rows of 5 spikes each.

You'll notice, as you're copying and pasting the spikes and adjusting their Z positions, that their X position will be shown as a dash in the Inspector, whereas the Z and Y positions show correctly. This is because they're all equal to each other. The dash indicates that the value is not the same across all of the currently selected GameObjects. This works the same way with other components that the GameObjects share, too – not just the Transform. This includes the variables of our own script components.

And there you have it – precisely positioned spikes, without copy-pasting all 25 of them one at a time. At this point, your Spike Trap should look like Figure 24-3.

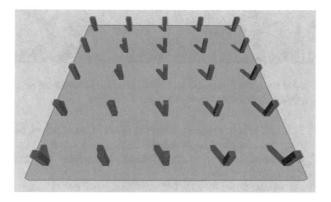

Figure 24-3. *Our Spike Trap with all of its spikes set up*

While you're at it, you can also remove the Box Collider component from all of the spikes at once. We don't need colliders for individual spikes – we'll use one collider that spreads over all of them. With all of the spikes selected (click the topmost Spike in the Hierarchy, then hold Shift and click the bottom one), remove the Box Collider component in the Inspector. Since they all have a Box Collider, Unity will delete them all at once for us.

Don't forget to also change the layer of the root Spike Trap GameObject to Hazard, and as always, agree to change all the children when Unity asks.

Raising and Lowering

We haven't yet set up our spikes fully. There's a new concept to be learned! Well, not so much a new concept as a side effect of an existing concept. We're going to achieve the effect of raising/lowering our spikes with a bit of magic involving pivot points and scaling.

Like I said before, there's a reason we made sure the bottom of each spike was vertically positioned to neatly line up with the Spikes GameObject.

Select your Spikes GameObject, switch to the scale transform tool (hotkey R), ensure that you are using the local pivot point (hotkey Z to toggle; the gizmos should appear at the base of the trap, not at the center of your spikes), and drag up the green box for the Y axis, increasing the Y scale. Alternatively, just set the Spikes GameObject's Y scale to something higher in the Inspector.

Since the spikes are all children of this empty GameObject, they all grow taller, as expected (see the left side of Figure 24-4). But the important thing is how the pivot point is scaling them "away from it."

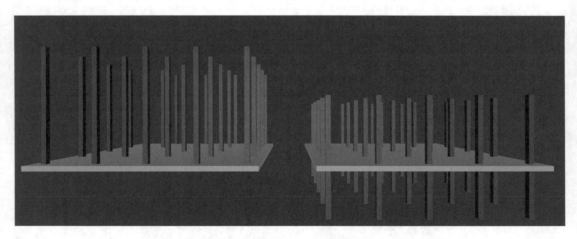

Figure 24-4. *Scaling up the Y axis of the Spikes GameObject to 5 (left) compared to scaling up the Y axis of each individual Spike to 5 (right). Both traps are at the same Y position*

Try to instead select all of the Spike instances within the Spikes GameObject, but don't select the Spikes GameObject itself. Scale up the Y axis again, just as you did before, and you'll get something more like the right side of Figure 24-4. The spikes scale up by their individual pivot points – the center of each spike – and thus stick out beneath the trap as well as above it.

The first option is what we want: the spikes should only go up, not down, when we raise the scale of the Spikes GameObject. That's why we've set our trap up in such a specific way. The spikes all have a Y scale of 1 and a Y position of 0.5. Since local position and scale are multiplied by the scale of the parent, this means they're exactly as many units tall as the Y scale of their pivot point – the Spikes GameObject – and they're exactly half that height above it, which keeps their bottoms precisely positioned at the pivot point. We can now define the height of all the spikes simply by setting the Y scale of the Spikes GameObject. We also need to only change the scale of one GameObject to raise or lower the spikes, rather than keeping all of the spikes in an array, looping over them with a "for", and changing each one individually.

Now that we're done demonstrating this concept, let's leave the Y scales where we want them to be by default. If you made any changes to the Y positions of the individual spikes, select them all and set their Y scale to 1 again, so they neatly copy the scale of their parent. Then, we're going to set the spikes to their "lowered" position by default by setting the Y scale of the Spikes GameObject (the parent of all the individual spikes) to 0.3.

Writing the Script

Now you know how we plan on raising and lowering our spikes. Let's implement the functionality now: the raising, the lowering, and the collisions. We'll add the actual collision boxes to our Spike Trap after we've made the script and seen how they'll be used in it.

Create a script named **SpikeTrap**. Add an instance of it to the Spike Trap root GameObject we made.

First, let's declare two "const" floats, depicting the height of the spikes when fully lowered and the height when fully raised. Declare them **right at the top** of the **SpikeTrap** script class:

```
private const float SpikeHeight = 4f;
private const float LoweredSpikeHeight = .3f;
```

Let's go over the process the trap will be playing out. The trap will have four states, which we define in an enum named State, declared **just under our two const variables**:

```
private enum State
{
    Lowered,
    Lowering,
    Raising,
    Raised
}
```

The states are somewhat self-explanatory:

- While **Lowered** or **Raised**, the spikes aren't moving. They're sitting still, either fully lowered or fully raised.

- While **Lowering**, the spikes are becoming shorter, starting at the maximum height and lowering down to the minimum height.

- While **Raising**, the spikes are growing taller, starting at the minimum height and raising up to the maximum height.

Initially, it will have its spikes in the Lowered position, so that's what we set the state to when we declare the variable, **just below the enum declaration**:

```
private State state = State.Lowered;
```

"Lowered" is also the first item in the enum, so that's what it would naturally be set to if we didn't provide a value when we declared the state variable. Just to be explicit, we'll provide the default value anyway.

Now let's declare the variables we'll be using, **just beneath the "state" variable**:

```
[Header("References")]
[Tooltip("Reference to the parent of all the spikes.")]
public Transform spikeHolder;
public GameObject hitboxGameObject;
public GameObject colliderGameObject;

[Header("Stats")]
[Tooltip("Time in seconds after lowering the spikes before raising them again.")]
public float interval = 2f;

[Tooltip("Time in seconds after raising the spikes before they start lowering again.")]
public float raiseWaitTime = .3f;

[Tooltip("Time in seconds taken to fully lower the spikes.")]
public float lowerTime = .6f;

[Tooltip("Time in seconds taken to fully raise the spikes.")]
public float raiseTime = .08f;

private float lastSwitchTime = Mathf.NegativeInfinity;
```

We have a reference to the Spikes GameObject, which is the master parent of all the spikes. We then have references to the GameObjects we'll add to the Spike Trap at the end, which will hold the colliders that either kill the player on touch when the spikes are Raising or block the player like an ordinary wall when the spikes are Raised or Lowering. The "hitbox" is the dangerous one (set up like any ordinary Hazard), while the "collider" is the one that behaves like a wall.

The hitbox will be active while Raising, and then we'll deactivate it and activate the wall once we hit the fully Raised position. Then, once we finish Lowering and become fully Lowered, both the hitbox and the normal collider will be off, allowing the player to safely walk over the spike trap – so long as they get off before it starts Raising again!

As for all the variables under the Stats header, the tooltips pretty much explain the purpose of each variable. The repeating process the trap will take is as follows:

- Begin raising over **"raiseTime"** seconds.
- Once raising finishes, wait **"raiseWaitTime"** seconds.
- Begin lowering over **"lowerTime"** seconds.
- Once lowering finishes, wait **"interval"** seconds.
- Repeat.

We'll also need a private variable that we'll use to track the "Time.time" that the trap started raising or lowering last, which is what the **"lastSwitchTime"** variable is for.

First, let's declare the methods that we'll be invoking to start raising and to start lowering:

```
void StartRaising()
{
    lastSwitchTime = Time.time;
    state = State.Raising;

    //Become deadly by activating our hitbox:
    hitboxGameObject.SetActive(true);
}
```

```
void StartLowering()
{
    lastSwitchTime = Time.time;
    state = State.Lowering;
}
```

Going by what we just discussed about the collisions, this should be starting to make sense. We mark the **"lastSwitchTime"** because we'll be using it to time the raising and lowering, we change the state accordingly, and when we start raising, we make sure our hitbox is active so the player dies if they touch.

Now we'll declare the logic, which raises and lowers the spikes, **in our Update method**:

```
if (state == State.Lowering)
{
    //Get the spike holder local scale:
    Vector3 scale = spikeHolder.localScale;
    //Update the Y scale by lerping from max height to min height:
    scale.y = Mathf.Lerp(SpikeHeight, LoweredSpikeHeight, (Time.time - lastSwitchTime) /
    lowerTime);

    //Apply the updated scale to the spike holder:
    spikeHolder.localScale = scale;
    //If the spikes have finished lowering:
    if (scale.y == LoweredSpikeHeight)
    {
        //Update the state and Invoke the next raising in 'interval' seconds:
        Invoke("StartRaising", interval);
        state = State.Lowered;
        colliderGameObject.SetActive(false);
    }
}
else if (state == State.Raising)
{
    //Get the spike holder local scale:
    Vector3 scale = spikeHolder.localScale;

    //Update the Y scale by lerping from min height to max height:
    scale.y = Mathf.Lerp(LoweredSpikeHeight, SpikeHeight, (Time.time - lastSwitchTime) /
    raiseTime);
    //Apply the updated scale to the spike holder:
    spikeHolder.localScale = scale;

    //If the spikes have finished raising:
    if (scale.y == SpikeHeight)
    {
        //Update the state and Invoke the next lowering in 'raiseWaitTime' seconds:
        Invoke("StartLowering", raiseWaitTime);
        state = State.Raised;

        //Activate the collider to block the player:
        colliderGameObject.SetActive(true);

        //Deactivate the hitbox so it no longer kills the player:
        hitboxGameObject.SetActive(false);
    }
}
```

The "if" and the "else if" both contain much the same code, with little changes to distinguish between raising and lowering. We use the **"Mathf.Lerp"** method, which is equivalent to Slerping with Vector3s and Quaternions, only it works on two float values instead of vectors or Quaternions. It takes three float parameters, moving the first float toward the second, using the third float as the fraction of the difference between the two.

While **Lowering**, we Lerp from the fully raised height of the spikes down to the fully lowered height.

While **Raising**, we Lerp from the fully lowered height of the spikes up to the fully raised height.

We saw this similar method being done when we Slerped the rotation of our Wanderers to their targeted rotation over a given amount of time. The same concept is being used here, it's just that we're working with floats instead of rotations. The current time ("Time.time"), minus the time we began ("lastSwitchTime"), gives us the total time we've been lowering/raising so far. This is divided by the time we wish the whole operation to take, giving us a value that starts at 0 and reaches 1 in that amount of time ("lowerTime" or "raiseTime").

As soon as the Lerp has brought the height to the exact height we seek, we change the state to Raised or Lowered, and then we use Invoke to kick off the next transition (StartLowering or StartRaising) in the correct amount of time. At this point, we also change whether our hitbox and collider are active...

- When the spikes first **begin raising**, we activate the hitbox collider, making the spikes a fully functioning Hazard that will kill the player on touch.

- When the spikes **finish raising**, the collider is made active to block the player without killing them, and of course, the hitbox will be deactivated so it won't be able to kill the player.

- When the spikes **finish lowering**, the collider that blocks the player without killing them will be deactivated, allowing the player to run over the spikes while they're down.

With this, all we need to do now is ensure that the process gets kicked off. Since we start out in the fully Lowered state, we'll need to call StartRaising at one point to set the whole repeating process in motion. We'll do this in our Start method, **right above** the **Update** method:

```
void Start()
{
    //Spikes will be lowered by default.
    //We'll start raising them 'interval' seconds after Start.
    Invoke("StartRaising", interval);
}
```

This creates a loop:

- On Start, we are Lowered, but we invoke StartRaising, which will set our state to Raising.

- Once Raising reaches the maximum height, we invoke StartLowering in "raiseWaitTime" seconds. This sets our state to Lowering.

- Once Lowering reaches the minimum height, we invoke StartRaising again.

Adding Collisions

Now all we have to do is set up our Hazard hitbox and our nonlethal collider:

- Right-click the Spike Trap and add a new empty GameObject child. Name it **"Hitbox"**. It should be in the **Hazard** layer.

- For the Hitbox, add a Hazard script component and a Box Collider. Make sure the Box Collider is marked as a **trigger** collider and give it a **Size** vector to fit the width and length of the plate, but make it a bit taller. Something like (9, 4, 9) will do. This will cause it to stick through the ground, since the collider pivot is at its center. We can raise it up by changing the **Center** vector to (0, 2, 0).

- Copy and paste the Hitbox. Rename this new one **"Collider"**, remove the Hazard component, and make its collider **not** a trigger. This is the one that will physically impede the character, but not kill them on touch. Switch its layer to **Default**, since it's equivalent to a wall.

- By default, make both the Hitbox and Collider GameObjects be **inactive** by selecting them and unchecking the checkbox at the left side of their name in the Inspector. The default state of the Spike Trap is Lowered, so neither collider should be active at the start.

Then, all you've got to do is set the references to the Hitbox and Collider in the SpikeTrap script, and don't forget the Spikes master parent GameObject should be referenced by the "spikeHolder" variable.

That'll do it. If you've set everything up correctly, the trap will now kill the player if they're standing on it when it's raising, and once it finishes raising, it will block the player until it fully lowers.

If you haven't already, don't forget to make a prefab for the Spike Trap. With all that spike set up, it would be extra painful to accidentally delete it with no way of getting it back!

Summary

This chapter gives us our final obstacle type, a deadly (if a bit blunt) spike trap that shows a unique behavior of toggling between a Hazard collider and a normal, nonlethal collider based on its state.

We've learned that when scaling a parent, the children scale relative to the pivot point. We've demonstrated how to introduce a pivot point to all of our spikes to not only scale them all at the same time, but also to make them scale how we want them to, preventing them from sticking through the bottom of our trap. We also exercised some tricks to quickly set up our spikes by row instead of creating each one separately.

This marks the final implementation of our first example project!

CHAPTER 25

Obstacle Course Conclusion

At last, we've reached the end of our first project. Let's go over the final steps you might take when finished with a project: "building" it so that others can play it. I'll leave you with some further ideas for features to add to the game as well.

Building the Project

Although our project is anything but a polished and pretty gem waiting to be distributed to the masses, we can still get some hands-on experience with the building of a Unity project.

We discussed this topic briefly already. Building a project converts it to a format acceptable for an end user who wants to play your game. It copies our Unity project into a set of files that can be run without the Unity editor. This is necessary if you ever want to make a game available to a base of players – you very well can't ask them all to download the Unity editor and play your game through it, and you certainly don't want to give out all of your code and assets to the players.

Building a project is a simple task. It's mostly done with a few button clicks. You've already seen the Build Settings menu (see Figure 25-1), opened with File ➤ Build Settings or with the hotkey Ctrl+Shift+B (Cmd+Shift+B on Mac). We used it to add our level scenes so they could be loaded from our level selection menu, which we used the top section of the build settings for.

© Casey Hardman 2024
C. Hardman, *Game Programming with Unity and C#*, https://doi.org/10.1007/978-1-4842-9720-9_25

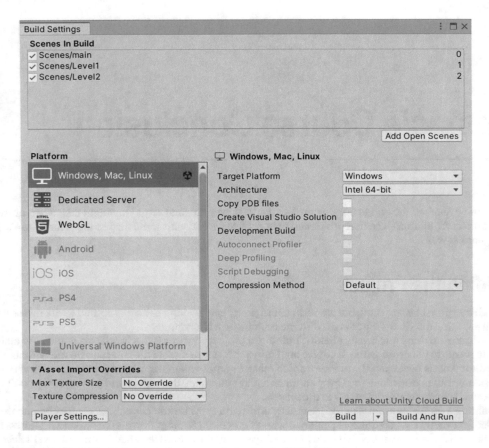

Figure 25-1. *The Build Settings menu for our project, set to build for Windows*

The section beneath the scenes is where you pick the target platform to deploy to (left) and related settings (right). By default, we're targeting Windows, Mac, and Linux. The project will be deployed to one of those particular operating systems based on the Target Platform field on the right side, which is a drop-down field.

Note that support for building to each operating system comes from a different Build Support module installed through the Unity Hub. If you want to build to a target platform that isn't listed, you probably don't have the module installed. All you have to do is go through the Unity Hub program and install the Build Support module for the operating system you want to target, which we talked about back in Chapter 1. Just open up Unity Hub, click the **"Installs"** tab on the left side, and then find your installed Unity version (if you have multiple versions installed, they'll all be listed), click the gear on its right-hand side, and then hit **"Add modules"** to bring up the module listing, shown in Figure 25-2.

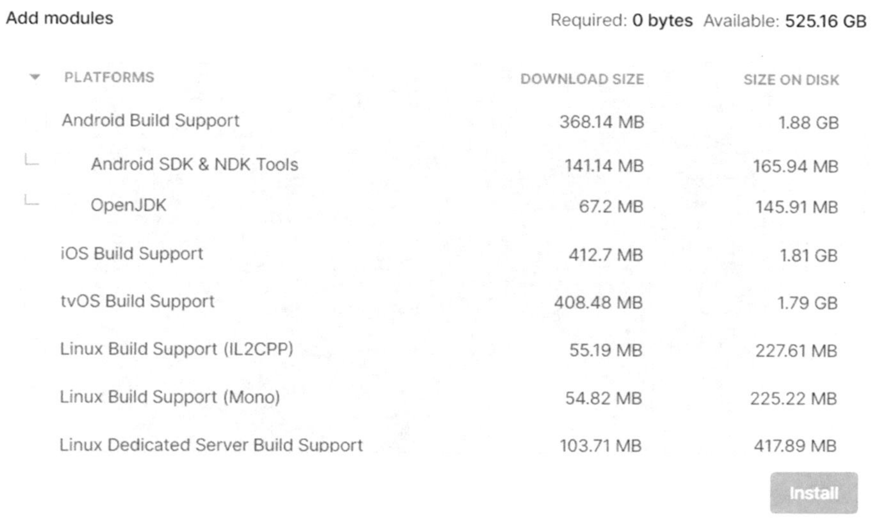

Add modules	Required: 0 bytes	Available: 525.16 GB
▾ PLATFORMS	DOWNLOAD SIZE	SIZE ON DISK
Android Build Support	368.14 MB	1.88 GB
└ Android SDK & NDK Tools	141.14 MB	165.94 MB
└ OpenJDK	67.2 MB	145.91 MB
iOS Build Support	412.7 MB	1.81 GB
tvOS Build Support	408.48 MB	1.79 GB
Linux Build Support (IL2CPP)	55.19 MB	227.61 MB
Linux Build Support (Mono)	54.82 MB	225.22 MB
Linux Dedicated Server Build Support	103.71 MB	417.89 MB

Install

Figure 25-2. The "Add modules" menu of Unity Hub is shown, scrolled down to show the Build Support modules

The **"PLATFORMS"** header shows all the different Build Support modules you can install. Simply select the ones you want, then click the Install button in the bottom-right corner and follow any further instructions the Unity Hub provides.

The remaining fields in the Build Settings aren't particularly relevant to the everyday user. All you should need to do is just click one of the two buttons in the bottom-right corner: Build or Build And Run, the only difference being whether or not the built project will be automatically executed when it finishes. Before building can begin, you'll have to select a folder to store the built project in. Unity will generate the necessary files within that chosen folder. I'd recommend keeping a specific folder with just the built project in it and nothing else, just to ensure that Unity has a clean environment to store the build in.

Player Settings

The Player Settings can be accessed with the button in the bottom-left corner of the Build Settings window (also shown in Figure 25-1). They can also be reached through Edit ➤ Project Settings and then by clicking Player in the listings on the left.

Player Settings relate to the built program. There are fields for a variety of different settings, but most of it doesn't really concern your average hobbyist user, and when you hit the point that it does concern you, there are plenty of places to learn about it. The most important area to look at is the **Resolution and Presentation** section, displayed in Figure 25-3.

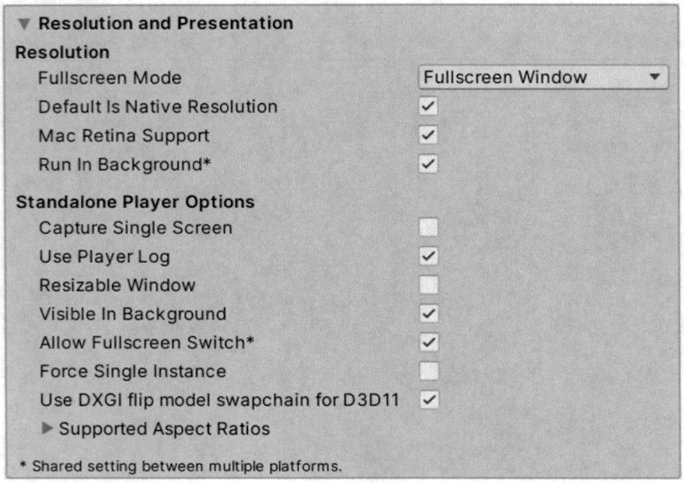

Figure 25-3. *The Resolution and Presentation section of the Player Settings when building for Windows*

Here's a quick overview of the fields that may interest you in this section – note that some may be slightly different if you're building to Mac or Linux:

- **Fullscreen Mode**

  Defines the default display for the window. Is it fullscreen or windowed by default? If it's windowed, it will be a movable window that is not fullscreen (not a "windowed fullscreen").

- **Default Is Native Resolution**

  If this box is checked, the game window will use the resolution of the user's computer by default. If you uncheck the box, two extra fields will appear, allowing you to set the default height and width of the game window yourself.

  If you've set Fullscreen Mode to Windowed, this field won't show, because you'll have fields for the window width and height already.

- **Run In Background**

  Check this box if the game logic (your scripts, physics, etc.) should continue to operate even when the user minimizes the window or loses focus on it. Alternatively, if the box is unchecked, the game will pause (freeze in place) whenever the user minimizes it. If it's windowed, it'll freeze in place when the user loses focus by clicking outside the window.

- **Resizable Window**

  If this box is checked, the window can be resized by the user clicking and dragging on the corners or edges. If it's not checked, the window will be stuck in the default size you've specified.

- **Force Single Instance**

  If checked, only one instance (window) of the game can be run at any time. Attempting to run a second one will simply bring focus to the already-running instance instead.

Aside from these features, there's also the option of defining a custom splash screen in the **Splash Image** folding section of the Player Settings, just beneath the Resolution and Presentation. The splash screen is a sequence of graphics that pop up when the game first runs, usually showing the logo of involved companies. You've probably seen this in games you've played before.

By default, your game will have a splash screen of the Unity logo, lasting a couple of seconds. If you're using the free license of Unity, you cannot disable this – you don't get a state-of-the-art game engine for free without giving a little credit! You can, however, add your own logos to the splash screen, customize the background color, and add a background image. Of course, this is probably not of much concern to you at this stage – but do remember that, if you want to lose the official Unity splash screen when your game runs, you have to have a paid version of Unity.

Recap

This project has been a great, big series of firsts, each one making you more comfortable and equipped with programming in Unity. Before we move on to the next project, let's take a quick overview of what major concepts we learned to use in this one:

- Moving with a **CharacterController** component, which we used for our player character.

- Moving with the simple **"Transform.Translate"** method, which we used for our projectiles.

- Turning a number value from "per frame" to "per second". If you want to move X units per second, move by "X ∗ Time.deltaTime" per frame.

- Slerping and Lerping positions, rotations, and float values. This is pretty much just moving value A toward value B by a fraction of the distance between the two. We've used it for smooth rotation transitions and for moving one value to another over a given amount of time.

- Calculating the time since an event happened. When the event first occurs, set a variable X to the current value of **"Time.time"**. After, use **"Time.time - X"** to get the seconds that have passed since.

- **Invoking** methods to run code after a specific duration has passed.

- Calling the **"GameObject.SetActive"** method to activate and deactivate GameObjects through code.

- Using a basic enum to depict the state of an object, then changing the way they behave based on this state.

- Calling the **"Random.Range"** method to generate a random value between two given numbers.

- How a **pivot point** can affect the scaling of a Transform.

- How to use **arrays** and **Lists**, and how to use a **"for" loop** to operate on each item in an array/List.

Additional Features

Now that you've got all this newfound experience, you can always add features to the project yourself. Thinking your way around a problem on your own is a great way to develop yourself as a programmer. Even if you bite off more than you can chew and attempt something too difficult, you're probably going to pick up at least a few tidbits of information that make you more knowledgeable – and who knows, they might help you solve a different problem in the future.

Striking out on your own to implement a feature in a game project doesn't mean you have to do it independently. A few Internet searches can make all the difference when it comes to solving problems or coding up new mechanics.

Getting an error message that doesn't make sense to you? Use your favorite search engine and type the error message out (you can even select an error in the Unity Console window and press Ctrl+C to copy the whole message). Chances are you'll find other people making a similar mistake to the one you've made, asking others for help figuring it out, and there you may find your answer.

Unsure how to go about implementing something? Search for it, and so long as it's not a particularly niche mechanic, you'll likely be able to find a guide or tutorial for it.

Dealing with a component type you're not used to? Search for it, and Unity's documentation page will likely be one of your first results. You can see all of the members of any built-in class and read the descriptions for individual variables or methods. Knowing what sort of relevant data and methods are at your disposal is often one of the first steps when it comes to planning your code. Unity's documentation also has manual pages that describe specific component types and concepts in a less technical and more guided way.

In this day and age, the information you need is probably just a couple well-chosen search terms away.

If you ever run into trouble that you can't seem to think your way around and you can't find a solution online, you can either set it down and come back to it when you've gotten better (there's no shame in this!) or head to some online community and ask for help with your particular problem.

If you're going to ask others for help, be thorough. You don't want your question to generate more questions! Describe what you're trying to accomplish, what's in your scene, and what's happening that you're trying to fix. If code is involved, copy-paste any of it that relates so others can check it for errors – particularly the subtle ones you may not have noticed.

Sometimes, the act of trying to describe your problem with enough detail that someone else may be able to solve it for you is enough to help you realize what's going wrong. One day, you'll realize you've gotten so good that you don't need other people's help. You're good enough at finding the answer yourself that you solve the hurdles before you ever hit the point of asking for help. Or perhaps the problems you face will be deep enough that properly explaining them so others can help is more trouble than figuring it out yourself.

I'll give you some ideas for features you might want to add to this project on your own:

- **Teleportation**

  Two teleporter pads are placed on the ground at different locations. Touch either one, and you'll get warped to the location of the other. Use an Inspector reference to the Transform of the other teleporter pad to link them together. That way you can move them around – even in-game – and it'll still work.

- **Checkpoints**

  Larger levels can have checkpoints spread throughout them. When the player touches the checkpoint, they unlock it, making it the current checkpoint. Whenever they die, they respawn at the current checkpoint (if they have one unlocked). Just make sure the player can't go back and unlock an earlier checkpoint by touching it again!

- **Lives**

  Give the player a limited number of lives. Whenever they die, take a life away. If they run out of lives, kick them back to the main menu and make them feel bad by telling them they're a loser. This way, they can lose their progress earned by reaching new checkpoints. Consider also rewarding them with more lives when they reach a new checkpoint.

If you're tired of doing what I say, don't be afraid to try to implement something that you think would be fun or interesting. You're likely to learn something in the process.

Or just keep following the book and save that for after!

Summary

In this chapter, we've handled some loose ends, leaving us ready to set aside our first example project and move on to the next. We learned how to use the Build Settings window to build our project, and we learned about the Player Settings window, which contains properties relating to the appearance and behavior of our project once it is built.

Next, we'll move on to a project that will give you plenty of practice working with object-oriented programming concepts like inheritance.

PART IV

■ ■ ■

Tower Defense

CHAPTER 26

■ ■ ■

Tower Defense Design and Outline

It's time to start our next project – a little tower defense game. We'll get some practice using inheritance, learn how to perform basic pathfinding for our enemy AI, get some experience with collision detection through scripts instead of colliders, and learn to use the Unity UI (uGUI) system, where we build our UI using GameObjects and components, rather than solely through code like we did in our last project.

Gameplay Overview

If you're unfamiliar with the genre, a *tower defense* is a game where the player places structures (towers) on the playing field which defend against oncoming enemy attackers, usually by automatically firing projectiles at them, like arrows and cannons and magic. One level at a time, enemies spawn in at a certain location and attempt to navigate their way to their goal. Whenever an enemy reaches the goal, you lose a life. This is sometimes referred to as "leaking." Once you lose all of your lives, you lose the game. Using money gathered from winning levels and slaying enemies, you build more and more towers to prevent enemies from leaking and to stay in the game.

Our tower defense will have a simple setup: the playing field is a rectangle, longer than it is wide, with the player camera hovering over it and pointing down at it, a camera orientation much like in our first project.

Enemies spawn at the top of the playing field – the **spawn point** – and navigate to the bottom, the **leak point**. Your towers sit between them and their goal. They will navigate around your towers using basic Unity **pathfinding**, which is the act of finding a route around all obstacles without touching or passing through them. Certain levels will instead have **flying enemies** which simply go over all our towers, no pathfinding involved, making them more challenging than normal enemies.

Our towers can be positioned to route enemies along specific paths, particularly in the interest of keeping them in range of our strongest towers for a longer duration. This is sometimes called **"mazing"** – the player will try to build an ideal maze that keeps the enemies in the right places for the longest time possible. Figure 26-1 shows the finished project with a small maze set up and some ground enemies navigating through it.

© Casey Hardman 2024
C. Hardman, *Game Programming with Unity and C#*, https://doi.org/10.1007/978-1-4842-9720-9_26

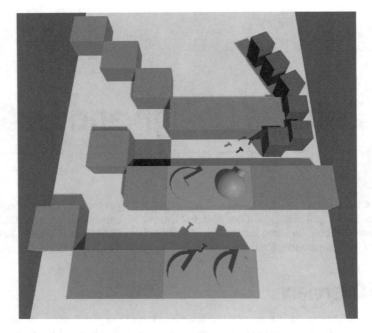

Figure 26-1. *Ground enemies resembled by red cubes navigate through our maze while our arrow and cannon towers (blue) fire at them. The basic pale-brown cubes are barricades used to cheaply expand the maze*

The game will transition back and forth between two states:

- **Build mode**, where there are no enemies spawning and the player can purchase and sell towers

- **Play mode**, where a round of enemies will spawn in sequence, one after the other, and attempt to reach the leak point

The game will start in build mode so the player can construct their first towers. Once the player is ready to begin the level, they must click a "Play" button. At this point, we perform our pathfinding to check what route the enemies will take to reach the goal. If pathfinding cannot find a route through the towers, the player will be warned, and they won't be able to start the level. Otherwise, if the player hasn't blocked the path, we enter play mode.

Play mode will spawn the enemies, each one following closely behind the last. The level ends as soon as all the enemies have either been slain or have leaked. If the player's health has dropped to 0 or below during this level, we gently break the news that they've lost. Otherwise, we enter build mode again, and the process can repeat itself.

Some tower defense games will have the enemies run through a path that the player can't build towers on – for example, the enemies might be down in a trench, while the towers can only be built on cliffs above. This solves the problem of the player being able to block enemies off with their towers and doesn't require any pathfinding. It's a game design thing, so I won't get into the differences between the two, but the concept of "mazing" isn't really a thing if you don't allow the enemies to mingle with the towers like we will. We want some practice with pathfinding anyway, so our method will suit us well.

The player earns money to build more towers as they slay enemies, as well as a chunk of extra money at the end of each round.

We'll implement a small variety of tower types:

- **Arrow Towers**, which rapidly fire a seeking projectile at a single targeted enemy at a time. Their projectiles are guaranteed to hit the target, homing in on them constantly. They can strike both ground enemies and flying enemies alike.

- **Cannon Towers**, which fire arcing projectiles at the ground where their target stands. Their projectiles deal damage in a radius, capable of hurting multiple enemies at once, but move slower and can be inaccurate. They do not fire at flying enemies. Since they fire at the ground location of their target, they might not even hit a target if it is quick enough.

- **Hot Plates**, which are flat towers that do not block enemies, allowing them to walk right over. They constantly apply damage to all enemies who stand on them. They're worthless against flying enemies.

- **Barricades**, which do not attack, but act as a cheap means of building a maze for enemies to navigate through. They're a price-efficient means of keeping enemies in range of your towers. Again, these are worthless against flying enemies.

Technical Overview

We're going to get into some new concepts in this project. It wouldn't be worth doing if it didn't challenge us in some new ways, right?

The camera movement will be handled first, some rudimentary stuff that isn't far off from what we've already done. The player is nothing but a floating camera in this project, since they don't have one character they're controlling, but that camera must be able to move around the stage. We'll implement basic camera controls: arrow key movement, movement by dragging the mouse, and the option to scroll in and out with the mouse scroll wheel.

After that, we'll get our first taste of **pathfinding**. The process of pathfinding is a complicated topic, but Unity makes it a bit simpler for us. Luckily, that means we won't have to implement a pathfinding algorithm ourselves – although they can be a bit of fun if you're into that stuff. We'll learn how to work with this system to give our enemies a path around the towers.

We'll also learn the concept of **raycasting**. It's a means of detecting if a collision occurs along a given line, starting at one Vector3 position and traveling along a given direction for a given amount of distance. This can be useful in a multitude of ways, but we'll be using it to detect the point on the playing stage beneath our mouse cursor so that we can point and click to where we want to place towers. In other words, we'll use it to get the world position on the stage beneath our mouse.

After that, we'll get some practice using **inheritance**. We learned about it before we started making our example projects, but this is the first time we'll put it to practical use. Using inheritance, we can reuse logic that certain towers share while still maintaining flexibility that allows us to define towers that behave differently than others (hot plates) or towers that don't do much of anything (barricades).

Our projectiles will also have varying forms that benefit from inheritance: some will seek a target and be guaranteed to hit it, while others will arc and flop down on a targeted ground location. They're both still projectiles, sharing some logic, but they differentiate in specific ways that are implemented in their lower types.

For our enemies, we'll have a base type that defines general stuff – notably, their health and the process of dying – and we'll implement lower types to contain the logic of ground enemies vs. flying enemies.

In build mode, we'll create UI a bit more polished and complex than our GUI experience with our last project.

We'll also get some experience with converting positions to points on a grid. All towers will have the same size, and we'll only allow the player to place them along increments of that size. You can place them perfectly side by side, with no space between them, or you can leave an entire tower's space between the two – but you can't do anything in between. This will require a bit of math-related tomfoolery, but it's not boring math. It's programming math – the fun sort.

At the end of every round, we'll give the player money for making it through, and we'll scale up the strength of our enemies. We'll have levels with flying enemies every fourth round, learning how to use a new operator to detect when that occurs.

Project Setup

To get started, create a new Unity project through the Unity Hub, using the 3D template and naming it **"TowerDefense"** as shown in Figure 26-2.

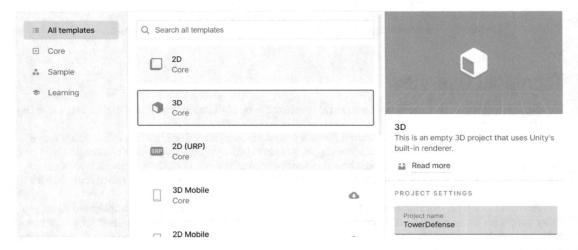

Figure 26-2. *Creating our project through the Unity Hub*

In the Project view, create folders for **Materials**, **Prefabs**, and **Scripts**, all inside the **Assets** folder, which should already have a Scenes folder inside it. While you're at it, rename the default SampleScene to **"main"**.

Summary

We've gone over how our project is expected to play and briefly considered the details of implementation. Simply put, it's a basic form of the tower defense genre with enemies spawning on one side of the stage and attempting to reach the bottom, while the player-built towers attempt to stop them. We'll explore a lot of important concepts in the making of this project, like inheritance, raycasting, and pathfinding, so let's jump right in and start implementing the pieces one by one.

CHAPTER 27

■ ■ ■

Camera Movement

The first thing we'll do for our project is get some camera movement in working order. The player has to be able to move around the stage to be able to see the whole thing, after all. We'll allow the player to move the camera with the arrow keys as well as by right-clicking and dragging with the mouse. We'll also provide the option to use the mouse scroll wheel to zoom in or out, which lets the player control how close their camera is to the stage.

All of the movement will be applied to a Vector3 variable called **"targetPosition"** instead of directly applying the movement to the camera Transform itself. We update this "targetPosition" vector with any changes in position we want to make to the camera. In every frame, we Slerp the camera toward that target position, allowing us to use the third parameter of the Slerp, the fraction of movement, to make the movement smooth and gradual.

It also makes it easy to restrict the camera to a certain area. Before we move the camera toward the target position, we'll ensure that each axis of the target position is within a certain range. We define variables for the minimum and maximum X, Y, and Z values we want to allow the camera within. By setting these, we can prevent the player from accidentally moving the camera so far away that they can't see the stage anymore and get lost in the endless void. It will also prevent them from zooming too far in or out.

Setting Up

With your default, main scene open, let's set a few things up before we get rolling on the code.

Create a Plane. Name it **"Stage"**. This will act as the floor. Set its position to (0, 0, 0) and set its scale to (7, 1, 20). I'll also create a material in our Materials folder, naming it Stage and applying it to the Stage GameObject. I'll give it a light-blue hex color of 9DE0F3.

There. We've designed our level, and it only took us mere seconds. We sure are talented.

Now let's set up the camera. The camera that comes with the scene by default will work. If you deleted it, just make a new one with GameObject ➤ Camera in the top toolbar. We'll rename it to **"Player Camera"** and have it positioned over the level, pointing down at it with a slight upward angle so it's not pointing straight down. A Y position of 54 will work just fine. We'll use an X rotation of 70. An X rotation of 90 will point straight down, so we just skew it 20 degrees off to give it that little tilt we want.

We'll make a **Player** script and attach it to the Player Camera GameObject.

You've been here before – let's declare the variables we're going to use in our Player script, and then go over any whose Tooltip attribute doesn't describe them already:

```
[Header("References")]
public Transform trans;

[Header("X Bounds")]
public float minimumX = -70;
public float maximumX = 70;
```

© Casey Hardman 2024
C. Hardman, *Game Programming with Unity and C#*, https://doi.org/10.1007/978-1-4842-9720-9_27

```
[Header("Y Bounds")]
public float minimumY = 18;
public float maximumY = 80;

[Header("Z Bounds")]
public float minimumZ = -130;
public float maximumZ = 70;
[Header("Movement")]

[Tooltip("Distance traveled per second with the arrow keys.")]
public float arrowKeySpeed = 80;

[Tooltip("Multiplier for mouse drag movement. A higher value will result in the camera
moving a greater distance when the mouse is moved.")]
public float mouseDragSensitivity = 2.8f;

[Tooltip("Amount of smoothing applied to camera movement. Should be a value between 0
and .99.")]
[Range(0, .99f)]
public float movementSmoothing = .9f;

//Current position the camera is moving towards:
private Vector3 targetPosition;

[Header("Scrolling")]
[Tooltip("Amount of Y distance the camera moves per mouse scroll increment.")]
public float scrollSensitivity = 1.6f;
```

First, we have the ever-familiar "trans" reference. This is all our camera will need to reference.

Next, we declare the minimum and maximum values to clamp our camera's position within, for each of the three axes. The Y axis will clamp our zooming in and out with the mouse scroll wheel, while the X and Z axes will clamp our movement either by right-clicking and dragging the mouse or by using the arrow keys.

The **"movementSmoothing"** determines what value we pass as the third parameter to our Slerp method: the fraction of distance we'll be moving the camera toward its target position each frame. A higher value will cause *more* smoothing, because the fraction we're actually going to pass for the third parameter is (1 - movementSmoothing), meaning our fraction of movement gets smaller (less movement per frame) as the smoothing gets higher. I'll explain further when we implement it.

You'll notice we have this new "Range" attribute declared above the "movementSmoothing" variable. This will change how the variable looks and behaves in the Inspector. We give this attribute the parameters 0 and 0.99f.

As always, the variable will show its current value in a field in the Inspector and allow us to type into the field to set a specific value. However, it will also show a slider bar that can be clicked and dragged to set the value within the range – anywhere between 0 and 0.99f. Most importantly, Unity will clamp the value between the given range, whether you use the slider bar or type in a value directly. This is nice for us, because as we'll discuss a bit later, we never want our "mouseSmoothing" value to go outside the range of 0 and 0.99f.

The **"targetPosition"** is what will actually be moved by our arrow keys, mouse dragging, and mouse wheel scrolling. After we ensure that it is within the bounds we declared earlier – the minimum and maximum X, Y, and Z values – we then Slerp the camera toward it, applying the "movementSmoothing" while we do so.

Now, save the changes to the script, go to the script component on the Player Camera GameObject, and set that "trans" reference so the camera is ready for testing as we implement its features.

We'll start by defining the methods we'll be calling to make things work. We'll use Start and Update, and we'll have some private methods that are called in Update. Just like with our Player script from the first project, we'll be doing this simply to split the code up into neat blocks, keeping things clean and separating the code by the feature it is implementing.

After we declare the methods, we'll write each one, one at a time. For now, though, we'll just leave them empty and make sure we're calling them in Update:

```
void ArrowKeyMovement()
{

}
void MouseDragMovement()
{

}
void Zooming()
{

}
void MoveTowardsTarget()
{
}

//Events:
void Start()
{

}
void Update()
{
    ArrowKeyMovement();
    MouseDragMovement();
    Zooming();
    MoveTowardsTarget();
}
```

This maps out our overall process. Just looking at the Update method, you can see how we plan on running things. With the methods named like they are, it practically spells itself out in plain English:

- First, check **arrow key movement**. If the player is pressing any arrow keys, the movement is applied to our "targetPosition" variable.

- Then add **mouse drag movement** to the "targetPosition" as well, checking if the player is holding right-click and moving their mouse.

- Now add up and down movement caused by **zooming**. In world directions, this movement is up and down, so the Y axis, but if you're looking through the camera, it's like going forward or back, since the camera is pointing down at the stage. We're calling it zooming because it gives the player a closer or further view of the stage.

- At last, we **move the camera toward the "targetPosition"**. We know the target position has been updated to match whatever input the player gave last, whether it be arrow key movement, mouse movement, or scrolling to zoom. Now we just restrict the target position to the bounds and then Slerp the camera toward the target position.

Arrow Key Movement

To implement the arrow key movement, we'll write a simpler take on the code we wrote for the player movement of our first project. We use the "Input.GetKey" method to check if a key is pressed and apply movement directly to the "targetPosition" if it is.

Before we get started, one thing that might slip the mind is that our target position is going to default to (0, 0, 0), since we declared it as a private Vector3 and assigned no value to it. This means the camera will always initially try to move to the world position (0, 0, 0) at the start of the game. To remedy that, all we need to do is set the target position to the camera position **in our Start method**:

```
void Start()
{
    targetPosition = trans.position;
}
```

This makes it so that whatever position we place the Player Camera at in the scene is the position it will start at.

Now, add this code **inside the ArrowKeyMovement method**:

```
//If up arrow is held,
if (Input.GetKey(KeyCode.UpArrow))
{
    //...add to target Z position:
    targetPosition.z += arrowKeySpeed * Time.deltaTime;
}
//Otherwise, if down arrow is held,
else if (Input.GetKey(KeyCode.DownArrow))
{
    //...subtract from target Z position:
    targetPosition.z -= arrowKeySpeed * Time.deltaTime;
}
//If right arrow is held,
if (Input.GetKey(KeyCode.RightArrow))
{
    //..add to target X position:
    targetPosition.x += arrowKeySpeed * Time.deltaTime;
}
//Otherwise, if left arrow is held,
else if (Input.GetKey(KeyCode.LeftArrow))
{
    //...subtract from target X position:
    targetPosition.x -= arrowKeySpeed * Time.deltaTime;
}
```

That'll do it. The "targetPosition" will have the arrow key movement applied to it, using "arrowKeySpeed" multiplied by "Time.deltaTime" to ensure it's "per second" instead of "per frame." For the up arrow, we apply positive Z movement; for the down arrow, we apply negative Z movement. Since our camera is pointing down at the stage from above, forward (positive Z) will move us up relative to the stage, and vice versa for backward (negative Z). This is much like our Player in the obstacle course project, only we aren't tracking velocity – we're just relying on Slerping toward our target position to keep things smooth for us.

The movement won't actually apply yet, though. Let's remedy that so we can test our features as we implement them.

Applying Movement

To apply the movement, we'll simply clamp each axis of our target position (X, Y, and Z) between the minimum and maximum values and then Slerp the camera position toward the target position.

Rather than using if and else blocks and clamping the value between a minimum and maximum ourselves, which would take multiple lines of code for each axis, we can use the "Mathf.Clamp" static method which takes three number parameters – the value, the minimum, and the maximum:

- If the **value** is below the **minimum**, the **minimum** is returned instead.

- If the **value** is above the **maximum**, the **maximum** is returned.

- Otherwise, if **value** is somewhere between, it is returned back to us unchanged.

Add this code **in the MoveTowardsTarget method**:

```
//Clamp the target position to the bounds variables:
targetPosition.x = Mathf.Clamp(targetPosition.x, minimumX, maximumX);
targetPosition.y = Mathf.Clamp(targetPosition.y, minimumY, maximumY);
targetPosition.z = Mathf.Clamp(targetPosition.z, minimumZ, maximumZ);

//If we aren't already at the target position, move towards it:
if (trans.position != targetPosition)
    trans.position = Vector3.Slerp(trans.position, targetPosition, 1 - movementSmoothing);
```

We set each axis of our "targetPosition" vector individually, calling "Mathf.Clamp" for each one. This results in three pretty repetitive lines of code, the only difference in each one being the axis we refer to throughout: the letter X, Y, or Z. When you type this out, double-check it to make sure you're getting it right – don't copy-paste and change only some of the Xs into Ys or Zs. That can cause some pretty confusing behavior, and it's surprisingly easy to overlook!

Moving on, the movement is only applied if the camera ("trans.position") is not (!=) already where it needs to be ("targetPosition"). This is just to ensure we aren't moving when we don't need to be, to save a little processing power. When moving, we set the position to the result of our Slerp call. That call will move the camera toward the target position.

As mentioned before, the fraction we pass in as our third parameter in the Slerp call isn't just the "movementSmoothing" variable given as is. Rather, we give it "1 - movementSmoothing" to ensure that, when we increase the "movementSmoothing", we're making the fraction smaller, which means the movement occurs over a longer duration – less movement toward the target per frame. This just makes more sense, given the variable name: you would expect, when increasing a variable that claims to be the amount of smoothing, that it gets smoother as the value gets higher, not the other way around.

By doing "1 - movementSmoothing", we ensure that, if the smoothing is something like 0.8f, we get 1 - 0.8f. That's 0.2f – a low value, resulting in more smoothing. In other words, we're pretty much "flipping" the value around when we pass it to the Slerp call so that it behaves like you'd expect given the variable name.

At this point, you can probably see why our Range attribute was set to keep the "movementSmoothing" value at a maximum of 0.99f instead of 1. If the smoothing were allowed to be 1, then we would simply be giving "1 - 1" as the fraction, resulting in 0. This would mean the camera would never move at all! By giving it a maximum value of 0.99f, we ensure that we never accidentally break the movement that way. If you can predict some situation where your code keels over and breaks, you should probably not trust yourself to remember that it's possible and avoid it in the future – because you probably won't remember it. And then some months later, you'll break it. And then you'll spend two hours and a few pulled-out tufts of hair trying to figure out what went wrong. And kick yourself when you realize what caused the problem.

At this point, you should now be able to test our arrow key movement in-game. Try playing with the smoothing value through the Inspector and note the difference when it's lower or higher. A very high value makes the movement very slow and slippery, while a very low value makes it snappy at the risk of being somewhat unpleasantly jarring.

Mouse Dragging

The next step is implementing camera movement by dragging the mouse.

Add this code **in the MouseDragMovement method**:

```
//If the right mouse button is held,
if (Input.GetMouseButton(1))
{
    //Get the movement amount this frame:
    Vector3 movement = new Vector3(-Input.GetAxis("Mouse X"), 0, -Input.GetAxis("Mouse Y"))
    * mouseDragSensitivity;
    //If there is any movement,
    if (movement != Vector3.zero)
    {
        //...apply it to the targetPosition:
        targetPosition += movement;
    }
}
```

This first method call hasn't been used yet: **"Input.GetMouseButton"**. This is a simple one, much like "Input.GetKey". It checks if a specific mouse button is currently being held down. It uses an integer value as its parameter, identifying which mouse button to check:

- **0** is the **left mouse button**.

- **1** is the **right mouse button**.

- **2** is the **middle mouse button** (which can be pressed down for a click in most all mice).

This will return true while the right mouse button is held down and false while it is not. Again, much like "Input.GetKey", there is also a version that checks if the mouse button was just pressed this frame: "Input.GetMouseButtonDown".

We then declare a local Vector3 named "movement". We use another new Input method here: **"Input. GetAxis"**. This is a more general means of reading input, where you provide a string as the means of identifying which kind of input you're after. In our case, we use "Mouse X" and "Mouse Y". These return what we call the "delta" for the mouse position, which means "how much it has moved this frame from its position last frame." For example, if the user didn't move the mouse left or right on this frame, "Mouse X" returns 0. If they did, it returns some fraction representing how much they moved the mouse.

The values will work opposite to how we want them to affect our target position, though:

- **Mouse X** will be **positive** when the mouse cursor goes **right** and **negative** when it goes **left**.

- **Mouse Y** will be **positive** when the mouse cursor goes **up** and **negative** when it goes **down**.

If we apply it directly to the target position movement, we get an awkward result where the camera movement follows the direction of the mouse cursor. That's opposite to how you normally expect it to work when you drag your camera around in games like this. It sort of goes against the idea of "dragging."

That's why we have the "-" sign before each "Input.GetAxis" call. It flips the returned values around: if the delta was positive, it becomes negative, and vice versa. In other words, if the mouse cursor moves right, the camera moves left, and so on for the other directions.

If you'd like to see for yourself, you can take out those "-" symbols before the "Input.GetAxis" calls and try it that way. You'll probably feel all sorts of wrong trying to move your camera with the mouse.

The "movement" vector we create is also correctly mapping the mouse axes to the actual 3D direction we want to move our camera. Remember, we're operating on world direction here, not a direction local to the camera. Again, the Mouse Y isn't actually "up and down" in-game, since the camera is pointing down. To go "up" from the perspective of the camera, we really need to go forward in world directions. Thus, the mouse Y movement needs to correspond to the Z axis when we move the camera, so we provide it as the Z axis when we create the "movement" vector, and we leave the Y axis at 0 so that no movement occurs there – only zooming with the mouse scroll wheel will affect our Y axis.

After the vector is created, we multiply it by our "mouseDragSensitivity" variable, giving us an easy way to adjust the amount of movement the mouse generates for the camera. Since it's tied to a variable like this, we could later implement a way for the player to set this themselves, such as through an options menu in-game.

After this, all that's left to do is apply the movement to "targetPosition", assuming there was any movement. We check that the movement vector is not equal to "Vector3.zero" – which is just shorthand for "new Vector3(0, 0, 0)" – and if so, add the movement directly to the target position.

That's all we need to make this feature work. You can now test it out if you like. Note how changing the sensitivity variable affects the movement.

Zooming

To implement the zooming, we need to detect mouse wheel scrolling. We can do this with a new member of Input by the name of **"mouseScrollDelta"**. This is a Vector2, which is just like a Vector3 except that it only has X and Y axes – no Z. The X axis corresponds to the mouse wheel being pressed left or right, which some mice support (but not all of them). It'll be -1 if the wheel was ticked left or 1 if the wheel was ticked right. But we don't need that function. The Y axis is what we're after: it measures how much the wheel has been scrolled up (positive) or down (negative) this frame.

Like with the mouse dragging, that value doesn't correspond to the movement we want. We want to go down toward the stage – which means we need to decrease our Y position – whenever the mouse wheel is scrolled up. We want to go up – increase our Y position – when the wheel is scrolled down. The way it is by default, we'll do the opposite. Again, we can just fix this by inverting, or "flipping," the Y value with a "-" sign.

You'll see it in the following code, which you'll be writing **in the Zooming method**:

```
//Get the scroll delta Y value and flip it:
float scrollDelta = -Input.mouseScrollDelta.y;

//If there was any delta,
if (scrollDelta != 0)
{
    //...apply it to the Y position:
    targetPosition.y += scrollDelta * scrollSensitivity;
}
```

As is usually the case with operator stuff, we could accomplish the same "flipping" effect if we subtracted the "scrollDelta" from the Y axis instead of adding it, changing that "+=" into a "-=". It doesn't really make a difference how we do it, just so long as we make sure it gets done!

With that in place, we now have all of our movement options up and running: arrow keys, right-click mouse dragging, and scroll wheel to zoom in and out. It's all clamped with our bounds variables, keeping the player within view of the stage at all times, and we use some configurable smoothing to add that feeling of luxury.

Summary

This chapter got our player camera movement working, exercising some concepts we've worked with already and teaching us a few new tricks, primarily relating to detecting mouse input. Here's a rundown of things to remember:

- The **"Mathf.Clamp"** method takes three number parameters (int or float): a value to clamp, a minimum, and a maximum. It will return the value, but will clamp it to never be lower than the minimum or greater than the maximum.

- The **"Input.GetMouseButton"** method returns true if a given mouse button is being held on this frame. It takes an int value to identify which mouse button is in question: 0 is the left mouse button, 1 is the right mouse button, and 2 is the middle mouse button.

- **Input.GetAxis("Mouse X")** returns the mouse X movement on this frame: **positive** when the cursor moves **right** and **negative** when it moves **left**.

- **Input.GetAxis("Mouse Y")** returns the mouse Y movement on this frame: **positive** when the cursor moves **up** and **negative** when it moves **down**.

- The **"Input.mouseScrollDelta"** property returns a Vector2 (a vector with just X and Y values) representing mouse scrolling that has occurred on this frame. The **X axis** is **left and right** movement, which not all mice support, and the **Y axis** is **forward and backward** scrolling – the standard scrolling that all mouse wheels should support.

With that out of the way, we can focus on the core mechanics of towers, projectiles, and enemies in our next chapters.

CHAPTER 28

Enemies and Projectiles

In this chapter, we'll set up the basis for both our enemies and the projectiles our towers will fire. We'll be getting into some inheritance to do this. Since we'll have **ground enemies** that move around our towers as well as **flying enemies** that go right over them in a straight line, we need to make sure we have a base class for our enemies that provides the common functionality that both enemy types will need – notably, taking damage and dying.

Similarly, our projectiles will come in two different forms: **seeking** and **arcing**. This means we'll want also a base class for functionality that all projectiles share: dealing damage, traveling at some speed, and targeting a specific enemy that the tower fired the projectile at.

Layers and Physics

Before we begin, let's set up our layers and our collision detection matrix so they'll be ready to use later. We did this in the last project, too, so this will look familiar. Since we've got a good idea of how our game will play and what we're going to need, we can set this stuff up early to avoid having to go back to add more layers as we implement new features.

In the top toolbar, navigate to Edit ➤ Project Settings ➤ Tags and Layers. On the right side, under the Layers field (click it if it's not showing you any layers), add these four layers:

- **User Layer 3**: Enemy
- **User Layer 6**: Tower
- **User Layer 7**: Projectile
- **User Layer 8**: Targeter

By the end, it should look like Figure 28-1.

© Casey Hardman 2024
C. Hardman, *Game Programming with Unity and C#*, https://doi.org/10.1007/978-1-4842-9720-9_28

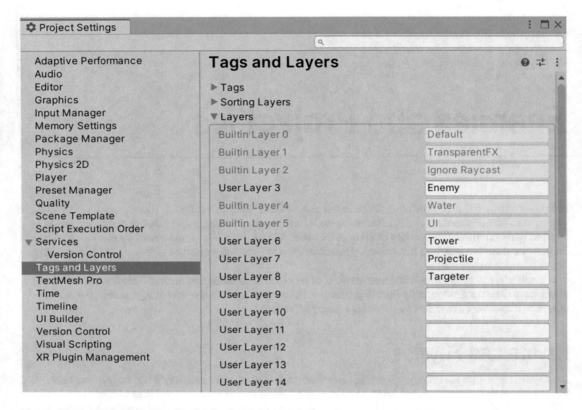

Figure 28-1. *Our layer settings in the Project Settings window*

While you've still got the Project Settings open, navigate to the Physics tab on the left to set up our collision detection matrix. If you forgot, it's how we make sure certain layers only collide with layers that relate to them. You'll find it by scrolling to the bottom of the Physics section, although it may initially be hidden. If you don't see it, it's probably folded up. Just click the "Layer Collision Matrix" field, which will be second to last, just above the "Cloth Inter-Collision" field.

We'll set ours up as shown in Figure 28-2. Targeters will be colliders that we use to detect enemies that come within range of towers, so we want them to only collide with the Enemy layer.

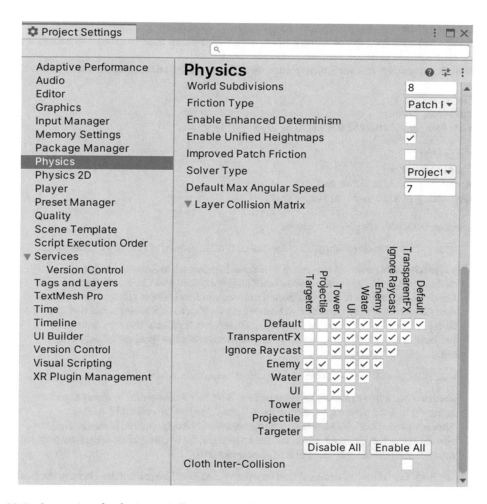

Figure 28-2. *Our settings for the Layer Collision Matrix field, found in the Physics tab of the Edit ➤ Project Settings window*

Aside from that, nothing else is that important. We'll make our Projectile layer only collide with Enemies and make our Enemies not collide with each other or with Towers. It isn't a big deal, anyway – we don't really plan on using collisions for this project. Our projectiles won't actually strike enemies as far as the collision system is concerned, because we're just scripting them to reach their targeted point and then disappear. Our enemies won't be stopped by collisions, since we're moving their Transforms directly along a predetermined path. But we'll set it up this way to be prim and proper.

Basic Enemies

For now, we'll be creating a **base class** for our enemies. This will hold logic that both ground enemies and flying enemies will use, but not the specific stuff that differentiates between them – notably, how they move. Every enemy needs to have health points and a means of taking damage. They'll also need to die when their health runs out. Since both types of enemies share this logic, we'll put that in the base class and implement their movement in separate inheriting classes. These inheriting classes are FlyingEnemy and GroundEnemy – but we'll be implementing them in a later chapter, so there's no need to make scripts for them yet.

Create an **Enemy** script in your Scripts folder, open it up, and let's declare some variables:

```
[Header("References")]
public Transform trans;
public Transform projectileSeekPoint;

[Header("Stats")]
public float maxHealth;
[HideInInspector] public float health;
[HideInInspector] public bool alive = true;
```

The first four variables are simple enough:

- **trans** – The ever-familiar quick reference to the Transform of the root GameObject.

- **projectileSeekPoint** – A reference to a Transform which will resemble what seeking projectiles should home in on. The Enemy script will be on the root GameObject, which will be positioned on the floor level, like we always do with our root GameObjects. We don't want homing projectiles to aim for our enemies' feet, though, so we want to expose a separate Transform, a child of the root, that our projectiles will aim for instead. This Transform is what the "projectileSeekPoint" variable will reference.

- **maxHealth** – Maximum amount of health an enemy can have.

- **health** – The current health the enemy has. We want our enemies to always spawn at maximum life, so we'll be setting their "health" to the "maxHealth" in Start. This is why we don't let ourselves set this variable in the Inspector, giving it the HideInInspector attribute. However, we keep it public so other classes can see how much health the Enemy has left if they ever need to.

Finally, we have the **"alive"** variable. When an enemy dies, we'll be calling the Destroy method to remove the enemy GameObject from the world. Sometimes, this doesn't necessarily happen instantly. It might take until the end of the frame (after all of our Update logic goes through) for the enemy, and thus its Enemy script and all of its other components, to be destroyed.

This means we might have a case where an enemy is technically dead, but not quite gone yet. Thus, we keep track of their state in this variable so we can always make sure they're actually alive before we do anything to them with other scripts, like towers. We can also use the "alive" variable to make sure they can't "die twice," so that if we wanted slaying enemies to give the player gold to buy towers, the enemy can't take damage again after dying (such as if two projectiles hit it in quick succession), causing it to give gold more than once.

As mentioned, we'll need the current health to be set to the maximum health in a Start method; otherwise, it'll stay at 0 all the time. Declare this method in your Enemy script:

```
protected virtual void Start()
{
    health = maxHealth;
}
```

This is a Start method, which means it behaves just like the normal "void Start()" method we've been using all along. However, we've given it two extra keywords before the "void".

We've heard of the **protected** keyword before, back in Chapter 9. It's used in place of **public** or **private** and means that this member can only be accessed by this class or any class which inherits from this class (and, technically speaking, other classes declared *inside* this class could also access its protected members). If we made it private, we'd be unable to access this method at all in the inheriting types we plan on declaring later, GroundEnemy and FlyingEnemy.

We've also briefly heard of the **virtual** keyword before, but we've waited on demonstrating it until now, where we can implement it with a proper use case.

The **virtual** keyword makes our method **overridable** by **lower types** (also called **inheriting types**). This means that a class which inherits from Enemy, such as a GroundEnemy or FlyingEnemy, can declare their own Start method that **overrides** this one.

Overriding a method allows the inheriting type to run its own logic when the method is called. The inheriting type can choose to call the upper type's method as well, or it can neglect to do so, completely overriding the method so that the inheriting type's code is the only code that gets to run when the method is called.

In other words, an inheriting type can determine if "Enemy.Start" should run first, then the inheriting type's "Start" code runs, or it can simply run its own code and totally ignore the "Enemy.Start" code.

This functionality is only possible if the method is marked as virtual – and the inheriting type has to have access to the method, which is why we made it protected instead of private. It could also be public, but we don't expect to have to call the method ourselves, and the Unity engine will call it on script startup regardless of its access modifier.

We'll see an example of how to override a method in a bit, but the point here is that we've made the method virtual to ensure that inheriting classes can still declare their own logic that happens on Start. Again, as a method named Start, it's still going to be called by Unity when the script is initialized. However, if we didn't make this method virtual, then declaring another method named Start in a script that inherits from this one would **"hide"** the original declaration. Only one of them would actually be called by Unity when the script is initialized – the lower type, the one that inherits from Enemy, would get called. Thus, we must declare the method as virtual to ensure that if one of our lower types wants to run their own Start logic, they can do so by overriding the method, rather than **hiding** it, which would cause the original Start not to run.

Again, we'll be overriding the method down the road, so we'll see exactly how the syntax looks.

Pressing on, let's declare a method in the Enemy script to make the enemy take damage. It's a simple method that takes life away from the enemy and then checks if the enemy has just lost the last of their remaining life. If so, it calls a second method, Die, which destroys the enemy and sets "alive" to false:

```
public void TakeDamage(float amount)
{
    //Only proceed if damage taken is more than 0:
    if (amount > 0)
    {
        //Reduce health by 'amount' but don't go under 0:
        health = Mathf.Max(health - amount, 0);

        //If all health is lost
        if (health == 0)
            Die();
    }
}
public void Die()
```

```
{
    if (alive)
    {
        alive = false;
        Destroy(gameObject);
    }
}
```

We don't allow the "amount" of damage to be under 0 so that we never accidentally "heal" an enemy by dealing negative damage. Aside from that, we use the "Mathf.Max" method again, decreasing the enemy health, but never letting it go beneath 0, since Max will return the highest of the two given parameters, so if "health - amount" is a negative value, Max will return 0 instead.

Again, we don't want to ever "kill the enemy twice," so we make sure they're alive before we proceed to Destroy the GameObject that the Enemy script is attached to, acquired with the "gameObject" member that all scripts have access to. The "gameObject" will be the root GameObject of the enemy, since that's what we'll be attaching the Enemy script component to.

Of course, we also mark their death by setting "alive" to false, preventing that "dying twice" scenario.

All that's left now is to create a temporary enemy to test with. We'll replace it with a more specific version down the road, but for now, we just want something we can test the Enemy script out on once we've got a tower to work with:

- Create an empty GameObject named **"Test Enemy"**. Position it anywhere on the Stage, keeping its Y value at 0.

- Add a Rigidbody, mark it as **kinematic**, and add a Box Collider. Set the collider **Size** to (5, 8, 5) and set its **Center** to (0, 4, 0). Do **not** check the Is Trigger checkbox in the collider.

- Add a Cube child to the Test Enemy. Remove its Box Collider component; we want the collider to be on the root only. Set its scale to the same size we gave the root's collider: (5, 8, 5). Set the local Y position to 4. It should now be covered by the collider. This collider is how our towers will detect when enemies come within firing range.

- Add the Enemy script to the Test Enemy. Assign the "trans" reference to the Test Enemy's Transform, and assign the "projectileSeekPoint" reference to the Cube Transform. This will make projectiles home in on the center of the cube; if we had made it the root Transform, they'd home in on the very bottom of the cube. Set the "maxHealth" to 12.

- I'll make an Enemy material and apply it to the Cube, giving it a dark orange color with a hex value of D0582D.

- Change the Test Enemy layer to Enemy, and agree to change the layer of its children, too.

- Make a prefab out of the Test Enemy in your Prefabs folder.

Projectiles

To implement projectiles, we'll be using inheritance again to declare a base Projectile class and then two separate subtypes: **SeekingProjectile** and **ArcingProjectile**. Every projectile deals a certain amount of damage, travels at a certain speed, and targets a certain Enemy that's being fired at. The difference is how they move and how they inflict that damage.

Seeking projectiles home in on the target enemy's "projectileSeekPoint" Transform, which we made a public reference to in the Enemy script for just this purpose. They move at a set speed, directly toward that point, until they reach it. Once they reach it, they damage the enemy and destroy themselves.

Arcing projectiles lock in their target location as soon as they are spawned. They aim for the base Enemy Transform, which is on the level with the Stage, because we want them to look as though they are being lobbed and landing on the floor, where they "blow up" (without any cool special effects, unfortunately) and deal damage to all enemies around that impact point. They won't be targeting flying enemies since they can't attack them by design, so we don't have to worry about how they react to enemies that aren't positioned on the floor.

Let's get started. Create a **Projectile** script. The first thing we'll do is add the **abstract** keyword to the class declaration line:

```
public abstract class Projectile : MonoBehaviour
```

This is an inheritance-related keyword. When we mark a class as **abstract**, we are implying that the class itself is not meant to have instances created and directly worked with. Rather, it acts as an upper type for more specific classes that inherit from it – but the class itself is never instanced directly. It merely serves as a base for other classes which share similar purposes.

Once you add the abstract keyword, save the script and go to the Unity editor. Try to drag and drop the Projectile script from your Project window onto a GameObject in your Hierarchy window. Once you drop it, Unity will give you a pop-up error message:

Can't add script behavior Projectile. The script class can't be abstract!

The class is abstract and thus should not be created directly. The only way to create an instance of a script class is by adding it as a component to a GameObject – but it's abstract, so Unity will prevent us from doing that. However, once we create our lower types, SeekingProjectile and ArcingProjectile, we'll make them inherit from Projectile without using the abstract keyword, so we will be able to add them as components.

As such, declaring a class as abstract not only makes it clear that it is not meant to be used as is, but also enforces that by preventing us (or others using our code) from misusing it at some point down the road.

Now let's write the contents of our base **Projectile class**:

```
[HideInInspector] public float damage;
[HideInInspector] public float speed;
[HideInInspector] public Enemy targetEnemy;

public void Setup(float damage, float speed, Enemy targetEnemy)
{
    this.damage = damage;
    this.speed = speed;
    this.targetEnemy = targetEnemy;

    OnSetup();
}

protected abstract void OnSetup();
```

First, you'll notice we have HideInInspector attributes given to our three variables. You might think that we would have the damage and speed variables show in the Inspector, but that's not how we'll be setting the values up. We don't want to tie the damage to our projectile script instances: we want the tower that spawns the projectile to set the data.

The variables explain themselves pretty well: the damage dealt on impact, the speed that the projectile travels per second, and the Enemy script of the enemy that the tower is firing the projectile at.

Next, you'll notice our intended method of applying our three variables to new projectiles: through this **Setup** method. It's like a constructor, taking a parameter named after each of our three variables and applying them with the "this" keyword. Since scripts don't have constructors, this is how we consistently apply the variables to each new projectile.

The Setup method will be called by the tower instance that fires the projectile, right after it Instantiates (creates an instance of) the projectile prefab. We want the towers to determine the damage and speed themselves. That way, we can have variations of towers which deal more damage or fire quicker projectiles, without having to create a separate projectile prefab with those settings on each one. For example, we might have a bunch of variations of arrow towers, where each one gets stronger, gaining more damage and firing quicker projectiles – but they all use the same projectile prefab, because they all fire the same arrow. If we set the damage on the Projectile script itself, we'd have to make a separate prefab for the arrow projectile for each type of arrow tower.

Similarly, if we ever get to a point where we want to change a tower's stats on the fly in-game, we can do so: since the tower passes the damage and speed to each projectile it creates, as soon as we change the tower's damage and speed, any new projectiles it creates will reflect that change. This would be useful if you wanted to, say, implement a tower that strengthens all towers within a certain range of it by boosting their damage.

And finally, after setting our variables in the Setup method, we call another method: **OnSetup**. This is a method we declare just below, but it's different than any other methods we've declared so far. It's marked with the **abstract** keyword, just like our class, and it has no code block coming after it. It has no curly braces – just a method declaration and then a semicolon.

An **abstract** method is much like a virtual method. It can be **overridden** by **inheriting types**, but unlike virtual methods, an abstract method cannot provide its own implementation – which is why it has no code block after it. As well as this, an abstract method can only go in an **abstract class**, and any inheriting classes **must** implement the abstract method. Even if the inheriting class doesn't actually want to run any code when the method is called, it still must declare the method; otherwise, you'll get a compiler error.

So this OnSetup method we declare is a means of giving our lower types a method that they can override to declare their own logic for what happens after the projectile sets up. By declaring the method, we give ourselves something that can be called, but we don't specify any code to run when it's called. That's for our lower types to decide. It's something like an event, akin to the Start and Update methods Unity provides us, except this time we've declared it ourselves.

Our SeekingProjectile doesn't actually need this logic, but our ArcingProjectile will. It needs to be told when its "targetEnemy" has been set so that it can mark the position of the enemy as soon as possible. That's how it knows where it will land. If we tried to put that logic in a Start method, the "targetEnemy" would still be null because the Setup method doesn't get called until after the Projectile is created by the tower.

We'll see how to override the method later.

We also mark this method as **protected**, giving our lower types access to it, but not **public** because other classes shouldn't be able to call it – they have no reason to.

Now let's implement the projectiles our arrow towers will use. Create a new script named **SeekingProjectile**. First off, we need to make it inherit from Projectile, so change the script class declaration line to this:

```
public class SeekingProjectile : Projectile
```

The only difference from the default is that we've made it inherit from our Projectile script instead of MonoBehaviour, the base class for all scripts. Now our script has the same members as the Projectile script: "damage", "speed", and "targetEnemy". As we've established, the projectile will be Instantiated (created) by the tower that's firing it, which will then immediately call the Setup method to set those three variables, so we know that part is being handled for us (well, not yet, but it will be once we've made towers work).

At this point, we'll get an error in our code because we have inherited from Projectile, but we have not implemented the abstract OnSetup method that Projectile expects us to. We'll handle that in a bit – first, let's see the code that makes our projectiles move toward their targeted Enemy and damage them on impact.

Here's the code we'll start with in our **SeekingProjectile** script class:

```
[Header("References")]
public Transform trans;

private Vector3 targetPosition;

void Update()
{
    if (targetEnemy != null)
    {
        //Mark the enemy's last position:
        targetPosition = targetEnemy.projectileSeekPoint.position;
    }

    //Point towards the target position:
    trans.forward = (targetPosition - trans.position).normalized;

    //Move towards the target position:
    trans.position = Vector3.MoveTowards(trans.position, targetPosition,
    speed * Time.deltaTime);

    //If we have reached the target position,
    if (trans.position == targetPosition)
    {
        //Damage the enemy if it's still around:
        if (targetEnemy != null)
            targetEnemy.TakeDamage(damage);

        //Destroy the projectile:
        Destroy(gameObject);
    }
}
```

We want the projectile to travel toward the "projectileSeekPoint" Transform of their "targetEnemy" until they touch it, then they'll deal their damage and destroy themselves. However, if the enemy dies while the projectile is traveling, we want it to continue to the point the enemy was at when it died. We don't want every projectile targeting an enemy to just vanish when the enemy dies, after all – this would look strange.

To accomplish this, we store the enemy "projectileSeekPoint" position in our own "targetPosition" variable every Update call to keep track of where the Enemy was last positioned, as long as the "targetEnemy" is not null – it'll become null as soon as the enemy is destroyed on death. Since we're moving toward our own "targetPosition" variable instead of the "projectileSeekPoint" Transform of the Enemy itself, we'll keep traveling even if the Transform has been destroyed. In other words, even if the enemy has died, we'll always have its last position stored, so we always know what position to travel toward.

Now, this is all the logic we need for the SeekingProjectile, but as I said, if we save and check the Unity Console, we'll see an error message:

CS0534: 'SeekingProjectile' does not implement inherited abstract member 'Projectile. OnSetup()'

As we discussed before, this is because when an upper class, like our Projectile script, has an abstract method declaration in it, all lower types, like SeekingProjectile, must provide an implementation of that method. They *have* to override it. Even if they don't want to actually run any code in that method, they still must have a declaration for it.

The declaration will be quite simple:

```
protected override void OnSetup(){}
```

Just write that line under your variable declarations. We declare the same method, OnSetup, with the same protected access modifier, but this time we specify it as an **"override"**. This means we're declaring it as an override to a method by the same name in the upper type. We can write whatever code we want in our version of the method, and whenever OnSetup is called, our code will run. But we don't want to actually do anything in the method call, so we simply put an empty code block {} at the end.

That should do it. We can't test our projectiles until we have towers to fire them, but let's set up an Arrow prefab so it's ready to use in our arrow tower.

We'll create a very blunt-looking arrow out of two cubes:

- Create an empty GameObject named **"Arrow"**.

- Attach a SeekingProjectile script instance to the Arrow. Set the "trans" reference to point at the Transform of the Arrow.

- Right-click the Arrow in the Hierarchy and create a child Cube. Name it **"Shaft"**. Set its local position to (0, 0, .75) and set its scale to (.4, .4, 1.5).

- Create another Cube, this time a child of the Shaft. Name it **"Head"**. Set its local position to (0, 0, .625). Set its local scale to (3, 1, .25).

- Since our SeekingProjectile script simply deals damage when it reaches the enemy position, it doesn't need its colliders. You can remove the Box Collider components found in both the Shaft and the Head.

- Change the Arrow layer to "Projectile" and allow Unity to change the layers of its children, too.

- I'll create an Arrow material and assign it to both cubes, giving the arrow a deep red color with a hex value of E50A3E.

When you're finished, it should look something like Figure 28-3.

Figure 28-3. *Our Arrow GameObject*

With that, we can create a prefab for the Arrow and remove it from the scene. Unfortunately, we can't actually see it inflict some damage on an enemy until we have our Arrow Tower set up, but we'll be doing that in the next chapter.

Summary

We now have the basis for projectiles and enemies ready to go, and our first projectile type, the SeekingProjectile, is ready – we just don't have a tower to fire it yet, which we'll implement next chapter.

Some points to remember from this chapter:

- A class marked as **abstract** is meant to serve as a base class for others to inherit from. You can't create instances of an abstract class. You're expected to inherit from the abstract class and create instances of the inheriting class.

- A method declared as **virtual** can be **overridden** by lower types to allow inheriting classes to provide their own implementation of the method.

- **Overriding** a virtual method is when an inheriting class declares a method with the same name and return type as the virtual method, but with the **"override"** keyword before the return type instead of the "virtual" keyword.

- A method declared as **abstract** is like a virtual method, but it has no implementation of its own (no code block after the declaration), and it must be part of an abstract class. Any inheriting classes must declare their own **override** version of the abstract method, or an error will be thrown.

CHAPTER 29

Towers and Targeting

Now that we have enemies and projectiles ready to go, we need towers to fire at them. In this chapter, we'll implement the framework that all of our towers will use, including a system that allows them to detect nearby enemies to target with their projectiles. We'll also implement the Arrow Tower as our first tower, giving us a means of seeing our projectiles being fired at the enemies. This foundation will make it easier for us to implement the remaining tower types in a future chapter.

Targeters

We'll use a system where our towers have a "targeter" to detect enemies within range, which they use to determine which enemies they will fire at. Using trigger collisions, targeters will detect when enemies touch their collider, which can be a sphere collider or a box collider, and will store those enemies in a List. When enemies leave the collider, it removes them from the List.

Each tower will have a Targeter GameObject nested inside it, which is an empty GameObject with the collider attached, as well as the **Targeter** script we're about to write.

Towers will use a reference to their Targeter to figure out which enemy they want to attack next. Arrow towers and cannon towers will have targeters that cover their attack range and will use the list of enemies as a collection of valid targets. In the case of the "hot plates" we'll be coding later, they'll use a box collider covering just the area taken up by the plate itself and constantly drain health from enemies detected by the targeter.

To detect when enemies touch the Targeter, we'll use the **OnTriggerEnter** event, which we used in the first project as well (to code the Hazard script). This event will be called whenever a new collider enters our trigger collider.

Create a new script named **Targeter**. We'll only need two variables:

```
[Tooltip("The Collider component of the Targeter. Can be a box or sphere collider.")]
public Collider col;

//List of all enemies within the targeter:
[HideInInspector] public List<Enemy> enemies = new List<Enemy>();
```

First, we have a reference to the collider of the Targeter. The **Collider** type is the base class for Unity's built-in collider components. In our case, we expect it to be a **SphereCollider** or a **BoxCollider**. If you'll recall from Chapter 11, these components are both lower types of the Collider class (they inherit from it), so the Collider-type field can store a reference to them. That's the magic of inheritance, and we'll be seeing more of it later. You can always store an object, like a BoxCollider or SphereCollider, as a reference in an upper, "less specific" type, like a Collider.

A BoxCollider is more specific than a generic Collider. It uses the members of a Collider, but also adds its own members and extra functionality itself. However, we can still store it as a Collider, because we know that it has all the same members as a Collider. Nothing is going to go wrong if we access those members. It's guaranteed to have them. But if we want to access the members specific to a BoxCollider, we have to **cast** it to a BoxCollider, because once we store it as a Collider, the compiler is no longer sure exactly what type it is. You'll see an example of how all this works in a second, when we actually interact with the Collider.

Second, we also declare a **List** we'll be using to store all enemies that are currently within that collider. If you'll recall, Lists are like arrays, but we can add and remove items from a List on the spot, and the size of the List automatically updates whenever we do. When an enemy touches the collider, we add them to this List. When an enemy leaves the collider, we remove them from this List. We initialize the List as a new instance when we declare it. Since it's a List, not an array, we don't have to specify the size. It can store however many enemies we need it to store.

We also make it hidden in the Inspector. Lists can be serialized and thus shown in the Inspector to allow us to set them up with an initial collection of items. While this can be useful, we don't want or need it in this case. We want the List to be handled in-game by our code only.

We'll also declare a handy property that returns true if there are enemies within the Targeter or false if there are not. Declare this just **beneath our variables**:

```
//Return true if there are any targets:
public bool TargetsAreAvailable
{
    get
    {
        return enemies.Count > 0;
    }
}
```

Your first idea of how to implement this might be to do an "if" to check if the Count is greater than 0 and, if so, return true or else return false.

But the way we've done it works too – and in just one line of code. Remember, the > operator simply takes a number on each side and returns true if the left number is greater than the right. The operator is already returning a bool – the data type our property should return. We can return the result of that operator as is, no if's or else's required.

This property may seem redundant, but it's a nice way to make your code read like plain English. Whenever a Tower needs to ask its Targeter if there are any targets available, rather than typing "if (targeter. enemies.Count > 0)", we can just type "if (targeter.TargetsAreAvailable)". It makes it obvious what we're asking – granted, it was already somewhat obvious, but more clarity never hurt anyone!

Moving on, we want to automate the way Towers set their Targeter size. Towers which fire projectiles will have a "range" stat of their own. Rather than fiddling with the size of their Targeter colliders to depict their range, we'll just set that "range" variable and have our scripts automatically size the colliders based on it. For that, we need a Targeter method that can set the size based on range.

The BoxCollider and SphereCollider types have different means of measuring their size. BoxColliders have a **"size"** Vector3 depicting the width, height, and length of the box. SphereColliders instead use a **"radius"** float depicting the radius of the sphere – in other words, the distance from the center of the sphere to its edge.

The Collider type itself doesn't deal with the size at all, and that's the type we store our reference "col" as. As far as the compiler is concerned, a Collider doesn't have those variables. A BoxCollider has a **size**. A SphereCollider has a **radius**. But a simple Collider has neither. So we'll have to cast the Collider reference to a BoxCollider or SphereCollider – whichever it actually is – to be able to access the size or radius member.

Let's observe how we can do this – declare this method beneath the variable and property declarations:

```
public void SetRange(int range)
{
    //Try to cast to a box collider:
    BoxCollider boxCol = col as BoxCollider;

    if (boxCol != null)
    {
        //We multiply range by 2 to make sure the targeter covers a space 'range'
        units in any direction.
        boxCol.size = new Vector3(range * 2, 30, range * 2);

        //Shift the Y position of the center up by half the height:
        boxCol.center = new Vector3(0, 15, 0);
    }
    else
    {
        //If it wasn't a box collider, try to cast to a sphere collider:
        SphereCollider sphereCol = col as SphereCollider;

        if (sphereCol != null)
        {
            //Sphere collider radius is the distance from the center to the edge.
            sphereCol.radius = range;
        }
        else
            Debug.LogWarning("Collider for Targeter was not a box or sphere collider.");
    }
}
```

First, we check if the collider is a box collider, using the **as** keyword. This attempts to cast to the given type (BoxCollider), returning null if the type is not compatible. We store the result in a local variable so we can easily check if it is indeed null. If it's not null, we now have a reference to it as a BoxCollider, giving us access to its more specific members: notably, its size and its center, two Vector3 members. We've effectively told the compiler to look at it as a BoxCollider, not a Collider.

The same process goes for the SphereCollider. If the collider isn't a BoxCollider, we'll instead check if it's a SphereCollider. If so, we do the same method, this time in the "else" block so that it only occurs if we failed to find a BoxCollider. We do the cast, and if it was not null, we reach in and access the "radius" member.

Finally, if that cast also failed, then we use "Debug.LogWarning" to give a warning in the Console window so we can be alerted if we ever failed to set up the collider of a Targeter correctly.

For box colliders, we always give them a height value of 30 units, which should cover enough space above the Targeter to reach any flying enemies we have later on. The center has to be adjusted to shift the collider upward by half the height, so its bottom lines up with the Targeter instead of the Targeter GameObject being at the center, which would cause half the collider to stick through the stage. This way, we can leave the targeters at a Y position of 0, aligned with the floor, and their colliders will size and position themselves appropriately.

With that out of the way, we now have a means of setting up the Targeter range with a method, and it'll automatically work regardless of whether the Targeter was given a box or sphere for its shape. We'll call it once we get around to implementing the towers themselves. We'll use spheres for the range of arrow towers and cannon towers, but our Hot Plate will need a box as its range, to accurately detect enemies standing on it.

Next, we need to keep track of enemies, properly adding and removing them from our List.

We'll write the **OnTriggerEnter** built-in Unity event in our Targeter script, **beneath the SetRange method**:

```
void OnTriggerEnter(Collider other)
{
    var enemy = other.gameObject.GetComponent<Enemy>();
    if (enemy != null)
        enemies.Add(enemy);
}
```

This is much like our Hazard script in the first project. When a collider enters the Targeter collider, we declare the "enemy" local variable which attempts to grab an Enemy component from the same GameObject that the collider was attached to. We use the shorthand "var" for the variable type, just to save a few letters. You'll recall that the compiler knows that we're expecting to get an Enemy returned to us, so it figures out what type we want the variable to be when it sees the "var" keyword.

The GetComponent method will return null if the component was not found. We check if we successfully found an Enemy component and, if so, add it to the "enemies" List.

When we set up our Test Enemy GameObject, we made sure that the Collider was part of the root GameObject, not attached to the Cube within. This was to ensure that it's easy for us to grab the Enemy component. Since they're both on the same GameObject, we can reliably call GetComponent on the same GameObject that the collider is attached to. If we had the collider attached to the Cube, then it wouldn't detect the Enemy component at all, because that's on the root GameObject.

A very similar process will be used to remove enemies from the List when they exit the collider. We write an **OnTriggerExit** method and use the same means to look for the Enemy component, but this time, call the **Remove** method of our List instead of the Add method. You can probably guess that the OnTriggerExit event is just like OnTriggerEnter, only it happens when a collider leaves the trigger collider.

```
void OnTriggerExit(Collider other)
{
    var enemy = other.gameObject.GetComponent<Enemy>();
    if (enemy != null)
        enemies.Remove(enemy);
}
```

The Remove method will remove the given instance from the List if it actually exists in the List. If not, it simply does nothing.

With the targeted enemies being tracked, we can now implement a method that our towers can use to find the enemy that's closest to them. We can do this by looping through the enemies in the List, checking the distance between their position and the Tower position, and keeping track of which Enemy had the lowest distance. We'll use a local variable for the lowest distance we found so far and another local variable to store the Enemy who had the lowest distance.

But we have another problem to solve. If an enemy dies while inside the List, the List won't automatically remove them. The Enemy will become "null" in the List, but it will still be an item in the List, taking up an index. Thus, we must be ready to deal with null references when we loop through the items in our List. We'll have to remove the null ones from the List as we go.

This brings forth another problem. When you remove from a List while looping through the List, you must be conscious about the effect that will have on the indexes stored in the List. Every item in the List that's stored "ahead" of the removed item will be shifted back to account for the removed item. Their indexes all decrease by 1 point.

We'll go over an example of this. Here's a basic loop that goes through the List of enemies, storing the current Enemy in a local variable and either removing them from the List if they're "null" or doing some code on them if they're not null:

```
//Loop through enemies:
for (int i = 0; i < enemies.Count; i++)
{
    var enemy = enemies[i]; //Current enemy
    //If the enemy has been destroyed:
    if (enemy == null)
    {
        //Remove it from the list:
        enemies.RemoveAt(i);
    }
    else //If the enemy is still around
    {
        // [do something with the enemy]
    }
}
```

The **RemoveAt** method of the List is like Remove, but instead of taking an Enemy instance to remove, it just takes the index of the item we want to remove. This is faster than Remove.

This might look like a fine way of doing it, but it messes with our indexes and causes some unwanted behavior. Let's say, for example, our List has indexes 0–5, totaling six enemies.

Now imagine indexes 0, 1, and 2 go by with no problem, but then, when our "i" is at 3, we find an enemy that's null. We now have indexes 4 and 5 ahead of us, still left to operate on.

So we remove that enemy at index 3. Now the enemies ahead of it are shifted back by the List. Index 4 becomes index 3. Index 5 becomes index 4.

Our "i" is still set to 3. Our loop iteration finishes, and the "for" increments "i" by 1 again. We're now at an "i" value of 4.

We've completely skipped an item! The item that was at index 4 was shifted to 3, but the loop has just iterated past index 3 and moved right along.

The solution is simple enough. We just subtract 1 from "i" after we remove the item from the List. Then, the "for" loop will add 1 when the iteration finishes, and we end up back at the same index instead of skipping it.

With that complication settled, let's write our method. Add this method to the Targeter script:

```
public Enemy GetClosestEnemy(Vector3 point)
{
    //Lowest distance we've found so far:
    float lowestDistance = Mathf.Infinity;

    //Enemy that had the lowest distance found so far:
    Enemy enemyWithLowestDistance = null;

    //Loop through enemies:
    for (int i = 0; i < enemies.Count; i++)
    {
        var enemy = enemies[i]; //Quick reference to current enemy
```

```
        //If the enemy has been destroyed or is already dead
        if (enemy == null || !enemy.alive)
        {
            //Remove it and continue the loop at the same index:
            enemies.RemoveAt(i);
            i -= 1;
        }
        else
        {
            //Get distance from the enemy to the given point:
            float dist = Vector3.Distance(point, enemy.trans.position);

            if (dist < lowestDistance)
            {
                lowestDistance = dist;
                enemyWithLowestDistance = enemy;
            }
        }
    }

    return enemyWithLowestDistance;
}
```

The method will return an Enemy, or null if no enemies are in the Targeter. It takes a single Vector3 argument, which is the point from which we want to calculate distance. We'll be using the tower position as the parameter when we call the method, which should be the same as the position of the Targeter GameObject anyway, but by using the parameter instead of just using the Targeter position, we make sure we can call this method to get the enemy closest to any point we want, if we ever need to.

The **"lowestDistance"** is where we'll store the distance between us and the Enemy that, so far, is closest to us. We start it at Infinity to ensure that the first distance we calculate is guaranteed to be set as the lowest.

The **"enemyWithLowestDistance"** explains itself: whenever we find an enemy whose distance is lower than "lowestDistance", we'll update "lowestDistance" and store the Enemy reference here.

Once we've looped through all enemies and checked their distance, we'll be left with "enemyWithLowestDistance" storing the one that was closest. We then just return that Enemy.

The loop starts off in the standard way when looping through an array or List: "i" begins at 0 and increases by 1 until it matches the Count of the List. We declare a local variable "enemy" to store the current enemy, which we grab from the List with "enemies[i]".

We then check if the enemy is null, or (the "||" operator); if it is not null, we check if it's dead. Remember, the exclamation mark "!" flips the value of the bool: if it was false, it becomes true, and vice versa. Thus, "!enemy.alive" is equivalent to "enemy.alive == false".

We do the same thing as before to remove the enemy, but this time, we decrease "i" by 1 to account for the indexes shifting back, as we just discussed.

If the enemy is not dead, we calculate the distance between them and the given "point" parameter using "Vector3.Distance". We compare that distance to the lowest distance we've found so far. If this one is lower yet, we update our lowest distance and store a reference to that Enemy, which will later be returned.

This method will also automatically handle a situation where the method gets called, but there are no enemies in the List. It will return null instead of throwing an error. The local variable "enemyWithLowestDistance" will be initialized to null. The for loop will do nothing at all if the List has a Count of 0, so it gets skipped completely. Then, we return that variable, which is still null.

With that, our Targeters are ready for use in towers. We'll just use them as an empty GameObject with a trigger SphereCollider or BoxCollider attached, in the Targeter layer. They'll be children of our root Tower GameObject so they go wherever the tower goes.

We'll set one up after we've coded our tower logic.

Tower Inheritance

For this chapter, the only tower we'll be fully implementing is the Arrow Tower. However, we'll be using inheritance to set up a system where future tower types we create will be able to reuse the portion of functionality that they share with the arrow tower.

We went over the towers we expect to implement: the Arrow Tower, Cannon Tower, Barricade, and Hot Plate. Let's review the scripts we'll be declaring to resemble those towers and how we'll get the effects we want for each tower by using those scripts.

Tower

Base class for all towers. It's a normal script, inheriting from the script class MonoBehaviour.

It defines how much the tower costs and how much of that cost is refunded to the player if they were to sell the tower. A mere Tower script will do nothing to hurt enemies, but will block them, forcing them to walk around it. We'll use it for barricades, since that's their only purpose, but all other towers will use lower types inheriting from Tower to implement their damage-dealing logic.

TargetingTower

Inherits from Tower.

This is a tower with a Targeter reference and a range variable (which is an int), both set in the Inspector. The range variable directly corresponds to the size of the Targeter, and we'll set the Targeter to that size in the Start method of the tower (using the SetRange method we declared for Targeter).

We won't use this type directly for any towers, but the Hot Plate tower can inherit from it to use the Targeter as a BoxCollider that detects enemies touching the plate. The Targeter will be sized the same as the tower itself, which will be a thin cube on the ground. Since the hot plate script will inherit from TargetingTower, it can access the Targeter reference we declare, reaching into it to loop through all targets and "burn" them all on every frame. We'll just give its targeter GameObject a collider that only covers the hot plate itself, which will be a thin square the size of a normal tower.

This means most of our hot plate logic is already handled by our Targeter. All we have to do with the script is make it deal damage to all enemies currently detected by its Targeter.

FiringTower

Inherits from TargetingTower.

This is the script we'll use for arrow towers and cannon towers. The logic of targeting a single enemy that's within range and periodically firing a projectile at them is handled here. We'll automatically assign a new target enemy whenever the targeted enemy dies or gets out of range. The closest enemy within range is targeted whenever we need to find a new target. Of course, we'll use the Targeter reference inherited from TargetingTower to find the closest enemy using the GetClosestEnemy method we declared earlier.

As far as firing projectiles goes, we'll have a reference to the projectile prefab we want to spawn. All we need to do is spawn it at the tower "projectile spawn point" Transform position and call its Setup method to pass in the damage, speed, and target enemy provided by the tower. The rest is handled by the projectile itself. If it's a seeking projectile (for arrow towers), it will home in on the targeted enemy. If it's an arcing projectile (for cannon towers), it will arc toward the initial position of the targeted enemy and impact there.

Upper Classes

This specification handles all of our use cases. We've planned out the inheritance in a way that lets us reuse functionality that needs to be shared between towers. If we coded each tower type individually, we'd have to give each one certain members that they all share anyway: how much gold they cost, how much gold they sell back for, the Targeter reference used by all but the barricade, and so on. Instead, we just inherit from the correct type, and those members are automatically shared. Most importantly, any future code that deals with towers now has the base class, Tower, that it can interact with to resemble any tower.

Let's get to it. Create a Tower script and write this code in the script class:

```
public int goldCost = 5;
[Range(0f,1f)]
public float refundFactor = .5f;
```

All we're giving our base towers is a gold cost (how much money we must pay to buy the tower) and a refund factor, which is a float between 0 and 1 resembling what fraction of the "goldCost" you are paid back when you sell the tower. That is, the user loses "goldCost" money when they buy the tower. When they sell it, they get back "goldCost * refundFactor". So if the "refundFactor" is 0.5f, then the user only gets back half of the money they spent for the tower. This is a common feature in tower defense games. If we gave the player back all their money whenever they sold a tower, they might as well just pawn back all their cannon towers before facing an air level and then make arrow towers instead, since cannon towers can't attack air enemies. This mechanic fixes that, punishing the player a bit for selling their old towers.

Other than that, we have no scripting to do for a basic tower. They have no functionality in and of themselves.

Moving down the line, let's make a TargetingTower script:

```
public class TargetingTower : Tower
{
    public Targeter targeter;
    public int range = 45;

    protected virtual void Start()
    {
        targeter.SetRange(range);
    }
}
```

First, we make sure to inherit from Tower, not MonoBehaviour, in the declaring line of the class, after the colon ":". We declare a Targeter reference and a range. We declare a Start method and make it virtual to ensure that lower types are able to override it if they need to. In this method, we call the SetRange method for our Targeter, setting it up with the correct range value as soon as possible.

That's all we need for our TargetingTower.

Arrow Towers

Before we script our arrow tower, let's set the GameObjects up so we know the hierarchy we'll be working with. Towers will always be 10 units wide and 10 units long at the base. They shouldn't exceed this size. This consistency will help us later with pathfinding and placing towers on the stage, and it keeps everything looking uniform.

When you're done, the arrow tower will look like Figure 29-1.

1. Create an empty GameObject. Name it **"Arrow Tower"**. Set its layer to **Tower**.

2. Right-click the Arrow Tower and create a child Cube named **"Base"**. Scale it to (10, 6, 10) and set its local position to (0, 3, 0). This will put its bottom at the position of the root Transform, as we've been doing.

3. Right-click the Base and create a child Cylinder. Set its local position to (0, .6, 0) and scale to (.8, .1, .8).

4. Right-click the Cylinder and create a child Cube. Name it **"Barrel"** (even though it's quite rectangular). Position it at (0, 2.2, .3) and scale it at (.2, 2.5, .65).

5. Right-click the Barrel and create an empty GameObject child. Name it **"Projectile Spawn Point"**. Position it at (0, 0, .5) and leave its scale as is. This will be used to make projectiles spawn at the tip of the Barrel.

6. You can remove the default collider components that come with the Base, Cylinder, and Barrel. Our enemies are going to use pathfinding to navigate around the towers, and the pathfinding won't use the colliders, so we won't need them.

7. Create an empty GameObject named **"Targeter"** that's a child of the root Arrow Tower. Change its layer to Targeter. Give it a **trigger** Sphere Collider and a **kinematic** Rigidbody.

8. Add an instance of our Targeter script to the Targeter. Set the "Col" field to reference the Sphere Collider of the Targeter.

9. I'll make a Tower material and give all of the visual pieces (the Base, the Cylinder, and the Barrel) a low-saturation blue color with a hex value of 7598B0.

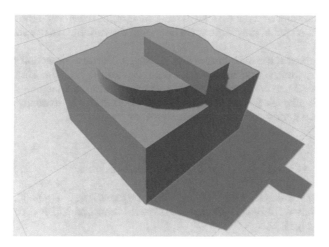

Figure 29-1. *Our Arrow Tower*

Let's move on and create a **FiringTower** script.

Be sure to change the declaring line to make it inherit from TargetingTower, and let's start with the variables:

```
public class FiringTower : TargetingTower
{
    [Tooltip("Quick reference to the root Transform of the tower.")]
    public Transform trans;
    [Tooltip("Reference to the Transform that the projectile should be positioned and
    rotated with initially.")]
    public Transform projectileSpawnPoint;

    [Tooltip("Reference to the Transform that should point towards the enemy.")]
    public Transform aimer;

    [Tooltip("Seconds between each projectile being fired.")]
    public float fireInterval = .5f;

    [Tooltip("Reference to the projectile prefab that should be fired.")]
    public Projectile projectilePrefab;

    [Tooltip("Damage dealt by each projectile.")]
    public float damage = 4;

    [Tooltip("Units per second travel speed for projectiles.")]
    public float projectileSpeed = 60;
    private Enemy targetedEnemy;
    private float lastFireTime = Mathf.NegativeInfinity;
}
```

You're an elite programmer now, so I'll let you read the tooltips to see what the purpose of each variable is. Even if you think you don't get it, don't fret. We'll be seeing the variables in use soon and going over how they're being used.

The two private variables at the bottom that don't have a tooltip are somewhat self-explanatory: the enemy we're currently targeting, which is the one we'll be shooting at, and the "Time.time" at which we last fired a projectile, which we'll use to know when it's time to fire our next projectile.

Our Update method will use a few separate methods to split the logic up neatly and reuse some of it. Let's start with that, to get a good overview of how it all works:

```
void Update()
{
    if (targetedEnemy != null) //If there is a targeted enemy
    {
        //If the enemy is dead or is not in range anymore, get a new target:
        if (!targetedEnemy.alive || Vector3.Distance(trans.position, targetedEnemy.trans.
        position) > range)
        {
            GetNextTarget();
        }
        else //If the enemy is alive and in range,
        {
            //Aim at the enemy:
            AimAtTarget();
```

```
            //Check if it's time to fire again:
            if (Time.time > lastFireTime + fireInterval)
            {
                Fire();
            }
        }
    }
    //Else if there is no targeted enemy and there are targets available
    else if (targeter.TargetsAreAvailable)
        GetNextTarget();
}
```

If there is a targeted enemy set, we then proceed to check if they are dead or otherwise outside of the tower's range. This is done with the trusty "Vector3.Distance" call, comparing our transform position to that of the targeted enemy. If the distance exceeds our "range" variable, we can't shoot that enemy anymore, so we call a method **GetNextTarget**, which will use the Targeter method GetClosestEnemy that we declared before to assign the enemy that should be targeted next.

Otherwise, if the enemy is alive and in range, we'll call **AimAtTarget**, which will rotate the portion of our tower that holds "the barrel" toward the target enemy. Then, we check if the current game time has gone over the time at which we last fired, plus the **"fireInterval"**, which is how long we want to wait between each projectile being fired. We've done this sort of thing before, so that's no big deal. We're calling another method we have yet to declare, **Fire**. That method will set **"lastFireTime"** to the current time and spawn the projectile.

Let's declare the AimAtTarget method. It's a little bulky, but simple enough:

```
private void AimAtTarget()
{
    //If the 'aimer' has been set, make it look at the enemy on the Y axis only:
    if (aimer)
    {
        //Get to and from positions, but set both Y values to 0:
        Vector3 to = targetedEnemy.trans.position;
        to.y = 0;

        Vector3 from = aimer.position;
        from.y = 0;

        //Get desired rotation to look from the 'from' position to the 'to' position:
        Quaternion desiredRotation = Quaternion.LookRotation((to - from).normalized,
        Vector3.up);

        //Slerp current rotation towards the desired rotation:
        aimer.rotation = Quaternion.Slerp(aimer.rotation, desiredRotation, .08f);
    }
}
```

The **"aimer"** will be set to the Cylinder on top of the tower, which is the parent of the Barrel, so the Barrel will spin with it too. We only want the Cylinder and Barrel to rotate toward our target and only along the Y axis, which spins without tilting it off the tower. Due to the way we set up the Barrel, it sticks out along the forward axis of the Cylinder. So as long as we point the cylinder directly toward the target enemy, the barrel will point there as well.

To make sure we're operating on the Y rotation axis only, we set up these two Vector3 variables **"from"** and **"to"** so that we can set their Y position to 0. Then we use them to get a direction to point from the "aimer" and toward the target enemy. By leveling their Y axis, we take it out of the equation. As far as the direction is concerned, everything is on the X and Z axes only – they're always equal on the Y axis, so that the "from" and "to" are never considered higher or lower than the other. This way, we don't look up or down at enemies, just outward, spinning in a circle atop the tower.

We use "Quaternion.LookRotation" to get the direction from "from" toward "to", as we've done before. You'll recall that LookRotation returns a rotation where the forward facing is pointing at the direction given as the first parameter, and the second parameter, "Vector3.up", is where the up axis should point. So we're saying "point the front of the cylinder at the target enemy, and keep the top pointing upward." If we did "Vector3.down" instead, the top of the cylinder would instead point straight down, which would flip it over.

We store that rotation in the **"desiredRotation"** variable. Then, we Slerp the "aimer" rotation toward that variable at a fraction of 0.08f per frame. This makes it nice and smooth.

Now we need GetNextTarget, which is just one line of code – but we need to use it twice, so why not make a method, right?

```
private void GetNextTarget()
{
    targetedEnemy = targeter.GetClosestEnemy(trans.position);
}
```

It just resets our **"targetedEnemy"** to the enemy that's closest to the tower. If there is no enemy within range, it'll return null, and according to the Update code, we'll wait until there are targets available before trying again.

Now, the most important bit is shooting arrows at the target:

```
private void Fire()
{
    //Mark the time we fired:
    lastFireTime = Time.time;

    //Spawn projectile prefab at spawn point, using spawn point rotation:
    var proj = Instantiate(projectilePrefab, projectileSpawnPoint.position,
    projectileSpawnPoint.rotation);

    //Setup the projectile with damage, speed, and target enemy:
    proj.Setup(damage, projectileSpeed, targetedEnemy);
}
```

We make sure to set the **"lastFireTime"** to the current "Time.time" – otherwise, we'd be shooting an arrow every single frame. We then spawn the Projectile instance using the Instantiate method, storing it in a local variable. The first parameter is the prefab to spawn, the second is the position to spawn it at (we use the Projectile Spawn Point position, at the tip of our Barrel), and the third is the rotation it should use (again, the same rotation used by the spawn point Transform, aligned with the Barrel).

This might seem a little off to you – we're Instantiating an entire prefab, but we're referencing just the Projectile script to do it. Remember, the **"projectilePrefab"** variable is of the Projectile type, not GameObject. Are we not just Instantiating a lonely Projectile script instance? Is that even possible? What would it be attached to?

Well, that's not what we're doing. Unity allows us to Instantiate prefabs and get back a reference to whatever part of them we actually want to interact with. When we Instantiate a script, we're really saying "I want to create this prefab, but when you're done, just return to me the Projectile script." This spares us having to call "GetComponent<Projectile>" after Instantiating the prefab.

You can do this with different component types, too – for example, you can store the prefab as a Transform variable if you need to interact with its Transform instead of its GameObject. It's just a little more convenient to have the Instantiate call return a reference to the component you want to interact with.

And as you can see, the reason we want to access the Projectile script is so we can easily call the Setup method afterward, passing in the tower damage and projectile speed and giving the projectile its targeted enemy.

That'll do it. Add a FiringTower script to the root Transform of our Arrow Tower, go over all the fields in the Inspector, and set the references we'll need. Don't forget to make a prefab out of the root GameObject. Figure 29-2 shows how the FiringTower script should look in the Inspector once you're done. We made the Arrow prefab in the last chapter, when we coded the Projectile script, and the other references point at the Targeter script on our Targeter child, and the Transform references we use in the script.

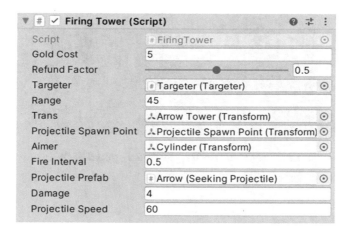

Figure 29-2. *A look at the FiringTower script of our Arrow Tower in the Inspector, with all the references correctly set*

Now you can put it all together and see it in action. Throw some arrow towers down with your prefab, or copy-paste the instances that are already in the scene. You can then use your Test Enemy GameObject that we set up in the last chapter – they won't try to get away, but as long as they're placed in range of the towers, they'll be shot and killed.

If your arrow towers aren't firing, make sure you've got everything in the correct layers: test enemies in the Enemy layer, towers in the Tower layer, and the Targeter of the towers in the Targeter layer. If you still experience problems, run through your script instances, like Enemy, FiringTower, and Targeter, and double-check that all of the references are set correctly. If you do find issues that you've fixed this way, be sure to apply those changes on the prefabs, too, so it doesn't happen again.

Figure 29-3 shows a setup with enemies and arrow towers in action.

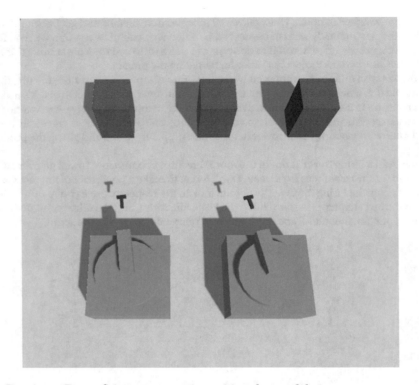

Figure 29-3. *Two Arrow Towers firing at test enemies positioned around them*

Summary

This chapter implemented our first tower type, the arrow tower, as well as the targeters that use trigger colliders to detect enemies within the firing range of the tower. Using inheritance, we've set a solid foundation for implementing the other tower and enemy types, setting us up for an easier time in the future. Next, we'll get some UI up and running to allow the player to build towers.

CHAPTER 30

■ ■ ■

Build Mode UI

In this chapter, we'll implement the user interface (UI) that shows during "build mode" to allow the user to buy new towers and sell old towers. Before we begin, let's outline the functionality we're going to implement. We'll go over what will they be able to do in build mode. After this, we'll do a quick primer of the important components and concepts behind Unity's UI. We'll then set up our own UI to look as it should in-game. In the next chapter, we'll implement the functionality of the UI, tying our buttons to code that handles building and selling towers.

Our finished Build Mode UI is shown in Figure 30-1. We'll be using **Unity UI** (also called **uGUI**) to design our UI out of GameObjects using appropriate components rather than coding using the GUI or GUILayout method like we did in our first project. Since the UI is a bigger part of the game this time, we'll put more effort into making it passable without creating any art for it ourselves. However, to keep the project from becoming unwieldy, we won't be making UI for a start screen or an in-game pause menu or anything of that sort. We did that in the first example project, and the tower defense project will function just fine for our purposes without it.

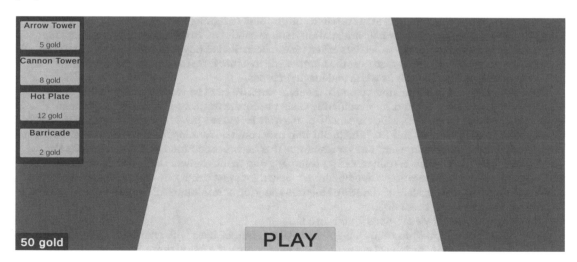

Figure 30-1. *End result of our Build Mode user interface*

The buttons on the left side are what we'll call the **build buttons**. Clicking any of these buttons will select the corresponding tower for building, and the button will change color to indicate that it is the currently selected button. One build button can be selected at a time, or none at all can be selected.

© Casey Hardman 2024
C. Hardman, *Game Programming with Unity and C#*, https://doi.org/10.1007/978-1-4842-9720-9_30

While a build button is selected, you can left-click the stage to attempt to build the tower at that location. Pressing Escape will deselect the button.

While there is no build button selected, you can instead left-click the stage to select an existing tower. This will show a little pop-up panel that provides us with an option to sell the tower. This panel will also have a little X button in its top-right corner that you can click to close the panel if you don't want to sell the tower – or you can press Escape. To continuously position this panel over the tower no matter how the camera is positioned, we'll learn how to convert a world position to its corresponding location on the screen – in other words, go from "world position" to "screen position." This way we can keep updating the location of the UI so that it always draws above the Tower.

Whenever a tower is bought, we'll use Unity's built-in pathfinding to check if the way is clear from the enemy spawn point at the upper end of the stage to the enemy leak point at the bottom end of the stage. If the way is not clear, we won't let the player start the level until they sell something to clear the path.

Build mode will be the initial state of the game when the player first starts playing. They'll start with some gold to spend on their first towers, and when they're ready, they'll hit Play. The enemies will spawn and move toward the leak point. Once all enemies are gone, we'll enter build mode again, and the cycle repeats.

In this chapter, we'll set up the UI itself, and in the coming chapters, we'll implement more and more of the features: building and selling towers, performing our pathfinding, and finally, entering Play mode to spawn enemies.

UI Basics

One could write an entire book about designing and implementing UI in Unity. This chapter won't go into that much detail, because that would be a very long chapter. We'll go over the basics of Unity's UI system and put it to use to make some basic buttons and panels. When we're done, our UI will be mapped out so we're ready to get it working with our code.

There are some considerations to make when you go about designing and implementing a user interface. You must ensure that the placement of elements is conducive to differing screen sizes and ratios.

A screen is made up of many small dots called **pixels**. Each dot is a tiny colored light on your screen. These many thousands of dots spread over the monitor will together form the picture that we see.

The **resolution** of a screen is its width and height in pixels.

Since different screens sometimes come in different sizes, we can't be sure just how much space we have to work with. Some monitors have a differing **aspect ratio**: the width-to-height ratio of a screen. Common HD monitors are 16:9, which means 16 pixels wide for every 9 pixels tall. Common resolutions for this aspect ratio are 1600×900 and 1920×1080. But your user could be running the game on a different aspect ratio, like 16:10, 5:4, 4:3, or some new ratio or resolution that becomes common after your game is released.

To deal with this, we have certain tools for positioning and sizing elements based on the screen width and height to ensure that there aren't any situations where things just don't show up on your screen. If you design your UI to have a constant, static size of 1600x900, any lower resolution will simply cut off part of your UI because the screen can't contain it.

We'll learn about Unity's solutions for this in a bit.

Unity's UI system represents each element of the UI as a GameObject with relevant UI components attached, depending upon the type of element. These elements can be found through **GameObject ➤ UI**. Remember, UI Toolkit is not the same thing: it's a separate feature for implementing UI.

We start with a **Canvas** GameObject. A Canvas will be the root of all of our UI: new UI elements we create will automatically be made children of a Canvas, and they must be a child of a Canvas in order to render. If you create a UI element without a Canvas in your scene, a new Canvas will be created, and the element you made will automatically be made a child of the new Canvas.

The Canvas represents the area that the UI is drawn in. Once you've created a Canvas, you'll see a white rectangle showing in your scene that resembles the Canvas. This is easiest to spot when you switch to 2D mode, accessed with the "2D" button on your Scene window toolbar, shown in Figure 30-2. It's also recommended to keep your Tool Handle Position and Rotation at **Pivot** and **Local**, shown also in Figure 30-2 (toggle these with the Z and X hotkeys).

Figure 30-2. *The Scene window with the Tool Handle Position set to Pivot, the Tool Handle Rotation set to Local, and 2D mode turned on*

Once you're in 2D mode, the Scene window will not allow you to use the Z axis, instead restricting you to the X and Y axes only, looking forward into the scene. This is ideal for editing UI, since it keeps a straight-on look at the Canvas. Similarly, if we were working on a 2D game, we'd keep this setting on all the time.

Create a Canvas with **GameObject ➤ UI ➤ Canvas**, then select the Canvas in the Hierarchy and press F to center your view on it. It will show a white rectangle that acts as the bounding box for all your UI. Any UI positioned outside of it will not be visible. As you add UI GameObjects to your Canvas, you'll notice that switching to Game mode allows you to see them onscreen as they'll show in-game.

When a Canvas is created, Unity will also create a new GameObject called **"EventSystem"** if one does not already exist. This handles input for elements that can be interacted with, like buttons. If all of your elements stop responding to your input, you may have accidentally deleted this GameObject. You can add a new one through **GameObject ➤ UI ➤ Event System**. There should only be one in your scene.

Since UI elements are GameObjects, their parenting will "attach" them to each other such that moving, rotating, and scaling a parent will affect its children as well. It also determines the order that elements are rendered in. Elements are drawn in a top-to-bottom order: those higher in the Hierarchy will be drawn first. This means if you have two elements that overlap each other, the one that's lowest in the Hierarchy will appear "on top" of the other, covering it.

You can change the order by dragging and dropping in the Hierarchy, just like with normal GameObjects. There are also methods in the Transform class that allow you to change order by code, if you should ever need to.

The Canvas GameObject has components that deal with the way the UI renders and scales with screen size.

The **Render Mode** field of the Canvas component has three possible settings that determine how the canvas and its elements are rendered:

1. **Screen Space – Overlay** will render elements over the screen with no fancy side effects. It's your average UI setup.

2. **Screen Space – Camera** is much like Overlay, but it references a target Camera and renders the UI as if viewed by that camera. You can use this to give the UI a perspective tilt.

3. **World Space** considers elements to be part of the world. This can be used to create interfaces that are meant to seem as if they are in the game world itself, such as a floating hologram menu or menus on an in-game computer screen.

The **Canvas Scaler** component handles the screen size and how the elements adapt to changes in the screen size. Most notable is the **UI Scale Mode** field, which has three possible options:

•   **Constant Pixel Size** will keep every element the same size in pixels, regardless of the size of the screen or the aspect ratio of the screen. This can cause elements to appear relatively large on small screens compared to large screens, or vice versa.

- **Scale With Screen Size** will provide us with a **Reference Resolution** field (a width and a height). This is the size the UI is designed for. If the screen is larger or smaller, the UI is scaled up or down proportionately. It also provides us with a **Screen Match Mode** field determining how the scaling reacts if the aspect ratio of the screen is different than that of our Reference Resolution. There are three options for this field:

    1. **Match Width or Height** will scale all elements by the difference in the width, the height, or a combination somewhere between. A resulting Match field between 0 and 1 determines how much a change in width will affect our UI sizing vs. how much a change in height will affect it. A value of 0 will cause the UI to only scale if the width is changed. A value of 1 will only scale if the height is changed. A value of 0.5 will provide an even mix of both.

    2. **Expand** will increase the size of the canvas, but never decrease it from the reference resolution.

    3. **Shrink** will decrease the size of the canvas, but never increase it from the reference resolution.

- **Constant Physical Size** will size UI elements by their physical size rather than a number of pixels. We specify a physical unit measurement to use, such as inches, centimeters, or millimeters, and the width and height of our elements will use this measurement instead of pixels.

When sizing your UI, a useful tip to remember is that you can always view your UI by switching to your Game window (even if your game is not currently running). While in your Game window, you can even test different screen resolutions by adjusting the aspect ratio setting using the drop-down found in the top bar of the Game window, which by default will use the "Free Aspect" setting. This can be used to view how your UI will show on different screen sizes.

The RectTransform

Rather than the Transform component that all other GameObjects use, UI elements will have a different, lower type (or *subtype*) of Transform called **RectTransform**. As a lower type, it has all of the members of a Transform, plus some of its own. Most notably, it adds a **width**, **height**, **pivot point**, and **anchoring**.

The **width** and **height** depict the size of the object, using the Canvas Scaler component's UI Scale Mode, mentioned earlier, to depict whether the size is in pixels or a physical measurement.

The **scale** then multiplies the size, meaning that increasing scale does not increase the actual value of the width or height, but does increase the visual size of the element.

The **pivot point** works just like pivot points we've used up until now – only instead of pivot points being changed by using parent GameObjects, we can directly change it with the Pivot field in the Inspector of the RectTransform component. It uses an X and Y axis, with (0, 0) being the bottom-left corner of the UI element and (1, 1) being the top-right corner. The values can be higher than 1 or negative to place the pivot off of the UI element. You could use this to spin UI elements around a distant point when they are rotated.

The position of a UI element will be (0, 0, 0) when its pivot point is located at the center of the Canvas. Increasing the X will go to the right, and increasing the Y will go up, and vice versa. The Z axis only affects your UI if the Render Mode of your Canvas is set to World Space, as described earlier.

The rect transform tool (hotkey T) can be particularly useful when positioning elements on the screen. We've used it before to move walls for our first project, so you're already familiar with it. The corners and edges of elements can be dragged to change their width and height, without affecting their scale.

While using the rect tool, the pivot point of the selected element is resembled by a circle icon, by default in the center of the element. You can change the pivot here by left-clicking and dragging this circle. It will snap to the edges of the element and the center of the width or height. Note that this only works while the

Tool Handle Position is set to Local, as shown before in Figure 30-2. If the circle is gray and not responding to clicks, you likely just need to press Z.

The RectTransform also employs a concept of **anchors**, which provide a means of fixing an element in a specific place relative to its parent element.

The anchors are visualized by four white triangular handles. By default for a new element, they'll all be positioned in the center of the Canvas, bundled up together, shown on the left side of Figure 30-3. You can click and drag the center of them to move them all at once or click an individual handle to pull it and separate it from the rest, shown on the right side of Figure 30-3. While pulling a single handle, two other handles react, keeping themselves aligned so that the four handles are always making a rectangular shape together.

Figure 30-3. *The four anchor handles for a UI element, all positioned together on the left, and the same four handles with some space between them on the right*

If you hold Ctrl before clicking an individual anchor handle, dragging will instead move all of them at once.

Each anchor corresponds to a corner of the associated element and how that corner is positioned within its parent element. The corner of the element will retain its position relative to the anchor point.

One common use for this is to anchor elements to one corner of the Canvas. If you leave your anchors at the center of the screen but place your elements at the edges of the screen, a change in screen size will likely mean your elements are no longer on the edge of the screen. To fix this, you can anchor them to the side of the screen you want them attached to. Our panel for build buttons in Figure 30-1, for example, is anchored to the top-left corner of the screen so that no matter the size or orientation of the screen, the elements are always tied to that corner. Similarly, our Play button is anchored to the middle of the bottom edge of the screen.

The Inspector has a handy means of easily assigning anchor presets, shown in Figure 30-4. This provides various options for assigning the horizontal and vertical anchors to the center or corners of the parent with a single click. You can also hold Shift or Alt while clicking, as depicted at the top of the Anchor Presets drop-down, to set the pivot and/or position of the element as well as its anchor, making it easy to dock elements to corners and edges of its parent – and if the Canvas itself is the direct parent of the element, this is effectively docking to the screen.

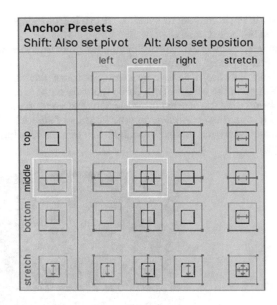

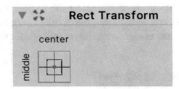

Figure 30-4. *The anchor preset button in the Rect Transform of the Inspector (left). When clicked, it shows the drop-down box of anchor presets (right)*

Building Our UI

With all that preliminary prattling out of the way, let's get back to the real world and start working on our own UI. Our UI is a simple mixture of panels (colored rectangles) and buttons with text inside them. Since UI elements are just GameObjects with certain components attached, we can make use of prefabs to define a consistent style that we can change all at once down the road if we want to. We can override the stuff we need to, like what the text says in a button, the size, the anchors, and so on, but keep things like color attached to the prefabs so we can easily make edits to all instances if we want to.

Before we begin, make sure you have an EventSystem and a Canvas in the scene (both can be created under GameObject ➤ UI), then let's set up the Canvas:

- Select your Canvas. In the Inspector, locate the Canvas Scaler.

- Change the UI Scale Mode field to Scale With Screen Size.

- Set the Reference Resolution to 1280×720. That's 1280 on the X axis and 720 on the Y axis.

- Set Screen Match Mode to Match Width or Height.

- Change the Match slider to 0.5.

Now let's create a generic button. Go to GameObject ➤ UI ➤ Button ➤ TextMeshPro. This will generate a pop-up window, shown in Figure 30-5, asking to import TextMeshPro assets into your project.

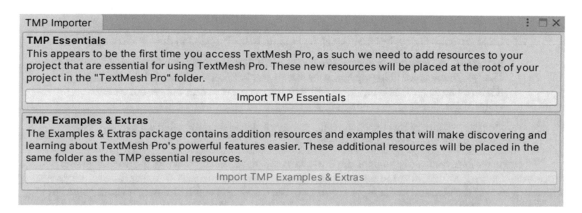

Figure 30-5. *TextMeshPro importer window, shown after attempting to make a UI-related GameObject with "TextMeshPro" mentioned in its name*

TextMeshPro is the newest and greatest rendering for text in the Unity engine. There are legacy options to render text, but this is the recommended. In order to use it, however, you'll have to click the **"Import TMP Essentials"** button in this window. This will automatically import what TextMeshPro features you need to use into your Assets folder, as described by the text in the window. Once you've clicked this, the **"Import TMP Examples & Extras"** button will become available to click as well, if you'd like to import extra examples of the usage of TextMeshPro features. You won't need to for the sake of this book, but you certainly can if you'd like to check it out.

If you opt out of the extra features and want them back later, you can navigate to Window ➤ TextMeshPro ➤ Import TMP Examples and Extras at any time.

Once you've imported the essentials, we can set up the button. It should already be in your scene (it'll be named "Button"), from the first time you tried to make it and the window popped up, but if not, just make the button again. Remember, it'll be made a child of your Canvas automatically upon creation.

- Select the Button and navigate to the Inspector. Ignore the Image component and focus instead on the Button component. Change its Normal Color field to an orange with a hex value of F0B683.

- Change its Highlighted Color to FFD6B2, a slightly paler variant. This will be the color used when the mouse hovers over the button.

- Change its Pressed Color to a slightly darker variant with a hex value of DA9E69. This color shows while the mouse button is held down over the button.

- Make its Selected Color match the Normal Color.

- The text within the button is represented by a child GameObject named "Text (TMP)". Select it and navigate to its TextMeshPro component in the Inspector. Set the Vertex Color field to a hex value of 0F1B64.

- Let's keep the UI in its own folder as we make prefabs for UI-related elements. In the Project window, make a "UI" folder in your Prefabs folder, then create the Button prefab in that folder by dragging it from the Hierarchy window and onto the folder in the Project window.

That will serve as the base for our buttons. The text inside isn't important; we'll override that when we implement the prefab. We just want to create a consistent template of colors so we don't have to set the same fields each time. You can delete this Button GameObject once you've made the prefab out of it.

Moving on, let's make a **generic panel**:

- Create a GameObject ➤ UI ➤ Panel. By default, it will be sized to the whole canvas.

- In the Image component, set the Color value to a dark blue with a hex value of 4B5374. In the color field pop-up, after setting the hex value, set the **"A"** field to 100 if it is not already. This is alpha – a value of 100 makes the color fully solid, while a value of 0 makes it totally transparent.

- Create a prefab for this panel as well. It's just a colored rectangle that we can lay elements on to group them up nicely.

We can use this instance of panel for the **build buttons** on the left side. Using the anchor preset drop-down for the RectTransform in the Inspector (shown prior in Figure 30-4), select the top-left preset, which will anchor the element to the top-left corner of the canvas. Its width and height should show in the Inspector after this. Change these to 180 width and 400 height. Then, apply the same top-left anchor preset again, but this time, hold Alt before you click the preset, which will snap the panel to the top left. Alternatively, you can use the rect tool (hotkey T), click within the panel, and drag to move it until its top-left corner is at the top-left corner of the Canvas. It should snap into place once you get close enough. Set the name of the Panel to **"Build Button Panel"**.

We want our build buttons to be a bit different than a normal button, since we need a tower gold cost displayed in them as well. We'll create a prefab variant of the Button to make these:

- Right-click the Button prefab in the Project and select Create ➤ Prefab Variant. Name the variant **"Build Button"**.

- Create an instance of the Build Button by dragging and dropping it from the Project onto the Build Button Panel in the Hierarchy, making the panel the parent of the new button.

- Change the button width to 160 and height to 80.

- Change the button anchor to the top-left preset.

- Change the name of the "Text (TMP)" child element to **"Tower Text"**.

- In the TextMeshPro component of the Tower Text, set the Font Style to Bold by clicking the "B" button of the Font Style field. Set the Font Size field to 22.

- For the Alignment field, you can hover your mouse over the individual buttons and wait for text to pop up depicting what value the button resembles. Select the "Center" button (second from right in the top row) and the "Top" button (leftmost in the bottom row). This will move the text to the top of the button and keep it horizontally centered.

- Copy and paste the Tower Name GameObject and change the name to **"Gold Cost"**. Find its TextMeshPro component in the Inspector and change the Font Style back to normal by clicking the "B" again, turning the bold style off. Leave the Alignment at the Center setting, but select the Bottom setting instead of Top, which is the third button from the left on the bottom row.

- At the top of the TextMeshPro component, use the text box to change the text to "XX gold" instead of "Button" and we'll fill in the gold cost on a per-tower basis.

- Our text is a little *too* close to the bottom, making it overlap the edge of the button a bit. At the bottom of the TextMeshPro component, click to expand the **Extra Settings**, then use the first field, **Margins**, and set the Bottom margin to 4, giving a little extra space between the text and the bottom of the button.

- Select the base Build Button GameObject. Using the **Overrides** drop-down near the top-right corner of the Inspector, click **Apply All** to apply the changes we made to our prefab variant.

Now that the generic build button is set up as a prefab, you can create the four buttons we need and fill the Build Button Panel with them. Making sure the first Build Button is a child of the Build Button Panel, use the rect tool (hotkey T) to left-click and drag within the Build Button so that it is at the top of the panel, with a little bit of margin so it's not *right* at the top. Ensure that it snaps horizontally to be centered within the panel.

Then, you can copy and paste it and drag each one down to fill the panel. Sized as the buttons and panel are, you should fit four of them – one for each tower. Just drag them on the Y axis with the move tool (hotkey W) or the rect tool, and keep the space between them roughly equal.

To keep things neat-looking and easy to find, we'll change each build button's GameObject name to correspond to the tower it will build. As seen before in Figure 30-1, the build buttons from top to bottom are in the order of Arrow Tower, Cannon Tower, Hot Plate, and then Barricade. Thus, we can change the names of our Build Button GameObjects, from top to bottom in the Hierarchy, to correspond: the topmost button will be named "Arrow Tower", the next will be named "Cannon Tower", and so on.

Now, set the **Tower Name** text and the **Gold Cost** text of each build button accordingly by editing their text in the TextMeshPro component of each one:

- An **Arrow Tower** will cost **5 gold**.

- A **Cannon Tower** will cost **8 gold**.

- A **Hot Plate** will cost **12 gold**.

- A **Barricade** will cost **2 gold**.

With that panel done, let's add the panel in the bottom-left that shows our **current gold**. We'll script it to function correctly later:

- Add an instance of the Panel prefab as a child of the Canvas. Name it **"Current Gold Panel"**.

- Set its **anchor** preset to **Bottom Left**, holding **Shift** and **Alt** when clicking to position it and its pivot point as well.

- Size it to 140 width and 52 height.

- Right-click the panel in the Hierarchy and select UI ➤ Text – TextMeshPro to add a Text element child. Name it **"Current Gold Text"**.

- Color the text a pure yellow (the color of sweet gold), with a hex value of FFFE00.

- Make the text **bold**, give it **30 font size**, and write **"50 gold"**. That's how much gold the player will start with. In the Alignment field, choose Center and Middle (second from the left in each row).

Now we'll create the **Play button** at the middle-bottom of the screen:

- Drag and drop an instance of the Button prefab onto the Canvas GameObject in the Hierarchy. Name it **"Play Button"**.

- Set its size to **240 width** and **70 height**.

- Set its **anchor** preset to **Bottom Center**, again holding **Shift** and **Alt** before clicking to position it at the bottom-middle of the screen.

- Click the **"B"** in the text Font Style, and change the **Font Size** to **54**. Just like for the gold cost, set the **Alignment** to **Center** and **Middle**. Change the text to say **"PLAY"** instead of "Button".

Lastly, we'll create an element that doesn't show all the time, **the Tower Selling Panel**, which we'll position over the selected tower constantly, using code to update its position even when the camera moves. It will show a button letting the user sell the tower, as well as an X button to deselect the tower and hide the panel again.

- Create an instance of the Panel prefab as a child to the Canvas. Name it **"Tower Selling Panel"**.

- Set its **anchor** to **Middle Center**.

- Set its **Pivot** to **(0.5, 0)**, placing the pivot point at the bottom-middle of the panel.

- Set its **width** to **186** and **height** to **68**.

- Set the Color field of the Image component to a lighter blue with a hex value of 8BB0D8.

- Add an instance of the Button prefab as a child to the Tower Selling Panel. Name it **"Sell Button"** and give it a **width** of **110** and a **height** of **58**. Set its **X position** to **-32** and its **Y** to **0**.

- Change the text in the button to read **"SELL"**, make it **bold**, give it a **font size** of **32**, and click the **Center** and **Top** buttons in the **Alignment** field.

- Copy-paste the SELL text GameObject, and rename it to **"Refund Text"**. Set its text to **"for XX gold"**; set its **Font Size** to **18**. Change its font style to normal by clicking the **"B"** in Font Style again. Set its **Alignment** to **Center** and **Bottom** to position it under the "SELL" text.

- Under the **Extra Settings** in the Refund Text's TextMeshPro component, add 4 to its Bottom Margin field like we did with the tower gold costs in the Build Panel, just to keep the text from slightly sticking out beneath the button.

- Add another Button prefab instance to the Tower Selling Panel. Name it **"X Button"**. Leave its **anchor** at **Middle Center** and set both its **width** and **height** to **38**. Set its **X position** to **60** and its **Y position** to **10**, placing it in the top-right corner of the selling panel.

- Set the X Button text to read just the letter **"X"**. Make it **bold** and set its **Alignment** to **Center** and **Middle**. Give it a **font size** of **34**.

- Finally, **deactivate** the Tower Selling Panel GameObject. We'll make it show by script when we need it to, but we don't want it to show by default.

The Refund Text will be updated to replace the "XX" with the actual refund value of the selected tower whenever the player selects a new tower, since the refund from selling the tower varies depending upon the tower type. When you're done, the Tower Selling Panel should look like Figure 30-6, and the other elements we've created should look like Figure 30-1 from the start of the chapter.

Figure 30-6. *The Tower Selling Panel*

At this point, we've put in the work to make our UI look how we want to. Let's create a prefab out of the entire Canvas, just to ensure we don't ever accidentally lose it.

You should now see your UI in-game, although it won't yet perform any of the functions it's intended for. Note that, in-game, our buttons will react to the mouse hovering over them, growing brighter, showing that the Event System is working, even if the buttons aren't actually doing anything yet when they're clicked.

Summary

It took some setup, but we've pieced together the UI for our game, learning the basics of using Unity UI to create UI GameObjects on a Canvas. With prefabs made for the various pieces of our UI, like the build buttons and the background panels, we can easily change colors and text styling across the board if we ever wanted to.

Now we can move on to scripting the functionality of the UI.

CHAPTER 31

Building and Selling

With our UI in place, it's time to hook it up with its functionality, giving our player the ability to build and sell towers. This will teach us how to handle events for our UI to respond to clicks on our buttons. We'll also be learning how to use a fundamental new type, the Dictionary, which will be a lifesaver for storing and retrieving towers we've built.

Events

UI elements that have some form of interaction with the user will have event fields exposed in the Inspector, such as a button having an "OnClick" event that occurs when the button is clicked. These fields allow us to attach functionality to the event so that some action is performed when the event happens.

We can add as many **actions** as we want to a single event for a single UI element. Each action we add will first ask us to reference some targeted object we want to interact with. Then, a drop-down field will appear that lets us point to some member on that object: a variable or a method.

If we drop a GameObject on this field, we can access members from any of the components attached to it or from the GameObject itself. For example, if we drop the Player Camera GameObject on the field, we can access members from the GameObject type as well as the Transform and Player script.

What happens next depends on what we point to within the object we referenced:

- **If we point at a variable**, a field will pop up that lets us set the value of the variable. When the event occurs, the variable value is set to whatever we put in that field. A major limit to this is that we cannot point at our own script variables – only members of built-in Unity types, like the name of a GameObject or the parent of a Transform.

- **If we point at a method**, it must be a public method with no more than one parameter, and the parameter must be of a type that's serializable – such as a basic value type, a script, or a built-in component. If the method declares a parameter, we'll get a field to set the parameter value. When the event occurs, the method is called, using the parameter value we provided in the field.

  Due to this, we *could* set our own script variables if we just declare a public method that takes a single parameter and sets our variable to that parameter value. It's not as convenient as setting the variable directly, but it works.

We'll use these actions to call methods from our script when it's time to implement the functionality of our buttons. We'll give each build button actions in their OnClick event to call methods that set the corresponding Tower prefab to build and give us a reference to the button so we can change its color back and forth when it's selected and deselected.

© Casey Hardman 2024
C. Hardman, *Game Programming with Unity and C#*, https://doi.org/10.1007/978-1-4842-9720-9_31

When our script is ready to build a tower, it can use that tower prefab variable to determine which tower to Instantiate, and since it's a Tower, it will have a "goldCost" variable we can use to determine if the player has enough money to build it.

Setting Up

When we place towers on the stage, we'll always keep them at a Y position of 0, with X and Z values at multiples of 10 (e.g., 10, 20, 30, and so on, including negative values). A tower is 10 units wide and long, so we're only allowing the player to place them along increments of the tower size. Ultimately, it's something like a grid of towers, where only one tower can be in a single cell of the grid at a time. In order to place a tower on the stage, we need to let the user point and click where they want it to go, though.

To do this, we'll be exploring a handful of new methods and concepts. We'll learn how to perform a **raycast**. This is a physics method that effectively "shoots a ray" out into the scene to test if hits any colliders. You define a point for the ray to start from, a direction for it to travel in, and a total distance for it to travel. If the ray hits anything, the method will give back information about what it hit.

To get the point on the stage that the player mouse cursor is hovering over, we can cast a ray starting at the mouse cursor position and shooting out at the stage. Conveniently, Unity has a built-in method in the Camera component that lets us convert a point on the screen to a **Ray** instance. The Ray is a type that stores an origin and direction of a ray, which we can provide to the raycasting method as a parameter.

Let's dive in. We'll start by giving the player an indication of where their mouse cursor is hovering over the stage. To do this, we'll raycast from the mouse and get the point the ray touched on the stage and then position a "highlighter" object there. But we don't want to just show the player the exact point on the stage that they touched. We want it to conform to multiples of 10 to show them the sort of grid pattern that towers will be placed in.

To start, we'll make our highlighter be a thin cube the size of a tower:

- Create a Cube with **no parent**. Name it **"Highlighter"**.

- Set its scale to (10, .4, 10).

- Set its layer to **"Ignore Raycast"** so that when trying to detect the stage with a raycast, we aren't hitting the highlighter instead.

- Create a material named Highlighter and give the cube a color with a hex value of FFFFFF – pure white. We'll also make it a bit transparent. After setting the hex value in the color picker, also change the **"A"** (alpha, meaning transparency) field (just above the hex field) to 60. That's it for the color, but we also need to change the **Rendering Mode** field at the very top of the material settings in the Inspector to **Transparent**. If you leave the Rendering Mode at the default setting of Opaque, the alpha will be ignored, and the object will always be fully solid.

- By default, **deactivate** the Highlighter GameObject.

This cube is now the size of a tower on the X and Z axes, so we just need to script it to position itself under the mouse cursor on the stage and to always snap to multiples of 10 with its X and Z position.

We're going to leave our Player script handling the camera movement and create a new script named "Game" to handle the game state, enemy spawning, and general gameplay mechanics like that.

So go ahead and create the **Game** script, create an empty GameObject also named **"Game"**, and attach an instance of the script to it.

Let's get started with the **Game** script:

```
using System.Collections;
using System.Collections.Generic;
using UnityEngine;
using UnityEngine.UI;
using TMPro;

public class Game : MonoBehaviour
{
    private enum Mode
    {
        Build,
        Play
    }
    private Mode mode = Mode.Build;

    [Header("Build Mode")]
    [Tooltip("Current gold. Set in Inspector to define starting gold.")]
    public int gold = 50;

    [Tooltip("Layer mask for highlighter raycasting.  Should include the layer of the
    stage.")]
    public LayerMask stageLayerMask;

    [Tooltip("Reference to the Transform of the Highlighter GameObject.")]
    public Transform highlighter;

    [Tooltip("Reference to the Tower Selling Panel.")]
    public RectTransform towerSellingPanel;

    [Tooltip("Reference to the Text component of the Refund Text in the Tower Selling
    Panel.")]
    public TextMeshProUGUI sellRefundText;

    [Tooltip("Reference to the Text component of the current gold text in the bottom-left
    corner of the UI.")]
    public TextMeshProUGUI currentGoldText;

    [Tooltip("The color to apply to the selected build button.")]
    public Color selectedBuildButtonColor = new Color(.2f, .8f, .2f);

    //Mouse position at the last frame.
    private Vector3 lastMousePosition;

    //Current gold the last time we checked.
    private int goldLastFrame;

    //True if the cursor is over the stage right now, false if not.
    private bool cursorIsOverStage = false;
```

```
    //Reference to the Tower prefab selected by the build button.
    private Tower towerPrefabToBuild = null;

    //Reference to the currently selected build button Image component.
    private Image selectedBuildButtonImage = null;

    //Currently selected Tower instance, if any.
    private Tower selectedTower = null;
}
```

First off, we have two extra "using" statements at the top of the script: **"UnityEngine.UI"**, which is where built-in UI components are declared, and **"TMPro"**, which is short for Text Mesh Pro and provides us with a type we assign to one of our variables below: **TextMeshProUGUI**. This is the name for the type of the TextMeshPro component used to draw text for our buttons and panels. We need to reference the component so we can change the text through code for the player's current gold and the tower selling panel's refund text, which tells the player how much gold they'll get back if they agree to sell a tower.

First off in the script class, we've got a simple enum to track if it's play mode or build mode, which we store in the "mode" variable – initially set to build mode so the player can set up their first towers at the start of the game.

Then we have our variables. Let's go over them and how we plan to use them:

- **gold** – The current gold will be handled by the Game script, since it also handles building and selling.

- **stageLayerMask** – A **LayerMask** is a built-in Unity type we haven't used before. It resembles a set of all of our collision layers (defined in our Project Settings) and allows us to check or uncheck each one individually. We'll pass it to our raycast call to define which layers the ray should collide with (the ones that are checked) and which it should ignore. In the Inspector, the layer mask field shows as a drop-down listing all layers, where each layer can be clicked to toggle it on or off.

- **highlighter** – A reference to the Highlighter's Transform, which we'll use to position it. We'll also go through this to get the GameObject so we can deactivate the highlighter when the mouse is not hovering over the stage, keeping it from hanging on the edge of the stage after the mouse has moved far away.

- **towerSellingPanel** – A reference to the RectTransform of the Tower Selling Panel. We'll use this to constantly position the panel above the selected tower.

- **sellRefundText** – As mentioned earlier, this is our TextMeshPro component for the refund text in the tower selling panel. It will say "for XX gold", but we'll change the "XX" to match the gold the Tower will give when sold.

- **currentGoldText** – Like the "sellRefundText", we use this to set the indicator of the player's current gold in the bottom-left corner.

- **selectedBuildButtonColor** – The color applied to the selected build button to distinguish it as the currently selected button. We initialize this to a default value of 20% red, 80% green, and 20% blue using the Color constructor, but since it's a public variable, we can change it in the Inspector if we want.

- **lastMousePosition** – We keep track of the mouse position each frame here. By comparing the mouse position from the last frame to the current mouse position, we can tell if the mouse moved this frame. We'll only perform our raycast if it's moved, just to save some unnecessary processing.

- **goldLastFrame** – We also keep track of the gold we had on the last frame, using this to detect when we need to update the "currentGoldText".

- **cursorIsOverStage** – If the raycast ever fails to find the stage, we'll set this to false and deactivate our highlighter so it stops showing up. Once the raycast finds the stage again, we'll reactivate the highlighter and set this back to true again.

- **towerPrefabToBuild** – A pointer to the Tower prefab we want to build. This will be set by a method that we'll hook up to the OnClick event for our build buttons, making them set this variable to the tower prefab associated with the build button. If this variable is not null, then a build button is selected, and clicking the stage will attempt to build this Tower. If it's null, no build button is selected.

- **selectedBuildButtonImage** – A pointer to the Image component of the build button that's currently selected. Again, this is set by the OnClick event we'll be setting up. We'll use this to change the color of the selected build button to distinguish it from the others.

- **selectedTower** – Currently selected Tower instance. This is what will be sold when the Tower Selling Panel "SELL" button is clicked. If it's null, there is no selected tower.

Once you've added the code and saved the script, go ahead and set up the references in the Inspector. Once you're done, the Build Mode variables of your Game script in the Inspector should look like Figure 31-1.

Figure 31-1. *The Build Mode settings of our Game script in the Inspector after all references have been set*

Note that for the Stage Layer Mask, we've unchecked all layers except for Default, which is the layer our Stage is in. **This is important!** By default, a layer mask will default to the "Nothing" setting. This will guarantee that your raycast won't collide with anything and probably leave you desperately wondering why, because it won't even throw an error.

Aside from that, the references point to components found in GameObjects named after the variable itself, so just drag and drop the GameObjects by name from the Hierarchy to the corresponding variable field.

Build Mode Logic

Let's declare a separate method to handle all of the build mode logic. We'll split it up into methods that we'll be declaring afterward. We'll call this method for build mode logic in the Update method, only while the "mode" is currently "Mode.BuildMode".

Add this code under the Game script variable definitions:

```
void BuildModeLogic()
{
    PositionHighlighter();
    PositionSellPanel();
    UpdateCurrentGold();

    //If the left mouse button is clicked while the cursor is over the stage:
    if (cursorIsOverStage && Input.GetMouseButtonDown(0))
    {
        OnStageClicked();
    }

    //If Escape is pressed:
    if (Input.GetKeyDown(KeyCode.Escape))
    {
        DeselectTower();
        DeselectBuildButton();
    }
}

void Update()
{
    //Run build mode logic if we're in build mode:
    if (mode == Mode.Build)
        BuildModeLogic();
}
```

This shows us the high-level overview of build mode logic:

- **PositionHighlighter** will raycast from the mouse cursor toward the stage. If it hits the stage, we'll update the highlighter position and ensure that it's active (visible). If it does not hit the stage, we'll deactivate the highlighter.

- **PositionSellPanel** will reposition the Tower Selling Panel to the screen position of the selected Tower, if there is presently a selected Tower. This way, the panel remains above the selected tower, even as the Player Camera moves around.

- **UpdateCurrentGold** will update the text of the gold indicator at the bottom-left corner to match the gold the player currently has.

- **OnStageClicked** will be called whenever the stage is clicked. We use the "cursorIsOverStage" bool we declared to only call the method when the cursor is actually hovering over the stage – which is set in the PositionHighlighter method, where the raycast is performed.

- **DeselectTower** clears out the selected tower and deactivates (hides) the Tower Selling Panel.

- **DeselectBuildButton** clears the selected tower prefab and reverts the color of the selected build button back to its normal state.

Let's start declaring these methods one at a time. First and foremost, let's position the highlighter and learn how to perform a raycast. I'll be declaring all of these next methods up above the BuildModeLogic method:

```
void PositionHighlighter()
{
    //If the mouse position this frame is different than last frame:
    if (Input.mousePosition != lastMousePosition)
    {
        //Get a ray at the mouse position, shooting out of the camera:
        Ray ray = Camera.main.ScreenPointToRay(Input.mousePosition);

        RaycastHit hit; //Information on what was hit will be stored here

        //Cast the ray and check if it hit anything, using our layer mask:
        if (Physics.Raycast(ray, out hit, Mathf.Infinity, stageLayerMask.value))
        {
            //If it did hit something, use hit.point to get the location it hit:
            Vector3 point = hit.point;

            //Round the X and Z values to multiples of 10:
            point.x = Mathf.Round(hit.point.x * .1f) * 10;
            point.z = Mathf.Round(hit.point.z * .1f) * 10;

            //Clamp Z between -80 and 80 to prevent sticking over the edge of the stage:
            point.z = Mathf.Clamp(point.z, -80, 80);

            //Ensure Y is always .2, half the height of the highlighter:
            point.y = .2f;

            //Make sure the highlighter is active (visible) and set its position:
            highlighter.position = point;
            highlighter.gameObject.SetActive(true);
            cursorIsOverStage = true;
        }
        else //If the ray didn't hit anything,
        {
            //... mark cursorIsOverStage as false:
            cursorIsOverStage = false;

            //Deactivate the highlighter GameObject so it no longer shows:
            highlighter.gameObject.SetActive(false);
        }
    }
    //Make sure we keep track of the mouse position this frame:

    lastMousePosition = Input.mousePosition;
}
```

We only perform the raycast if the mouse position is different on this frame than it was on the last frame. At the very end of the method, we'll set the "lastMousePosition" to its current position so it's ready for next frame. This is just to avoid unnecessary raycasts, saving processing power.

We declare a Ray variable. To get the camera that's tagged **"MainCamera"** in the scene, we reference **"Camera.main"**. The camera included in the scene by default will have this tag, but if not, it should be set in the Inspector, just beneath the name field for the Player Camera and to the left of the Layer field, shown in Figure 31-2.

Figure 31-2. *The tag field in the head of the Inspector for our Player Camera GameObject*

Using the "Camera.main" member gives us an easy way to grab this Camera component on the fly. The Camera method we call, **ScreenPointToRay**, returns a new Ray instance that resembles a ray shooting out of the camera, originating at a specific screen position. The parameter we give is the screen position we want to use. We get a Ray that starts at the mouse position and shoots out of the camera.

After this, we declare another local variable: a **RaycastHit** named "hit". We then call **"Physics.Raycast"**, and as you can see, we provide the "hit" as a parameter, but we use a new keyword before it: **"out"**.

A parameter in a method can be declared as an "out" parameter, which means that the value is passed in as a reference, so that any modifications made to it will be reflected in our variable.

To understand what this means, you need to realize the distinction between **value types** and **reference types**.

A **reference type** is created by declaring a **class**. When we reference an instance of a class, we are pointing at a single instance of the type. A variable and a parameter will both point to the same instance, and any modifications made to either one will automatically affect the other – because, again, they're both pointing at the exact same data. If you create a class instance and store it in variable A, then create many other variables that all reference the variable A, and then everything points to the same, single instance of the class. Change one, and you change them all.

A **value type** is created by declaring a **struct** (short for structure), which is similar to a class except that it is treated differently when passed around (among other things). Whenever a struct is referenced, such as when assigning a variable or passing a variable into a method call as a parameter, the struct is copied and a new instance is given. If you create a struct instance and store it in variable A, then create many other variables that all reference the variable A; each variable will store its own instance of the struct. Each assignment copies the struct. Changing one of the variables will change *only* that variable, unlike with classes.

This distinction may not be something you've put much thought into so far due to it just feeling intrinsic, but the most obvious examples of struct types are **string**, **float**, **int**, and **bool**, which we've been using copiously since the start of our programming journey.

If we declare an int variable and assign it some value, and then pass it to a method call as a parameter, any changes made to that parameter within the method won't affect our variable, right? For example:

```
void ChangeNumber(int number)
{
    number += 5;
}
int someNumber = 5;
ChangeNumber(someNumber);
Debug.Log(someNumber); //Still logs 5.
```

This is because int is a value type. It's a struct, not a class. When you give your "someNumber" variable as a parameter, you're really creating a copy of it and passing that into the method call, so that any changes the method makes to the parameter are not reflected on our variable. They don't point to the same data.

A parameter marked with **"out"** is a way of navigating around this. RaycastHit is a struct, and thus, it's passed as a value type. But the Raycast method declares the RaycastHit parameter as "out", and thus, any changes made to it in the method will affect the same data we pass in. Our variable and the parameter will both point to the same instance, as if it were a class, not a struct. If the Raycast method detects a hit, it can then fill up the RaycastHit with information that we can access through our variable.

This does not function this way just because *we* put the "out" keyword there in our Raycast call. Rather, the Raycast method put the "out" keyword there in its declaration. We simply have to also put it there – kind of like acknowledging that we're aware that it's an "out" parameter.

With that out of the way, the parameters we give to our "Physics.Raycast" call are in the order of

- The **Ray** to cast

- The "out" **RaycastHit** to fill with data about the hit, if one occurs

- The maximum **distance** to cast the ray, which we give "Mathf.Infinity"

- The value of the **layer mask** to use

When you give a layer mask to a method like this, it usually doesn't ask you for the LayerMask instance itself. It asks for an int value. To get this, just reference the "value" member of the LayerMask, and it will work its magic behind the scenes.

You can call "Physics.Raycast" with many different kinds of parameters – it has over 10 overloads. We touched on overloads before, but to recap, an overload is a separate implementation of a method that takes a different set of parameters. You can declare multiple methods by the same name, but with different parameters for each method – these are overloads, where each has its own implementation using its own set of declared parameters. With the overloads provided in the Raycast method, we can leave out the "hit", we can substitute a Ray for its individual components (origin and direction), and other such odd cases. However, the overload we're using gives us all the control we need.

The Raycast method is wrapped in an "if" because it returns true if it hits something and false if it does not. Using this, we can react accordingly: if the ray didn't hit the stage, we deactivate the highlighter and set "cursorIsOverStage" to false. If it did hit the stage, we use the only member of "hit" we need to concern ourselves with: "point". This is the position that the ray struck on the collider it hit (the stage).

We use some math to round the number out to a multiple of 10. The equation isn't terribly complex: we multiply the value by 0.1f first, so that, for example, a value of 14 becomes 1.4 instead. Then we round that value, moving to the nearest multiple of 1 – so 1.4 would become 1 instead. After that, we can just multiply by 10 to scale it back up. Thus, 14 goes to 1.4, then is rounded to 1, and then back to 10. We do this for both axes, but the Z axis then gets clamped between -80 and 80. This prevents the user from placing towers on the bottom 2 rows and top 2 rows of the stage, to give the spawn point and leak point some reserved space and to prevent the player from building directly atop the spawn/leak point.

We set the Y value to 0.2, which is half of the height of our Highlighter cube. That keeps it nice and flush against the stage.

After performing our math and setting the position up, we certainly wouldn't want to forget to actually apply it to the Highlighter GameObject. We also make sure the highlighter is active and "cursorIsOverStage" is set to true.

This gives us a small portion of the functionality we need. There's still much to do to make our build mode work like we want it to – but since we've just conquered raycasts and set up one piece of the functionality, let's see it in action.

We have those five other methods that we're calling in BuildModeLogic but haven't declared yet, so we simply have to declare basic, empty methods for them as placeholders to quiet the compiler and let us play our game. Throw these down under the PositionHighlighter method for now, and we'll replace them with proper methods later:

```
void PositionSellPanel(){}
void UpdateCurrentGold(){}
void OnStageClicked(){}
void DeselectTower(){}
void DeselectBuildButton(){}
```

Save your script and try playing the game. You'll notice the highlighter popping into place as you move your mouse, moving only when the mouse is past any of the edges of the highlighter.

The Dictionary

Let's press on. To store towers that have been built, we're going to use a new type of collection – not a List or an array, but a **Dictionary**. It's a very useful type of collection that stores items not by an index, but by a "key." While the List takes only one generic type, which is the type stored in the List, the Dictionary takes two generic types when declared: the **key** type and the **value** type.

The keys are what identify the values (items) stored within the Dictionary. Whenever you want to store an item in a Dictionary or get an item from a Dictionary, you always supply a key. Rather than giving an int index like in arrays and Lists, we give an instance of the key type and get back the associated value. If there is no value stored in the Dictionary by that key, we get an error.

Shortly put, the key is how we identify the value. Every item in the Dictionary is paired with a key, and there's only one value per key. If you assign a value to a key that already has a different value assigned to it, you'll overwrite the old value. The same key cannot exist more than once in a Dictionary.

In our case, the key is a Vector3 for the tower position, and the value is the Tower script instance itself. Let's declare this Dictionary beneath the other private variables in the **Game** script:

```
//Dictionary storing Tower instances by their position.
private Dictionary<Vector3, Tower> towers = new Dictionary<Vector3, Tower>();
```

The first generic type supplied between the "<" and ">" braces is the key. The second type, Tower, is the value. This means we store our Tower instances by their Vector3 position on the stage. Whenever we add a tower, its key is simply the "Tower.transform.position".

This works perfectly for us, because we know that there will only ever be one Tower in the same position at a time – we don't plan on allowing users to build towers inside of each other, after all. It also means that all we need to do to grab a Tower instance at a location is to pass in the location as a key to our Dictionary. If a tower exists there, we'll get it. And since we're neatly rounding the position of our highlighter to multiples of 10 – exactly what we'll be doing when positioning our towers – we can use its position to get the Tower at its location (if there is one).

Getting and setting from a Dictionary is done with **indexing**, just like arrays and Lists, using the **[]** syntax. Instead of putting an index in, we put a key. Of course, the key must match the generic type we declared for the key when we made the Dictionary, or we'll get a compiler error.

This means that, if we want to get the Tower at our highlighter position, we can simply type:

```
towers[highlighter.position]
```

To set a Tower instance at a position when we build it, we can type:

```
towers[somePosition] = someTower;
```

But we need to know if a tower exists at a location before we allow the user to build there. To do this, the Dictionary provides us with the **ContainsKey** method. This method takes a key and returns true if there is a value associated with it or false if there is not.

To check if a tower exists at Vector3 "somePosition", we need only do this:

```
//Check if the tower exists:
if (towers.ContainsKey(somePosition))
{
    //If it does exist, we can safely grab it:
    var tower = towers[somePosition];
}
```

But enough theory – let's just use our Dictionary to see it in action. We'll implement the OnStageClicked method, which we already set to call whenever the user left-clicks while "cursorIsOverStage" is true.

In this method, we behave based on whether or not a build button is currently selected.

If a build button is selected, clicking the stage should attempt to build the tower, assuming we have enough money to do so.

If no build button is selected, then clicking the stage will select the tower under the cursor, if there is one. Later, we'll position the Tower Selling Panel over the selected tower, but for now, we just need to set "selectedTower", make sure the Tower Selling Panel is active (and thus visible), and reset the refund text to read the correct amount of gold.

Remember, we declared those five empty methods before so we could get the compiler off our back for calling them without declaring them. OnStageClicked is one of them, so be sure to replace the empty method declaration with this; otherwise, we'll have two (and that won't do):

```
void OnStageClicked()
{
    //If a build button is selected:
    if (towerPrefabToBuild != null)
    {
        //If there is no tower in that slot and we have enough gold to build the
        selected tower:
        if (!towers.ContainsKey(highlighter.position) && gold >= towerPrefabToBuild.goldCost)
        {
            BuildTower(towerPrefabToBuild, highlighter.position);
        }
    }

    //If no build button is selected:
    else
    {
        //Check if a tower is at the current highlighter position:
        if (towers.ContainsKey(highlighter.position))
        {
            //Set the selected tower to this one:
            selectedTower = towers[highlighter.position];
```

```
                //Update the refund text:
                sellRefundText.text = "for " + Mathf.CeilToInt(selectedTower.goldCost *
                selectedTower.refundFactor) + " gold";

                //Make sure the sell tower UI panel is active so it shows:
                towerSellingPanel.gameObject.SetActive(true);
            }
        }
    }
```

The **BuildTower** method is a new one, which we'll declare in a second. It takes the Tower prefab to build and the position to build it at, and does just what you'd expect – Instantiates the Tower instance and places it at the position.

Since we don't work with fractions of gold, we call **"Mathf.CeilToInt"** when we calculate the refund amount. The term "Ceil" is short for *ceiling* and simply means "round the fraction up." If there's even a tiny fraction, it gets rounded up – for example, 2.004f becomes 3. The "ToInt" in the method name implies that we want the float to get converted to an int when it's returned. There is an alternative that's just "Mathf. Ceil" which rounds the fraction up just the same, but returns a float instead. There's also "Mathf.FloorToInt" which would round the fraction down – but we'll be nice to the player and give them that extra golden coin if there's a fraction.

When selecting towers, we change the "sellRefundText" to say "for […] gold", where the […] is the gold cost of the tower multiplied by its refund factor, which determines the percentage you get back when selling.

Let's declare BuildTower to get the compiler to stop chiding us. I'll put it right below the OnStageClicked method:v

```
oid BuildTower(Tower prefab, Vector3 position)
{
    //Instantiate the tower at the given location and place it in the Dictionary:
    towers[position] = Instantiate(prefab, position, Quaternion.identity);
    //Decrease player gold:
    gold -= towerPrefabToBuild.goldCost;
    //Update the path through the maze:
    UpdateEnemyPath();
}
```

Here we see the assignment of a value in the "towers" Dictionary. We use the position as a key and assign a Tower reference as the value, for which we Instantiate a new prefab instance. You don't need to call a method to add to a Dictionary – just assign using the indexer, and the value is assigned to the key, whether the key was in the Dictionary already or not.

We subtract the gold cost from our current gold and then call a method named **UpdateEnemyPath**. We'll declare that method later and implement it in the next chapter, when we start working on spawning enemies and pathfinding. We call it here to update the path that the enemies will take through the maze – after all, whenever a new tower is placed (or sold), the path might be able to change to a more optimal route.

OnClick Event Methods

With that in place, we still have no way of building a tower. We need to declare methods to call when our build buttons are clicked, and then we must hook those methods up to the OnClick events of our individual build buttons.

As we established at the start of the chapter, any public method with a single parameter of a serializable type, or no parameters at all, can be called through a UI event. We have two things to do when a build button is clicked: set the selected button Image component so we can change its color and set the "towerPrefabToBuild". Since we can't use two parameters for a single method call, we'll have to split the functionality into two separate methods, down **beneath the BuildTower method**:

```
public void OnBuildButtonClicked(Tower associatedTower)
{
    //Set the prefab to build:
    towerPrefabToBuild = associatedTower;

    //Clear selected tower (if any):
    DeselectTower();
}
public void SetSelectedBuildButton(Image clickedButtonImage)
{
    //If we have a build button already, make sure its color is reset:
    if (selectedBuildButtonImage != null)
        selectedBuildButtonImage.color = Color.white;
    //Keep a reference to the Button that was clicked:
    selectedBuildButtonImage = clickedButtonImage;
    //Set the color of the clicked button:
    clickedButtonImage.color = selectedBuildButtonColor;
}
```

To ensure that the Tower Selling Panel disappears and the selected tower clears when we click a build button, we run **DeselectTower**, which is currently just an empty method placeholder, but we'll get around to it soon.

We also store the Image component of the clicked build button. This Image component has its own "color" field that works in conjunction with the various color fields present in the Button component. By default, the Image color is white, which doesn't affect the color of the button. Whatever the Button defines as the color is what it will be. But by setting this color, we can mix the Image color with the Button color instead, giving us an easy way to tint the color without having to set all of the various color fields of the Button component, since it has colors for normal, highlighted (meaning moused over), pressed, and so on. This way, we don't have to remember what to set the colors back to when we want to revert the color to its normal state. We just set the Image color back to white, and the Button colors take over.

We also set the Image color back to white for the currently selected image, if any, before we replace the currently selected image with the newly selected one.

Notice that we've made the methods public. We won't be able to assign them in the OnClick event if they're private.

To be able to access our methods, we need to compile the code so the methods are detected. Once again, we're trying to call methods that we haven't declared yet – notably, UpdateEnemyPath – so let's declare it as an empty method and then get the button events hooked up to our method calls:

```
void UpdateEnemyPath(){}
```

With that, we should have no errors left to trudge through when we save and return to the editor.

For now, all we'll be setting up is our Arrow Tower build button, since we don't have the other towers or their prefabs set up yet. In the Hierarchy, select the **Arrow Tower build button**, a child of the Build Button Panel in our Canvas. Head to the bottom of the Button component in the Inspector:

- Where the **OnClick** event is listed, click the little plus (+) icon in the bottom right to add an event.

- Beneath the drop-down field with "Runtime Only" selected, there should be an Object field set to None. Drag the Game GameObject (the one with our Game script attached) from the Hierarchy onto this field.

- The field titled "No Function" will become available. By clicking it, you'll see options for GameObject, Transform, and Game. These are the components on the Game GameObject that we can interact with through the event.

- Click the Game option – this is referring to our Game script instance, not the GameObject of the same name. More options will unfold, each one a variable or method that we can interact with. Select our method **OnBuildButtonClicked**.

- A field will pop up for the Tower prefab associated with the button. This is the parameter of our OnBuildButtonClicked method. Drag the Arrow Tower prefab from the Project window onto this field.

- Again, click the plus to make us a second event and reference the Game GameObject, then use the drop-down to select the **Game ➤ SetSelectedBuildButton** method. Scroll up in the Inspector and drag the Image component from this build button, dropping it onto the parameter field.

When you're done, the OnClick event should look like Figure 31-3.

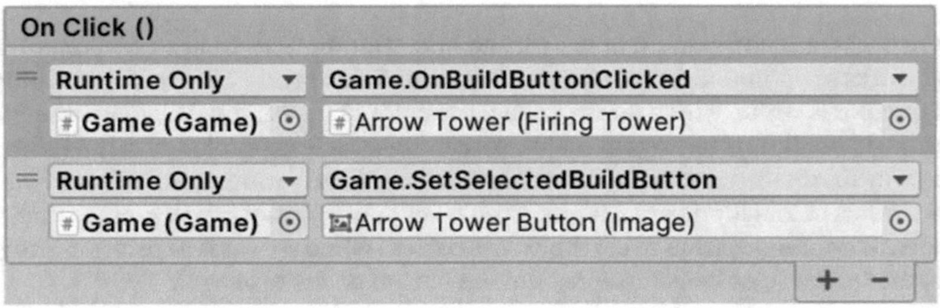

Figure 31-3. The OnClick event with our two actions set up to call methods in our Game script

At last, a portion of the functionality is operational. Playing now, you should be able to click the Arrow Tower button in-game to make it turn green, indicating that it is selected. Clicking the stage will then build an instance of the Arrow Tower where the highlighter is positioned.

However, our gold isn't updating in the bottom-left panel of the UI yet, and pressing Escape won't deselect the build button because we haven't implemented **DeselectBuildButton** yet.

Let's implement that method. It's another one that we declared earlier to get the compiler off our back, but we never filled it with code, so make sure you find the empty declaration instead of writing it again:

```
void DeselectBuildButton()
{
    //Null the tower prefab to build, if there is one:
    towerPrefabToBuild = null;
```

```
    //Reset the color of the selected build button, if there is one:
    if (selectedBuildButtonImage != null)
    {
        selectedBuildButtonImage.color = Color.white;
        selectedBuildButtonImage = null;
    }
}
```

This short method is already being called when we press Escape, through our BuildModeLogic method. It nulls out the variables associated with the currently selected build button and reverts the Image component back to the default white color so the button doesn't appear selected anymore.

Now let's implement **UpdateCurrentGold** – again, replace the old, empty method with this:

```
void UpdateCurrentGold()
{
    //If the gold has changed since last frame, update the text to match:
    if (gold != goldLastFrame)
        currentGoldText.text = gold + " gold";

    //Keep track of the gold value each frame:
    goldLastFrame = gold;
}
```

With that in place, building a tower should immediately cause our gold to decrease in the bottom-left corner. The "currentGoldText" is being set to the int value of our "gold" variable, then we're adding a space and the word "gold" so it shows as, for example, "50 gold" instead of just "50".

We still can't sell towers, though. We need to position the sell panel constantly to keep it above the selected tower by implementing the **PositionSellPanel** method – yet again, remember we have a placeholder method already, so replace it:

```
void PositionSellPanel()
{
    //If there is a selected tower:
    if (selectedTower != null)
    {
        //Convert tower world position, moved forward by 8 units, to screen space:
        var screenPosition = Camera.main.WorldToScreenPoint(selectedTower.transform.position
        + Vector3.forward * 8);
        //Apply the position to the tower selling panel:
        towerSellingPanel.position = screenPosition;
    }
}
```

Here, we use a new Camera method: **WorldToScreenPoint**. It takes a position in world space and converts it to a point on the screen. The position we give is the selected tower position, but we move it forward by 8 units to place the panel somewhere "above" the Tower on our screen – since a tower moving forward will move it up the stage, this is equivalent to moving it up in relation to our camera.

We already set the "selectedTower" variable to any tower that gets clicked while no build button is selected and the highlighter is at the position of the tower. With this in place, you should be able to play the game, click the Arrow Tower build button, click the stage to build one, press Escape to deselect the build button, and then click the tower you built to select it. The panel should show above it, showing the correct amount of gold refund in the text, shown in Figure 31-4.

Figure 31-4. *The Tower Selling Panel showing above an Arrow Tower*

Since we haven't set up the Sell or X button to do anything yet, clicking them will be somewhat disappointing. Let's change that.

We need to implement the methods we plan on calling with our button events. First off is a method that occurs when the Sell button is clicked:

```
public void OnSellTowerButtonClicked()
{
    //If there is a selected tower, sell it:
    if (selectedTower != null)
        SellTower(selectedTower);
}
```

And, of course, we must implement that **SellTower** method we're trying to call:

```
void SellTower(Tower tower)
{
    //Since it's not going to exist in a bit, deselect the tower:
    DeselectTower();
    //Refund the player:
    gold += Mathf.CeilToInt(tower.goldCost * tower.refundFactor);

    //Remove the tower from the dictionary using its position:
    towers.Remove(tower.transform.position);

    //Destroy the tower GameObject:
    Destroy(tower.gameObject);
```

```
    //Refresh pathfinding:
    UpdateEnemyPath();
}
```

We CeilToInt the refund value and add the money back to the player's current gold. To remove the Tower from our "towers" Dictionary, we call the **Remove** method. It takes the key of the value we want to remove. Since the key is the position of the associated tower, all we need to do is reach into the given Tower parameter and reference its "transform.position".

Then we Destroy the tower GameObject.

Since a tower just got removed from the stage, we need to update the enemy path again to ensure that it finds the easiest path through the stage, in case that tower was blocking a more ideal route.

We also need to code the contents of our method to deselect a tower. We have a placeholder for this one, too, but make sure you **make it public** when adding the code; otherwise, we can't access it in our UI event:

```
public void DeselectTower()
{
    //Null selected tower and hide the sell tower panel:
    selectedTower = null;
    towerSellingPanel.gameObject.SetActive(false);
}
```

Now we just need to add the event. This will be done just the same way we did for our build button. In the Hierarchy, find your **Sell Button** in your **Tower Selling Panel**, and add an OnClick event that calls Game ➤ OnSellTowerButtonClicked.

For the **X Button** (a sibling of the Sell Button, so it should be close in the Hierarchy), add an event that calls Game ➤ DeselectTower.

Neither of these methods has a parameter to reference, so we just need to point at the method and be on our way.

With that, the core functionality of Build Mode will be operational:

- Clicking a Build Button will select it, turning it green (unless you changed the color in the Game script). For now, the other three build buttons aren't wired up with their events because we haven't made their towers yet, so they won't do anything, but the Arrow Tower will. Now, we know how to set the others up when we get to that point.

- Clicking the stage with a build button selected will build the tower there, if the player has the money to do so.

- Pressing Escape with a build button selected or a tower selected will clear the selection.

- Clicking a tower without a build button selected will select the tower, showing the sell panel above it. Clicking Sell will sell the tower and refund us, while clicking the X button will deselect the tower so the panel stops showing.

- Clicking the build button while a tower is selected will also clear the tower selection.

- Any change in gold from buying or selling a tower will update the gold indicator in the bottom left.

Summary

This was a significant chapter with many new concepts to explore. We learned how to...

- Attach **actions** that occur on certain **events** in a UI element. This gives us the ability to call a method from a script or component or to set the value of a property in a component or GameObject. If you want to call a method through an action, the method must be **public** and must have **no more than one parameter**.

- Perform a **raycast** to test for a collision from a starting point, moving along a direction for a maximum amount of distance.

- Convert to a screen position from a world position using the Camera method **WorldToScreenPoint**.

- Use a **LayerMask** to define the layers a raycast can collide with. Layer masks can be conveniently set up in the Inspector.

- Get a **Ray** that shoots out of the Camera from a given screen position, using the Camera method **ScreenPointToRay**.

- Use a **Dictionary** to store objects by key/value pairs: to add a value, you must also associate it with a key. The key and value type are provided as generic types when declaring and constructing the Dictionary instance using the "<" and ">" braces.

At last, we can start working on our enemy pathfinding and spawning for Play Mode, giving those towers something to shoot – then it's on to implementing the last three tower types.

CHAPTER 32

Play Mode Logic

In this chapter, we'll get ready to spawn enemies and make them move by setting up some preliminary play mode logic: the **spawn point** where enemies are Instantiated whenever play mode is first initiated, the **leak point** they'll be pathfinding toward, and the actual path we expect them to run along to get to the leak point. In the last chapter, we set up the **UpdateEnemyPath** method in the Game script, which does nothing as of now, but gets called whenever towers are sold or bought. We'll do our pathfinding there, creating a new path whenever we need one.

If a path cannot be found, we'll prevent the player from starting the level by blocking the Play Button with a Panel, making it unable to be clicked. We'll also show some text letting the player know what the problem is. They'll have to sell towers to unblock the path so the enemies can get through; otherwise, they won't be able to play the next level.

Spawn and Leak Points

Let's set up the spawn point and leak point at each side of our Stage plane. Our enemies will be 5 units wide and long, so we'll make "plates" on the floor that are the same size:

- Create an empty GameObject. Name it **"Spawn Point"**. Set its position to (0, 0, 96).

- Add a child Cube. Set its position to (0, .1, 0) and its size to (5, .2, 5).

- Copy-paste the Spawn Point and rename it to **"Leak Point"**. Make sure you've selected the root itself (not the Cube inside it) when you do this. Set its position to (0, 0, -96) to put it at the bottom side of the stage instead of the top.

- I'll create Spawn Point and Leak Point materials and apply them to their corresponding cube, giving the spawn point a dark orange color with a hex value of D4983D and a red color with a hex value of FF2227 for the leak point.

Once you're finished, you'll have a plate at each end of the Stage plane. Let's declare variables in our **Game** script to reference the two points so we can use their positions when pathfinding – I'll put these variables up above the ones we've already declared:

```
[Header("References")]
public Transform spawnPoint;
public Transform leakPoint;
```

Save and return to the editor to set these references so they're ready to go when we need them.

© Casey Hardman 2024
C. Hardman, *Game Programming with Unity and C#*, https://doi.org/10.1007/978-1-4842-9720-9_32

Locking the Play Button

Let's get the UI elements we want to use to lock the Play button ready: a Panel to cover the Play Button and some text above the Play Button describing why the next level can't be played.

Once the Panel is in place, we'll reference it in the Game script, from which we can activate it if the path is blocked and deactivate it once it's unblocked. The text message associated with the panel will be a child of it so that it also gets activated and deactivated.

Let's create the panel:

- Right-click the **Canvas** GameObject in your Hierarchy and add a **UI ➤ Panel**. Name it **"Play Button Lock Panel"**. Remember that all UI elements will render in order from top to bottom in the Hierarchy. Those which render later (lower in the Hierarchy) will render over (or "on top") of those above them in the Hierarchy. The Play Button Lock Panel that we just added will be at the bottom of all its siblings in the Hierarchy, meaning it will render over the top of our Play Button, which will also cause it to block the Play Button from being clicked – the Panel will receive the clicks, not the Play Button.

- Set the **anchor** preset to **Bottom Center**, holding **Shift** and **Alt** while doing so, causing the Panel pivot point and position to also move.

- Size the panel to **240 width** and **70 height**.

- Change the **Color** field of the panel **Image** component to a red with a hex value of FD5757. Change the **"A"** (alpha) of the color to 70, making it partially transparent.

The panel will act as something of a screen that lays out over the button, adding a washed-out red color to it. Figure 32-1 compares the Play Button with and without the panel showing over it.

Figure 32-1. *The Play Button in its normal state (top) vs. when the Lock Panel is active (bottom)*

Now let's add the text that will show above the Play Button while the panel is active:

- Right-click the Play Button Lock Panel and add a child **UI ➤ Text ➤ TextMeshPro**. Change its size to **340 width** by **80 height**. Set its **Y position** to **85**.

- Give the text a **font size** of **22**.

- Type this message into the text box in the **Text** component: *"Towers are blocking enemies from reaching the leak point! Can't play until a path is cleared!"*

- Set the text **Vertex Color** to a pale red with a hex value of FF4949.

When you're finished, the button should look like Figure 32-2 while the panel is active. By default, make the panel inactive so it doesn't show when the game first starts.

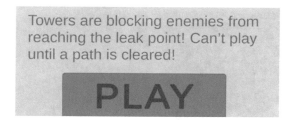

Figure 32-2. The Play Button in-game while the Play Button Lock Panel is active

We'll be needing a reference pointing to the GameObject of the panel so we can activate and deactivate it.

Add this reference to the **Game** script:

```
[Tooltip("Reference to the Play Button Lock Panel GameObject.")]
public GameObject playButtonLockPanel;
```

And of course, don't forget to return to the editor and set the reference by dragging the Play Button Lock Panel from the Hierarchy onto the field in the Game script component in the Inspector.

Pathfinding Setup

Unity provides options for pathfinding and associated AI, like local avoidance – which is AI that prevents navigating objects from bumping into each other while moving toward their goal. It even has solutions for dealing with slopes and open space that can be jumped over. We don't need this sort of functionality for our game, though. We just want to find a path around our towers on our flat stage, no jumping or slopes involved, and we want to move our enemies with our own scripts. Luckily, the fancy features won't get in our way. We'll be able to call a method that calculates a path from point A to point B and gives us the resulting points along the path in sequence. In the next chapter, we'll utilize that sequence of points to move our enemies from the start to the finish.

In order to access the navigation features we need, the **AI Navigation** package must be installed. We'll do this right from the Unity editor by using the top toolbar to navigate to **Window ➤ Package Manager**, as shown in Figure 32-3.

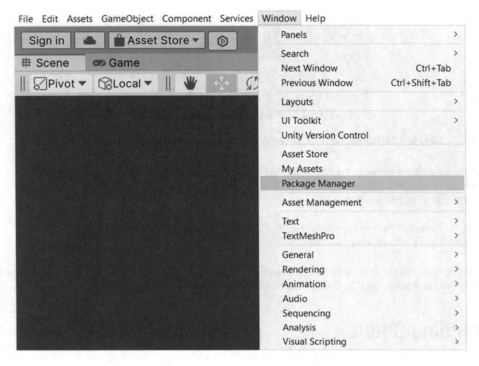

Figure 32-3. *Accessing the Package Manager window using the top toolbar*

In the Package Manager window, you'll see the listing of packages at the left side. These packages provide additional, optional features to your project and can be added, removed, and updated to their latest version right here in the window. Clicking one of these packages will populate the right side of the window with details about the package.

Let's find the AI Navigation package and install it:

- Ensure that the drop-down button just beneath the Package Manager window tab (outlined in the upper left of Figure 32-4) is set to the **Unity Registry** setting. This means it will show all of the packages in the registry, not just packages within your project.

- Find the search bar (outlined in the top-right corner of Figure 32-4) and type **"AI Navigation"** into it.

- Click the **AI Navigation** package on the left side.

- Click the **Install** button, just beneath the search bar (also outlined in Figure 32-4).

- Wait for the package to finish installing and then close the Package Manager window.

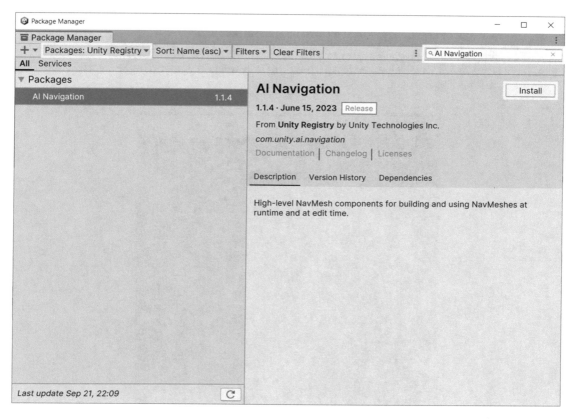

Figure 32-4. *The Package Manager window, set to view packages from the Unity Registry (outlined in the top left) and searching "AI Navigation" (outlined in the top right)*

With that, the navigation features we require will be available to use in our project.

Let's continue our setup by navigating to **Window➤ AI ➤ Navigation** using the top toolbar, which will open up the Navigation window. This window has two tabs at the top: **Agents** and **Areas**. We're only concerned with the **Agents** tab.

An **agent** is the term for an object that's using the navigation. They are resembled as cylinders, and we can use the Navigation window to create different types of agents as well as view and edit their settings.

By default, we'll have a **Humanoid** agent, although more can be added by clicking the plus-shaped button located at the bottom-right corner of the agent type listing.

Let's go over the settings and set them up how we want – by the end, your Navigation window should look like Figure 32-5:

- **Agent Name** is used to identify different types of agents. Change it to **"Enemy"**.

- **Agent Radius** is the distance from the center of the cylinder to the edge. Since our enemies are 5 units wide and long, a radius of 2.5 would make the agents the same size as the enemies. We'll set it instead to a value of **3** to give a little extra space between the enemies and the towers.

- **Agent Height** is the number of units tall the cylinder is. Our enemies are **8** units tall.

- **Step Height** is the maximum height an agent can step up or down. This doesn't matter in our case, so leave it at the default value of **0.4**.

- **Max Slope** is the highest angle of a slope the agent will be able to walk up. Our stage is totally flat, so we'll just set this to **0** because Unity will give us a warning about it if we leave it as is.

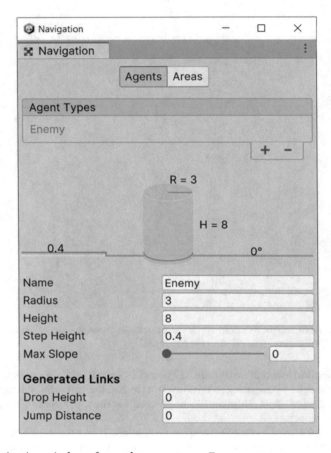

Figure 32-5. *The Navigation window after we have set up our Enemy agent type*

The next step is to ensure the navigation system counts our Stage GameObject as a navigable surface:

- Find and select your **Stage GameObject** in the Hierarchy.

- At the bottom of the Inspector, click the **Add Component** button and use the search bar to search for **"NavMeshSurface"**. Press Enter to add the component. Alternatively, you can add the component using the top toolbar: **Component ➤ Navigation ➤ NavMeshSurface**.

- Leave the component settings as they are, and click the **Bake** button at the bottom-right corner.

This will generate a **Nav Mesh Data** asset, which stores navigation information about the surface within your scene. The asset will be stored in a new folder named after your scene, placed in the same folder as your scene in the Assets menu. You don't really have to concern yourself with the asset – it is automatically linked to the NavMeshSurface component on your Stage GameObject. If you ever accidentally delete this asset, you can generate it again by clicking that same Bake button in your NavMeshSurface component.

There's just one step left to set up our pathfinding. We still haven't defined our towers as obstacles that block navigation. The navigation system doesn't automatically qualify any collider as an obstacle. We have to add a **NavMeshObstacle** component to our towers to specify them as an obstacle that should be navigated around:

- Open the **Arrow Tower** prefab by double-clicking it in the Project window. Add a **NavMeshObstacle** component to its root GameObject: **Component ➤ Navigation ➤ Nav Mesh Obstacle** in the top toolbar.

- In the Inspector, navigate to the NavMeshObstacle component. Set its **Center** to **(0, 3, 0)** and the **size** to **(10, 6, 10)**. This will cover the base cube of the tower.

- Check the **"Carve"** field. This field resembles whether or not the NavMeshObstacle should carve out a space from the NavMesh – in other words, should it actively act as an obstacle in the NavMesh itself? If this was set to false, the obstacle would not affect the NavMesh itself, but would be avoided by any agents using Unity's built-in NavMeshAgent component. We aren't using the component – we're just finding a path on the NavMeshSurface and navigating that path using our own script. This means the obstacle won't do anything for us unless we enable the Carve feature.

- Save the prefab and return to the scene.

We'll do this for all of our other tower types as well; otherwise, enemies will navigate right through them. We aren't making those tower types until we actually *have* some enemies navigating our stage, though.

Finding a Path

In the previous chapter, we declared an empty method called **UpdateEnemyPath** and ran it whenever a tower was built or sold. This is where we'll do our pathfinding.

Because the path relates to ground enemies, we're going to declare the path as a **static** variable in the GroundEnemy script. You'll recall from Chapter 9 that a static variable is a variable that is tied not to each instance of the class, but to the class type itself. With static variables, one instance of the variable exists for the whole class, and any instance of the class which uses this variable will be pointing to the same thing. Since the GroundEnemy is what will actually be running along that path, we'll put the static variable in its script class.

Let's put this to practice. Create a **GroundEnemy** script, open it up, and give it this code:

```
using System.Collections;
using System.Collections.Generic;
using UnityEngine;
using UnityEngine.AI;

public class GroundEnemy : Enemy
{
    public static NavMeshPath path;
}
```

To access necessary navigation-related stuff, we'll need to write this **"using UnityEngine.AI"** at the top of the script file, among the default usings that all scripts have. This gives us access to the **NavMeshPath** type, which resembles a path given to us by the navigation system – we use this type when we declare our static variable **"path"**. This is our static variable pointing to the path that our ground enemies will take. Since they'll all take the same path anyway, it wouldn't make sense to give them an instanced (non-static) variable that has to be set for each ground enemy when it is spawned into the game. With our static variable, we can set the path up in our Game script, and our GroundEnemy instances will have access to it at all times to begin moving along the path as soon as they spawn.

Note also that our script is inheriting from the base **Enemy** class to give it the standard functionality that every enemy should have, like health points and dying.

That's it for the GroundEnemy script, although we'll be coming back to it when we make them actually move along the path we generate for them.

Moving along, we'll need to update the path once at the start of the game to ensure that if the player starts the level without building any towers (like a madman), the path will still be set up to go from the spawn point to the leak point.

Simple enough – just open up your **Game** script and add this Start method to it:

```
void Start()
{
    UpdateEnemyPath();
}
```

Now, let's make the pathfinding happen. First, we'll need to also add the **"using UnityEngine.AI;"** line to the top of the **Game** script so we can access the **NavMesh** class there.

This NavMesh class has the static method **CalculatePath**, which is a simple means of pathfinding from one point to another and storing the path in a given **NavMeshPath** instance.

We need to call this method from the **UpdateEnemyPath** method. However, if we simply call the method there, we'll run into a problem. The effects of creating and destroying the towers don't always happen immediately. It might take until next frame for our NavMeshObstacle to start or stop affecting the NavMesh. Thus, we can't just run the CalculatePath method immediately, because it might still calculate the path before the obstacle is added or removed. We need to do it shortly *after* the UpdateEnemyPath method is called.

To accomplish this, we'll declare a **PerformPathfinding** method and simply Invoke it to perform after a brief wait in the UpdateEnemyPath method:

```
void UpdateEnemyPath()
{
    Invoke("PerformPathfinding", .1f);
}

void PerformPathfinding()
{
    //Ensure the GroundEnemy.path has been initialized:
    if (GroundEnemy.path == null)
        GroundEnemy.path = new NavMeshPath();

    //Pathfind from spawn point to leak point, storing the result in GroundEnemy.path:
    NavMesh.CalculatePath(spawnPoint.position, leakPoint.position, NavMesh.AllAreas,
    GroundEnemy.path);
```

```
    if (GroundEnemy.path.status == NavMeshPathStatus.PathComplete)
    {
        //If the path was successfully found, make sure the lock panel is inactive:
        playButtonLockPanel.SetActive(false);
    }
    //If the path is blocked, activate the lock panel:
    else
        playButtonLockPanel.SetActive(true);
}
```

Due to some of the quirks of the way Unity's scripts serialize data, we have to make sure that we don't create the "new NavMeshPath()" instance in the GroundEnemy script variable declaration for the "path". So to create the path for the first time, the first "if" checks if the path has not yet been constructed and does so if it hasn't. After that, we can use the same instance for every CalculatePath call.

Here we see our **"NavMesh.CalculatePath"** method, as mentioned before. The first parameter is the start point of the search, and the second parameter is the end point of the search. We use the position of our spawn point and leak point.

The third parameter is asking for an **area mask**. This is like the layer mask we used in our Raycast method in the last chapter, but it corresponds to **area types** that we can set up in the Navigation window. These types allow you to specify different types of ground, each one with its own "cost" value. The pathfinding operation will account for the cost of areas when trying to find the ideal path. This can be used to define areas of ground that are walkable, but more costly to walk on than others – for example, swampy ground might slow down soldiers running through it, so it would have a high cost, and thus, the pathfinding might choose to go around it rather than cutting through it. We don't have a need for this feature, so we just reference the static member **"NavMesh.AllAreas"** to fill this parameter.

Lastly, we give "GroundEnemy.path" as the path to fill with data.

Afterward, we can reference the path **".status"** member, which is an enum **NavMeshPathStatus** that will depict whether or not the path made it to the destination. If it did, the status will be **PathComplete**. If the path could not make it all the way to the end point, it will be **PathPartial**.

We activate or deactivate the Play Button Lock Panel based on whether or not the path was complete.

At that, you should be able to play the game and see the effects. If you build a line of towers blocking the path, the lock panel will activate, preventing you from clicking Play, as depicted in Figure 32-6.

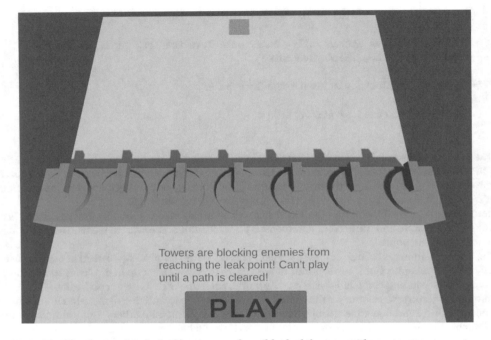

Figure 32-6. *The Play button has locked because we have blocked the way with our towers*

Selling one of these towers to unblock the way will cause the button to unlock.

Summary

We've got ourselves set up with a point to spawn the enemies at and a leak point where they'll be destroyed in order to take lives from the player. We learned how to run basic pathfinding for our ground enemies whenever a tower is built or sold and how to lock the Play button from being pressed by rendering a panel over it when pathfinding fails to find a route through the maze. Now we're finally set up to make the Play button actually start the level and send some enemies our way.

Here are some points to remember from this chapter:

- Meshes in your game world that you want to pathfind over must be given a **NavMeshSurface** component whose **Bake** button has been clicked to generate a **Nav Mesh Data** asset storing navigation information about the surface.

- **NavMeshObstacle** components with the **"Carve"** checkbox ticked will carve a hole out of the NavMeshSurface where they are, preventing the pathfinding from going over that space.

- A **static** variable in a class will be a single instance attached to the class itself, rather than each instance of the class having their own copy of the variable.

- **"NavMesh.CalculatePath"** calculates a path between two points. It takes four parameters: the start point of the search, the end point of the search, an area mask resembling which areas are valid to walk over, and a **NavMeshPath** to fill with the path data. In order to access the NavMesh class, you must include a **"using UnityEngine.AI;"** at the top of your script file.

- **"NavMeshPath.status"** returns a **NavMeshPathStatus** enum that can be used to determine if a path made it all the way to the end point. It will be **".PathComplete"** if it reaches the end point or **".PathPartial"** if the way was blocked and it could not reach the end.

CHAPTER 33

Enemy Logic

Pathfinding is happening automatically to generate our GroundEnemy path around towers, we have arrow towers, and we have our base Enemy script class to build our GroundEnemy and FlyingEnemy scripts off of. Let's get to making our Play Button initiate the spawning of enemies, then implement our two enemy types. We'll have our GroundEnemy following the path generated by the pathfinding, while our FlyingEnemy simply navigates from the spawn point to the leak point.

Play Mode Setup

The Play button will start the level when it is clicked and begin spawning enemies. We'll spawn one enemy at a time until a certain number of enemies have been spawned. Enemies will either die to towers or leak by reaching the leak point. Either way, they get destroyed. Once all enemies have finished spawning and no enemies are left in the game, the level is complete. If the player has no health left, they've lost, so we'll toggle on a panel that covers the screen, telling them how disappointing they are. If not, we just return to build mode, give the player some gold as a reward for their victory, and increase the current level by 1.

Let's declare the relevant variables for all of this logic at once in the **Game** script. We'll make a new heading, down beneath all of the build mode–related variables, and add these variables:

```
//Play Mode:
[Header("Play Mode")]

[Tooltip("Reference to the Build Button Panel to deactivate it when play mode starts.")]
public GameObject buildButtonPanel;

[Tooltip("Reference to the Game Lost Panel.")]
public GameObject gameLostPanel;

[Tooltip("Reference to the Text component for the info text in the Game Lost Panel.")]
public TextMeshProUGUI gameLostPanelInfoText;

[Tooltip("Reference to the Play Button GameObject to deactivate it in play mode.")]
public GameObject playButton;

[Tooltip("Reference to the Enemy Holder Transform.")]
public Transform enemyHolder;

[Tooltip("Reference to the ground enemy prefab.")]
public Enemy groundEnemyPrefab;
```

© Casey Hardman 2024
C. Hardman, *Game Programming with Unity and C#*, https://doi.org/10.1007/978-1-4842-9720-9_33

```
[Tooltip("Reference to the flying enemy prefab.")]
public Enemy flyingEnemyPrefab;

[Tooltip("Time in seconds between each enemy spawning.")]
public float enemySpawnRate = .35f;

[Tooltip("Determines how often flying enemy levels occur.  For example if this is set to 4,
every 4th level is a flying level.")]
public int flyingLevelInterval = 4;

[Tooltip("Number of enemies spawned each level.")]
public int enemiesPerLevel = 15;

[Tooltip("Gold given to the player at the end of each level.")]
public int goldRewardPerLevel = 12;

//The current level.
public static int level = 1;

//Number of enemies spawned so far for this level.
private int enemiesSpawnedThisLevel = 0;

//Player's number of remaining lives; once it hits 0, the game is over:
public static int remainingLives = 40;
```

The first chunk of variables are all references to various things, which we'll need to set up now:

- **buildButtonPanel** should be set to the Build Button Panel in our Canvas so we can deactivate and activate it accordingly when entering play mode or build mode.

- **gameLostPanel** will be a UI panel we'll create that lays over the screen when the player has lost all their lives. We'll create it in a bit.

- **gameLostPanelInfoText** is a text element inside the Game Lost Panel that tells us how many lives we had left (so we know how badly we lost) and what level we lost at. We'll have to set the text when the player loses to make it have the proper information.

- **playButton** points to the Play Button. Like the "buildButtonPanel", we'll be deactivating it in play mode to hide it and reactivating it when build mode begins again.

- **enemyHolder** should be set to a new, empty GameObject named Enemy Holder. We'll use this as the parent to all enemies. We can use the number of children it has to know when all of the enemies have been destroyed and the level has ended.

- **groundEnemyPrefab** and **flyingEnemyPrefab** will be set later, after we've created the associated prefabs for enemies, and we'll use them to Instantiate the enemies when spawning them.

The remaining variables are explained in their tooltips. We have a means of changing the time between each enemy spawning, how many ground levels must pass before a flying level occurs, how many enemies will spawn in each level, and how much gold the player earns at the end of the level. We also have a static variable for the current level and the lives remaining and a private variable that we'll use to track how many enemies we've spawned so we know when to stop.

Let's create the Game Lost Panel so it's ready to use when we need it:

- Add an instance of the Panel prefab as a child to the Canvas. Name it **"Game Lost Panel"**. It should automatically cover the whole Canvas. If not, open the anchor presets drop-down, hold Alt, and click the bottom-right "Stretch" option.

- Add a child UI ➤ Text ➤ TextMeshPro element to the Game Lost Panel. It should be centered on the panel. Name it **"Game Over Text"**. Give it a **width** of **340** and a **height** of **50**. In the TextMeshPro component, make the text read **"Game Over"**, give it a **font size** of **48**, make it **bold**, set its **Alignment** to **Center** and **Middle**, and give it a **Vertex Color** with a hex value of FFA800.

- Add another child TextMeshPro GameObject to the Game Lost Panel. Name it **"Info Text"**. Give it a **Y position** of -**160**, a **width** of **340**, and a **height** of **180**. Give it **24 font size**, set its **Alignment** to **Center** and **Top**, and give it a **Vertex Color** with a hex value of FFC044. Clear the text out; we'll set it through script later.

Once you've finished, deactivate the Game Lost Panel by default and drag and drop a reference to it and the Info Text into your Game variables. Make sure the Game Lost Panel is the **lowest child** of the **Canvas** in the Hierarchy, since we want it to draw over the top of everything else.

Again, make sure you've set up your Enemy Holder (just an empty GameObject with no parent) and set the reference to it in the Game script, as well as setting the Build Button Panel and the Play Button to their corresponding references.

Now, let's declare play mode logic for our Update method. We'll do much the same thing we did with the BuildModeLogic method. We'll adjust our Game script's Update method to add an "else" that calls PlayModeLogic when it's not build mode:

```
void Update()
{
    //Run build mode logic if we're in build mode:
    if (mode == Mode.Build)
        BuildModeLogic();
    else
        PlayModeLogic();
}
```

Beneath all of your methods relating to build mode in the Game script, declare the PlayModeLogic:

```
public void PlayModeLogic()
{
    //If no enemies are left and all enemies have already spawned
    if (enemyHolder.childCount == 0 && enemiesSpawnedThisLevel >= enemiesPerLevel)
    {
        //Return to build mode if we haven't lost yet:
        if (remainingLives > 0)
            GoToBuildMode();

        //Or if we have lost...
        else
        {
            //Update game lost panel text with information:
            gameLostPanelInfoText.text = "You had " + remainingLives + " lives by the end
            and made it to level " + level + ".";
```

```
            //Activate the game lost panel:
            gameLostPanel.SetActive(true);
        }
    }
}
```

To detect when the level is finished, we use the Enemy Holder, checking its **"Transform.childCount"** member, which tells us how many children it has. If it has no children and we've already spawned all of the enemies we plan on spawning for that level, we count the level as finished.

If we haven't run out of lives yet, we run **GoToBuildMode** to switch back to build mode. We'll declare it soon.

If we have run out of lives, the Game Lost Panel will ruin our fun by sprawling across our screen and preventing us from seeing anything or hitting any buttons.

Let's declare a GoToPlayMode to define the logic that occurs when it's time to switch from build mode to play mode:

```
void GoToPlayMode()
{
    mode = Mode.Play;

    //Deactivate build button panel and play button:
    buildButtonPanel.SetActive(false);
    playButton.SetActive(false);

    //Deactivate highlighter:
    highlighter.gameObject.SetActive(false);
}
```

We don't want the highlighter or Build Button Panel to show during play mode, so we just deactivate them.

Now, let's switch back to build mode from play mode, which we already scripted to occur when the level ends and we still have lives left:

```
void GoToBuildMode()
{
    mode = Mode.Build;

    //Activate build button panel and play button:
    buildButtonPanel.SetActive(true);
    playButton.SetActive(true);

    //Reset enemies spawned:
    enemiesSpawnedThisLevel = 0;

    //Increase level:
    level += 1;
    gold += goldRewardPerLevel;
}
```

We reactivate the Build Button Panel and Play Button. The highlighter will reactivate itself on its own when we mouse over the stage again, as it always does in build mode, so we needn't worry about it. We also want to be sure to reset the number of enemies spawned so far in the level, then give the player their gold reward, and increase the level number.

Now, declare a **StartLevel** method that we'll hook up to our Play Button OnClick event:

```
public void StartLevel()
{
    //Switch to play mode:
    GoToPlayMode();

    //Repeatedly invoke SpawnEnemy:
    InvokeRepeating("SpawnEnemy", .5f, enemySpawnRate);
}
```

It's just two lines of code, but the second line is new to us. Let's talk about what it does. To repeatedly spawn an enemy, we'll use this new form of invoking: the **InvokeRepeating** method. This method will keep invoking a method at a given rate. You'll recall that the Invoke method just calls a function on the script by a name, given as a string, and provides us with a second parameter that lets us wait a given number of seconds before the call actually occurs.

InvokeRepeating is similar, but it takes three parameters:

- The **method name** of the method to invoke, as a string.

- The **initial wait time** in seconds. The first call takes this long to occur after we call InvokeRepeating.

- The **interval time** in seconds. After the first call occurs, this is the time between each call thereafter.

InvokeRepeating will keep invoking our method until we cancel it by calling the **CancelInvoke** method. We can simply write a line of code with nothing but "CancelInvoke();" to cancel all ongoing method invokes for the script, or we can give the CancelInvoke call a string parameter for the name of a single method we want to stop invoking. We'll be doing that once we've spawned the last enemy required, based on the "enemiesPerLevel" variable we've already declared.

This means we have to declare that SpawnEnemy method, but before we do that, let's make the StartLevel method get called when we click the Play Button. We've hooked this up before with our arrow tower build button: find the **Play Button GameObject** in the Hierarchy (a child of the Canvas, as with all our UI elements), select it and view its **Button** component in the Inspector, scroll down to the **OnClick** event, and click that plus-shaped button to make a new action to occur on this event.

Drag and drop the **Game GameObject** from the Hierarchy onto the field that is currently set to None. Click the **"No Function"** drop-down and select **Game ➤ StartLevel()**. That's all – the Play Button will now let us start the game.

If you don't see StartLevel in the Game's list of variables and methods, be sure you've declared the StartLevel method as public and have saved the script in your code editor since declaring it.

Spawning Enemies

Initiating play mode is great and all, but all it's going to do is give us messages in the Console window about how we never even declared the method we're invoking. Let's get to it.

Our SpawnEnemy method will spawn either the ground enemy prefab or the flying enemy prefab based on the level, using an operator we haven't used yet: the **"%"** symbol, called a **modulus operator**. This operator takes a number value on either side and returns the remainder of dividing the two numbers. If the numbers are equally divisible, it'll return 0. If not, it will return the remainder that cannot be divided.

For example, in 15 % 5, the 15 can be divided by 5 three times, leaving a 0 remainder. However, if it was 15 % 6, the 15 can be divided by 6 twice, leaving us with a remainder of 3.

Let's see it in action and declare the method we're invoking:

```
void SpawnEnemy()
{
    Enemy enemy = null;

    //If this is a flying level
    if (level % flyingLevelInterval == 0)
        enemy = Instantiate(flyingEnemyPrefab, spawnPoint.position + Vector3.up * 18,
        Quaternion.LookRotation(Vector3.back));
    else
        enemy = Instantiate(groundEnemyPrefab, spawnPoint.position, Quaternion.
        LookRotation(Vector3.back));

    //Make enemy a child of the enemy holder:
    enemy.trans.SetParent(enemyHolder);

    //Count that we spawned the enemy:
    enemiesSpawnedThisLevel += 1;

    //Stop invoking if we've spawned all enemies:
    if (enemiesSpawnedThisLevel >= enemiesPerLevel)
        CancelInvoke("SpawnEnemy");
}
```

We declare a null variable for the enemy we plan on spawning, and then we spawn either a ground or flying enemy prefab, assigning the new enemy to that variable. As you may recall, the Instantiate method takes arguments in the order of prefab to spawn, position to spawn it at, and rotation to spawn it with. Our flying enemies are spawned at the spawn point, plus 18 units in the global up direction so they're actually in the air. We also make sure to make enemies look at the global back direction, which points them toward the leak point (straight down from the player's view in-game).

Our equation to ask "Is this a flying level?" is "level % flyingLevelInterval". The "flyingLevelInterval" will be 4 by default, so let's observe the behavior as the "level" value increases.

For levels 1, 2, and 3, the left-side number in our modulus operator is less than the right-hand value (4), so it can't be divided at all. The left-hand value is returned in this case. The result is 1, 2, and 3. We are not on an air level, because the result is not 0.

Once we hit level 4, the left-side number is now equal to the right-hand value, so the values are divisible, leaving a remainder of 0. That means it is a flying level.

Then the level becomes 5, then 6, and then 7. For these, the right-hand value (4) can still be divided only once before the remainder is too low to divide anymore, so the remainder gets returned. Again, we get 1, then 2, and then 3. Then we hit 8, and the right-hand value is divided twice now, leaving 0 again – another flying level.

And so, the flying levels will come at levels 4, 8, 12, 16, and so on, simply by automatically spawning a different prefab when the level is a multiple of 4 (or whatever the "flyingLevelInterval" is set to).

Aside from that, the method then makes the new enemy a child of the Enemy Holder, which is how we'll track how many enemies are left alive. Then we count +1 spawned enemy and cancel the repeating invoke with the **CancelInvoke** call if we've reached the target number of enemies spawned.

Now we need to code the GroundEnemy and FlyingEnemy to make them function correctly.

Before we do this, let's change the way they set their health. In the base **Enemy** script, we'll give them a "healthGainPerLevel" variable, declared under their "maxHealth":

```
public float healthGainPerLevel;
```

We'll change the Enemy's Start method to set the max health to the base value it is given in the prefab, plus the health gained per level, which, of course, we must multiply by the current level:

```
protected virtual void Start()
{
    maxHealth += healthGainPerLevel * (Game.level - 1);
    health = maxHealth;
}
```

We multiply by "level - 1" so that at level 1, the max health is the base value given in the prefab, and only levels won after that will add to enemy health.

While we're at it, we can also declare a method we'll be using in a bit: a Leak method for the base Enemy class that we'll call from our lower classes when they reach the leak point.

Declare this in the **Enemy** script class:

```
public void Leak()
{
    Game.remainingLives -= 1;
    Destroy(gameObject);
}
```

We take away a life from the player, referencing the static variable to do so. We also Destroy the enemy.

Enemy Movement

Let's make our GroundEnemy movement, and then we'll work on our FlyingEnemy. We already made our GroundEnemy script earlier, but we never implemented an Update method to make it move.

First, we'll need some variables. We'll add some extra variables below the "path" that we declared earlier, making our GroundEnemy script look like this:

```
public class GroundEnemy : Enemy
{
    public static NavMeshPath path;

    [Tooltip("Units moved per second along path.")]
    public float movespeed = 22;

    private int currentCornerIndex = 0;

    private Vector3 currentCorner;
```

```
    private bool CurrentCornerIsFinal
    {
        get
        {
            return currentCornerIndex == (path.corners.Length - 1);
        }
    }
}
```

The **NavMeshPath** stores the path as an array called **"corners"**. Each "corner" in the array is just a Vector3 for a point along the path. To make them move along the path, we just need to move them along these points, from index 0 to the last index in the array. We'll store an int for the current index of the corner we're moving toward, as well as a Vector3 for the current corner so we don't have to get it from the array every time.

We also declare a simple property that provides a shorthand to test if the current corner is the last one in the "path.corners" array.

Now, we can finally get around to overriding the virtual Start method we declared in our Enemy class. Add this Start method declaration to the **GroundEnemy**:

```
protected override void Start()
{
    base.Start();
    currentCorner = path.corners[0];
}
```

The **"base"** keyword refers to the upper class, the Enemy. We can then call its protected virtual Start method, ensuring that the code there is run before our implementation runs. Then, all we have to do for our implementation is just one line of code: start the current corner off at the first corner in the path.

All you have to do to override a virtual method in an upper type is use the **"override"** keyword. After that, if you don't want to *completely* override the method and provide your own, sole implementation of it, you can then call the method on the "base" – the upper type. Usually, this is done, as you often declare virtual methods to allow functionality to be *added* onto that of the upper type(s), not *replaced* entirely.

Anyway, the reason we're using the Start method is to apply the first corner in the path (which will always be the starting point of the path, which is the spawn point) as our "currentCorner"; otherwise, the "currentCorner" will default to "Vector3.zero", which would cause our enemies to always run to the center of the stage first.

Now we'll implement an Update method to move and point toward the current corner. Once we've reached the corner, we check the "CurrentCornerIsFinal" property to see if we just reached the last corner in the array. If so, we Leak. If not, we GetNextCorner, which we'll also declare:

```
private void GetNextCorner()
{
    //Increment the corner index:
    currentCornerIndex += 1;

    //Set currentCorner to corner with the updated index:
    currentCorner = path.corners[currentCornerIndex];
}
```

```
void Update()
{
    //If this is not the first corner,
    if (currentCornerIndex != 0)
        //Point from our position to the current corner position:
        trans.forward = (currentCorner - trans.position).normalized;

    //Move towards the current corner:
    trans.position = Vector3.MoveTowards(trans.position, currentCorner, movespeed * Time.
    deltaTime);

    //Whenever we reach a corner,
    if (trans.position == currentCorner)
    {
        //If it's the last corner (positioned at the path goal)
        if (CurrentCornerIsFinal)
            Leak();
        else
            GetNextCorner();
    }
}
```

The reason we only point at the corner if it is not the first one is because the first corner will be at the position of the spawn point, where we are already. Trying to point at a position that's exactly where we already are can cause some odd flipping behavior, so we avoid that with the first "if" in the Update call.

Now we have our GroundEnemy script functioning, so let's implement the GroundEnemy. If you still have that Test Enemy prefab from before, skip the following list and just drop an instance of the Test Enemy into the scene, rename it to "Ground Enemy", remove the Enemy script from the Test Enemy, and then move on to adding the following GroundEnemy script.

If you need to make it from scratch, however:

- Create an empty GameObject named **"Ground Enemy"**. Change it to the **Enemy** layer.

- Add a Box Collider sized (5, 8, 5) with a center of (0, 4, 0). Do **not** check the Is Trigger checkbox.

- Add a **kinematic** Rigidbody.

- Add a Cube child sized and positioned the same as the box collider: a scale of (5, 8, 5) and a center of (0, 4, 0).

- I've made a material named "Enemy" to apply to the Cube and given it a hex value of D0582D – a dark orange.

Now, add a GroundEnemy script instance to the root. I'm giving mine a Max Health of 12, Health Gain Per Level of 2, and Movespeed of 22. Set the "trans" reference to the Ground Enemy Transform, as always, and then set the "projectileSeekPoint" reference to the child Cube Transform so seeking projectiles hit it in the center, not at its feet.

Then, create a prefab for the Ground Enemy. If you made the prefab out of the old Test Enemy, agree to create a new, original prefab when Unity asks if you'd rather do this or create a new prefab variant.

Also, don't forget to reference the Ground Enemy prefab in the Game script's "groundEnemyPrefab" variable so it can spawn them in.

At this point, you should be able to play the game for the first three levels to see the ground enemies in action, although without our flying enemies, you'll get errors in the fourth level and nothing will spawn.

So, let's implement the flying enemies next. They'll be simpler than the ground enemies, since they just travel through the air from the spawn point to the leak point.

Create a **FlyingEnemy** script and let's write it:

```
public class FlyingEnemy : Enemy
{
    [Tooltip("Units moved per second.")]
    public float movespeed;

    private Vector3 targetPosition;

    protected override void Start()
    {
        base.Start();

        //Set target position to the last corner in the path:
        targetPosition = GroundEnemy.path.corners[GroundEnemy.path.corners.Length - 1];

        //But make the Y position equal to the one we were given at start:
        targetPosition.y = trans.position.y;
    }

    void Update()
    {
        //Move towards the target position:
        trans.position = Vector3.MoveTowards(trans.position, targetPosition, movespeed *
        Time.deltaTime);

        //Leak if we've reached the target position:
        if (trans.position == targetPosition)
            Leak();
    }
}
```

This makes for a similar but simplified script. It simply uses the last corner in the "GroundEnemy.path" as its "targetPosition", set once on Start. It overrides the "targetPosition.y", which would normally be on the ground level, to instead set it to the Y position that the Game script spawned the FlyingEnemy at. This keeps our Y position unchanged when our Update method moves us toward the "targetPosition".

Once it reaches the target position, it calls Leak.

Setting up the prefab is similar to the ground enemy, but we'll add a second cube to act as somewhat crude-looking "wings":

- Create an empty GameObject named **"Flying Enemy"** and set its layer to **Enemy**.

- Add a Box Collider with a size of (3, 3, 3), add a **kinematic** Rigidbody, and add a **FlyingEnemy** script. Set both the "trans" reference and the "projectileSeekPoint" to point at the Flying Enemy. I'll set the Max Health to 8, Health Gain Per Level to 3, and Movespeed to 19.

- Add a Cube child named **"Body"**. Remove its collider and set its scale to (3, 3, 3).

- Add another Cube as a child of Body. Name it **"Wings"**, remove its collider, and set its scale to (3, .15, 1).

- Apply the Enemy material to both cubes, or make a new material if you'd like to color your flying enemies something else.

When you're done, create a prefab out of the Flying Enemy and delete the instance from the scene. Your enemy should look something like a very crude airplane (or a plus symbol), shown in Figure 33-1.

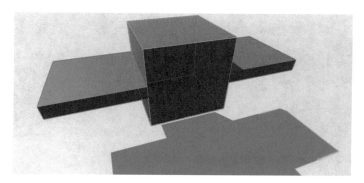

Figure 33-1. *The Flying Enemy*

Now, reference the Flying Enemy prefab in the Game script's "flyingEnemyPrefab" variable, right alongside the "groundEnemyPrefab". With both prefabs referenced, test out our newly implemented features! Figure 33-2 shows our ground enemies navigating around our towers.

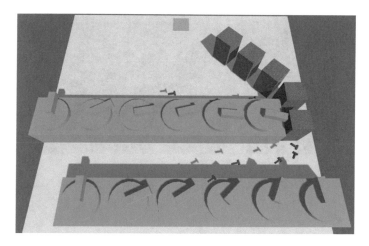

Figure 33-2. *A level with arrow towers firing at ground enemies. The ground enemies are seen moving around the arrow towers*

Figure 33-3 shows the flying enemies in action, soaring over our arrow towers.

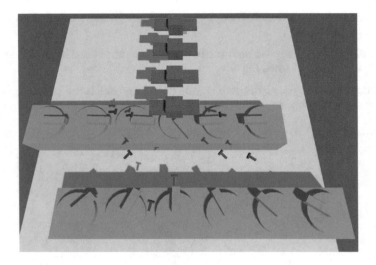

Figure 33-3. *A level with arrow towers firing at flying enemies*

And finally, our lose condition: if you let the enemies leak until you lose your default setting of 40 lives, you'll be greeted with the "game over" screen shown in Figure 33-4. It waits until all enemies are gone to end the game, so that the user can see how many lives they would've needed to stay in the game.

Figure 33-4. *Game Over screen, depicting a loss with -5 lives at level 3*

Summary

This chapter got our core mechanics in place at last: both of our enemy types, a game loop of transitioning from build mode to play mode and then back again, enemies "leaking" to take lives from the player if they reach the end of the stage, and a "game over" screen if the player loses all of their lives.

Some points to remember are as follows:

- **InvokeRepeating** can be used within a script to continuously Invoke a script method at a given rate, only stopping when **CancelInvoke** is called.

- A **virtual** method can be **overridden** by lower types with the **"override"** keyword.

- An overridden method must use the **"base"** keyword to reference its upper type and call the method of the same name. If not, the upper type's implementation of the method will not run, causing the override to completely replace the method functionality.

CHAPTER 34

More Tower Types

At last, it's time to implement our final three tower types: **Cannon Towers**, for which we'll need to implement a projectile that arcs; **Hot Plates**, which will be surprisingly easy; and **Barricades**, which will be even easier yet.

Arcing Projectiles

Our Cannon Tower projectile is intended to curve downward as it travels toward its mark. It's far from a grand flourish, but it will give a little extra sense of weight to our so-called cannonballs.

The projectile will use its "speed" value to determine how fast it travels toward its target on the X and Z axes – outward from the tower. Its Y axis will be handled separately, following a curve from the spawn position (the barrel of the cannon tower) to the floor over the duration it takes to reach the destination on the X and Z axes.

Let's create a new **ArcingProjectile** script, which will inherit from Projectile:

```
public class ArcingProjectile : Projectile
{
    public Transform trans;

    [Tooltip("Layer mask to use when detecting enemies the explosion will affect.")]
    public LayerMask enemyLayerMask;

    [Tooltip("Radius of the explosion.")]
    public float explosionRadius = 25;

    [Tooltip("Curve that should go from value 0 to 1 over 1 second.  Defines the curve of
    the projectile.")]
    public AnimationCurve curve;

    //Position we're aiming to travel to.  Will always have a Y value of 0.
    private Vector3 targetPosition;

    //Our position when we spawned.
    private Vector3 initialPosition;

    //Total distance we'll  travel from initial position to target position, not counting
    the Y axis.

    private float xzDistanceToTravel;
```

```
//Time.time at which we spawned.
private float spawnTime;

private float FractionOfDistanceTraveled
{
    get
    {
        float timeSinceSpawn = Time.time - spawnTime;
        float timeToReachDestination = xzDistanceToTravel / speed;
        return timeSinceSpawn / timeToReachDestination;
    }
}
}
```

I'll let the comments and tooltips speak for themselves and explain just the stuff that's new.

The **AnimationCurve** is a built-in class that's going to resemble the curve the projectile takes to reach its destination. Unity has a special little pop-up editor that lets us set up the curve ourselves using visual tools in the Inspector. We can then reference our AnimationCurve in our code and call its **Evaluate** method, passing in a float parameter. That float resembles the time, anywhere from the start of the curve to the end, and the method returns the value that the curve has at that point. You'll see how the curve looks in a moment, and we'll go over how it works in more detail. We'll be using it to resemble the arc the projectile takes.

The **"FractionOfDistanceTraveled"** member is a shorthand means of getting a value from 0 to 1 resembling how much of the distance toward our target we have traveled so far. "timeSinceSpawn" is the number of seconds that have passed since the projectile spawned. "timeToReachDestination" is the total distance we need to travel (X and Z axes only) divided by the units we travel per second, which results in the number of seconds it takes to reach our target position. Thus, we divide the time since the projectile spawned by the time we expect it to take to reach the destination, giving us a value of 0 when the projectile first spawns, rising to 1 when it has reached its destination.

We'll override the protected abstract OnSetup method given in the Projectile base class. We made the Projectile call this method after it is set up with its "speed", "damage", and "targetEnemy" variables. We'll use it to set up the private variables we'll use to get things done:

```
protected override void OnSetup()
{
    //Set initial position to our current position, and target position to the target enemy
    position:
    initialPosition = trans.position;
    targetPosition = targetEnemy.trans.position;

    //Make sure the target position is always at a Y of 0:
    targetPosition.y = 0;

    //Calculate the total distance we'll need to travel on the X and Z axes:
    xzDistanceToTravel = Vector3.Distance(new Vector3(trans.position.x, targetPosition.y,
    trans.position.z), targetPosition);

    //Mark the Time.time we spawned at:
    spawnTime = Time.time;
}
```

To set **"xzDistanceToTravel"**, we use a simple "Vector3.Distance" call, but since we don't want the Y position of the projectile to play into the equation, we just create a new Vector3, giving it the X and Z values from our Transform, but leaving its Y position at 0. Since the "targetPosition" Y value is set to 0 just beforehand, we know that they're both equal on the Y axis, meaning it won't affect the distance between them.

Save that code and head to the Unity editor. Let's set up the projectile that will hold the script and check out this AnimationCurve member while we're at it:

- Create a Sphere and name it **"Cannon"**. Set its scale to (4, 4, 4) and put it in the **Projectile** layer.

- Remove the Sphere Collider component and attach an **ArcingProjectile** script component. Set the "trans" reference to the Transform component. For the Enemy Layer Mask, check **only** the **Enemy** layer and leave the others unchecked.

- If you'd like, you can create a material for the Cannon, but I'm going to use the Arrow material to keep it the same color as our arrows.

When you click the "curve" field in our ArcingProjectile script in the Inspector, a pop-up Curve editor will show. Inside this editor a graph of sorts is visible, which is where the curve will be laid out – although there won't be a curve at all by default. The buttons on the bottom of the editor are presets which can be clicked to fill the graph in with a curve. Click the third preset from the left so that your Curve editor looks like Figure 34-1.

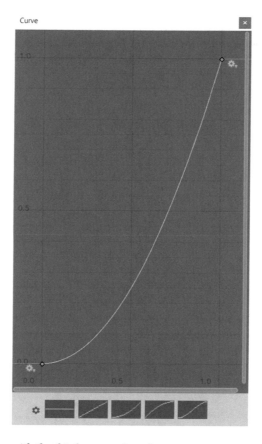

Figure 34-1. *The Curve editor with the third preset selected*

The horizontal axis (left to right) resembles **time**, and the vertical axis (up and down) resembles the **value**. Each axis has number values on the bottom, showing what the time or value is at that point on the axis.

The bottom left is 0 value and 0 time. The top right is 1 value and 1 time.

To make use of the curve, we simply pass in a time and get back the value corresponding to that time. The equivalent of this, in person, is to place your finger somewhere on the bottom axis, like on the 0.5 mark (halfway through the curve). Then, trace your finger up until it touches the green line of the curve. After that, just trace your finger straight left until you hit the vertical axis. Whatever the value is at that point, that's your result.

That's what the "AnimationCurve.Evaluate" method does: we give it a float parameter for the time, and it gives us the corresponding value.

The "time" doesn't have to be 1 second, though – by using our "FractionOfDistanceTraveled" property, we've given ourselves an easy transition from 0 (the left side of the curve) to 1 (the right side of the curve) over the time it takes to reach our destination, based on our actual speed and the distance to the destination.

The AnimationCurve doesn't only have these relatively straightforward curves found in the presets on the bottom – you can make more complicated ones by adding **keys**. Right-click somewhere near the line of the curve within the Curve editor and select "Add Key" to put an extra point at that position within the curve. You can pull any of these keys around, and the curve will pass through each one in order, from left to right. Each key also has two **tangents** sticking out of it, which are visible when the key is selected by clicking it. These can be moved by clicking and dragging them, like the key, but they're attached to the key and affect the slope the curve takes on each side of the key, giving you more control.

You can right-click keys to delete them, edit their time and value explicitly with float number fields, and even change the way the key and its tangents behave. Using multiple keys and settings, you can create more specific curves to match whatever you are using them for – an example of a less straightforward curve can be seen in Figure 34-2.

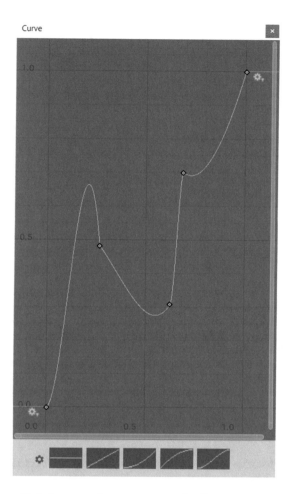

Figure 34-2. *A curve with multiple keys, creating a more complex line*

This isn't what we're after, though – I just wanted you to know what you can do with an AnimationCurve. The third preset, which we selected in Figure 34-1, is exactly what we want for our curve. We'll use the Evaluate return value as the fraction to Slerp the Y value of the projectile toward the Y value of the target position (which will be 0, the floor level). It will start at 0 (the bottom left of the curve), and over time, it will raise to a value of 1.

Okay, once you've assigned the curve, go ahead and create a prefab out of the Cannon and remove it from the scene. Now let's declare our Update method for the ArcingProjectile and see exactly how this Slerp call is going to work:

```
void Update()
{
    //First, we'll move along the X and Z axes.
    //Get the current position and zero out the Y axis:
    Vector3 currentPosition = trans.position;
    currentPosition.y = 0;
```

```
//Move the current position towards the target position by 'speed' per second:
currentPosition = Vector3.MoveTowards(currentPosition, targetPosition, speed * Time.
deltaTime);

//Now set the Y axis of currentPosition:
currentPosition.y = Mathf.Lerp(initialPosition.y, targetPosition.y, curve.Evaluate(Fract
ionOfDistanceTraveled));

//Apply the position to our Transform:
trans.position = currentPosition;

//Explode if we've reached the target position:
if (currentPosition == targetPosition)
    Explode();
}
```

First, we get the position of our Transform in a new Vector3. We'll apply this value to the Transform after we've modified it. We set its Y position to 0 and then use MoveTowards to travel only on the X and Z axes toward the target position.

Then we handle the Y axis. In each frame, we set our Y position to the result of the Slerp call starting at the initial Y position (when we first spawned) and moving toward the target Y position (the floor). Thus, we want the fraction (third parameter) to start at 0, our position, and raise to 1 (the floor position) over the duration it takes to reach the target position. If we just passed in FractionOfDistanceTraveled, it wouldn't curve, though. It would take a straight line. So we pass that value into the "curve.Evaluate" method. With the time going from 0 to 1 over the duration of the projectile's path, it works out perfectly: the curve takes our Slerp value from 0 to 1 in a fancy way.

But before we can test, we need to declare the Explode method to damage enemies in a radius:

```
private void Explode()
{
    //Get enemy colliders in the explosion radius:
    Collider[] enemyColliders = Physics.OverlapSphere(trans.position, explosionRadius,
    enemyLayerMask.value);

    //Loop through enemy colliders:
    for (int i = 0; i < enemyColliders.Length; i++)
    {
        //Get Enemy script component:
        var enemy = enemyColliders[i].GetComponent<Enemy>();

        //If we found an Enemy component:
        if (enemy != null)
        {
            float distToEnemy = Vector3.Distance(trans.position, enemy.trans.position);
            float damageToDeal = damage * (1 - Mathf.Clamp(distToEnemy / explosionRadius,
            0f, 1f));
            enemy.TakeDamage(damageToDeal);
        }
    }
    Destroy(gameObject);
}
```

Here, we use a new method: **"Physics.OverlapSphere"**. This tests for collisions against colliders in a sphere at the position given in the first parameter, sized by the radius given in the second parameter, and using a layer mask given in the third parameter – which is where we use our "enemyLayerMask" to make sure we're only getting Enemy instances. It returns an array containing all the Colliders touched by the sphere.

We then loop through these colliders, grab their Enemy script component, and calculate the distance from the projectile to the Enemy. Using that, we can calculate a value from 0 to 1 resembling how far the enemy is from the center of the explosion radius, where 0 is right in the middle of the projectile and 1 is at the very edge. This is just "distToEnemy / explosionRadius".

However, we want to do full damage to enemies in the center and less as they grow further from the center, so we need to "flip" the value by subtracting it from 1. That gives us a multiplier for the damage to deal. Just to be safe, we "Mathf.Clamp" the value between 0 and 1 – we're dealing with the center of the Enemy, so if their collider was just clipped at the edge, they may actually be *further* from the explosion than our "radius" variable. This Clamp call accounts for those odd cases.

We then deal the damage to the enemy with the TakeDamage method that we declared when we first coded the base Enemy class. After doing this for each touched enemy, we Destroy the projectile.

Cannon Tower

Let's get our Cannon Tower prefab ready to test our ArcingProjectile script:

- Create an empty GameObject. Name it **"Cannon Tower"** and place it in the **Tower** layer. To ensure it blocks ground enemy movement, give it a **NavMeshObstacle** component with a size of (10, 6, 10) and a center of (0, 3, 0). Make sure to check the **"Carve"** box.

- Add a Cube child named **"Base"**. Scale it to (10, 6, 10) and set its local position to (0, 3, 0).

- Add a Sphere child to the root Cannon Tower GameObject. Name it **"Dome"**. Position it at (0, 6, 0) and scale it to (7, 7, 7).

- Add a Cylinder child to the root Cannon Tower GameObject. Name it **"Barrel"** and give it a 90 X rotation to point it forward. Give it a position of (0, 7.5, 3) and a scale of (2, 1, 2). Now make it a child of the Dome so that it turns when the Dome turns.

- Add an empty GameObject as a child of the Barrel. Name it **"Projectile Spawn Point"** and give it a position of (0, 1, 0) to put it at the end of the barrel. To point its forward axis out from the barrel, give it an X rotation of 270.

- You can remove the colliders from the Base, Dome, and Barrel, since enemies navigate around our towers anyway due to the NavMeshObstacle component.

- Open your Arrow Tower prefab and locate the Targeter we made for it. Copy it with Ctrl+C or by right-clicking and clicking Copy in the context menu. Return to the scene and paste the Targeter, make it a child of the root Cannon Tower GameObject, and set its local position to (0, 0, 0).

- Add a **FiringTower** script component to the root Cannon Tower GameObject. Set the references. The Targeter should reference our own Targeter child, "aimer" should be the Dome, and the "projectilePrefab" should be the prefab for the Cannon we created earlier. You know what to do with the "trans" and "projectileSpawnPoint" references.

- Set the Gold Cost to 8, Range to 30, Fire Interval to .75, Damage to 9, and Projectile Speed to 80.

- Apply the Tower material to all the individual pieces – or create a new material if you'd like your cannon towers to have a different color than the rest.

- Create a prefab out of the root Cannon Tower GameObject and then remove it from the scene.

When you're done, your Cannon Tower should look something like Figure 34-3.

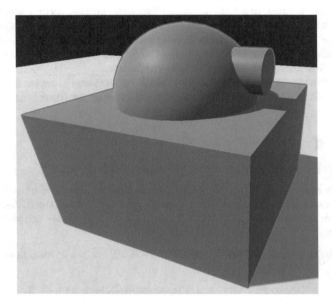

Figure 34-3. *Our Cannon Tower*

And your Cannon Tower's FiringTower script should look like Figure 34-4.

▼ # ✓ Firing Tower (Script)		❼ ⇄ ⋮
Script	# FiringTower	⊙
Gold Cost	8	
Refund Factor	●──── 0.5	
Targeter	# Targeter (Targeter)	⊙
Range	30	
Trans	⌁ Cannon Tower (Transform)	⊙
Projectile Spawn Point	⌁ Projectile Spawn Point (Transform)	⊙
Aimer	⌁ Dome (Transform)	⊙
Fire Interval	0.75	
Projectile Prefab	# Cannon (Arcing Projectile)	⊙
Damage	9	
Projectile Speed	80	

Figure 34-4. *The FiringTower script of our Cannon Tower in the Inspector*

One final step: The Build Button for our Cannon Towers needs its OnClick events set up so that we can build the tower to test it.

You know how to do this. Find the Cannon Tower Build Button GameObject tucked away in the Canvas (within the Build Button Panel) and set its Button component up with two events in the Inspector, each pointing at the Game GameObject. One calls **"Game.OnBuildButtonClicked"** and provides the Cannon Tower prefab as a parameter. The other calls **"Game.SetSelectedBuildButton"** and provides the Image component of the same GameObject (the build button) as its parameter. When you're done, the OnClick event should look like Figure 34-5.

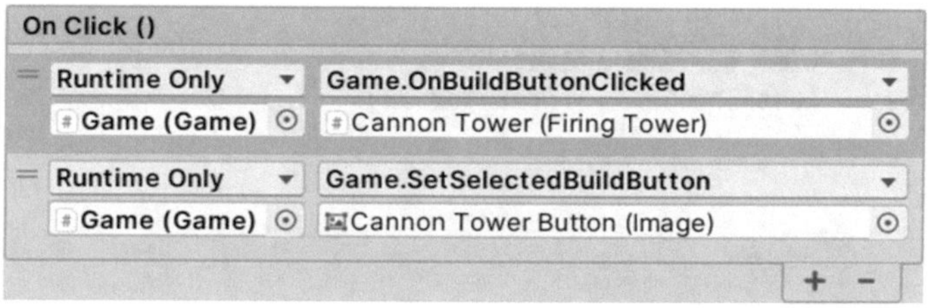

On Click ()

Runtime Only ▾	Game.OnBuildButtonClicked ▾
▪ Game (Game) ⊙	▪ Cannon Tower (Firing Tower) ⊙
Runtime Only ▾	Game.SetSelectedBuildButton ▾
▪ Game (Game) ⊙	▨ Cannon Tower Button (Image) ⊙

Figure 34-5. The OnClick event in the Inspector, at the bottom of the Button component of our Cannon Tower build button

With that, you should now be able to hop into the game, select the Cannon Tower build button, and place some Cannon Towers. Once you play the level, you'll see the cannon towers firing. Particularly when you watch from an angle in the Scene view, you can tell how the projectiles curve toward the ground instead of taking a straight line toward it.

If you want to watch it very closely to see the effect of our AnimationCurve, you can click the Pause button beside the Play button in the Unity editor, get your camera in position in the Scene view, and use the "step" button beside the pause button (hotkey Ctrl+Alt+P) to "step" one frame forward at a time. Hold the hotkey to play out the frames in quick succession.

Since we use an AnimationCurve to define the arc of the Cannon projectiles, you could even change the curve to something with more of an upward arc, if you'd like.

There's just one final step. Our Cannon Towers can still attack flying enemies. We didn't want that. Only Arrow Towers should fire at flying enemies.

To implement this, we'll go to our **FiringTower** script. First, add a variable to the script that specifies if the tower can or cannot attack flying enemies:

```
[Tooltip("Can the tower attack flying enemies?")]
public bool canAttackFlying = true;
```

In the **Update** method of the **FiringTower**, locate this block:

```
else //If the enemy is alive and in range,
{
    //Aim at the enemy:
    AimAtTarget();

    //Check if it's time to fire again:
    if (Time.time > lastFireTime + fireInterval)
    {
        Fire();
    }
}
```

And update it to this:

```
else //If the enemy is alive and in range,
{
    //If we can attack flying enemies, or the enemy is a GroundEnemy:
    if (canAttackFlying || targetedEnemy is GroundEnemy)
    {
        //Aim at the enemy:
        AimAtTarget();

        //Check if it's time to fire again:
        if (Time.time > lastFireTime + fireInterval)
        {
            Fire();
        }
    }
}
```

We've added an "if" that checks whether the tower can attack flying enemies, or if it can't, we check that the targeted enemy is a GroundEnemy.

Now we just need to go uncheck the **"canAttackFlying"** field in the Cannon Tower prefab so they can't attack flying enemies.

And with that, our cannon towers are complete!

Hot Plates

Two tower types to go. I promised this one would be easy. Create a script named **HotPlate** and give it this code:

```
public class HotPlate : TargetingTower
{
    public float damagePerSecond = 10;

    void Update()
    {
        //If we have any targets:
        if (targeter.TargetsAreAvailable)
        {
            //Loop through them:
            for (int i = 0; i < targeter.enemies.Count; i++)
            {
                //Quick reference to current enemy:
                Enemy enemy = targeter.enemies[i];

                //Only burn ground enemies:
                if (enemy is GroundEnemy)
                    enemy.TakeDamage(damagePerSecond * Time.deltaTime);
            }
        }
    }
}
```

You'll notice the script inherits from TargetingTower, which means it will already have its Targeter collider set up and tracking enemies within it – we just need to give it a "range" to match the size of the Hot Plate, and then, in our Update method, we "burn" all targeted enemies for constant damage per second. Since the Targeter will find flying enemies as well, we need to make sure we only burn an enemy if it's a GroundEnemy.

Let's set up the prefab and build button:

- Create an empty GameObject named **"Hot Plate"**. Put it in the **Tower** layer and give it a **HotPlate** script. Set the Gold Cost to 12 and Range to 5. Its damage per second should also be at 10. The reason we set Range to 5 is because, if you'll recall, we've set the Range field up to mean "how far away from the center of the Tower." Thus, it needs to be half of the size of the plate, not the full size! The plate will be the size of all towers, so 10 units by 10 units on the X and Z axes.

- Add an empty GameObject child to the Hot Plate. Name it **"Targeter"** and put it in the **Targeter** layer. Give it a **trigger** Box Collider, a **Targeter** script component with the "col" field set to a reference to that Box Collider, and a **kinematic** Rigidbody.

- Add a Cube as a child to the Hot Plate, positioned at (0, .2, 0) with a scale of (10, .4, 10). You can delete the Cube's collider. I'll also apply a new material named "Hot Plate" to mine with a bright-orange color using a hex value of FF6034.

- Don't forget to set the Targeter reference in the HotPlate script.

- Create a prefab for the Hot Plate and then delete it from the scene.

Then, set up the build button the same way we set up the Cannon Tower build button – but, of course, reference the Hot Plate prefab.

That's it. Our Hot Plates won't have a NavMeshObstacle component because they are meant to be walked over by enemies, not navigated around.

Barricades

Barricades are just Towers with nothing else to them. They'll be a simple cube with no cool turret on top:

- Create an empty GameObject named **"Barricade"** and put it in the **Tower** layer.

- Add a base **Tower** script with a Gold Cost of 2.

- Once again, give it a **NavMeshObstacle** component with a size of (10, 6, 10), a center of (0, 3, 0), and with the **"Carve"** box checked.

- Add a Cube child and give it the same position (0, 3, 0) and scale (10, 6, 10) as the NavMeshObstacle. You can remove the Box Collider component.

- Since they don't blow things up, I'm making a material named "Barricade" and giving them a drab, brown color with a hex value of A6843F.

You know the drill. Make a prefab, delete the instance from the scene, and set up the build button, just like the last two towers.

Summary

With that, we've implemented all four of our tower types and hooked them all up to their corresponding build buttons. We learned how to use the **AnimationCurve** and how to test for all Colliders touching an imaginary sphere using the **"Physics.OverlapSphere"** method.

Figure 34-6 shows a little maze set up with all four tower types involved.

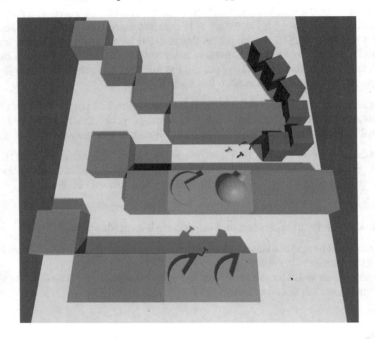

Figure 34-6. *A little maze with Barricades, Arrow Towers, a Hot Plate, and a Cannon Tower*

CHAPTER 35

Tower Defense Conclusion

We have at last concluded our second project. It's no finished game, but we've learned quite a lot along the way. Let's get a quick refresher on it all and then review some ideas for additional features you could try to implement on your own.

Inheritance

A major focus of this project was inheritance. We talked about it in the first part, but this project puts it to work. We used base classes like Tower and Projectile to define a set of variables and logic that can be implemented in different ways:

- A Tower can be bought and sold. To implement that, we need not concern ourselves with what specific type of Tower it is. We can reference it as a Tower to grab its gold cost and refund factor. We don't know what it does, but we don't need to. We just need to let the player put it on the stage or take it off and adjust the player's gold accordingly.

- A Projectile stores a travel speed and damage and is always spawned with a certain enemy as its target. When creating a projectile, we need not worry about whether it's an Arcing or Seeking projectile. We just give it a speed, damage, and target enemy and let the subclass do the rest.

This demonstrates one of the important takeaways of inheritance: that you can reference an upper type like Tower or Projectile even if a lower type is actually stored in the reference. If you only need the features of a Tower, like gold cost and refund factor, you can look at any more specific version as a Tower. If you ever need to make the distinction of what exact type it is, you can do so with **casting**. We demonstrated this with the Targeter, casting the Collider type to BoxCollider or SphereCollider.

We also put **abstract classes** to use, which is a means of making a class that cannot have instances of itself created. These classes are never intended to be used as is, instead acting as base classes that we inherit from to get use out of them. You'll only ever create instances of the lower types of the abstract class, not the abstract class itself.

This led us to using **abstract methods** and **virtual methods**. You declare the method, marking it either as "abstract" or "virtual" on the upper type:

```
public class UpperType
{
    public virtual void Setup()
    {
```

© Casey Hardman 2024
C. Hardman, *Game Programming with Unity and C#*, https://doi.org/10.1007/978-1-4842-9720-9_35

```
        //[setup code for the upper type goes here]
    }
}
```

You can then declare the method on a lower type to allow it to extend the method with its own logic. This is done with the **override** keyword:

```
public class LowerType : UpperType
{
    public override void Setup()
    {
        //Call the upper type's version of the method:
        base.Setup();
        //[setup code for the lower type goes here]
    }
}
```

You'll recall that abstract methods can only be declared on abstract classes, and the abstract method declaration won't give its own code block. The lower type **must** declare an override for the abstract method and provide a code block for the implementation (even if it's just an empty code block). However, with virtual methods, lower types are **not** forced to declare an override.

UI

We put Unity's UI system to use to make something a bit more than just the bare minimum. We learned that this UI system operates through GameObjects and components, making use of the hierarchical structure of parents and children. All our UI elements are children of the **Canvas** and can further be nested inside each other. Using pivots, we can determine how individual elements and their children rotate and scale.

Of course, most UI requires some form of responsiveness to the user. We learned how to add functionality by responding to **events**, using **OnClick** events found in the Inspector to call methods on our Player script when our build buttons were clicked. You can use this to call methods or set built-in variables on a GameObject or any of its scripts or components. But if you're trying to call a method you declared on one of your scripts, that method **must** be public, and it **must** either have no parameters or have one parameter of a serializable type like a script, a built-in type, or a component.

Raycasting

We learned how to use **"Physics.Raycast"** to fire a ray that will strike any colliders of a given **LayerMask**, returning true if an object was hit. Using this, we detected objects under the mouse by converting mouse position to a ray shooting out of the Camera with the **ScreenPointToRay** method. The LayerMask lets us set it up in the Inspector to select which collision layers we want our ray to hit, and which we want to ignore.

If you visit the official Unity scripting API for the Raycast method, you'll see that it has many overrides allowing you to call it with different parameters. You can avoid using the **Ray** and **RaycastHit** types that we used and opt to instead simply give a Vector3 for the ray start point and a Vector3 for the direction it travels in:

```
if (Physics.Raycast(origin, direction))
{
    //...
}
```

336

If this method is used, the "maxDistance" parameter defaults to "Mathf.Infinity", so the ray will travel infinitely in the direction it was cast. If you'd rather give a maximum distance yourself, you can provide a third parameter (a float).

Alternatively, you can use another similar override with an "out RaycastHit" as a third parameter and a "maxDistance" as a fourth parameter. Pretty much any combination you could need is covered!

Pathfinding

We learned how to perform some basic pathfinding to give us a series of points for our ground enemies to travel along to take them through the player's maze. Through the **Navigation** window, we marked our Stage plane as **Navigation Static**, updated the **Agent** settings to match the size of our enemies, and **Baked** the settings to the scene. This allows us to call **"NavMesh.CalculatePath"** to fill an existing **NavMeshPath** instance with the points that make up the path.

By making our path a static variable in the GroundEnemy class, we allowed ourselves to access it from other classes without requiring a reference to an instance of a GroundEnemy.

Additional Features

You might already be cracking your knuckles in preparation to tweak numbers for the game, like enemy health and speed, tower damage and rate of fire, and gold costs and rewards. Those things can be fun to play with, and our current settings certainly don't make the game particularly challenging. I'll leave that design stuff to you and suggest some features that require a bit of coding and implementation.

Health Bars

One feature of polish we're missing is an indication of enemy health. It's not very satisfying to watch our cannon towers shooting at our enemies when we can't even see their damage "splashing" to nearby enemies! The obvious answer would be to give each enemy a health bar above its head.

You can do this with **world space** UI. You'll need to add a separate **Canvas** to the scene and change its **Render Mode** to **World Space**. You'll also want to change the **"Reference Pixels Per Unit"** field of the **Canvas Scaler** component to something lower, like 10.

Health bars can then be positioned in world space, but they still must be children of the world space Canvas, or they won't render. Since health bars can't be children of their corresponding Enemy, you'll have to make the Game script create a health bar prefab instance for each Enemy when it is spawned and then script the health bars to position themselves above the enemy's head every frame and to automatically destroy themselves when the enemy dies. Alternatively, you could put a health bar prefab instance in the enemy prefabs, so they spawn with their own health bar, and then script the bar to make itself a child of the World Canvas after – but this means you'd have to place a health bar on each enemy prefab separately.

You can use a Panel as a dark-red background for the health bar and then use a bright-red Panel inside that one as the "fill". Size the "fill" to completely cover the background. In every frame, set the X axis of the "fill" scale to the percentage of life remaining on the enemy the health bar is associated with: "enemy.health / enemy.maxHealth". That would be done with a script attached to the health bar, with a reference to the RectTransform of the "fill" panel. Once the enemy loses health, the fill begins to shrink, but the background panel will be there to show behind it.

You can determine how the fill panel shrinks by setting its origin with the rect tool (hotkey T). The origin is that blue circle we talked about, which can be clicked and dragged while using the rect tool. If you leave the origin in the center of the panel, the shrinking will pull the left and right sides of the panel in toward the center until nothing remains. If you put it at the left side, then the right side will shift toward the left until nothing remains.

Types for Armor and Damage

Some tower defense games make use of differing types of armor and damage. In each level, enemies will use a different armor type from a selection of, say, three, like metal, wood, or magic. Each tower could then be assigned a damage type, and each damage type is strong against certain armor types, but weak against others. This encourages the player to have a range of towers that deal damage in all the types so that no enemies are particularly difficult to handle.

More Complex Pathing

Make the ground enemies touch little points on the stage along the way to the leak point. Rather than running from the spawn point to the leak point, put a few extra points between the two, designated by similar colored plates (flat cubes or cylinders). For example, enemies could go from the spawn point to the first plate, then to the second plate, and then to the leak point.

This is a fun little mechanic that gives the player something to maze around. If you know your enemies will have to touch certain spots on the stage before they continue, you can maze laboriously around those points and place your most important towers within range of them to ensure they get used as much as possible. Enemies will have to navigate through the maze, touch the point, and then navigate back out. It adds an extra layer of tactics to the game.

To implement this, ground enemy pathfinding would have to be changed. You can't just pathfind from the spawn point to the leak point anymore. You could implement this with a **List<Vector3>** to store all the points. Pathfind from the spawn point to the first plate. Add the corners to the List. Then, pathfind from the first plate to the second plate, and add those corners to the List. Then, pathfind from the second plate to the leak point, and add the corners.

That can be done using the List instance method **AddRange**. It adds the items from an array or List to the end of another List. For example:

```
var points = new List<Vector3>();

// [Perform pathfinding]

//Add points:
points.AddRange(path.corners);
```

This adds the path corners to the "points" List.

You would also need to make sure that towers can't be built directly on top of the points. Since enemies must touch the point, placing a tower on top of it makes the path impossible. Each point should be centered at a position a multiple of 10, placing it directly in the slot a tower would normally go. Then you can update the tower building logic to not allow placing towers when the highlighter is on top of one of these points.

Range Indicators

Give the player some indication of the range that firing towers have. You could make a thin Cylinder with a semitransparent material, named "Range Highlighter". When the player puts their normal highlighter at the position of a tower, make that the highlighted tower. Whenever the highlighted tower changes, make sure it's a FiringTower by performing a cast. If so, size the range highlighter Cylinder to match the tower's range and center the Cylinder on the tower. If it's not a FiringTower, hide the range highlighter by deactivating it.

Upgrading Towers

Give the player a means to upgrade existing towers, paying some gold to make them stronger. You could change the Tower Selling Panel to give it an "Upgrade" button and some text for the tower name and current level. When the player upgrades a tower, charge them some gold and strengthen some of the tower's stats based on what type of tower it is: damage, projectile speed, and range could all rise. Or you could make the player upgrade individual stats and track the level of each stat separately.

Summary

Now that we've gone over the important stuff you've learned throughout this project and given you some ideas for additional features to implement, it's up to you to decide if you want to linger on this project and try to expand it yourself or move on to our next project to continue the book. This project has taken us a long way with programming fundamentals like inheritance and working with collections like the List and the Dictionary. In the next project, we'll be dealing with physics and 3D movement systems more in-depth.

PART V

Physics Playground

■ ■ ■

CHAPTER 36

Physics Playground Design and Outline

For our third example project, we'll be tackling some new topics pertaining to the physics of the Unity engine. We'll implement a mouse-aimed camera with 3D movement for our player, including jumping, gravity, and wall jumping. We'll play with some objects using proper Rigidbody-controlled physics, giving our player a means of pushing and pulling them from a distance. We'll also tinker with joints to attach Rigidbodies to each other and "force fields" to play with adding forces to Rigidbodies and/or our player on the fly.

Feature Outline

This project will play less like a game and more like a testing ground. We'll get our hands dirty with different aspects of the physics engine, as well as work with fully 3D player controls, since up until now our projects have used top-down camera angles.

Camera

Our camera will have two modes: **first-person** and **third-person**. You're probably comfortable with these terms already. First-person is "through the eyes of the character," turning left, right, up, or down as the mouse moves. Third-person is "over the shoulder," hovering behind the character and orbiting around them as the mouse moves.

We'll allow the player to switch between these modes on the fly with the press of a hotkey, smoothly moving the camera from one mode into the other. We'll have proper smoothing applied to our camera's rotation, configurable in the Inspector to allow us to select how much smoothing we want. This not only makes first-person rotation smoothly respond to the mouse, but also the third-person orbiting.

The player will also be able to change how far the third-person camera will hover behind their character by using the scroll wheel of their mouse to draw the camera closer or pull it further away. We'll limit this to a certain minimum and maximum distance to keep the player from going crazy with it.

Player Movement

Since we have a mouse-aimed camera, we'll be implementing a "more 3D" movement system than our first project: the WASD keys to move local to the direction the camera is pointing, Space while grounded to jump, and Space while midair to attempt to "wall jump" off of a nearby surface. Once we're midair, whether by jumping or running off a ledge, we'll carry with us any ongoing velocity. Once we become grounded again, that velocity will drag out over time, if we aren't using WASD to move.

Wall jumps are performed by pressing Space while midair with a surface anywhere near the sides of our character. It can be behind, in front, left, or right; it doesn't matter. It just has to be close enough.

A wall jump will provide upward and outward momentum. If we're not holding any WASD keys when we perform a wall jump, it just goes straight up. If we are holding WASD keys, we'll also "push off" in that local direction – for example, holding W when performing a wall jump will move us forward as well as upward.

To implement this, we'll be using a different method of tracking our player velocity, employing only one velocity variable that handles velocity given by movement as well as external forces like force fields pushing us. This will demonstrate a handful of new and useful concepts for working with vectors.

Pushing and Pulling

To experiment with applying forces to Rigidbodies, we'll give our player a **telekinesis** power, allowing them to point at an object that has a Rigidbody and either hold **left-click** to **pull** the object toward them or hold **right-click** to **push** it away from them.

This power will be limited so that it only works on objects that are close enough to the player. We'll draw a simple, colored square at the center of the screen to demonstrate where the mouse is pointing and change its color to respond to what the telekinesis is currently doing. It will be **gray** when the player is not pointing at something that can be affected by telekinesis, **white** if the player is pointing at something valid that's in range, **orange** if the object is valid but not in range, and **green** while we are actively pulling or pushing something.

Moving Platforms

By default, our player will simply remain still even if the object they're standing on is moving. If you want to have floating platforms that move around, you probably want the player to move with the platform, rather than the platform sliding out from underneath the player. We'll code a means of setting up a platform that other objects will "attach" to when they land on it. With that in place, we'll code a script that makes a platform move back and forth between two points. The player can jump or walk onto these moving platforms and will begin to move with the platform as you would expect. They will also be able to move around as they normally do on solid ground, even while platform moves and carries them with it.

Joints and Swings

We'll learn how to create a series of linked objects, assembling something like a chain to hold up a swinging sphere. The player can use their telekinesis to push and pull the sphere to make it swing like a wrecking ball. They can even apply telekinesis to individual links in the swing.

Force Fields and Jump Pads

We'll implement two similar systems: **force fields** that constantly add velocity in a given direction to all objects that remain within them and **jump pads** that apply a sudden change in velocity to any object when it first touches the pad. Both of these systems can be adjusted to make them work on GameObjects with a Rigidbody, the player, or both. Since the player velocity is handled by our own script, not a Rigidbody, we'll have to react differently when the player touches the field as opposed to an object controlled by a Rigidbody.

Project Setup

Let's get our project ready before we begin. With Unity Hub, create a new project using the 3D template, just like we did for the last two projects. I'll name mine **"PhysicsPlayground"**.

Once the project finishes creating and opens up for us, click any GameObject in the scene, click its Layer drop-down at the top right in the Inspector, and then click "Add Layer…" and let's set up three layers:

- **3: Player** – Only the player character will use this layer.

- **6: Force Field** – Jump pads and force fields will use this layer.

- **7: Unmovable** – We'll make the player's "telekinesis" work on all layers except this one. If we ever want a GameObject that's controlled by a Rigidbody, but can't be pulled and pushed by the player, we can put it in this layer.

When you're done, your layer settings should look like Figure 36-1.

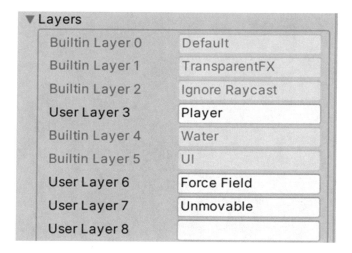

Figure 36-1. *Our layer settings*

As with the first two projects, I'll also use the Project window to rename the default scene to **"main"** and create these folders:

- Materials

- Prefabs

- Scripts

Summary

With a general idea of how our project will play and the features we expect to implement, let's press on and start adding mechanics one by one. When we're done, we'll have hands-on experience with the fundamental concepts and components of Unity's built-in physics.

CHAPTER 37

Mouse-Aimed Camera

Before we give the player any means of moving around, we're going to provide them with a first- and third-person camera system that lets them turn their character and camera with the mouse. Both systems will be handled by one script, and the player will be able to press a hotkey to smoothly switch from one to the other.

Coding the first-person camera will be a bit simpler. We position it where the player's eyes would be, and we rotate it based on changes in the mouse position. Move the mouse left, the camera and the player will turn left, and so on.

The third-person camera requires some extra legwork. We want it to be positioned a certain distance behind the player at all times, orbiting around the player as the mouse moves, but always looking at a certain point on the player. We also want to prevent it from passing through walls in its way, so that it instead slides along the surface of the wall.

Player Setup

Let's get the player all set up in the scene:

- Create an empty GameObject named **"Player"**. Position it at (0, 0, 0). Apply the **Player** layer to it.

- Add a child empty GameObject to the root Player GameObject. Name it **"Model Holder"**. Remember, you can right-click the Player and select "Create Empty" to add a child directly to it. It should automatically have the **Player** layer. Keep its local position and rotation at (0, 0, 0).

- Add a Capsule child to the Model Holder. Set its local position to (0, 3, 0) and scale it to (2, 3, 2). This makes it 6 units tall and puts its bottom right at the root Player position.

- Remove the Capsule Collider component from the Capsule. We'll be using a CharacterController for collisions instead, which will be set up in the next chapter.

- Add another empty GameObject as a child of the root Player GameObject. Name it **"Camera X Target"**. Leave its local position at (0, 0, 0). We'll just be using it for its Transform.

- Copy and paste the Camera X Target and rename this new instance to **"Camera Y Target"**.

- In the Hierarchy, locate the "Main Camera" GameObject that's included in the scene by default. Drag it onto the Player to make it a child of the root Player GameObject, just like the Model Holder and the Camera Targets. If you've deleted the Main Camera, you can just right-click the Player and create a new Camera instead.

- Change the camera layer to Player and name it **"Player Camera"**. In the **Clipping Panes** field of the Camera component, set the **Near** value to 0.01 instead of the default value of 0.3. Set its local position to (0, 5.4, 0), placing it up near the top of the player's Capsule model.

How It Works

The root Player GameObject holds all of the others. This one never rotates. It should remain at (0, 0, 0) rotation at all times. The Model Holder is what we apply rotation to, keeping it facing forward along the facing direction of the camera, but only on the Y rotation axis, which is what turns it left and right. We don't want to affect its X rotation, which would tilt it up toward the sky or down toward the ground. If you were working with a player model, you wouldn't want their whole body to tilt up and down when they raise or lower their head, right? You would, however, likely want to have their upper body bend forward or back as they look down or up, but our player is just a capsule, so we don't need to worry about that.

The two Camera Target GameObjects will play several important roles in our camera system. You can effectively look at them as one entity, the Camera Target, but we have them as two separate Transforms, one for X rotation and one for Y rotation, to avoid problems down the road that would occur if we applied both axes of rotation to the same Transform. When we use their rotation, we'll get the X and Y rotations and combine them as one Vector3.

Let's detail the purpose of our Camera Target:

- Whenever the player moves the mouse, we'll immediately apply that rotation to the Camera Target. X rotation is applied to Camera X Target, and Y rotation is applied to Camera Y Target.

- **In first-person mode**, the actual camera will have its rotation Slerped toward that of the Camera Target to add some smoothing to the first-person camera movement.

- **In third-person mode**, the **target position** is where, in relation to our character, we want the third-person camera to be positioned. This is determined by raycasting, starting at an **orbit point** and pointing directly backward along the Camera Target rotation. The orbit point will be a Vector3, set in our Inspector, that determines the local position (relative to the player's position) that we want the third-person camera to spin around (orbit) as the mouse moves. If the raycast hits a wall, the target position is placed at the point where the ray struck the wall. Otherwise, if no wall was struck, the target position is placed at the end of the range of the ray, which is determined by a variable we can change in the Inspector. With that in place, we just constantly Slerp the third-person camera position toward the target position, smoothly moving it into the place it should be.

As you can see, our whole process revolves somewhat around the Camera Target. In every frame, we'll check mouse movement and rotate the Camera Target first based on that: left and right mouse movement applies to the Camera Y Target, while up and down mouse movement applies to the Camera X Target. Then we run logic based on whether we are in first- or third-person mode. Either way, that logic is going to rely on the Camera Target to determine how the camera moves and rotates: first-person mode just smoothly follows the rotation of the Target, and third-person mode determines its target position based on the Target facing and then Slerps toward that position, while constantly looking at the orbit point.

Since the third-person camera looks at the orbit point and the raycast originates at the position of the orbit point, the Camera Target position is not important. The Target's facing direction is all we use it for.

The orbit point will be local to the Model Holder so that as the Model Holder rotates with the third-person camera movement, the orbit point remains at the same position relative to it. This allows us to place the orbit point somewhere off to the side of the character model, such as beside one of their shoulders, and the point will always remain relative to the model rotation.

Script Setup

Let's get to it. In your Project, create a **PlayerCamera** script in your Scripts folder.
Let's start off with the variables:

```
public class PlayerCamera : MonoBehaviour
{
    //References:
    [Header("References")]
    [Tooltip("The base Transform of the player, which should never rotate.")]
    public Transform playerBaseTrans;

    [Tooltip("Set this to the Transform that has the Camera component (which should also
    have the PlayerCamera component).")]
    public Transform trans;

    [Tooltip("Reference to the Camera X Target Transform.")]
    public Transform cameraXTarget;

    [Tooltip("Reference to the Camera Y Target Transform.")]
    public Transform cameraYTarget;

    [Tooltip("The Transform holding the model. This is what will rotate on the Y axis to
    turn left/right as the camera turns.")]
    public Transform modelHolder;

    //Movement and Positioning:
    [Header("Movement and Positioning")]

    [Tooltip("How quickly the camera turns. This is a multiplier for how much of the mouse
    input applies to the rotation (in degrees).")]
    public float rotationSpeed = 2.5f;

    [Tooltip("The amount of smoothing applied to the third-person camera. A higher value
    will cause the camera to more gradually turn when the mouse is moved.")]
    [Range(0, .99f)]
    public float thirdPersonSmoothing = .25f;

    [Tooltip("The third-person camera will be kept this many units off of walls it touches.
    Setting this higher can help prevent the camera from clipping with bumpy walls.")]
    public float wallMargin = .5f;
```

```
[Tooltip("The amount of smoothing applied to the first-person camera. A higher value
will cause the camera to more gradually turn when the mouse is moved.")]
[Range(0, .99f)]
public float firstPersonSmoothing = .8f;

[Tooltip("Position, local to the Model Holder, for the camera to use when in first-
person mode.")]
public Vector3 firstPersonLocalPosition = new Vector3(0, 5.4f, 0);

[Tooltip("Position, local to the Model Holder, for the camera to orbit around when in
third-person mode.")]
public Vector3 thirdPersonLocalOrbitPosition = new Vector3(0, 5.4f, 0);

//Bounds:
[Header("Bounds")]
[Tooltip("Minimum distance from the for the third person camera to have from its orbit
point.")]
public float minThirdPersonDistance = 5;

[Tooltip("Maximum distance from the for the third person camera to have from its orbit
point.")]
public float maxThirdPersonDistance = 42;

[Tooltip("Resembles the current third person distance. Set this to whatever you want the
initial distance value to be.")]
public float thirdPersonDistance = 28;

[Tooltip("Multiplier for scroll wheel movement. A higher value will result in a greater
change in third-person distance when scrolling the mouse wheel.")]
public float scrollSensitivity = 8;

[Tooltip("X euler angles for the camera when it is looking as far down as it can.")]
public int xLookingDown = 65;

[Tooltip("Y euler angles for the camera when it is looking as far up as it can.")]
public int xLookingUp = 310;

//Misc:
[Header("Misc")]
[Tooltip("The layer mask for what the third-person camera will be obstructed by, and
what it will ignore and pass through. You'll probably want this to include environmental
objects, but not smaller entities.")]
public LayerMask thirdPersonRayLayermask;

[Tooltip("The key to press to change from first-person to third-person, or vice
versa.")]
public KeyCode modeToggleHotkey = KeyCode.C;

[Tooltip("The key to hold down to hold the camera still, unlock the mouse cursor, and
allow mouse movement.")]
public KeyCode mouseCursorShowHotkey = KeyCode.V;
```

```
[Tooltip("Is the camera currently in first-person mode (true) or third-person mode
(false)? This can be set to determine the default mode when the game starts.")]
public bool firstPerson = true;

//Is the mouse cursor currently showing?  Toggled on by holding the
mouseCursorShowHotkey.
private bool showingMouseCursor = false;

//Target position for the third-person camera.
private Vector3 thirdPersonTargetPosition;

//Gets the third-person camera orbit point in world space.
private Vector3 OrbitPoint
{
    get
    {
        return modelHolder.TransformPoint(thirdPersonLocalOrbitPosition);
    }
}

//Gets the rotation of both the X and Y Camera Targets together.
private Quaternion TargetRotation
{
    get
    {
        //Construct a new rotation out of Euler angles, using the rotation of the X
        target and Y target together:
        return Quaternion.Euler(cameraXTarget.eulerAngles.x, cameraYTarget.
        eulerAngles.y, 0);
    }
}

//Gets a direction pointing forward along the TargetRotation.
private Vector3 TargetForwardDirection
{
    get
    {
        //Return the forward axis of the TargetRotation:
        return TargetRotation * Vector3.forward;
    }
}
}
```

Pay attention to the tooltips and the comments to explain the purpose of the variables, and if any of the variables are confusing to you, they'll be explained once they come into play in the following code.

Now, let's get the script ready to run when the time comes. Add the PlayerCamera script component to the Player Camera GameObject and set the references so that it looks like Figure 37-1. Be sure to set the Third Person Ray Layermask field to only include the Default layer. If you don't set it, it will include no layers at all, so the third-person camera will never slide against walls like we want it to.

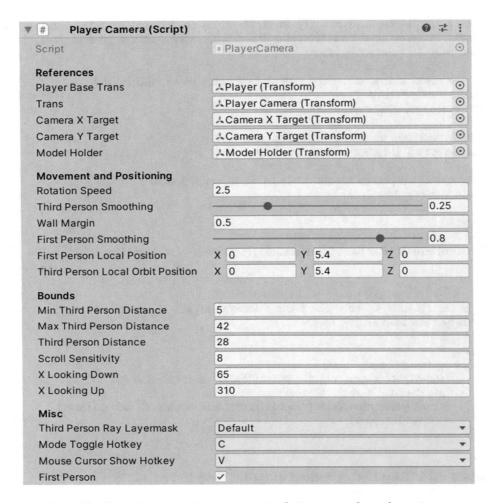

Figure 37-1. *View of the Player Camera script component in the Inspector after we've set it up*

With that done, let's do our usual routine and map out the basic functionality with some private methods that are called in our Unity event methods:

```
void Start()
{
    //By default, don't show the mouse:
    SetMouseShowing(false);
}

void Update()
{
    //Process hotkeys:
    Hotkeys();
}
```

```
//LateUpdate occurs after all Update calls.
void LateUpdate()
{
    //Update camera target rotation, so long as we're not showing the mouse cursor:
    if (!showingMouseCursor)
        UpdateTargetRotation();

    //Perform positioning logic based on the mode we're in:
    if (firstPerson)
        FirstPerson();
    else
        ThirdPerson();
}
```

This outlines the general behavior of our camera with private methods we'll be writing one by one next.

First, the Start method will call **SetMouseShowing**. If **false** is passed as a parameter, this will hide the mouse cursor and allow mouse movement to move the camera. If **true** is passed instead, the camera will not respond to mouse movement, and the mouse cursor will show.

The Update method calls only one method: **Hotkeys**. This is where we handle the pressing of our mode toggling hotkey (to switch between first-person and third-person) and our mouse showing hotkey.

Next, we're using a Unity event method that we haven't yet used: **LateUpdate**. This is just like Update, in that it is called every frame – however, all scripts will first call their Update, and then all scripts will call their LateUpdate. This way, if you want to be sure something happens after the rest of your scripts occur, you can place it in LateUpdate instead, because by the time LateUpdate is being called, every script will have already run its Update for that frame.

Our LateUpdate method will call **UpdateTargetRotation** to handle mouse input and update the rotation of the Camera Targets based on that, but only while the cursor is showing (in other words, while the mouse showing hotkey is not held down). It will then call either the **FirstPerson** or the **ThirdPerson** method based on which mode we are in.

We've put this logic in a LateUpdate, rather than an Update, so that any movement the player makes will happen first, before we, for example, raycast using a position relative to our Model Holder to determine our target position. This just ensures the camera operations occur after the player movement. If instead the player always moved after the camera determined its target position, then the target position would be "one frame behind" the player movement, which could be noticeable, particularly if the framerate drops low enough.

Hotkeys

Let's start with our **Hotkeys** and **SetMouseShowing** methods, up above the Unity event methods we just declared:

```
void Hotkeys()
{
    //Toggling first and third-person mode:
    if (Input.GetKeyDown(modeToggleHotkey))
    {
        firstPerson = !firstPerson;
    }

    //Toggling mouse mode:
    if (Input.GetKeyDown(mouseCursorShowHotkey))
```

```
        //Whenever the mouse cursor hotkey is pressed
        SetMouseShowing(true); //Show the mouse

    if (Input.GetKeyUp(mouseCursorShowHotkey))
        //Whenever the mouse cursor hotkey is let go of
        SetMouseShowing(false); //Don't show the mouse
}

void SetMouseShowing(bool value)
{
    //Enable or disable the cursor visibility:
    Cursor.visible = value;
    showingMouseCursor = value;

    //Set the cursor lock state based on 'value':
    if (value)
        Cursor.lockState = CursorLockMode.None;
    else
        Cursor.lockState = CursorLockMode.Locked;
}
```

Whenever the **"modeToggleHotkey"** is first pressed down, we use "firstPerson = !firstPerson;" – in other words, we flip the bool value of "firstPerson".

After that, the camera will automatically Slerp itself to the position it should be at, which will be implemented in the FirstPerson and ThirdPerson methods, so we don't have to do anything else to make the mode transition.

We also ensure that whenever the **"mouseCursorShowHotkey"** is first pressed down, we call **SetMouseShowing** (declared below Hotkeys) to true, so that the cursor shows and the camera stops responding to mouse movement; when the hotkey is released, we undo that, hiding the cursor again and relieving control to the camera.

Moving on, in the SetMouseShowing method, we use a few static members of the Unity class **Cursor** to fiddle with our cursor.

"Cursor.visible" is a built-in static member we can set to hide (false) or show (true) the cursor. But if we just set that, the hidden cursor would still hit the edge of the screen and stop going if the player moved it too far in one direction, and if the game was running in windowed mode, the cursor would begin showing again once the mouse left the screen.

We use **"Cursor.lockState"** to remedy this. It stores an enum called **CursorLockMode**. A value of **Locked** will lock the cursor at the center of the screen. Even though you can't see it, it will be kept there, which lets us move the mouse as much as we want without it hitting the edges of the game window.

The reason we want a way to easily toggle off the hiding of the cursor is so that we have a way to click somewhere else in the Unity editor while testing, such as to change a value in the Inspector or click the Play button to stop playing. If you had UI in the game, you would also want to start showing the cursor whenever the player opens a menu that requires clicking with their mouse while in-game, such as a pause menu or an inventory menu.

Mouse Input

With the cursor hiding and showing out of the way, let's code our **UpdateTargetRotation** method to handle the Camera Targets:

```
void UpdateTargetRotation()
{
    //The X rotation we should be receiving uses the mouse Y because rotating along the X
    axis makes us look up/down.
    float xRotation = Input.GetAxis("Mouse Y") * -rotationSpeed;

    //The Y rotation we should be receiving uses the mouse X because the rotating along the
    Y axis makes us look left/right.
    float yRotation = Input.GetAxis("Mouse X") * rotationSpeed;

    //Apply the rotation to the camera:
    cameraXTarget.Rotate(xRotation, 0, 0);
    cameraYTarget.Rotate(0, yRotation, 0);

    //Prevent camera from looking too far up or down:
    //If the X rotation is anywhere between 180 and 360
    if (cameraXTarget.localEulerAngles.x >= 180)
    {
        //If it's less than the looking up value, set it to the xLookingUp:
        if (cameraXTarget.localEulerAngles.x < xLookingUp)
            cameraXTarget.localEulerAngles = new Vector3(xLookingUp, 0, 0);
    }
    //If the X rotation is anywhere between 0 and 180
    else
    {
        //If it's past the x looking down value set it to the xLookingDown:
        if (cameraXTarget.localEulerAngles.x > xLookingDown)
            cameraXTarget.localEulerAngles = new Vector3(xLookingDown, 0, 0);
    }
}
```

First, we create both an **"xRotation"** and a **"yRotation"** variable. The "x" and "y" in the names refer to the axis of rotation that the Camera Target will be receiving. This doesn't correlate to the X and Y axes of the mouse movement, though, so it might look like we have it backward at first:

- **X rotation** tilts the Transform up toward the sky (negative) or down toward the ground (positive).

- **Mouse Y input** is up (positive) and down (negative). Thus, the Y input is used for the X rotation, but it has to be flipped so that up is negative and down is positive.

- **Y rotation** turns the Transform to the right (positive) or left (negative).

- **Mouse X input** is left (negative) and right (positive). This maps nicely to the Y rotation as is, so we don't have to flip it.

We also multiply the input by the **"rotationSpeed"** variable we declared, which can be raised or lowered to change the mouse sensitivity.

The rotation is then applied to the corresponding Camera Target Transform. Each axis of rotation is performed on a separate Transform to avoid any twisting that would come with applying both rotations to the same Transform.

Afterward, we make sure the X rotation value of the X target is clamped between the two variables we declared before: **"xLookingDown"** and **"xLookingUp"**.

The **"localEulerAngles"** member of a Transform is the "rotation" Vector3 you'll see in the Inspector when you view the Transform. An X rotation of 0 points the camera directly forward, which is equivalent to 360, where it resets to 0 again. The value can also be depicted as a negative amount, rotating in the opposite direction: a rotation of -10 is equivalent to 350, for example, because a rotation that's less than 0 (a negative rotation) will double back to 360 and decrease from there. Thus, you can depict the same rotation as a negative or positive value: -90 is equivalent to 270, for example. The "eulerAngles" member will always use positive values to represent its rotation, though – although it will let us set a negative value, in which case it would just convert it to the equivalent positive value for us.

These two variables define the X rotation values we want to prevent the Target from going past: if looking down as far as possible, it should not be able to tilt any further down than an X rotation of "xLookingDown"; looking up as far as possible, it should not be able to look any further up than an X rotation of "xLookingUp".

Figure 37-2 shows the camera on the player, viewed from the right side. From left to right, we see the camera looking down at the maximum amount, then looking up at the maximum amount, and then with both of these angles together, showing the cone that the camera is allowed to move within. The blue arrow for the Z axis and the overlapping red line is what we're paying attention to here, since that's the local forward direction of the camera. The green arrow has been removed in the rightmost depiction, showing only the forward axis when looking down/up.

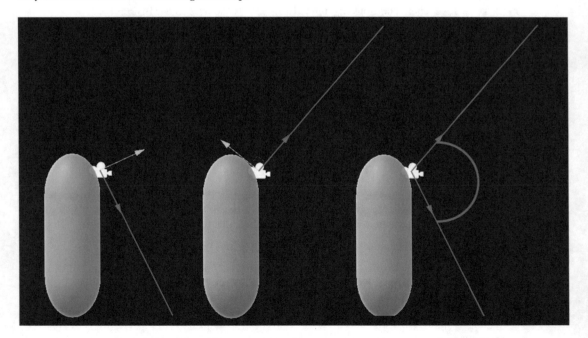

Figure 37-2. *Viewing the player and camera from the right side shows the camera looking all the way down (left), all the way up (middle), and both at once, showing the cone of X rotation allowed (right)*

Figure 37-3 provides a visualization of the angles involved when viewing the player from the same right-side angle. A rotation of 0, which is equivalent to 360, will point the camera straight forward. Adding to the angle will rotate clockwise, pointing the camera further and further down, while subtracting from it will point it further upward. If it rotates lower than 0, it resets to 360, and likewise, if it rotates higher than 360, it resets to 0. Figure 37-3 also depicts where our "xLookingDown" and "xLookingUp" angles lie.

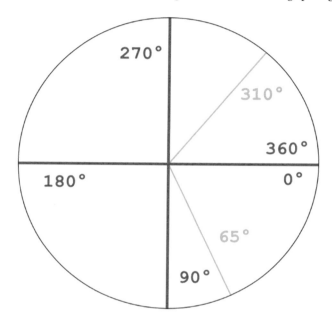

Figure 37-3. *Visualization of a single axis of rotation, separated into increments of 90 degrees (red). In green, angles of 65 degrees and 310 degrees are also shown to visualize our default "xLookingDown" and "xLookingUp" values*

This should help make sense of why we have to be more particular when we clamp the rotation. Just using a clamp method to clamp the rotation between 65 and 310, for example, would do precisely what we don't want to do. Thus, we separate the logic into two conditions. If the rotation is on the bottom half of that circle – between 0 and 180 – we don't let it raise past "xLookingDown", which is set to 65. If the rotation is on the upper half of that circle – between 180 and 360 – we don't let it go below the "xLookingUp value", which is set to 310.

This accounts for the "doubling back" that occurs when the camera X rotation goes from, say, 5 degrees to 355 degrees.

First-Person Mode

With the Camera Targets properly rotating, we can implement the first-person camera mode. This will do two things: if it's not there already, Slerp the camera toward the local position we want it to be at, which is defined by the **"firstPersonLocalPosition"** variable; and then update the camera rotation by Slerping it toward the current rotation of the Camera Target, which is acquired using the **"TargetRotation"** property (combining the X Target and Y Target rotations into one Quaternion).

This will all occur in the **FirstPerson** method we're already trying to call in Update, which we'll declare now:

```
void FirstPerson()
{
    //Get the position the first-person camera needs to be at:
    Vector3 targetWorldPosition = modelHolder.TransformPoint(firstPersonLocalPosition);

    //If the camera isn't at the first person camera location yet, Slerp it there:
    if (trans.position != targetWorldPosition)
    {
        trans.position = Vector3.Slerp(trans.position, targetWorldPosition, .2f);
    }

    //Get the rotation of the camera, slerped towards the target rotation:
    Quaternion newRotation = Quaternion.Slerp(trans.rotation, TargetRotation, 1.0f -
    firstPersonSmoothing);

    //Apply just the X and Y axes to the camera:
    trans.eulerAngles = new Vector3(newRotation.eulerAngles.x, newRotation.
    eulerAngles.y, 0);

    //Make the model face the same direction as the camera, but with the Y axis removed from
    the direction:
    modelHolder.forward = new Vector3(trans.forward.x, 0, trans.forward.z);
}
```

First, the camera is moved toward the position we want it to be at while in first-person mode, if it's not already there. This is how we smoothly transition the camera from third-person mode to first-person mode, moving it from its location behind the player to the local position it's expected to have when in first-person mode. To do this, we use the **TransformPoint** method to make the position relative to the "modelHolder" position, rotation, and scale. For example, if a value of (0, 5.4, 0) is passed into the TransformPoint call, it goes from "5.4 units above the world origin" to "5.4 units above the modelHolder."

This system works fine for our purposes, since we'll have our "firstPersonLocalPosition" variable set to (0, 5.4, 0). If we had an X or Z value that was not 0, this could cause the first-person camera to lag slightly behind where it should be when the player is moving their mouse. This is because the model holder is spinning on the Y axis (left and right) as the mouse moves left and right. That doesn't affect the result of transforming the Y position from local to world space, but it will affect the X and Z positions. Thus, the target position changes as the model turns when there is a nonzero value in the X or Z, so it will constantly be smoothing into that position.

For example, imagine you wanted the "firstPersonLocalPosition" to be a foot or two to the right side of the character's head. Maybe they're a strange alien with a very sideways neck, so their head is actually over their right shoulder. As the model holder spins, the head is pivoting around, and thus, the camera would be following behind it the whole time, rather than locking into place once the transition finishes – remember, the camera is a child of the root Player GameObject, not the Model Holder, so it won't automatically spin with the model as the rotation occurs.

Like I said, that won't be a problem for us, but if we did have some model with a head positioned forward or to the side and we wanted to line our first-person camera up with it properly, it could make for an awkward experience.

A workaround to that would be to use a "transitioning" bool variable, marking it as true when we begin transitioning from third-person to first-person. While "transitioning" is true, use the Slerp to move the camera to the target position, and check if it's reached the position yet (or come within a short distance of it). Once it has reached the point, mark "transitioning" as false. While "transitioning" is false, the camera should be locked in place, so just set its position without using Slerp. This keeps the smooth transition when first switching to first-person mode, but after the transition completes, it locks the camera in that place so it doesn't lag behind the point it should be when the model spins.

Anyway, after the movement is handled, we move on to the first-person camera rotation. When we Slerp the camera rotation, we calculate the result of the Slerp call from current rotation, toward "TargetRotation", and store it in the **"newRotation"** local variable. We then apply only the X and Y angles of that result to the camera, to make sure no odd Z rotation occurs. We don't want Z rotation because it would tilt the camera to the left or right, as if the player were cocking their head (imagine the camera doing a barrel roll; that's Z rotation).

We also apply the rotation of our first-person camera to the Model Holder GameObject. We're using directions here, not angles, so we take the forward-facing direction of the camera, exclude the Y axis, and make that the Model Holder Transform's new forward direction.

Third-Person Mode

Our third-person logic will use the **"OrbitPoint"** property that we declared earlier to define the origin of a ray and the **"TargetRotation"** property to determine the direction that our wall detection raycast will travel in. Since the "TargetRotation" is always pointing in the direction the camera should be looking forward at, we'll point the ray directly backward from that rotation, traveling only as far as the **"thirdPersonDistance"** variable. If it hits a wall, we'll set the target position to that point. Otherwise, we set the target position to the end of the ray.

Once we set the target position, we also need to smooth the camera position toward the target position with a Slerp afterward.

Let's declare the method and see how it looks:

```
void ThirdPerson()
{
    //We'll calculate the third-person target position by casting a ray backwards from the
    orbit point.
    //Make a new ray at the position of the orbit point, pointing directly backwards from
    the camera target:
    Ray ray = new Ray(OrbitPoint, -TargetForwardDirection);
    RaycastHit hit;

    //Cast the ray using thirdPersonDistance plus the wallMargin to account for walls just
    outside the distance:
    if (Physics.Raycast(ray, out hit, thirdPersonDistance + wallMargin,
    thirdPersonRayLayermask.value))
    {
        //If the ray hits something, set the target position to the hit point:
        thirdPersonTargetPosition = hit.point;

        //We'll offset it back towards the cameraTarget by 'wallMargin' distance:
        thirdPersonTargetPosition += TargetForwardDirection * wallMargin;
    }
```

```
    else //If the ray didn't hit anything
    {
        //Set the target position to 'distance' units directly behind the camera target
        thirdPersonTargetPosition = OrbitPoint - (TargetForwardDirection *
        thirdPersonDistance);
    }

    //Slerp the camera towards the target position using our smoothing settings:
    trans.position = Vector3.Slerp(trans.position, thirdPersonTargetPosition, 1.0f -
    thirdPersonSmoothing);

    //Now that the camera has been moved properly, make it look at the orbit point:
    trans.forward = (OrbitPoint - trans.position).normalized;

    //Make the model face the same direction as the camera, with no Y axis position
    influence:
    modelHolder.forward = new Vector3(trans.forward.x, 0, trans.forward.z);
}
```

If you check what the **"OrbitPoint"** property is returning, you'll see that it's just calling TransformPoint with the "modelHolder" to get the "thirdPersonLocalOrbitPosition" as a world position, no longer relative to the Model Holder, much like we did with the first-person local position earlier. Rather than typing out that bulky line each time, we give ourselves a more concise name: "OrbitPoint".

We also use the **"TargetForwardDirection"** property we declared before, which uses a simple trick of creating a Quaternion (rotation) out of the combined Euler angles of our X Target and our Y Target and then multiplying that by a direction: forward. This results in a direction that travels forward along the rotation. The property pretty much points in the direction the first-person camera should be pointing, and the opposite direction of this is where the third-person camera aims to be.

We then use the **Raycast** method, explored in our second project. The ray and the "out hit" are passed in, which we just created beforehand. The third parameter is the ray distance, and the fourth is the layer mask value to use.

You may be wondering why the ray distance parameter has the **"wallMargin"** added to it. Think about it like this: if we set our camera up to have a wall margin of 2, that means we're expecting our camera to distance itself 2 units away from walls behind it. However, if the ray was only as long as the "thirdPersonDistance", and we positioned our camera at the end of the ray whenever there was no wall there, what if a wall was a mere 1 unit, or 0.005 units, away from the end of the ray? Then our camera would be closer than 2 units to the wall. By extending the ray, we ensure that if a wall is just a little further away than the tip of the ray, it'll still get detected and the camera will be kept "wallMargin" units away from it as a result, just as expected.

If the ray hits anything, we set the target position to the hit point and then move it away from the wall using the "TargetForwardDirection", which is the opposite direction that we sent the ray in. We also use "wallMargin" here to determine how far from the wall it should be moved. If "wallMargin" was set to 0, the target position would simply remain exactly at the hit point. This could cause awkward clipping where part of the camera's view "sticks through" walls, particularly if the wall is bumpy – that's why we added this ability to define a wall margin in the first place.

If the ray did not hit anything, we still have to set the target position. We set it to the "OrbitPoint", traveling backward from the Camera Target – the same direction we used to cast the ray – by the desired "thirdPersonDistance".

After that, we just have to make sure we're Slerping the camera position to the target position at all times, using the same "1 - smoothing" equation we used before (ensuring that a *higher* smoothing value makes for *smoother* movement, as you'd expect when setting the variable).

We also have to make sure the camera is always pointing at the "OrbitPoint", so we use the same equation we've used multiple times to get the direction pointing from one position to another:

```
(to - from).normalized
```

So our equation gets a direction from the camera position to the OrbitPoint and makes that the "forward" direction of the camera.

Finally, we spin the Model Holder to always point forward with the camera, like we do with the first-person camera, and we use the same system we used with the first-person camera. Since we only want the model holder to spin left and right, not tilt up and down, we construct a new Vector3 and "cut out" the Y direction of the camera's forward facing. This gives us a direction that mimics the camera's forward facing, but only on the X and Z axes, preventing the possibility of any upward or downward tilting.

Now all that's left is giving our player a means of changing the third-person distance, which we can tie to the scroll wheel. Since we already have our Hotkeys method handling basic input like this, we can add a little chunk of code that changes the distance variable when the scroll wheel is detected.

This won't be complicated at all – just get the scroll wheel input this frame and apply it to the "thirdPersonDistance" variable, using the "scrollSensitivity" variable to modify it.

We'll add this code underneath the existing code **in our Hotkeys method**:

```
//Scroll wheel for third-person camera distance:
if (!firstPerson)
{
    //Get scroll wheel delta this frame:
    float scrollDelta = Input.GetAxis("Mouse ScrollWheel");

    //Subtract delta from thirdPersonDistance, multiplying it by the scroll sensitivity:
    thirdPersonDistance = Mathf.Clamp(thirdPersonDistance - scrollDelta * scrollSensitivity,
    minThirdPersonDistance, maxThirdPersonDistance);
}
```

We subtract the "scrollDelta" rather than adding because we want to go **further away** from the player, meaning a **higher** "thirdPersonDistance", when **scrolling back**, but the scroll wheel input will be **negative** when scrolling back.

Testing

You should now be able to playtest your camera and watch it in action, but it won't do us much good if we don't have anything in our scene to indicate that the camera is actually moving – plus we'd like some walls near the player to demonstrate the third-person camera moving forward to keep from passing through objects.

Add a Plane named **"Floor"** to the scene, positioned at (0, 0, 0) with a (100, 1, 100) scale. You can then just add a tall Cube and position it near the Player to give you something to test the third-person camera with.

Remember, our default hotkeys are C to switch between camera modes and holding V to show your cursor again and freeze the camera in place. Once you click away from the Game window (e.g., to the Inspector or Hierarchy), you can let go of V, and the camera will remain frozen until you click back into the Game window and tap V again.

You may also want to play with the smoothing variables of the Player Camera script. If you don't notice the smoothing much, turn it up high in the Inspector, and it will become much more obvious.

Summary

With that, we've implemented a camera that can switch smoothly between first- and third-person modes. Our Camera Targets have the rotation applied to them every frame, and the actual camera GameObject uses that rotation to determine first-person rotation and third-person target position. We smooth the first-person camera rotation toward its target rotation every frame. For the third-person camera, it is constantly moved toward its target position, orbiting around the OrbitPoint, and kept facing forward at the OrbitPoint.

CHAPTER 38

Advanced 3D Movement

In this chapter, we'll be implementing the movement system for our player. This includes using the WASD keys to move, pressing Space to jump, and gravity to make the player fall back to the ground. In the next chapter, we'll also implement a wall jumping mechanic that allows the player to "push off" of a nearby wall to gain extra upward and outward momentum while midair.

How It Works

Let's get an overview of how we expect this system to work before we start poking into the code. This movement system will operate with a few concepts that are similar to that of our player movement in the first project:

- Momentum is gained in the direction held by the WASD keys.

- Ongoing momentum is lost over time when no WASD keys are held.

- Attempting to move against ongoing momentum will provide an increase in momentum gain so the player can more easily reverse the direction they're traveling in.

We'll also use a **CharacterController** component to perform our movement, just like in the first project. This time, however, we have to account for that pesky Y axis – the player has to fall when they run off of a ledge, so we'll need to make them accumulate downward momentum when they're midair.

To make things more realistic, we'll keep any ongoing momentum when the player becomes midair, whether by jumping or falling off a ledge. This means that all velocity they have acquired through movement will keep going in the same direction after they jump or step off a ledge. The velocity won't begin to drag out until they land on the ground again. Because this can feel a bit sticky, we'll still allow them to influence their movement with the WASD keys while midair, but we'll use a multiplier for midair movement so we can decrease how effective it is. We want them to be able to draw back if they've made a poor jump or wiggle toward a wall if they didn't jump straight enough at it, but we don't want them to have the same control that they have on the ground.

This time, we have to make the movement local to our player model. In our previous projects, our movement systems used world space directions because the camera never rotated. This time, the player model will be facing whatever direction the player is looking toward. The WASD keys are no longer going to provide velocity in consistent directions. They'll have to be local to the facing of the player.

We can achieve this in a few different ways. Your first idea might be to simply store movement velocity as local to the player. We could do it much the same way as we did in our first project, maintaining a **"movementVelocity"** variable where the Z axis corresponds to the W and S keys and the X axis corresponds

© Casey Hardman 2024
C. Hardman, *Game Programming with Unity and C#*, https://doi.org/10.1007/978-1-4842-9720-9_38

to the A and D keys. For example, if we are traveling straight forward, we might have a "movementVelocity" of (0, 0, 26). This vector represents 26 units of forward (Z axis) momentum per second.

Since our CharacterController expects us to move it by giving a world space vector, not local to the Transform facing, this means we would have to make our "movementVelocity" local to the facing of our Model Holder, supplying the result to our "CharacterController.Move" method.

For example, when our "movementVelocity" is (0, 0, 26), we see it as "26 units of forward momentum, relative to the direction our Model Holder is facing." But the way we want to look at it is not the way our CharacterController will see it. The **"CharacterController.Move"** method moves in world space, so it would see the vector as "26 units forward in world space," which could also be considered "north." It disregards the direction our Model Holder is facing and creates a very awkward experience for our player.

Thus, we have to make the "movementVelocity" local to our Model Holder, using the Transform method **TransformDirection**. This method takes a Vector3 direction that is meant to be local to the Transform and then returns it as a world space direction. In other words, it handles the conversion from local to world space for us. If we transform "movementVelocity" from local to world space when it is (0, 0, 26), and our Model Holder is actually looking backward (south), the "movementVelocity" becomes (0, 0, -26), which takes us south instead of north. This goes for any direction the Model Holder faces. If we are facing directly right, it would become (26, 0, 0) instead or (-26, 0, 0) if we are facing directly left, or any shade between.

This is viable, and doing it this way can work. We can handle the velocity the same way we did in our first project, the only difference being that we must use TransformDirection to convert it from local to world space before we supply it to our CharacterController to actually perform the movement.

But maintaining this is not as easy when it comes to things like falling off of ledges and jumping. Remember, with the movement local to our Model Holder facing, the player can obtain forward momentum and then easily steer it by turning the mouse. Whatever way they are facing, that is where the velocity takes them. But once they become midair, we want them to no longer be able to turn their camera to adjust their momentum. If we just operated on local velocity the whole time, the player could run forward, leap into the air, and then turn their mouse to completely change their direction. They could jump off a ledge, then turn around midair and safely land where they started the jump. This makes for a rather unrealistic movement system.

So things become more complicated. We would have to convert our "movementVelocity" to world space whenever we become midair. This way, it gets locked into the world direction we were facing when we started the jump and is stuck that way. But then what happens when we land? More complications! The world velocity will have to be converted back to local "movementVelocity" once we land, so that we can steer our momentum again.

This all adds a layer of complexity to the management of our velocity, and it becomes more awkward when you consider how you might have external velocities applied to the player that are not capped by their maximum movement speed, like if something shoved the player or if the player performed a "dash" move like the one we implemented in our first project.

To simplify things, we'll use a different approach. Rather than looking at how much we're moving on each individual axis, we'll look at what is known as the **magnitude** of our "worldVelocity" Vector3. The magnitude of a vector is a math equation you can perform to get what can be seen as the distance that the vector traverses. It is also sometimes referred to as the **length** of the vector. We can get the magnitude of a vector by simply using the **"Vector3.magnitude"** property. It returns a float. We don't really need to know what the math equation is, because the plain English version is simpler anyway: it returns "how far the vector travels." If you were to add Vector3 "A" to a Vector3 position "B", then "B" will be moving "A.magnitude" units of distance from where it was.

Then there is the **"Vector3.normalized"** member, which is a property that returns a new vector, going in the same direction as the original, but with its magnitude scaled down to 1. In other words, it is effectively "converting the vector to a direction."

We've already seen the "normalized" member in our past projects – we used it in the "(to - from). normalized" equation, which is how we get the direction to point from a position of Vector3 "from" to another position of Vector3 "to". For example, to get a direction pointing from an enemy to the player, do this:

```
(playerPosition - enemyPosition).normalized
```

A direction is still a Vector3; it's just that it has a magnitude of 1. Thus, it can be multiplied by a float to scale the magnitude to whatever that float value is. This is why ".normalized" can be considered turning the vector into a direction. Once you've normalized a Vector3, you can then multiply it by a float to get a Vector3 that travels that many units in that direction.

We're about to make use of these concepts to code our movement system. Our velocity will be stored in a single vector depicting the world space velocity our player currently has. This is *always* depicted in world space and never gets converted back and forth between world and local space, using some clever tricks regarding the magnitude of the velocity.

When we check for input of the WASD keys, we don't manage our velocity in "units per second." We just get the local direction that the movement keys are held down in. For example, the local direction is (0, 0, 1) if just W is held, it's (1, 0, -1) if D (right) and S (backward) are held, and so on.

We can then convert that local direction to a world space direction using the **TransformDirection** method with our Model Holder reference, which will be turning as the player moves their mouse to aim their camera. We'll apply our velocity gain per second (a float), in the world space direction, to our "worldVelocity".

To cap the movement at a maximum speed, we'll use the magnitude of our "worldVelocity". If the magnitude is equal to our "movespeed" variable, we are already moving "movespeed" units per second in the direction we are traveling – whatever that direction is – so we won't allow our player to go any faster in that direction.

Enough of the theory – now that you have a general overview of how our process will work and, notably, how it differs from our first project, let's get started with piecing it together so we can see these concepts in action.

Player Script

We already set up our Player GameObject in the previous chapter, so we only need to make a few tweaks to get it ready for implementing the movement.

Add a **CharacterController** component to the root **Player** GameObject. Set the CharacterController's **Center** to (0, 3, 0), its **Height** to 6, and its **Radius** to 1, which will make it match the Capsule we added to our Model Holder before.

Now, create a **Player** script in your Scripts folder. Let's get it started by declaring our variables and an outline of the methods that split up our Update logic:

```
//Variables
[Header("References")]
[Tooltip("Reference to the root Transform that has the Player script.")]
public Transform trans;

[Tooltip("Reference to the Model Holder Transform. Movement will be local to the facing of
this Transform.")]
public Transform modelHolder;

[Tooltip("Reference to the CharacterController component.")]
public CharacterController charController;
```

```csharp
[Header("Gravity")]

[Tooltip("Maximum downward momentum the player can have due to gravity.")]
public float maxGravity = 92;
[Tooltip("Time taken for downward velocity to go from 0 to the maxGravity.")]
public float timeToMaxGravity = .6f;

//Property that gets the downward momentum per second to apply as gravity:
public float GravityPerSecond
{
    get
    {
        return maxGravity / timeToMaxGravity;
    }
}

//Y velocity is stored in a separate float, apart from the velocity vector:
private float yVelocity = 0;

[Header("Movement")]
[Tooltip("Maximum ground speed per second with normal movement.")]
public float movespeed = 42;

[Tooltip("Time taken, in seconds, to reach maximum speed from a stand-still.")]
public float timeToMaxSpeed = .3f;

[Tooltip("Time taken, in seconds, to go from moving at full speed to a stand-still.")]
public float timeToLoseMaxSpeed = .2f;

[Tooltip("Multiplier for additional velocity gain when moving against ongoing momentum. For
example, 0 means no additional velocity, .5 means 50% extra, etc.")]
public float reverseMomentumMulitplier = .6f;

[Tooltip("Multiplier for velocity influence when moving while midair. For example, .5 means
50% speed. A value greater than 1 will make you move faster while midair.")]
public float midairMovementMultiplier = .4f;

[Tooltip("Multiplier for how much velocity is retained after bouncing off of a wall. For
example, 1 is full velocity, .2 is 20%.")]
[Range(0, 1)]
public float bounciness = .2f;

//Movement direction, local to the model holder facing:
private Vector3 localMovementDirection = Vector3.zero;

//Current world-space velocity; only the X and Z axes are used:
private Vector3 worldVelocity = Vector3.zero;

//True if we are currently on the ground, false if we are midair:
private bool grounded = false;
```

```csharp
//Velocity gained per second.  Applies midairMovementMultiplier when we are not grounded:
public float VelocityGainPerSecond
{
    get
    {
        if (grounded)
            return movespeed / timeToMaxSpeed;

        //Only use the midairMovementMultiplier if we are not grounded:
        else
            return movespeed / timeToMaxSpeed * midairMovementMultiplier;
    }
}

//Velocity lost per second based on movespeed and timeToLoseMaxSpeed:
public float VelocityLossPerSecond
{
    get
    {
        return movespeed / timeToLoseMaxSpeed;
    }
}

[Header("Jumping")]
[Tooltip("Upward velocity provided on jump.")]
public float jumpPower = 76;

//Update Logic:
void Movement(){}
void VelocityLoss(){}
void Gravity(){}
void Jumping(){}
void ApplyVelocity(){}

//Unity Events:
void Update()
{
    Movement();
    VelocityLoss();
    Gravity();
    Jumping();
    ApplyVelocity();
}
```

To define gravity, we declare **"maxGravity"**, the maximum downward velocity value that can be applied by gravity, and **"timeToMaxGravity"**, the time we want it to take, in seconds, to reach that maximum downward velocity. Decrease the "timeToMaxGravity" variable, and gravity will take full effect on your player faster. Increase it and the player will be more "floaty," taking longer to begin falling after they have jumped or stepped off an edge.

The actual Y velocity is stored as a float in the private **"yVelocity"** variable, while the X and Z axes of our velocity will be stored in the **"worldVelocity"** Vector3. This is so we can track the magnitude of our outward velocity for movement, without the Y axis affecting it. It'll make more sense why we do it this way when we apply our movement to the velocity.

Our movement variables are similar to those of our first project. The **"movespeed"** is the maximum velocity on the X and Z axes that we want to be able to have just by moving while grounded. External forces might make us move faster than that, but if we're just moving around while grounded, we won't be able to pick up any more speed than "movespeed".

We also use **"timeToMaxSpeed"** and **"timeToLoseMaxSpeed"** which are used in the "VelocityGainPerSecond" and "VelocityLossPerSecond" properties, just like in the movement system of our first project.

The **"reverseMomentumMultiplier"** is also the same concept we used in our first project, although we'll be implementing it a little differently. It is a multiplier for our movespeed which is added as bonus speed when we are working to move against ongoing velocity – trying to go west when we are already traveling east, for example. The higher you set it, the quicker the player can switch directions.

The **"midairMovementMultiplier"** is how we prevent the player from gaining as much velocity from midair movement as they would with grounded movement. We apply it when getting the **"VelocityGainPerSecond"** property, but only while **"grounded"** is false (meaning we're midair).

The **"bounciness"** is a new variable that we use to determine how hard the player bounces off of walls that they hit while midair. We don't want the player to slide against walls that they strike while midair. If they did, then they would keep sliding against a wall, and if they rose up over the wall, they would keep going. Thus, you could jump at a wall, face-plant into it for a second, and then rise up over it and keep going forward as if you didn't just smack into the wall. To avoid that, we'll redirect the player's momentum away whenever they strike a wall. Alternatively, you could set "bounciness" to 0 to make the player completely stop traveling outward when they hit a wall – they won't bounce off of it, they'll just plop against it like a ball of wet paper.

Beneath the variables, our process is outlined with our empty methods:

- **Movement( )** will check if the player is holding the WASD keys, updating the **"localMovementDirection"** vector based on which keys are held. If any keys are held, it will convert the local movement direction to world space based on the direction the Model Holder is facing and then apply "VelocityGainPerSecond" to "worldVelocity" in that direction. Since this occurs first, other methods can use the "localMovementDirection" to check which movement keys are held, if they need to.

- **VelocityLoss( )** causes our ongoing velocity to "drag out" while we are grounded, assuming we are either not holding any movement keys, or our velocity magnitude is greater than "movespeed".

- **Gravity( )** subtracts from "yVelocity" as long as we are midair, but only if our downward velocity has not exceeded "maxGravity".

- **Jumping( )** checks for the Space key being pressed while grounded. If so, it adds "jumpPower" upward momentum by adding to "yVelocity".

- **ApplyVelocity( )** puts our "worldVelocity" and "yVelocity" together and applies it as movement per second with the CharacterController. We'll use some information given to us by the CharacterController to determine if we touched ground during that movement, and if so, we'll set "grounded" to true; otherwise, we'll set it to "false". Conversely, we'll also check if we bumped our head during the movement. If so, we'll lose our upward velocity so we start falling as soon as we hit our head, rather than sliding against the surface until gravity begins to pull us down.

To make sure things are ready when we begin, go ahead and add an instance of the **Player** script to the root Player GameObject. Set the three references: "trans" should point to the root "Player" Transform, the Model Holder can be dragged from the Hierarchy onto the corresponding field to reference it, and the CharacterController you just added to the Player GameObject can be dragged to the Char Controller field through the same Inspector view.

Movement Velocity

Let's start with basic grounded movement and work up from there. First, we'll fill in the code for our Movement method, which will make our WASD keys affect our "worldVelocity":

```
void Movement()
{
    //Every frame, we'll reset local movement direction to zero and set its X and Z based on
    WASD keys:
    localMovementDirection = Vector3.zero;

    //Right and left (D and A):
    if (Input.GetKey(KeyCode.D))
        localMovementDirection.x = 1;
    else if (Input.GetKey(KeyCode.A))
        localMovementDirection.x = -1;

    //Forward and back (W and S):
    if (Input.GetKey(KeyCode.W))
        localMovementDirection.z = 1;
    else if (Input.GetKey(KeyCode.S))
        localMovementDirection.z = -1;

    //If any of the movement keys are held this frame:
    if (localMovementDirection != Vector3.zero)
    {
        //Convert local movement direction to world direction, relative to the model holder:
        Vector3 worldMovementDirection = modelHolder.TransformDirection(localMovementDirect
        ion.normalized);

        //We'll calculate a multiplier to add the reverse momentum multiplier based on the
        direction we're trying to move.
        float multiplier = 1;

        //Dot product will be 1 if moving directly towards existing velocity,
        // 0 if moving perpendicular to existing velocity,
        // and -1 if moving directly away from existing velocity.
        float dot = Vector3.Dot(worldMovementDirection.normalized, worldVelocity.
        normalized);

        //If we're moving away from the velocity by any amount,
        if (dot < 0)
            //Flipping the 'dot' with a '-' makes it between 0 and 1.
            //Exactly 1 means moving directly away from existing momentum.
```

```
            multiplier += -dot * reverseMomentumMulitplier;

    //Calculate the new velocity by adding movement velocity to the current velocity:
    Vector3 newVelocity = worldVelocity + worldMovementDirection * VelocityGainPerSecond
    * multiplier * Time.deltaTime;

    //If world velocity is already moving more than 'movespeed' per second,
    // we'll Clamp the new magnitude to that of our existing velocity:
    if (worldVelocity.magnitude > movespeed)
        worldVelocity = Vector3.ClampMagnitude(newVelocity, worldVelocity.magnitude);

    //Else if we aren't moving over 'movespeed' units per second yet,
    // we'll Clamp the magnitude at a maximum of 'movespeed':
    else
        worldVelocity = Vector3.ClampMagnitude(newVelocity, movespeed);
    }
}
```

First, we set up the **"localMovementDirection"** to point in the direction the player is holding with the WASD keys. The X and Z axes are all we're using, and they'll either be 0, 1, or -1. This is the direction the player is attempting to move in, local to the facing of the Model Holder.

We convert this from a direction local to the Model Holder to a direction in world space by calling the **TransformDirection** method, storing the result in the variable named **"worldMovementDirection"**. With this, we know the direction we want our velocity to be influenced toward by our movement, and since it's in world space, we can use it to add to our "worldVelocity".

We **normalize** our "localMovementDirection" when we pass it into the TransformDirection method, which we discussed when implementing the dashing mechanic in our first project, back in Chapter 20. Technically, the magnitude is not exactly 1 for our world direction vector if two movement keys are being held. For example, the magnitude of a vector like (1, 0, 1) is not 1, it's a little higher – about 1.41 – because it traverses a little more distance than a vector that's just, for example, (0, 0, 1) or (1, 0, 0). Thus, if we used it as is, we would actually get a little more movement when we move diagonally, so we normalize it. This just makes it so that diagonal movement is not "more effective" than moving directly forward, backward, left, or right.

Before we apply the change in velocity using that world direction, we calculate the **"multiplier"** variable, which is how we apply the reverse momentum influence. This uses a static Vector3 method, **Dot**, which is new to us. It returns what is known as the **"dot product"** of two Vectors. It should be given two normalized vectors – which means two vectors with a magnitude of 1. As the comments describe, the dot product will be 1 if vector A points in the same direction as vector B, 0 if it points perpendicular (a 90-degree angle away), and -1 if it points in the exact opposite direction. It's not just one of those three values, though – it's a fraction anywhere between them. So if A points in almost the same direction as B, but not exactly, it might return something a little lower than 1, like 0.9.

We'll use the "dot" to determine how much of our "reverseMomentumMultiplier" gets added to the "multiplier" we declared. First, we check if "dot" is less than 0. If it's greater than 0, it's traveling in a direction no more than 90 degrees off of the direction the world velocity is taking us. Thus, it's not really reversing momentum, so we don't apply any extra multiplier. Since we declare "multiplier" with a default value of 1, this means it's not going to affect the movement at all.

However, if it's less than 0, we add to the multiplier, using "dot" as a fraction for how much of the "reverseMomentumMultiplier" is used. We use a "-" operator to flip "dot" so that it's anywhere between 0 and 1, not -1 and 0. If we don't do that, it would decrease the value of "multiplier" since we'd be adding a negative value. Of course, you could also just subtract the value without flipping "dot" if you changed the line to this instead:

```
multiplier -= dot * reverseMomentumMulitplier;
```

Both versions do the same thing in slightly different ways. I'm sticking to the "+=" way demonstrated in the original example because the multiplier is only ever going to be added to by this equation, so it makes more sense in my head to see the "+=" there – but really, the effect is the same either way, so it's not a big deal.

After that calculation, our multiplier will be anywhere from 1.0 to 1.6, if "reverseMomentumMultiplier" is at its default value of 0.6.

After that, we perform a little vector trickery to apply the velocity. We first calculate the new velocity in a separate vector. This is done by starting with the existing "worldVelocity" and adding the velocity we want to add on this frame. We use the world movement direction we calculated earlier and multiply that by the velocity we want to gain per second; plus, we apply the "multiplier" we just calculated, and as always, "Time. deltaTime" shows up again, since we want this to be "velocity gained per second."

When we apply the new velocity, we have to make sure we aren't increasing the velocity above the magnitude it should be allowed to have. Since we aren't handling each individual axis separately as we were in our first project, we have to do this differently. The simple solution is to use the **"Vector3. ClampMagnitude"** static method. It takes a Vector3 and a float for the maximum magnitude we want that vector to be allowed. It returns back the same vector, but if the magnitude was greater than the float value, it will be scaled down to the float value. If the magnitude was not greater, the vector is returned as is.

We clamp the magnitude in two different ways. If it's already at something greater than "movespeed", then that means some external force may have given us a shove. We don't want to constantly clamp our magnitude at "movespeed" because then this isn't possible anymore. External forces which push us harder than we are able to move on our own will immediately be diminished if we constantly clamp our world velocity to "movespeed" magnitude. Instead, we want to drag any extra momentum from external forces out over time, so the player takes longer to "skid" to a stop in these situations. We'll handle this case in our "VelocityLoss" method (empty for now, but we'll get to it soon).

But if we aren't moving any faster than "movespeed", we want to clamp the magnitude to a maximum of "movespeed" so that, while running about normally, we can't move faster than we should.

This allows us to apply the velocity so that our momentum is adjusted in the direction our movement takes us, but without ever allowing our ongoing momentum to be greater than "movespeed". The same concept applies when the magnitude is greater than "movespeed". Say we're shoved by something, like an enemy striking us or a force field pushing us. Let's also say we have 60 movespeed, but our world velocity magnitude is now 90 due to the external force.

If we move against the momentum, then the clamping of the magnitude doesn't matter, because we'll be decreasing the world velocity magnitude by moving against it anyway. We're fighting against the existing momentum, bringing our magnitude down to 0 as we change directions.

But if we move in the same direction instead, our movement won't give us more speed, since the magnitude is prevented from raising over its current value.

Effectively, we're preserving the existing magnitude of "worldVelocity" when it's higher than "movespeed", but still allowing the player to move against it to fight the momentum.

Applying Movement

Let's apply the movement to our player so we can see it in action. We'll fill out the code for the last method we call in Update, the **ApplyVelocity** method:

```
void ApplyVelocity()
{
    //While grounded, apply slight downward velocity to keep our grounded state correct:
    if (grounded)
        yVelocity = -.1f;

    //Calculate the movement we'll receive this frame:
    Vector3 movementThisFrame = (worldVelocity + (Vector3.up * yVelocity)) * Time.deltaTime;

    //Calculate where we expect to be after moving if we don't hit anything:
    Vector3 predictedPosition = trans.position + movementThisFrame;

    //Perform the movement:
    charController.Move(movementThisFrame);

    //Checking grounded state:
    if (!grounded && charController.collisionFlags.HasFlag(CollisionFlags.Below))
        grounded = true;
    else if (grounded && !charController.collisionFlags.HasFlag(CollisionFlags.Below))
        grounded = false;

    //Bounce off of walls when we hit our sides while midair:
    if (!grounded && charController.collisionFlags.HasFlag(CollisionFlags.Sides))
    {
        worldVelocity = (trans.position - predictedPosition).normalized * (worldVelocity.
        magnitude * bounciness);
    }

    //Lose Y velocity if we're going up and collided with something above us:
    if (yVelocity > 0 && charController.collisionFlags.HasFlag(CollisionFlags.Above))
        yVelocity = 0;
}
```

Because we'll be asking our CharacterController "Did we hit something below us the last time we called Move()?" to determine if we are grounded or not, we apply a constant, negligible amount of downward velocity while we are grounded. This way, if we move while grounded, we'll go down a little bit, causing us to touch the floor beneath us. If we didn't do this, we'd move directly outward, and the CharacterController would not think we were grounded because our bottom didn't touch anything.

We store the vector we will be moving on this frame in a variable and later pass that into the Move call with our CharacterController. The velocity is calculated by taking "worldVelocity", which is just our X and Z velocity, and then adding a "Vector3(0, yVelocity, 0)" to that. Remember, "Vector3.up" is just a shorthand way of typing "new Vector3(0, 1, 0)". Multiplying a float by "Vector3.up" is just saying "go up by this amount."

We also store a vector for the position we expect to have after moving, if nothing gets in our way. This is used to calculate bouncing direction.

After we move, we can then use the **"CharacterController.collisionFlags"** member to check which parts of the capsule making up our controller had collisions during the last move call.

This is a **bit mask**, which behaves like a layer mask. Remember how layer masks are essentially a list of "checkboxes" for each layer? Each individual layer can be true or false. This is how the collision flags work, except instead of layers, we have collision directions: **Below**, **Sides**, and **Above**. We can use the **"HasFlag"** method to return true if a collision occurred Below, at the Sides, or Above. A collision can occur on one or more of these in a single Move call, so each one could be either true or false at any time.

If we are currently not grounded, and we hit something below us, then we become grounded.

After that, we check if we are grounded, but did not hit anything below us. In that case, we must become midair (not grounded).

We also perform our "bouncing" here. When we hit something from our side while midair, we adjust our velocity. This is done by redirecting it from the predicted position to the actual position we ended up at. We then multiply that direction by the magnitude, which is affected by our "bounciness" variable. If the "bounciness" is 1, we get the full magnitude redirected. If it were 0.5 instead, we'd only get 50% of the magnitude, causing some of our momentum to be lost when we hit the wall.

After that, we check also for collisions at our top. If we struck something above us, we lose all positive "yVelocity". If we didn't implement this, we would keep rising up against anything above us until gravity dropped our "yVelocity" below 0. This way, it immediately drops to 0 once we bump our head, causing us to start falling.

With that, you can test movement by using the WASD keys. Of course, we still have to actually make the movement stop once we let go of the WASD keys; otherwise, we'll just keep moving.

Losing Velocity

Let's implement the **VelocityLoss** method so we can move without worrying about being set into perpetual motion:

```
void VelocityLoss()
{
    //Lose velocity as long as we are grounded, and we either are not holding movement keys,
    or are moving faster than 'movespeed':
    if (grounded && (localMovementDirection == Vector3.zero || worldVelocity.magnitude >
    movespeed))
    {
        //Calculate velocity we'll be losing this frame:
        float velocityLoss = VelocityLossPerSecond * Time.deltaTime;

        //If we're losing more velocity than the world velocity magnitude, zero out velocity
        so we're totally still:
        if (velocityLoss > worldVelocity.magnitude)
        {
            worldVelocity = Vector3.zero;
        }

        //Otherwise if we're losing less velocity than our current magnitude...
        else
        {
            //Apply velocity loss in the opposite direction of the world velocity:
            worldVelocity -= worldVelocity.normalized * velocityLoss;
        }
    }
}
```

We first check for the situation when velocity loss should occur:

- We must be grounded, not midair.

- We must not be holding any of the WASD keys. To determine this, we use the "localMovementDirection" vector which we set in the Movement method every frame.

- Alternatively, if we are holding any of the WASD keys, we will still lose velocity if our world velocity magnitude is greater than "movespeed".

Notice the set of parentheses that surround the "||" operator and its values in that first "if" statement. If the parentheses were not there, the "&&" operator would apply to "grounded" and "localMovementDirection == Vector3.zero", which would totally break the condition.

To apply the velocity loss, we first calculate how much magnitude we should lose on this frame in a quick variable. Then, we must apply it one of two ways. If the magnitude we are losing on this frame is greater than the magnitude of our world velocity, then applying it should just end all momentum, so we set "worldVelocity" to "Vector3.zero".

Otherwise, if we aren't going to lose all velocity magnitude on this frame, we apply the velocity loss as momentum in the opposite direction that the "worldVelocity" is currently traveling in. Seeing this, it should become a bit clearer why we must differentiate between the two methods of applying the velocity. If we just did the latter method every frame, then we would never actually stop moving completely. We would apply velocity in the opposite direction until our momentum reversed; then we'd do it again and again, constantly reversing the direction because we're constantly adding some amount of velocity every frame.

That should now allow us to move around in-game and, once we let go of the WASD keys, lose all of our velocity over time.

Gravity and Jumping

Now all that's left is the vertical axis. First, we'll fill in the **Gravity** method, which is a simple few lines of code:

```
void Gravity()
{
    //While not grounded, decrease Y velocity by GravityPerSecond, but don't go
under -maxGravity:
    if (!grounded && yVelocity > -maxGravity)
        yVelocity = Mathf.Max(yVelocity - GravityPerSecond * Time.deltaTime, -maxGravity);
}
```

Since "maxGravity" is set as a positive value depicting the "maximum downward momentum we can have due to gravity," we have to do a little flipping when we apply it to "yVelocity". If "yVelocity" is positive, we'll go up. If it's negative, we'll go down. Thus, the gravity needs to subtract from our "yVelocity". We use Max to ensure that it cannot drop below "-maxGravity".

We only do this if our "yVelocity" is not already less than "-maxGravity". This makes sure that external forces can drive us downward harder than gravity can, but should that happen, gravity will not keep applying and capping the downward momentum as it does.

With that, you can add a big cube to your scene to walk on, position your player on top of it, and then play and walk off the edge. You should start falling as soon as your figurative feet leave the cube.

Let's give ourselves a way to get back up onto the cube, though, by implementing jumping:

```
void Jumping()
{
    if (grounded && Input.GetKeyDown(KeyCode.Space))
    {
        //Start traveling 'jumpPower' upwards per second:
        yVelocity = jumpPower;

        //Stop counting ourselves as grounded since we know we just jumped:
        grounded = false;
    }
}
```

Again, not too complicated. We only allow jumping while grounded, and it occurs when you press Space. Since we know we're grounded and will have no downward velocity (except the default -1 to keep ground detection functioning correctly), our "yVelocity" can simply be set to the "jumpPower" with an "=" rather than adding to it with a "+=".

You might wonder why it's necessary to bother setting "grounded" to false when a jump occurs. While grounded, we constantly set our "yVelocity" to -1 in the ApplyVelocity method, which is called just **after** the Jumping method. If we didn't set "grounded" to false here, then this would still occur immediately after a jump, which would make jumping do nothing – the "yVelocity" we apply here would be reverted back to -1 right after by the ApplyVelocity method.

With that, you can test again and try jumping with Space. You'll rise and fall based on the gravity settings and the jump power. How high the jump takes you is dependent upon a combination of all those variables: the maximum gravity, the time taken to apply maximum gravity, and the jump power.

Summary

In this chapter, we learned some more advanced tricks for working with vectors to implement player movement, jumping, and gravity in a mouse-aimed setup. Some key things to remember are as follows:

- The **magnitude** (also called **length**) of a vector is the amount of distance it traverses.

- A **normalized** vector is a vector with a magnitude of 1. This can be looked at as a "direction." Multiply it by float "X" to go X units in the given direction.

- After calling Move with a CharacterController, you can test where collisions occurred on the collider using its **"collisionFlags"** member. Use the **"collisionFlags.HasFlag"** method and supply the **"CollisionFlags"** enum as a parameter, which has the values **None**, **Sides**, **Above**, or **Below**.

CHAPTER 39

■ ■ ■

Wall Jumping

With our player movement, gravity, and jumping implemented in the last chapter, we'll move on to give our player the ability to push off a nearby wall for an extra midair jump.

There are different ways to design a wall jumping mechanic. You might only allow a wall jump to be performed in the opposite direction that the player's velocity is traveling in, to enforce the idea that they are "pushing off" of the wall and redirecting their momentum.

Our system will be a bit more allowing. We'll simply test for collisions with walls near the player, and if we can find any, we'll allow the wall jump. The wall jump will go straight up if the player is holding no WASD movement keys; if they are holding any movement keys, it will also push off in the local direction they're holding. For example, holding S will wall jump backward, D will wall jump toward the player's right side, and so on – assuming there's a nearby wall to jump off.

Variables

First off, let's declare the variables that relate to wall jumping. Everything's going in the **Player** script. Declare these variables beneath the existing ones:

```
[Header("Wall Jumping")]
[Tooltip("Outward velocity provided by wall jumping.")]
public float wallJumpPower = 40;

[Tooltip("Upward velocity provided by wall jumping.")]
public float wallJumpAir = 56;

[Tooltip("Maximum distance from the player's side that a wall can be detected for a wall
jump.")]
public float wallDetectionRange = 2.4f;

[Tooltip("Cooldown time for wall jumps, in seconds.")]
public float wallJumpCooldown = .3f;

[Tooltip("Only layers included in this mask will count as walls that can be jumped off.")]
public LayerMask wallDetectionLayerMask;

//Time.time when we last performed a wall jump.
private float lastWallJumpTime;
```

© Casey Hardman 2024
C. Hardman, *Game Programming with Unity and C#*, https://doi.org/10.1007/978-1-4842-9720-9_39

```
//Returns true if wall jump is not on cooldown, false if it is on cooldown.
private bool WallJumpIsOffCooldown
{
    get
    {
        //Current time must be greater than the last wall jump time, plus wall jump
        cooldown:
        return Time.time > lastWallJumpTime + wallJumpCooldown;
    }
}
```

- **"wallJumpPower"** is the velocity we'll be applying on the X and Z axes when a wall jump occurs. This is only applied if any of the WASD keys are held when the jump is first ordered.

- **"wallJumpAir"** is the upward velocity, which will always be applied regardless of the WASD keys.

- **"wallDetectionRange"** depicts the maximum distance away from the player a wall can be when we wall jump off it. Anything that's further from the player than this will not be detected for wall jumping.

- **"wallJumpCooldown"** is a short cooldown we'll apply to wall jumps so the player can only perform one every 0.3 seconds. This is a public variable, so it can always be changed in the Inspector, if you want to limit the player's movement a little more.

- **"wallDetectionLayerMask"** will be used when we check for walls near the player. These are the layers the player can jump off. Any colliders in a layer that's not in this mask will not count as a nearby wall.

- **"lastWallJumpTime"** will be set to the current "Time.time" whenever we perform a wall jump. It will be used to check if the wall jump is on cooldown.

- **"WallJumpIsOffCooldown"** is a shorthand property for checking if the wall jump is off cooldown and available to use (true) or on cooldown and unavailable (false).

Once you've written these variables, be sure to save the script and go set up that layer mask in the Inspector for your Player. We'll make it include just the **Default** layer, not any of the others. Remember, if you don't do this, the layer mask will be set to "Nothing" by default, meaning we won't be able to wall jump off of anything.

In the Inspector, our new Wall Jumping variables will look like Figure 39-1 when finished.

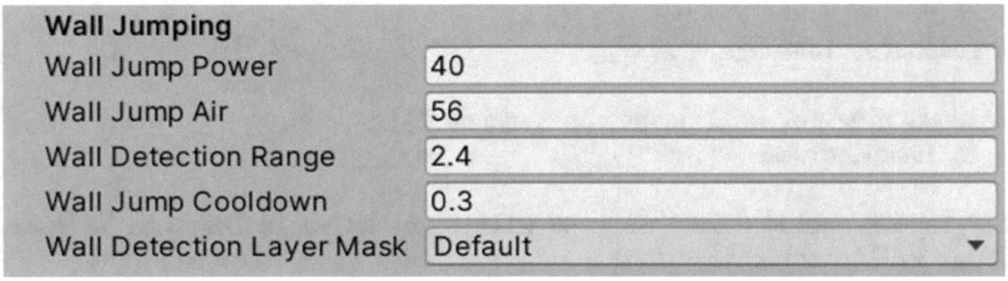

Wall Jumping	
Wall Jump Power	40
Wall Jump Air	56
Wall Detection Range	2.4
Wall Jump Cooldown	0.3
Wall Detection Layer Mask	Default ▼

Figure 39-1. *The Wall Jumping variables of our Player script in the Inspector*

Detecting Walls

We'll need to know if a wall is near us before we allow a wall jump to occur. To detect if a wall is nearby, we'll call the method **"Physics.OverlapBox"**. This takes some parameters defining an invisible box in world space. It tests if any colliders are inside this box or touching it, gathers them all in a "Collider[]" array, and then returns that array.

We used a similar method, "Physics.OverlapSphere", when we implemented our Cannon Towers in the second project. This method is just like that, but it tests for collisions in a box shape instead of a sphere shape.

All we'll need to know is if at least one collider is returned to us. We don't really need to mess with the returned array. We just need to check if its "Length" member is greater than 0. To do this, we can define a **WallIsNearby** method that performs the check using OverlapBox and then returns true if the returned array length is greater than 0 or false if it is not.

If we're clever about it, this can be done in a single line of code within the WallIsNearby method, but your first instinct is probably to do it in more than one line. I'll give a few code samples that you don't have to write into your Player script yet, just to demonstrate the point.

The following code sample shows one way of doing it, with the parameters of the OverlapBox call excluded just to keep the extra clutter out of the way for now:

```
private bool WallIsNearby()
{
    Collider[] colliders = Physics.OverlapBox();

    if (colliders.Length > 0)
        return true;
    else
        return false;
}
```

Pretty cut and clean, right? Store the returned array in a local variable and check the "Length" member to determine if we should return true or false. It's not necessarily wrong, it's just doing it in more lines of code than necessary.

Here is how you might do the same thing with one line of code in the method instead:

```
private bool WallIsNearby()
{
    return Physics.OverlapBox().Length > 0;
}
```

As you can see, we are calling OverlapBox, but we're not storing the returned array in a local variable before we access it. We're simply reaching directly into the returned array after the closing parenthesis ")" of the OverlapBox method call. Doing this, we can grab the "Length" member of the array and use the ">" operator to get a bool value: true if the array has any members in it, and false if it does not.

This comes out to one simple equation that can be returned as is, no variables required.

With that out of the way, let's write the actual method, including the parameters we'll use to define the OverlapBox. To spread the method call out so it's a little more comfortable to read, I'll put each parameter on its own line of code.

Let's declare it in the **Player** script, down beneath all of the wall jumping variables we just declared:

```
private bool WallIsNearby()
{
    return Physics.OverlapBox(
        trans.position + Vector3.up * (charController.height * .5f),
        Vector3.one * wallDetectionRange,
        modelHolder.rotation,
        wallDetectionLayerMask.value).Length > 0;
}
```

This is something you may see when method calls have lots of parameters or when the parameters are large and unwieldy. Each parameter is given with its comma at the end to separate it from the next parameter, but we also add a line break after the comma, spreading our parameters out and making it easier to read each one.

Let's go over what these parameters are.

The **first** parameter is a Vector3 depicting the **world position** of the **center** of the box. We start at the root Transform position, which is at the floor level, right at the bottom of our Capsule model. We add a vector going straight up by half of our CharacterController's Height setting, which we've set in the Inspector to a value of 6. So effectively, the box center is halfway up the height of the player.

The **second** parameter is the **"half extents"** of the box. This is a Vector3 depicting half of the size of the box. X is width, Y is height, and Z is length. It is given as "half extents" instead of the full size of the box.

For this parameter, we use "Vector3.one", which is shorthand for "new Vector3(1, 1, 1)". We multiply it by the "wallDetectionRange". This is effectively the same as typing this:

```
new Vector3(wallDetectionRange, wallDetectionRange, wallDetectionRange)
```

It's just a bit shorter. Ultimately, this parameter depicts that each side of the box will be "wallDetectionRange" away from the center. Thus, the total size of the box is double the "wallDetectionRange", if you measure it from one side to the opposite (which is why it's called "half extents" and not just "size").

The **third** parameter is a Quaternion for the **rotation** of the box. We give the box **"Quaternion.identity"** for its rotation, which just means "no rotation." It will point forward along the world forward direction, just as if you had created a new Cube in the Scene.

Lastly, the **fourth** parameter is our **layer mask** value, which lets us define which layers constitute as walls that can be jumped off. This works just like it does with the Raycast method.

After the OverlapBox call, we then reach into the returned array and ask if its "Length" is greater than 0, as described earlier. This means as long as at least one collider was detected, our WallIsNearby method will return true; if no colliders were detected, it will return false.

Performing the Jump

With everything set up, let's add an extra method to check for the Space key being pressed and perform the wall jump if applicable.

We'll add a Wall Jumping method amid our existing Update logic methods we've declared in the past, **between Gravity and Jumping**:

```
void Movement() {...}
void VelocityLoss() {...}
void Gravity() {...}
```

```
void WallJumping()
{
    //If midair and wall jump is not on cooldown:
    if (!grounded && WallJumpIsOffCooldown)
    {
        //If space is pressed:
        if (Input.GetKeyDown(KeyCode.Space))
        {
            //Make sure a wall is nearby to jump off:
            if (WallIsNearby())
            {
                //If any movement keys are held, apply outward movement by converting local
                movement direction to world-space,
                // relative to the model holder, and multiplying by wall jump power:
                if (localMovementDirection != Vector3.zero)
                    worldVelocity = modelHolder.TransformDirection(localMovementDirection) *
                    wallJumpPower;

                //If we're falling, all downward momentum is replaced with the wall jump air:
                if (yVelocity <= 0)
                    yVelocity = wallJumpAir;

                //If not falling, just add wall jump air to existing velocity:
                else
                    yVelocity += wallJumpAir;

                //Apply wall jump cooldown:
                lastWallJumpTime = Time.time;
            }
        }
    }
}
void Jumping() {...}
void ApplyVelocity() {...}
```

And we'll have to be sure to call it in the Update method. We want it to occur **before the Jumping method**:

```
void Update()
{
    Movement();
    VelocityLoss();
    Gravity();
    WallJumping();
    Jumping();
    ApplyVelocity();
}
```

The first three "if" blocks in WallJumping amount to "while midair and wall jump is off cooldown, when the Space key is first pressed, and if a wall is nearby." On those conditions, we perform the wall jump.

To apply outward momentum, we transform the local movement direction (which WASD keys are held) to world space, as we learned how to do in the last chapter, and multiply that by the "wallJumpPower". We directly set the "worldVelocity" to this value with an "=" operator rather than adding the velocity as extra.

This means if you jump off a wall, all existing outward velocity will be ended, and the wall jump velocity will replace it.

For example, this way the player can jump directly at a wall, then wall jump backward in the opposite direction. If we just added the wall jump velocity to the world velocity, then attempting to go backward with a wall jump wouldn't be as effective, since it would be working against ongoing momentum. The two would likely just cancel each other out, unless your "wallJumpPower" was sufficiently high.

If you would rather have ongoing momentum be retained when a wall jump occurs, you can change the line to include the current world velocity magnitude as well as the jump power:

```
worldVelocity = modelHolder.TransformDirection(localMovementDirection) * (wallJumpPower +
worldVelocity.magnitude);
```

This is the same thing, but rather than just multiplying by "wallJumpPower", we multiply by the power plus the ongoing magnitude of our "worldVelocity". In other words, however fast the velocity was moving before is added to the wall jump power, but it's all directed along the wall jump direction instead of whatever direction we were traveling before.

This can make for more convincing wall jumps if you were, say, pushed by an external force. Rather than all of your momentum being replaced by the wall jump power, which could look awkward if the wall jump power was less than the momentum you had, your existing momentum gets redirected and the wall jump power is also added to it as extra velocity. Wall jumping back and forth between two walls repeatedly this way could "stack up" a lot of velocity, though, and it would look rather awkward if you were to be flying at a wall at high speed, only to wall jump in the opposite direction (now at even *higher* speed, since "wallJumpPower" is also added in).

In the end, it's just a matter of how you want to implement the mechanic. For our purposes, I'll be leaving it at the first example, with no "worldVelocity.magnitude" involved. If you think it's more fun the second way, go ahead and replace the line.

After we add that outward velocity, we then add the upward velocity. This is done one of two ways. If we're falling, we want the wall jump to counteract that downward momentum, so we directly set "yVelocity" rather than adding to it. This overrides any negative velocity we already had.

Otherwise, if we wall jump when we're already rising, we just add extra upward velocity, so that existing upward momentum is retained and added onto by the momentum gained from "kicking off the wall," so to speak.

Lastly, we set the "Time.time" at which the last wall jump was performed, which puts it on cooldown automatically due to our "WallJumpIsOffCooldown" property.

With that, you can go and test out the new features. Try creating some cubes and making them tall enough to jump up against and wall jump off. You can stand next to the wall, jump with no WASD keys held, and press Space again while midair to just go straight up. The default cooldown is low enough that you can keep doing this to go up and up as far as you need to get over a wall of any height (although you can raise the cooldown if that sort of power frightens you).

You can also put two tall cubes next to each other and wall jump back and forth between them. You may want to make some materials of varying colors to apply to your floor and the cubes, just so everything doesn't blend together into one color.

Remember, if you forgot to set up the "wallDetectionLayerMask" variable in the Inspector, the walls around the player might not be detected, preventing you from performing wall jumps. Similarly, if you didn't change the Player's layer, then it might still be in the Default layer, causing them to count as a wall themselves, which would allow wall jumping even if no wall is nearby.

Summary

In this chapter, we learned how to use the "Physics.OverlapBox" method to test for colliders within a box-shaped area. Using this, we allow the player to press Space while midair with a wall nearby to push off the wall for an extra aerial jump, adding another option for movement and allowing the player to scale walls with ease.

■ ■ ■

CHAPTER 40

Pulling and Pushing

In this chapter, we'll make use of raycasting to allow the player to point their camera at a GameObject with a Rigidbody and hold left-click to pull the object toward them or right-click to push it away from them. Rather than pulling and pushing by moving the Transform directly, we'll apply force to the Rigidbody so that the physics system handles the motion for us. This will demonstrate how to manipulate Rigidbodies by applying forces to them.

Script Setup

The pushing and pulling features will be implemented in a separate script that we'll attach to the Player GameObject, just to keep it separate from the player movement logic.

Start off by creating a **Telekinesis** script in the Scripts folder of your project. Open it up, and let's declare our variables:

```
public class Telekinesis : MonoBehaviour
{
    public enum State
    {
        Idle,
        Pushing,
        Pulling
    }
    private State state = State.Idle;

    [Header("References")]
    public Transform baseTrans;
    public Camera cam;

    [Header("Stats")]
    [Tooltip("Force applied when pulling a target.")]
    public float pullForce = 60;

    [Tooltip("Force applied when pushing a target.")]
    public float pushForce = 60;

    [Tooltip("Maximum distance from the player that a telekinesis target can be.")]
    public float range = 70;
```

```
[Tooltip("Layer mask for objects that can be pulled and pushed.")]
public LayerMask detectionLayerMask;

//Current target of telekinesis, if any.
private Transform target;

//The world position that the target detection ray hit on the current target.
private Vector3 targetHitPoint;

//Rigidbody component of target.  For something to be marked as a target, it must have a
Rigidbody.
//So as long as 'target' is not null, this won't be null either.
private Rigidbody targetRigidbody;

//If there is no current target, this is always false.  Otherwise, true if the target is
in range, false if they are not.
private bool targetIsOutsideRange = false;

//Gets the Color that the cursor should display based on the state and target distance.
private Color CursorColor
{
    get
    {
        if (state == State.Idle)
        {
            //If there is no target, return gray:
            if (target == null)
                return Color.gray;

            //If there is a target but it's not in range, return orange:
            else if (targetIsOutsideRange)
                return new Color(1, .6f, 0);

            //If there is a target and it is in range, return white:
            else
                return Color.white;
        }
        //If we're pushing or pulling, return green:
        else
            return Color.green;
    }
}
```

In every frame, we'll cast a ray using the **"detectionLayerMask"** with infinite distance (range). If a valid target is found with the ray, we'll set the related variables:

- target

- targetHitPoint

- targetRigidbody

- targetIsOutsideRange

This gives us all we need to know about our target, if we have one. We still target objects that are outside of our "range" variable, but we have the "targetIsOutsideRange" bool to tell us if the target can actually be pulled or pushed.

We then check for input: holding the left mouse button while we have a valid, in-range target will pull the target toward us, while right-click will push the target away.

We'll set our "state" based on what we were doing on this frame: nothing (Idle), pushing, or pulling.

Our **"CursorColor"** property reacts to the **"state"** as well as **"targetIsOutsideRange"**, returning a different Color based on these factors:

- If there is no target, it returns **gray**.

- If there is a target but it is outside the range, it returns **orange**.

- If there is a target and it is inside range, it returns **white**.

- While we are pushing or pulling a target, it returns **green**.

The "cursor" will be a small rectangle drawn in the center of the screen, where the raycast originates. It will use "CursorColor" to define its color. This will make it automatically update based on the situation, to give the player some indication of when they have a valid target, when the target is outside range, and when they're actively pulling or pushing their target.

Before we continue, let's set up the Telekinesis script. First, add an instance of the script to your root Player GameObject (the same one that has the Player script instance). Set the "baseTrans" reference to the Player Transform and drag and drop the Player Camera GameObject onto the "cam" reference field. Make sure to also set the layer mask to include only the **Default** layer. When you're done, your script should look like Figure 40-1 in the Inspector.

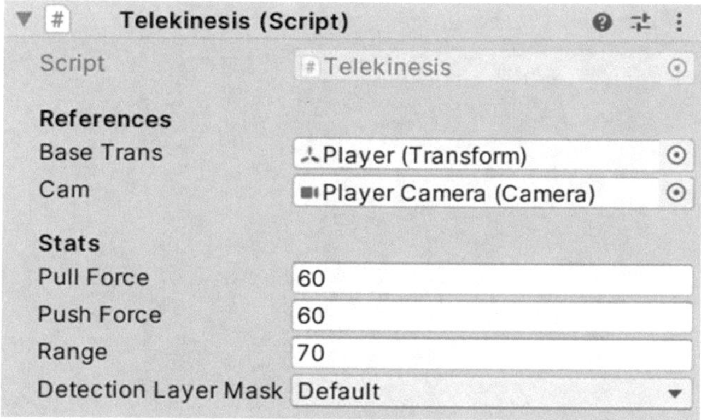

Figure 40-1. *Our Telekinesis script with all of its fields correctly set in the Inspector*

Moving on, let's map out our basic functionality with some methods:

```
//Update logic:
void TargetDetection(){}

//FixedUpdate logic:
void PullingAndPushing(){}

//Unity events:
void Update()
```

385

```
{
    TargetDetection();
}
void FixedUpdate()
{
    PullingAndPushing();
}
```

You'll notice we're using a new built-in Unity event here: **FixedUpdate**. This is where the actual pulling and pushing will be performed, while the raycast for target detection will instead occur in the normal Update event that we're so used to.

FixedUpdate

The **FixedUpdate** method is like Update, but you should use FixedUpdate instead if you intend on interacting with the physics system through code. Notably, applying forces to Rigidbodies should be done through FixedUpdate instead of Update. It occurs not once per frame, but at a set interval with the same amount of time between each FixedUpdate. Unexpected results can occur in physics components if you interact with them in Update instead of FixedUpdate.

How frequently the physics updates are called is dependent on a value that you can set by navigating to the Edit ➤ Project Settings window, clicking the **Time** tab, and locating the **Fixed Timestep** value, shown in Figure 40-2. By default, the value is set to 0.02, which means FixedUpdates are called 50 times per second.

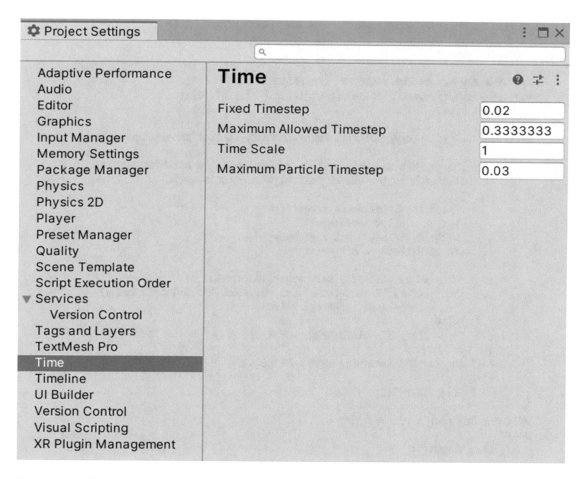

Figure 40-2. *The Time tab is open in the Project Settings window, where the Fixed Timestep field can be found*

Setting the value lower will generate more updates per second, but comes at the cost of performance. Setting it higher will save on performance, but may make physics less accurate, even downright choppy at particularly high values.

Within a FixedUpdate call, "Time.deltaTime" will still work the same way, returning the Fixed Timestep value always. You can also access "Time.fixedDeltaTime" to get this value within your code. You can even set it in-game to dynamically change the update frequency of physics.

Target Detection

Before coding our FixedUpdate logic, let's get our target detection working so we know what we're dealing with.

We'll fill in the **TargetDetection** method we declared before with this code:

```
void TargetDetection()
{
    //Cast a ray out of the center of the screen:
    var ray = cam.ViewportPointToRay(new Vector3(.5f, .5f, 0));
    RaycastHit hit;

    if (Physics.Raycast(ray, out hit, Mathf.Infinity, detectionLayerMask.value))
    {
        //If the ray hit something with a Rigidbody that's not kinematic:
        if (hit.rigidbody != null && !hit.rigidbody.isKinematic)
        {
            //Set the telekinesis target:
            target = hit.transform;
            targetRigidbody = hit.rigidbody;
            targetHitPoint = hit.point;

            //Based on distance, set targetIsOutsideRange:
            if (Vector3.Distance(baseTrans.position, hit.point) > range)
                targetIsOutsideRange = true;
            else
                targetIsOutsideRange = false;
        }
        //If the ray hit something with no Rigidbody
        else
            ClearTarget();
    }
    //If the ray didn't hit anything
    else
        ClearTarget();
}
```

Here, we use the **"Camera.ViewportPointToRay"** method. This method is just like the **"ScreenPointToRay"** method that we used in our second project to detect where to place our tower building highlighter. It returns a Ray that shoots out of the camera, originating at a specific point on the screen.

The only difference is that it operates by the **"viewport"** instead of by a pixel position on the screen. It's just a different way to locate a position on the camera view. Rather than specifying pixels, such as half of the width and height of the screen, we specify a fraction between 0 and 1 for the X and Y values. The X is left and right, and the Y is up and down, just like with pixels, but we don't have to concern ourselves with the screen width and height. (0, 0) is the bottom-left corner of the camera, and (1, 1) is the top-right corner. Thus, (.5f, .5f) will get us the center. Since we don't have to plug the mouse position into the method, this one will suit us just fine as an easy way to get a ray shooting out of the center of the screen. It's just a bit simpler than using ScreenPointToRay and calculating half of the "Screen.width" and "Screen.height".

The Z axis doesn't do anything, so we just leave it at 0.

We cast the ray in an "if" statement, as always. If the ray hit anything, the Raycast call will return true and the "hit" will be filled with data about what was hit, as we've come to understand about raycasting.

We'll only mark something as a target if it has a Rigidbody, and only if that Rigidbody is not kinematic. You'll recall that a kinematic Rigidbody is not controlled by the physics system. We can't apply forces to such a Rigidbody anyway, so they don't make for valid targets.

When we mark the target, we must set our four target-related variables for future reference: the target Transform, the target Rigidbody, the position where the ray struck the target, and whether or not the target is out of our telekinesis range.

If the target did not have a non-kinematic Rigidbody, or if the ray simply didn't hit anything in the first place, we call the **ClearTarget** method.

Let's declare that method. It's a simple one that just resets the values of the variables to null and false. I'll put it down below the **"CursorColor"** property:

```
void ClearTarget()
{
    //Clear and reset variables that relate to targeting:
    target = null;
    targetRigidbody = null;
    targetIsOutsideRange = false;
}
```

That does it for target detection. We can now expect our camera to constantly be shooting a ray out of the center of its view, striking only the layers defined in our "detectionLayerMask". It will detect and store information about the target the ray strikes, if any. Otherwise, it clears the target.

Pulling and Pushing

Now we can fill in the method that does the interesting part: detecting mouse buttons and applying forces to pull or push the target.

We'll fill in the **PullingAndPushing** method with this code:

```
void PullingAndPushing()
{
    //If we have a target that is within range:
    if (target != null && !targetIsOutsideRange)
    {
        //If the left mouse button is down
        if (Input.GetMouseButton(0))
        {
            //Pull the target from the hit point towards our position:
            targetRigidbody.AddForce((baseTrans.position - targetHitPoint).normalized *
            pullForce, ForceMode.Acceleration);
            state = State.Pulling;
        }
        //Else if the right mouse button is down
        else if (Input.GetMouseButton(1))
        {
            //Push the target from our position towards the hit point:
            targetRigidbody.AddForce((targetHitPoint - baseTrans.position).normalized *
            pushForce, ForceMode.Acceleration);
            state = State.Pushing;
        }
        //If neither mouse buttons are held down
        else
            state = State.Idle;
    }
```

```
//If we don't have a target or we have one but it is not in range:
else
    state = State.Idle;
}
```

The target Rigidbody is accessed so we can call its **AddForce** method. This method takes a Vector3 for the amount of force to apply, as well as a **ForceMode** enum that defines how the force applies to the Rigidbody.

To apply the force, we use that familiar equation to get the direction we desire:

```
(to - from).normalized
```

Then we multiply that direction by the force we want to apply, either **"pullForce"** or **"pushForce"** based on which one we're doing. You'll notice we aren't multiplying the forces by "Time.deltaTime". When dealing with forces in FixedUpdate like this, we don't need to do that. Remember, FixedUpdate is occurring at a fixed number of times per second, and Unity is accounting for that automatically in its built-in physics methods like AddForce.

The **ForceMode** enum has four possible values that change two factors of how the force is applied:

- Does it happen as a constant push, like one object pressing against another, or a strong wind; or as a sudden impact, like an explosion?

- Is it affected by the mass of the Rigidbody?

Those four possible values are

- **Force**, which is a **constant** push that is **affected** by mass

- **Acceleration**, which is a **constant** push that **ignores** mass

- **Impulse**, which is a **sudden** push that is **affected** by mass

- **VelocityChange**, which is a **sudden** push that **ignores** mass

Our selection, Acceleration, ensures that the force we apply is not going to be an instant impulse, as if the object was being hit by a wave of force from an explosion or something of the sort. It is more like a gradual, constant influence pulling it toward us or pushing it away from us.

It is also ignoring the mass, which means if we pull or push a Rigidbody with a very high mass, the force will still affect the Rigidbody just as much. This makes it so you can make heavy objects and still allow the player to pull and push them.

Aside from applying the force, we also manage the "state" enum so that it always reflects what we were doing during the last FixedUpdate call.

With that in place, we can now pull and push Rigidbodies, but we still need to draw our cursor so we can see the center of our screen, where the ray is being cast from.

Cursor Drawing

We'll draw a basic, colored square in the center of the screen that gives the player indication of where their telekinesis ray is being cast from, with a color that responds to the situation.

To do this, all we need is one line of code in an **OnGUI** event method. As you may remember from our first project, we can call **GUI** methods from the built-in OnGUI event to draw 2D user interface elements to the screen. In our situation, this will be a quick and easy way to draw a simple square of color to the screen through code, rather than setting up a Canvas with a UI element for our cursor.

We'll write our **OnGUI** method beneath the FixedUpdate method:

```
void OnGUI()
{
    //Draw a rectangle of the CursorColor at the center of the screen:
    UnityEditor.EditorGUI.DrawRect(new Rect(Screen.width * .5f, Screen.height * .5f, 8, 8),
    CursorColor);
}
```

We're reaching into the **UnityEditor** namespace to access this method because it's only available through **EditorGUI**, not the normal GUI. You could put a "using UnityEditor;" line at the very top of the script file and cut out the "UnityEditor" part of the reference, if you want, but since we're only using one UnityEditor reference in the script, it won't save us much typing.

One thing to note is that you won't be able to build a game if you're running EditorGUI methods in your game code. The methods are really only meant for use in the Unity editor, which is fine for our purposes. If you were coding for a real game instead of just testing features like we are, you would want to implement the cursor with an actual UI element, like a Panel, and you'd change its color through a reference. You could also use an image file for your cursor and use the "GUI.DrawTexture" method to draw that image to the screen – however, since we're focusing on code and not working with images, the DrawRect method will get the job done just fine.

The method we're calling is a basic one that just draws a rectangle with a given solid color. It takes a Rect as its first parameter and the Color as the second.

You may remember our usage of the Rect data type (short for rectangle) from our first project:

- The first parameter is the X position of the left side of the rectangle.

- The second parameter is the Y position of the top side of the rectangle.

- The third parameter is the width, in pixels.

- The fourth parameter is the height, in pixels.

A value of 0 in the X position is the left edge of the screen, while a value of "Screen.width" would put it all the way at the right edge of the screen.

Similarly, 0 for the Y axis is the bottom edge, while "Screen.height" is the top.

We simply put our rectangle right in the center of the screen by using half of the screen width and height as its position. We make it 8x8 pixels, although you could change this if you wanted it smaller or larger.

With that, all of our telekinesis features are in place. To test them out, try creating three cubes on the ground near the player. Give each one a **non-kinematic** Rigidbody and set each Rigidbody's Mass value higher than the last one. You can make the scale match the mass too, if you want – make the second cube have a scale of (2, 2, 2) and a mass of 2, for example. Then, point at them with the center of your camera and try to pull (left-click) and push (right-click). You'll see how the Rigidbody takes over the physics, causing the object to turn and bounce as it moves. The position on the cube that your cursor is pointing at will affect how the force is applied to it, allowing you to see the difference when you shove or pull at the edges, corners, or center.

One final note: do your Rigidbodies seem to be in slow motion as they move and, particularly, as they fall? This is likely because, roughly speaking, we've been using feet as our measurement for things like the size of our player and, as such, the size of cubes in relation to our player. However, Unity's gravity is, by default, set up to look realistic with a measurement of meters.

This can be changed easily in Edit ➤ Project Settings ➤ Physics, where the first field is **"Gravity"**. By default, it is set to -9.81, meaning 9.81 units of downward momentum per second – this is accurate to the real world, but only when measuring with meters.

Since we're measuring with feet, we can adjust the gravity to -32.18, as shown in Figure 40-3, to get an approximately similar amount of gravity, measured in feet instead of meters.

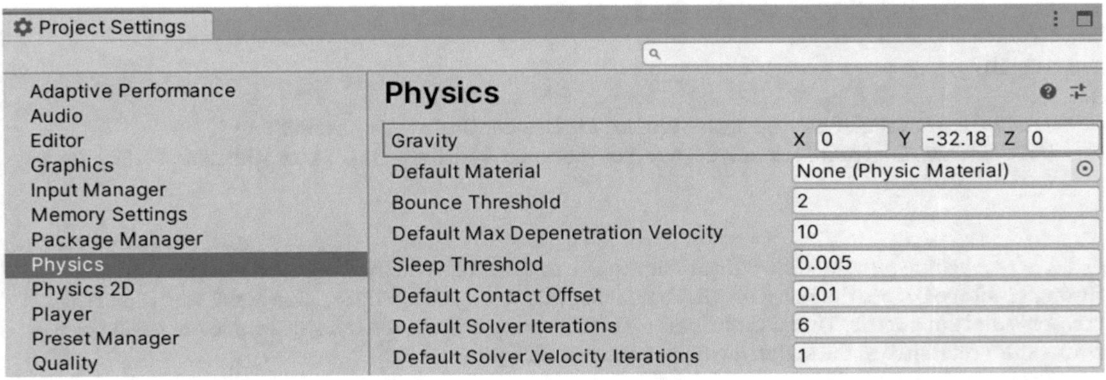

Figure 40-3. *The Project Settings window is shown, with the Physics tab selected and the Gravity Y field set to -32.18*

Summary

This chapter taught us how to apply external forces to Rigidbodies using the **AddForce** method, as well as the four different options for applying force that Unity provides to us. We also learned that Unity's physics simulations occur at a fixed timestep, not "once per frame" like the Update method. Any code that interacts with the physics system constantly, such as by applying forces to a Rigidbody, should occur in a **FixedUpdate** event, not Update.

■ ■ ■

CHAPTER 41

Moving Platforms

In this chapter, we'll implement a moving, floating platform that travels back and forth between two locations, and we'll implement a simple system that allows the Player to stand on these platforms and ride them as they move. This will be done by making the platform become the parent of the Player when the Player lands on the platform.

We'll also allow individual objects controlled by a Rigidbody to stick to the platform as it moves.

Platform Movement

First, we need a script that makes a platform move back and forth between two positions. We'll make its initial position in the scene be its starting point, and we'll expose a Vector3 in the Inspector that will act as the targeted position – the point it travels to. It will repeatedly travel back and forth between the initial position and the targeted position, with the option of staying stationary for a given amount of time whenever it reaches a point, giving the player time to step onto it.

This won't be anything groundbreaking, now that you've come this far already, so let's get it done. Make a new script named **PlatformMovement** in your Scripts folder, and let's start off with our variables and properties:

```
private enum State
{
    Stationary,
    MovingToTarget,
    MovingToInitial
}

private State state = State.Stationary;

[Header("References")]
[Tooltip("The Transform of the platform.")]
public Transform trans;
[Header("Stats")]

[Tooltip("World-space position the platform should move to.")]
public Vector3 targetPosition;

[Tooltip("Amount of time taken to move from one position to the other.")]
public float timeToChangePosition = 3;
```

© Casey Hardman 2024

C. Hardman, *Game Programming with Unity and C#*, https://doi.org/10.1007/978-1-4842-9720-9_41

```
[Tooltip("Time to wait after moving to a new position, before beginning to move to the next
position.")]
public float stationaryTime = 1f;

//Returns the units to travel per second when moving.
private float TravelSpeed
{
    get
    {
        //Distance between the two positions, divided by number of seconds taken to change
        position:
        return Vector3.Distance(initialPosition, targetPosition) / timeToChangePosition;
    }
}

//Gets the current position we're moving towards based on state.
private Vector3 CurrentDestination
{
    get
    {
        if (state == State.MovingToInitial)
            return initialPosition;
        else
            return targetPosition;
    }
}

//World position of platform on Start.
private Vector3 initialPosition;

//State for the platform to use next - either MovingToTarget or MovingToInitial.
private State nextState = State.MovingToTarget;
```

The only variable that might not have a clear purpose to you is probably the **"nextState"**. This variable is used to store the state we want to switch to after we wait the **"stationaryTime"**. Since our **"state"** will be set to **Stationary** during this time, we need a second State variable to store whether we must move toward the target position or the initial position once the stationary time ends.

Let's see the variables in action with the rest of the code:

```
//Transitions 'state' to the 'nextState'.
void GoToNextState()
{
    state = nextState;
}

//Unity events:
void Start()
{
    //Mark the position of the platform at start:
    initialPosition = trans.position;
```

```
    //Invoke the first transition in state after 'stationaryTime' seconds:
    Invoke("GoToNextState", stationaryTime);
}

void FixedUpdate()
{
    if (state != State.Stationary)
    {
        trans.position = Vector3.MoveTowards(trans.position, CurrentDestination, TravelSpeed
        * Time.deltaTime);

        //If we've reached the destination
        if (trans.position == CurrentDestination)
        {
            //Based on our current state, determine what the next state will be:
            if (state == State.MovingToInitial)
                nextState = State.MovingToTarget;
            else
                nextState = State.MovingToInitial;

            //Become stationary and invoke the transition to the next state in
            'stationaryTime' seconds:
            state = State.Stationary;
            Invoke("GoToNextState", stationaryTime);
        }
    }
}
```

Here, we declare the **GoToNextState** method to give us something we can Invoke to initiate movement again once we've become stationary. Then, we make sure to set our "initialPosition" in the Start call, and since our "state" variable is set to Stationary by default, we also have to set off the process by Invoking the first call to GoToNextState. By default, the "nextState" is set to "State.MovingToTarget", which works out perfectly because we want the platform's initial position to be where it is placed in the scene by default.

GoToNextState will start moving the platform toward its target, which occurs in the **FixedUpdate** method. Using FixedUpdate instead of Update synchronizes the platform movement with the physics system. Since we'll have Rigidbodies and the player's CharacterController riding the platform, this will avoid any odd kinks in the system that might occur if we used Update instead.

The movement of the platform is done with a simple **"Vector3.MoveTowards"** call, which we've seen quite a few times already: we move our current position toward the **"CurrentDestination"** by **"TravelSpeed"** units per second. The "CurrentDestination" property will automatically return either the "initialPosition" or the "targetPosition" based on the current value of "state".

Once we've reached the destination, we set the "nextState" to move toward the other destination, then we become Stationary and Invoke the next state change.

This creates a neat little loop of movement back and forth.

Let's build a moving platform GameObject. It's a pretty simple setup, but one caveat is that we want the platform to have an empty GameObject as its root, with the actual platform as a child. This is because we'll be making the platform become the parent of anything that wants to "ride" it, so we want a clean scale of (1, 1, 1) so that its scale does not mess with its children at all – particularly, it would cause major problems with anything controlled by a Rigidbody if we didn't do this.

- Create an empty GameObject named **"Moving Platform"**. Give it a **kinematic** Rigidbody and an instance of the **PlatformMovement** script, with the "trans" reference pointing to that of the Moving Platform.

- Add a child Cube to the Moving Platform, with a local position of (0, 0, 0) and a scale of (25, .5, 25).

- Position the Moving Platform where you want it to start. Set its Target Position field to the same as its position, but add about 50 units to the X or Z axis.

Now the platform should move back and forth. You can tweak the timing variables in the Inspector if you'd like it to move faster or slower, or if you'd like to change how long it waits before it begins moving again after it stops.

Platform Detection

If we just use our PlatformMovement script, the platform will move without bringing the player with it. This is because there isn't really any *physics* going on here. As we've established, Unity's physics system takes over when a GameObject has a **non-kinematic** Rigidbody attached, causing objects to realistically bump into each other, succumb to gravity, and so on, and in order to interact with these objects, we must add forces to their Rigidbodies. However, there are no non-kinematic Rigidbodies involved in our setup: our platform has a **kinematic** Rigidbody, and our player uses a CharacterController. All we're doing is directly adjusting the Transform position of our platform. Thus, if we want our player to move with our platforms, we'll have to implement that ourselves. Let's get to it.

We'll provide two methods of allowing GameObjects to be attached to a platform. One method will operate via a trigger collider, which we'll use for the player – when the trigger touches the platform, it makes the platform the parent of the Transform, and when the trigger stops touching the platform, it makes the parent null again, effectively "detaching" the player from the platform.

The other method will respond to normal, physical collisions and can be used to allow, for example, a Cube under the control of a Rigidbody to attach to platforms on touch.

Regardless of how the GameObject gets attached to platforms, all it will need is a simple script that we'll create now, named **PlatformDetector**, to enable this feature:

```
public class PlatformDetector : MonoBehaviour
{
    [Tooltip("Transform to move with the platform.")]
    public Transform trans;
}
```

This script pretty much only exists to alert a platform that the GameObject holding the script wants to be attached to the platform.

The actual work will be done by the script that we'll attach to anything we want to act as a moving platform. Make a script named **Platform** and give it this code:

```
public class Platform : MonoBehaviour
{
    void OnTriggerEnter(Collider other)
    {
        var detector = other.GetComponent<PlatformDetector>();

        if (detector != null)
            detector.trans.SetParent(transform);
    }
```

```
    void OnTriggerExit(Collider other)
    {
        var detector = other.GetComponent<PlatformDetector>();
        if (detector != null)
            detector.trans.SetParent(null);
    }

    void OnCollisionEnter(Collision col)
    {
        var detector = col.gameObject.GetComponent<PlatformDetector>();
        if (detector != null)
            detector.trans.SetParent(transform);
    }

    void OnCollisionExit(Collision col)
    {
        var detector = col.gameObject.GetComponent<PlatformDetector>();
        if (detector != null)
            detector.trans.SetParent(null);
    }
}
```

Pretty repetitive, right? All we're doing is providing the same code for trigger collisions as well as for physical collisions. The Platform script will detect collisions occurring with it, and if it finds a PlatformDetector script attached to whatever just collided with it, then it knows that the GameObject that touched it wants to attach to platforms. It becomes the parent of the other Transform when the colliders touch and sets the parent to null when they stop touching.

It uses the PlatformDetector's "trans" reference when setting the parent. We expose the Transform whose parent should be changed as a variable instead of just using the Transform that the PlatformDetector script is attached to because this allows for a collider that acts as a platform detector to be used as a child GameObject, pointing at the root Transform.

You'll see what I mean, because we're about to do just that with the Player:

- Create an empty GameObject as a child of the Player, and name it **"Platform Detector"**. Keep its local position and scale at (0, 0, 0).

- Give it a **Sphere Collider**, check the **Is Trigger** checkbox, change the **Radius** to **1**, and set its **Center Y** position to **0.8**, which will make it stick out a little bit beneath the capsule that acts as the player model.

- Give it a **kinematic** Rigidbody and a **PlatformDetector** script with the "trans" field set to that of the root Player GameObject.

This provides us with a little sphere trigger collider at the "feet" of the player. Since it has a PlatformDetector script attached to it, any Platform scripts that it touches will see this and use the "trans" reference to parent the Player to the Transform of the Platform.

Now all we need to do is add a **Platform** script component to the root Moving Platform GameObject. Then you can play, run along to the Moving Platform, and jump onto it. The Player will move with it, and if you walk off or jump, you'll detach from it. You can watch in the Hierarchy as the Player switches from being a child of the Moving Platform and back to an "orphan," so to speak (a Transform with no parent).

We can also make a box that attaches to the platform without the use of any trigger colliders. Just create a new Cube, add a Rigidbody that's **not** kinematic, and add a PlatformDetector. Set the "trans" of the PlatformDetector to the Cube Transform, and position it atop your Moving Platform. Since the Platform script uses both trigger and non-trigger collision events, it will work with objects like this without any further setup.

Summary

We now have a simple moving platform script, as well as a means of attaching the Player to these moving platforms, allowing them to ride the platform as it moves. Objects controlled by a Rigidbody can also be given the PlatformDetector script to cause them to attach to the platform when they touch it.

CHAPTER 42

■ ■ ■

Joints and Swings

This chapter will go over an example of some basic usage of a physics component called the **Configurable Joint**, which can be used to bind GameObjects together with the physics system. We'll use it to create a chain of objects, each one attached to the one above it to create something like a rope. At the bottom of the rope, we'll attach a sphere that will swing with the rope. Our player can use their "telekinesis" to pull the sphere or its joints, making it something like a wrecking ball.

Swing Setup

Let's set up the GameObjects of our swing first so they're all ready to be connected by joints. The swing will consist of a hovering cube that remains stationary and cannot be pulled or pushed. Beneath this cube, three identical "chain links" will hang below. Each chain link is a little sphere with a long, slender cube hanging beneath it. Each sphere will connect to the cube of the chain link above it. The finished product is shown in Figure 42-1.

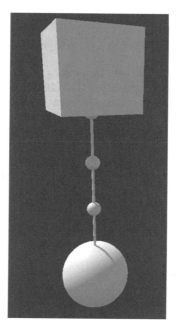

Figure 42-1. *The full Swing GameObject, consisting of a hovering cube on top, three chain links hanging below it, and a larger sphere connected at the bottom*

© Casey Hardman 2024

C. Hardman, *Game Programming with Unity and C#*, https://doi.org/10.1007/978-1-4842-9720-9_42

399

Start by creating an empty GameObject named **"Swing"** with no parent. We'll use this as a root for the Swing. We'll be able to select it to move the whole Swing and all its pieces wherever we want.

- Add a Cube child to the **Swing**. Name it **"Hovering Cube"**. Set its scale to (10, 10, 10) and its local position to (0, 35, 0). Set its layer to **Unmovable**.

- Add an empty child GameObject, also a child of the **Swing**. Name it **"Chain Link"** and set its local position to (0, 30, 0).

- Add a Sphere child to the Chain Link. Leave its local position at (0, 0, 0) and set its scale to (2, 2, 2).

- Add a Cube child, also to the Chain Link. Set its scale to (0.3, 5, 0.3) to make it slender and long. Set its local position to (0, -3.5, 0) to place it just beneath our Sphere.

After we set this one Chain Link up, we'll be copy-pasting it to create the others. But first, let's make sure it has the components we need so we aren't adding them and setting them up three times.

We'll need each Chain Link root GameObject (not the Sphere or Cube within) to have a **Rigidbody** and a **Configurable Joint** added. Go ahead and add each of those now and give the Rigidbody a **Mass** value of **1.5**.

You might think we should add a Rigidbody not to our Chain Link, but to both the Sphere and the Cube within it, but this isn't necessary.

The Rigidbody of the Chain Link will detect the Box Collider and Sphere Collider of its child GameObjects and will consider them fused together to form a single body, acting as if both of those colliders are part of the same object. We can effectively think of them as two pieces of metal welded together. If the Cube is struck by something, then it moves and the Sphere pivots with it – and vice versa.

These are known as **compound colliders** and can be used to represent a more complex object by shaping it out of "primitive" collider types. Primitive colliders are the colliders for basic built-in shapes: Box Collider, Sphere Collider, and Capsule Collider. By creating a parent GameObject with a Rigidbody attached, then adding children with primitive colliders, we create one whole object with a more complex shape than just a cube, sphere, or capsule.

You can do this to "summarize" the shape of a more complex mesh with a combination of primitive shapes.

Moving on to our Configurable Joint, we have a few values to set.

The **Configurable Joint** component is attached to the GameObject that you want to connect another GameObject to, and the Rigidbody of the other GameObject is referenced in the Configurable Joint. So when making a chain out of these Chain Link objects, this means that the Configurable Joint component will be on the upper (higher) link in the chain, and the link beneath that chain will be referenced as the **"Connected Body"** member of the Configurable Joint (the first member listed in the Inspector).

The **Anchor** value of the Configurable Joint is a Vector3 depicting from where the Connected Body pivots. The location is local to the Transform of the GameObject that holds the Configurable Joint component.

Go ahead and set our **Anchor** to a value of **(0, -6, 0)**.

The position of the anchor is shown in the Scene as a dark-gray set of position handles. With our Anchor setting, this will place it at the bottom of the cube, shown in Figure 42-2.

Figure 42-2. *The Chain Link is shown sticking out of the bottom of our Hovering Cube. The Configurable Joint Anchor location is visible at the bottom of the Chain Link Cube as a small set of arrows*

This will ensure that the Chain Link we position below this one will be pivoting around the bottom of this link, not the center of the Sphere (which would be quite awkward).

Moving on, the six **Motion** and **Angular Motion** drop-down fields in the Configurable Joint are all we have left to set.

Each of these fields represents a single axis: X, Y, or Z. Each one can be set to **Locked**, **Limited**, or **Free**. The Motion fields represent whether the Rigidbody can change position on that axis. The Angular Motion fields represent whether the Rigidbody can rotate on that axis:

- When **Locked**, the axis is not changed by the joint at all.

- When **Limited**, the axis is affected, but limited by the other fields that can be customized down below.

- When **Free**, the axis can move as much as warranted with no limitations.

For our purposes, we'll set all three of the Motion fields to Locked because we don't want the joints to cause movement, just rotation – they pivot around each other.

As for the Angular Motion fields

- If we allow **angular X motion**, the chain links can swing **forward and back**.

- If we allow **angular Y motion**, the chain links can **twist sideways**, allowing the platform to turn.

- If we allow **angular Z motion**, the chain links can swing **right and left**.

The swinging will be more controlled if you only allow it to pivot on the X or Z axis and lock the other two. The Y axis isn't all too important, simply depicting whether we'll see the cubes twisting and turning from the forces applied to them.

In our case, we'll set the **Angular X Motion** to **Free** and set both the **Angular Y Motion** and **Angular Z Motion** to **Locked**. This will allow it to swing forward and back only, something like a pendulum. Since this is all local to the Transform, if you want it to swing left or right instead, you can just rotate the entire Swing on the Y axis instead of changing the Configurable Joint settings.

The rest of the fields beneath the Motion fields won't need any tampering. At this point, Figure 42-3 shows how your Rigidbody and Configurable Joint components should look in the Inspector. Note that your **Connected Anchor** value may differ from what is shown in Figure 42-3, but that's fine – it will change once we hook the joints up to each other anyway.

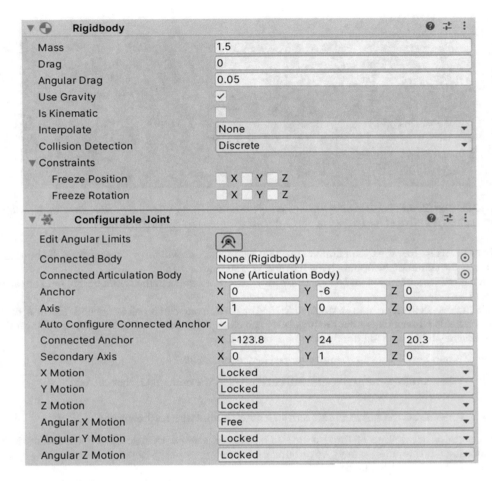

Figure 42-3. *Our Rigidbody and Configurable Joint components shown in the Inspector*

Now, let's continue the setup:

- Select the Chain Link and copy-paste it. We'll need this Chain Link to be **7 units lower** on the **Y axis** than the last, which will position it so that the bottom of its Sphere is just beneath the Cube of the upper link. To do this, you can select the copy and type "-7" **after** the **current Y position** value in the field (making it "30-7" in this case), and Unity will calculate the new value as soon as you click away from the field. If you'd rather type the value in yourself, it should be a Y position of 23.

- Again, copy and paste the Chain Link we just made, and apply the same -7 units to the Y axis so the Y position is 16.

We now have three Chain Links, all touching at their tips to create – you guessed it – a chain. They stick out the bottom of our Hovering Cube, as shown in Figure 42-4.

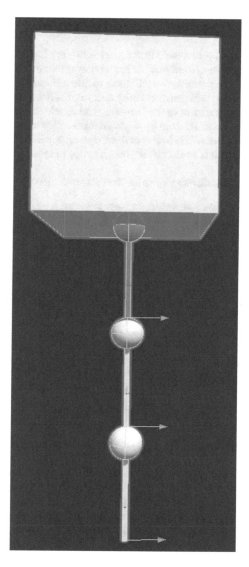

Figure 42-4. *Our entire Swing object while selected. Each Configurable Joint Anchor is also shown at the bottom of each Cube*

Now we just need the ball at the end of the chain:

- Add a Sphere child to the **Swing** GameObject. Set the **scale** to **(10, 10, 10)** and the **position** to **(0, 5, 0)** so it's just beneath the lowest Chain Link.

- Add a **Rigidbody** component to the Sphere. Set the **Mass** to **4** to give it some extra weight when it knocks into other Rigidbodies.

With that, our setup of the bits and pieces of our swing is complete, which means your swing should at last look like it does in Figure 42-1 from before.

Connecting the Joints

In order to connect the joints to each other, we'll first want to connect the upmost Chain Link to the Hovering Cube itself. This will require a Configurable Joint component on the Hovering Cube.

To add a Configurable Joint component, you will have to add a Rigidbody as well. Trying to add one without a Rigidbody already attached will result in Unity automatically adding one.

Go ahead and add a Configurable Joint to the Hovering Cube, which will also give it a Rigidbody. Since we don't want our Hovering Cube to be affected by any collisions or forces, we'll constrain its position and rotation through the Rigidbody. Check all six boxes of the Constraints field of the Rigidbody. You can also uncheck the Use Gravity field, since it wouldn't make much sense to apply gravity when we've already frozen our Rigidbody in place.

The Rigidbody settings should look like Figure 42-5 when you're done.

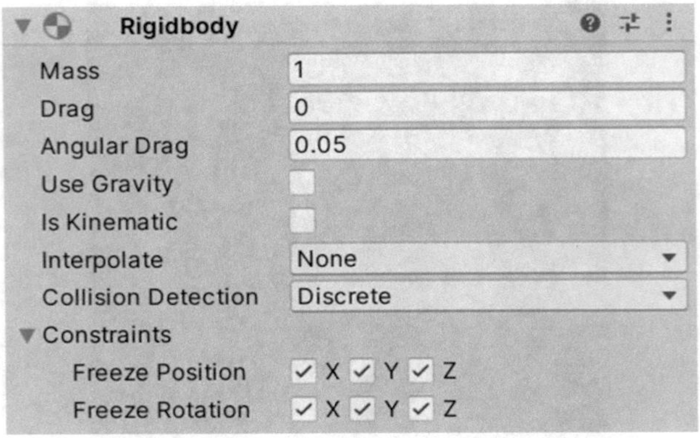

Figure 42-5. *Rigidbody settings in the Inspector for our Hovering Cube*

Now we have the Hovering Cube anchored in place above the ground, so all the Chain Links can hang from it.

There are a few settings we need to apply to the Configurable Joint component on our Hovering Cube. Set the **Anchor** to the bottom of the cube with a value of **(0, -0.5, 0)**. Remember, the Anchor position is local to the Transform, so each unit in the Anchor is multiplied by the Transform scale. For our Chain Links, the scale was (1, 1, 1) so the Anchor value was effectively in world units, but since our Hovering Cube is scaled to (10, 10, 10), that means each unit in the Anchor setting is worth 10 world space units. That's why it's -0.5 to put it at the bottom of the Cube, not -5. Think of it as "50% of the height of the cube," not "0.5 units."

We also need to lock our **Motion** values in the Configurable Joint of the Hovering Cube. Following the same settings you used on the Chain Links, shown before in Figure 42-3, apply them again to the Hovering Cube, but this time, instead of setting the Angular X Motion to Free, set it to **Limited**.

This means the fields below that pertain to limiting the X angle will be active. We're going to apply a limit to the rotation of this top link, to prevent the chain from going too crazy and looping around the Hovering Cube itself.

This can be done with the two folding fields called **"Low Angular X Limit"** and **"High Angular X Limit"**. Unfold each field, and in the **Low** limit, set its Limit field to -60; in the **High** limit, set the Limit field to 60. Figure 42-6 shows Angular X Limit fields.

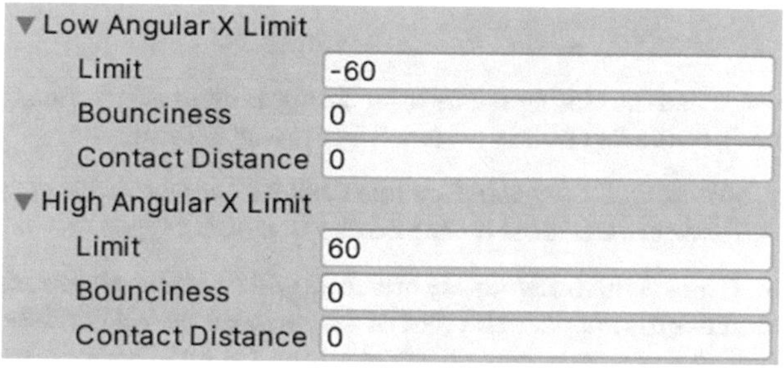

Figure 42-6. *The Low Angular X Limit and High Angular X Limit fields of the Configurable Joint of our Hovering Cube in the Inspector*

The Limit fields resemble the degrees of rotation allowed on the X axis. We're giving it a range of 60 degrees in either direction; after which the top Chain Link will lock up, preventing it from rotating any further.

Now let's attach each link to the one above it. Remember, the **Connected Body** field of the Configurable Joint should be set to the link that is **lower** to the ground. If you haven't changed the Chain Link names after copy-pasting them, their names should be as follows:

- **Chain Link** is the highest one.

- **Chain Link (1)** is the middle one.

- **Chain Link (2)** is the lowest one.

So first, select the **Hovering Cube** and drag **Chain Link** (the topmost one) from the Hierarchy onto the "Connected Body" field of the Configurable Joint. This binds the first Chain Link to the Hovering Cube. Since the Hovering Cube is suspended in the air, the Chain Link will never fall, but it will still be affected by gravity so that even if we pull or push it with our Telekinesis script, it will always be pulled by gravity, causing it to hang down from the Hovering Cube.

Now we can go down the chain and attach each lower link to the upper link:

- Chain Link should have its Connected Body set to the Rigidbody of Chain Link (1).

- Chain Link (1) should be set to Chain Link (2).

- Finally, Chain Link (2) should have the Sphere Rigidbody as its Connected Body, which binds the Sphere to the bottom link.

At that, you should be able to play the game, run over to your Swing with the Player, and try pulling and pushing the Sphere or the Chain Links with the Telekinesis feature. You can raise the Swing up however high you want. If it's given a Y position of 0, the Sphere will bump into the ground as it swings, so you may want to lift the whole Swing up a bit to give it room. Try stacking up some cubes, each with a Rigidbody attached, and use your Telekinesis to swing the wrecking ball into them.

Remember, the swing has been set to only swing on the X axis, which is forward and backward, local to the rotation of the Swing. This means it's like a pendulum, swaying back and forth in only one direction. Trying to pull and push it from the wrong side won't generate much of a reaction.

If you'd like to allow it to swing in both directions, select the Hovering Cube and all three Chain Links at once in the Hierarchy, locate the Configurable Joint component in the Inspector, and then switch the Angular Z Motion to Free.

Summary

This chapter taught us how to use the Configurable Joint component to attach two Rigidbodies such that they pivot around each other. Some key points to remember are as follows:

- Box Colliders, Sphere Colliders, and Capsule Colliders are considered **primitive** collider types. These are the most basic and cheap collider types.

- A parent GameObject with a Rigidbody attached will consider all its children with primitive Collider components to be part of the same whole object. When one collider is struck, it's as if they were all struck, since the Rigidbody considers them one attached unit.

- The **Configurable Joint** component should be attached to the GameObject to which the other Rigidbody is attached. The **"Connected Body"** field refers to the Rigidbody that should be attached to the GameObject with the Configurable Joint component.

CHAPTER 43

■ ■ ■

Force Fields and Jump Pads

In this chapter, we'll be implementing a configurable **ForceField** script that pairs with a trigger collider to apply force to Rigidbodies and/or the player. Based on a variable set in the Inspector determining the type of force to apply, we'll either apply it constantly while the trigger is touched or once when the trigger is first entered. In other words, based on the force mode you choose, you could make an object either get pushed as if by a large fan, or get shoved up like a "jump pad" thrusting them all at once.

Script Setup

Let's start by creating a script named **ForceField** in the Scripts folder and declaring our variables:

```
public class ForceField : MonoBehaviour
{
    [Tooltip("Should the force field affect the player?")]
    public bool affectsPlayer = true;

    [Tooltip("Should the force field affect Rigidbodies?")]
    public bool affectsRigidbodies = true;

    [Tooltip("Method of applying force.")]
    public ForceMode forceMode;

    [Tooltip("Amount of force applied.")]
    public Vector3 force;

    [Tooltip("Should the force be applied in world space or local space relative to this
    Transform's facing?")]
    public Space forceSpace = Space.World;

    //Gets the force in world space.
    public Vector3 ForceInWorldSpace
    {
        get
        {
            //If it's world-space we can just return 'force' as-is:
            if (forceSpace == Space.World)
                return force;
```

```
        //If it's local space, we use our transform to convert 'force' from local to
        world space:
        else
            return transform.TransformDirection(force);
    }
  }
}
```

This gives us a setup that allows each script to control how it behaves with some tweaking of the variables in the Inspector. We can make the force field affect only the player, only Rigidbodies, or both. We can change the force mode, the amount of force applied, and whether the force is applied locally ("Space.Self") or in world space ("Space.World"). We also have a property giving us a quick way to grab the amount of force to apply, automatically converting it to a world space direction relative to the Transform that the ForceField is attached to if the **"forceSpace"** is "Space.Self". This is done with the **"Transform. TransformDirection"** method that we used before. It takes a Vector3 and converts it from being local to the Transform to instead be depicted in world space.

This way, instead of using "force" directly, we can use the **"ForceInWorldSpace"** when calling "Rigidbody.AddForce", and we'll know it's applying the force in the correct direction in world space (which is what "Rigidbody.AddForce" expects).

When we learned how to pull and push Rigidbodies for our Telekinesis script, we went over the four different ForceMode settings. To sum it up, the **Force** and **Acceleration** modes apply constant force, where **Force** is affected by the Rigidbody mass and **Acceleration** is not. Conversely, the **Impulse** and **VelocityChange** modes apply a sudden shove, where **Impulse** is affected by Rigidbody mass and **VelocityChange** is not.

Force Field Setup

Let's set up a simple Force Field GameObject so it's ready to roll when we've finished coding it:

- Start by creating an empty GameObject as a root. Name it **"Force Field"** and set its layer to **Force Field**. Add a Rigidbody, mark it as **kinematic**, and add the **ForceField** script.

- Add a Cube child to the Force Field. Leave its scale at (1, 1, 1) and set its local position to (0, .5, 0). This puts the bottom of the cube at the position of the root Force Field GameObject.

- Check the **Is Trigger** box for the Cube's Box Collider component.

- Create a material named "Force Field" in your Materials folder. Change the first field, **Rendering Mode**, to **Transparent**. I'll apply a green-blue color with a hex value of AAFFE3 and give it 75% transparency by setting the A (alpha) field to 25. Apply the material to the Cube we made.

- Drag and drop the Force Field root GameObject from the Hierarchy to the Prefabs folder in the Project view to create a prefab.

This gives us a little semitransparent box with a trigger collider attached, shown in Figure 43-1. We can use the prefab to create a force field of any size. Scaling up the root Transform will increase the size of the force field while keeping it at the same position on the ground.

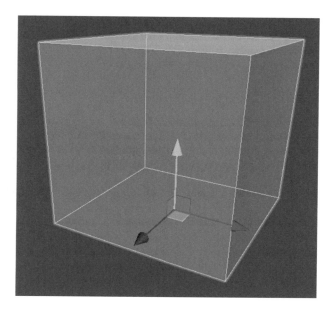

Figure 43-1. *The Force Field GameObject*

Adding Velocity to the Player

Before we make the ForceField apply its force, we still need some method of applying force to our Player. Since the Player doesn't use a Rigidbody, we must implement this ourselves. Luckily, it won't be hard at all. We'll add this method in our **Player** script, just beneath our old **WallIsNearby** method:

```
public void AddVelocity(Vector3 amount)
{
    //Add the velocity X and Z to our 'worldVelocity':
    worldVelocity += new Vector3(amount.x, 0, amount.z);

    //Add the velocity Y to our 'yVelocity':
    yVelocity += amount.y;

    //Ensure that we become midair if our Y velocity was raised above 0.
    //If we don't do this, it will be set to -.1f again in ApplyVelocity if we are grounded.
    if (yVelocity > 0)
        grounded = false;
}
```

This method exposes a simple process of adding velocity in all three axes to the Player, working with our existing system. You'll recall that the Player "worldVelocity" is a Vector3, but it is for the X and Z axes only, keeping a value of 0 at its Y axis. The "yVelocity" float handles the Y axis instead. Thus, we can't just add the velocity to our "worldVelocity", so we create a new Vector3 that applies only the X and Z axes when we add the velocity to "worldVelocity". We then separately add the "amount.y" to our "yVelocity".

You might recall that, in the **ApplyVelocity** method which makes the Player move by their velocity per second, we constantly apply a -0.1 "yVelocity" while the Player is grounded. Thus, if we had a ForceField shoving the player upward when the player is already grounded, it would immediately be overridden by the Player setting their velocity back to -0.1 before moving. That's why we must make sure we set "grounded" to false if the Y velocity has become a positive value.

Applying Forces

To apply forces to touching objects, we'll need two separate trigger collider events. **OnTriggerStay** will handle the **Force** and **Acceleration** force modes, making them apply their force constantly at a rate of "force" per second while the trigger is being touched. **OnTriggerEnter** will handle the **Impulse** and **VelocityChange** force modes, making them apply the "force" not per second, but only once when the trigger is first touched.

Each of these events provides us with a single parameter pointing at the other Collider that was touched.

Heading back over to the **ForceField** script, let's declare those methods:

```
void OnColliderTouched(Collider other)
{
    //If we affect the player,
    if (affectsPlayer)
    {
        //Check for a Player component on the other collider's GameObject:
        var player = other.GetComponent<Player>();

        //If we found one, call AddVelocity:
        if (player != null)
        {
            //If the force mode is a constant push mode, use Time.deltaTime to make the
            force "per second".
            if (forceMode == ForceMode.Force || forceMode == ForceMode.Acceleration)
                player.AddVelocity(ForceInWorldSpace * Time.deltaTime);
            //Otherwise, use the force as-is.
            else
                player.AddVelocity(ForceInWorldSpace);
        }
    }

    //If we affect Rigidbodies,
    if (affectsRigidbodies)
    {
        //Check for a Rigidbody component on the other collider's GameObject:
        var rb = other.GetComponent<Rigidbody>();

        //If we found one, call AddForce:
        if (rb != null)
            rb.AddForce(ForceInWorldSpace, forceMode);
    }
}
```

```
void OnTriggerEnter(Collider other)
{
    //Impulse and VelocityChange modes will apply force only when the trigger is first
    entered.
    if (forceMode == ForceMode.Impulse || forceMode == ForceMode.VelocityChange)
        OnColliderTouched(other);
}

void OnTriggerStay(Collider other)
{
    //Acceleration and Force modes will apply force constantly as long as the collision
    stays in contact.
    if (forceMode == ForceMode.Acceleration || forceMode == ForceMode.Force)
        OnColliderTouched(other);
}
```

We detect the collider being touched with an Enter and a Stay method, and each one calls the same **OnColliderTouched** method.

This method checks for a Player component on the GameObject of the touching Collider if the **"affectsPlayer"** bool is true, and if it finds one, it adds force to the player. Whether or not we use "Time. deltaTime" in the force depends on the ForceMode, since Force and Acceleration modes are expected to apply "per second" through the OnTriggerStay method, while Impulse and VelocityChange are expected to apply only once through the OnTriggerEnter method.

Roughly the same thing is done with Rigidbodies: if the **"affectsRigidbodies"** bool is true and there is a Rigidbody attached, apply force. For Rigidbodies, we don't need to use "Time.deltaTime" to apply the constant force. The "Rigidbody.AddForce" method will automatically look at the force as "per second" if we use either the Force or Acceleration mode.

With that, you can set up some force fields in your Scene and try them out. They're somewhat small by default, but we can set their scale value to whatever we want or simply use the scale tool (hotkey R) to scale them by eye.

Set the "force" vector to something noticeable: try a Y value of 200, for example. Using Force or Acceleration mode will cause the touching entities to hover upward while they remain in the force field. Using Impulse or VelocityChange will apply the force all at once, causing the entity to jerk upward instead. This would be useful for making a "jump pad" of sorts, allowing the player to reach high places by stepping on it or to launch objects far distances by pushing or pulling them onto it with the Telekinesis feature.

You can also place force fields sideways on walls and switch the Force Mode to Self to apply the force relative to the Force Field–facing direction. Just remember to keep track of where your axes are pointing when you set the "force" variable. The arrows shown by the position tool (hotkey W) when you select your Force Field will point in the local direction of each axis, so you can know which axis to apply force in.

If the arrows are pointing along the world directions, just press the X hotkey to make them local to the selected Transform. For example, Figure 43-2 shows a rotated Force Field on the side of a wall, with the position tool arrows showing local to the Force Field. In this case, if you want the Force Field to shove entities away from the wall, you would set your force as the Y axis (the green arrow) of the "force" vector.

411

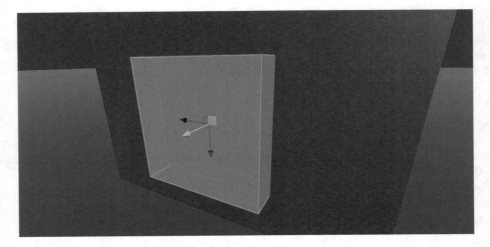

Figure 43-2. *A Force Field is shown sticking off the side of a wall, with its local Y axis pointing away from the wall*

Summary

In this chapter, we implemented a Force Field script that can be used for a sudden shove, like a jump pad for our player or a constant force. We combined our knowledge of adding forces to Rigidbodies, as well as trigger colliders and their associated collision detection events: **OnTriggerStay**, **OnTriggerEnter**, and **OnTriggerExit**.

CHAPTER 44

Conclusion

This chapter marks the conclusion of our final example project and this book. We've come a long way and learned a lot since we started, and I applaud you for coming this far!

That said, don't even begin to think of getting bored yet. C# is an old language rich with features, and we've hardly demonstrated all that the Unity game engine is capable of. There's plenty more to learn. Don't stop seeking out new information and adding tools to your belt!

Let's get a summary of what we went over with this project, and then we'll part with some ideas on where to take your learning from here. Even if you decide not to structure your learning very rigidly past this point, just trying to implement new things can take you a long way. If you've followed this book from start to finish, you ought to have an understanding of the environment you're working in that allows you some room to wiggle and try out stuff you're really interested in. You might not have as much guidance this way, but working out solutions yourself can help you become better at problem-solving. Keep trying new things, and if you get in over your head, take a step back and reevaluate. You can always come back to a lofty project some time down the road, when you've learned new things and become a better programmer – and working on things you care about most will help to keep your interest piqued.

Physics Playground Recap

This project gives us experience dealing with Unity's 3D physics system, as well as some new concepts on how to deal with vectors and 3D motion. Here's a summary of the major takeaways:

- The **magnitude** of a vector is a float value depicting how much distance the vector travels. It can also be called the **length** of a vector. The **"Vector3.magnitude"** member is a property that returns the magnitude.

- **Normalizing** a vector makes it point in the same direction it did before, but makes it only have a magnitude of 1. This means that multiplying a normalized vector by an int or float will travel that many units in the direction the vector points.

- Physics updates are not synchronized with normal frame updates. Each physics update will occur at a set interval, with the default being **50 updates per second** (once every 0.02 seconds). If necessary, they might happen multiple times per frame, or they might happen every other frame, or every three frames – it all depends on the framerate. The gist of it is that the updates will occur 50 times per second whether the game is running slow (low framerate, choppy) or fast (high framerate, smooth).

- Scripts which interact on every frame with physics components like the Rigidbody should use the **FixedUpdate** built-in event method, not Update. FixedUpdate occurs every physics update, so 50 times per second by default.

© Casey Hardman 2024
C. Hardman, *Game Programming with Unity and C#*, https://doi.org/10.1007/978-1-4842-9720-9_44

- If a GameObject is to be controlled by a Rigidbody, you should not move its Transform directly through scripts. Instead, add forces with the **"Rigidbody. AddForce"** method.

- **Primitive** collider types are the colliders for basic shapes: Box Collider, Sphere Collider, and Capsule Collider.

- To create a Rigidbody with a shape defined by multiple primitive colliders, use a root GameObject with a Rigidbody component attached, and then attach Colliders to child GameObjects. This is a **compound collider**. Only the root GameObject needs a Rigidbody component. All Colliders will count as part of the same whole object controlled by the root Rigidbody.

Further Learning for Unity

Let's go over some loose ends pertaining to the Unity engine that you may be interested in checking out. These are a few things we didn't get into during our projects to keep things from getting bloated. If you're interested in learning about a feature of the engine, the Unity Manual pages on the official Unity site offer a good starting point.

Your favorite search engine should have an easy time guiding you to Manual pages. Just search for "unity manual" and tack on the feature you're interested in at the end, such as "unity manual coroutines."

The Asset Store

The Asset Store is a place where other Unity developers can upload products for use within the engine, including scripts for code extensions and game functionality, 3D models or 2D graphics, music, sound effects, and so on. As the name depicts, anything that could be used as an asset in your Project window could be placed on the Asset Store.

The Asset Store contains both free and paid assets. If you're in need of something that you can't quite make yourself, you might just be able to find it there.

The Asset Store can be accessed by visiting it on the Web at this URL:

```
https://assetstore.unity.com/
```

A quick search of "unity asset store" with your favorite search engine should also find it, if that link doesn't work.

Coroutines

The **coroutine** is a concept that can be employed to provide some timing-related functionality for method calls that you can't quite achieve with Invoke calls. A coroutine is a method that can **yield** with a special line of code. Yielding can stop execution of the code for some given amount of time – a number of seconds or until the next frame or until some condition is true. After the wait, the code continues execution at the same line, with all the same local variables in the same state. This can be useful for handling more delicate processes without the need for Invoking many different methods. It can also be used to perform a strenuous task bit by bit to prevent from generating a drop in framerate or a lengthy pause in gameplay: for example, a loop with very many iterations can "yield" until the next frame every five to ten iterations so that it "runs in the background" instead of doing it all at once.

The MonoBehaviour class (base class for all script components) is the entry point for calling coroutines. This is done with the **StartCoroutine** method – however, in order for a method to qualify for being called as a coroutine, it must return the type **IEnumerator**.

Let's observe an example in which we declare a coroutine that logs a message, waits three seconds, and then logs another message:

```
//Declare the coroutine like any other method, but with the 'IEnumerator' return type.
private IEnumerator MyCoroutine()
{
    Debug.Log("Coroutine executing.");

    //Within the coroutine, use "yield return" to pause execution.
    yield return new WaitForSeconds(3);

    Debug.Log("Coroutine finished.");
}
```

Here, we see the **yield** keyword before our **return** keyword. Whenever you wish to suspend the execution of the coroutine, you must use the "yield return" keywords.

What we actually return is a **yield instruction**, specifically, the **WaitForSeconds** instruction. It does just what the name implies: it causes the coroutine to wait the given number of seconds, supplied as a parameter, before it continues execution, starting with the next line after the **yield return** statement.

In order for this to work, you must use the **StartCoroutine** method, as described before:

```
StartCoroutine(MyCoroutine());
```

Note that the coroutine supplied to the StartCoroutine method must be called like any other method, complete with a set of parentheses. This provides another advantage of coroutines over Invoked methods: they support parameters.

Here is an example of a coroutine that uses parameters to log a message depending upon whether or not a given Transform was moved within a given amount of time after the coroutine was started:

```
private IEnumerator TrackTransform(Transform trans, float waitTime)
{
    Vector3 initialPosition = trans.position;

    yield return new WaitForSeconds(waitTime);

    if (trans.position != initialPosition)
        Debug.Log("The Transform moved!");
    else
        Debug.Log("The Transform did not move.");
}

private void Start()
{
    //Log whether or not the Transform of this script's GameObject moved within 3 seconds:
    StartCoroutine(TrackTransform(transform, 3));
}
```

We create a local variable to mark the position of the Transform **"trans"** when the coroutine is first called. We then yield and wait, using the **"waitTime"** to determine how long. After that, we log a different message depending upon whether or not the Transform moved.

Coroutines can also be **nested** – a coroutine may **yield return** a **StartCoroutine** call to initiate another coroutine and wait for the second coroutine to finish before continuing:

```
private IEnumerator MyCoroutine()
{
        Debug.Log("Coroutine executing.");
        yield return StartCoroutine(MyOtherCoroutine());
        Debug.Log("Coroutine finished.");
}

private IEnumerator MyOtherCoroutine()
{
        Debug.Log("Other coroutine executing.");
        yield return new WaitForSeconds(2);
        Debug.Log("Other coroutine finished.");
}
```

In this case, if you call **StartCoroutine(MyCoroutine())**, then you will end up with the messages logged in this order:

```
Coroutine executing.
Other coroutine executing.
Other coroutine finished.
Coroutine finished.
```

An important note here is that we use **yield return** when starting the nested coroutine. If we simply called StartCoroutine without the "yield return", then it would independently start the second coroutine (MyOtherCoroutine) without suspending the first coroutine (MyCoroutine).

Using coroutines and nested coroutines can give you a lot more power over the execution of your methods than the Invoke method, so it's a great tool to consider if you require more precise control over a complicated sequence.

Script Execution Order

Under the Edit ➤ Project Settings window, there is a tab called Script Execution Order which we never had a reason to use in our example projects. It may prove useful to you at some point in the future, so it's good to know what it's for.

The name entails its purpose pretty well: it allows you to specify a consistent order in which your scripts receive event calls like Update or Start. You can make the event calls for one script to always occur before another if the order is important for some specific reason in your project.

Further Learning for C#

Polishing up your skills with the programming language you use can be a good way to expand your horizons. Knowing all you're capable of doing with the language may guide you to solutions you wouldn't have found otherwise. This section will provide an overview of some of the features we didn't get to go over in detail with our example projects.

Delegates

Delegates provide a means of declaring a variable that can point at methods, something like a way to reference a method as if it were an object instance. The variable can be called like a method, without knowing exactly which method is attached to it.

To sum up the process

- Declare a delegate, giving it a name, return type, and any number of parameters. This is like a template or a blueprint that methods must follow.

- You can now declare a variable that uses the delegate name as the variable type.

- Any method which matches the delegate return type and parameters can be assigned to the variable. The variable can then be called like a method.

Let's review the syntax involved in each of these steps:

```
//Declare the delegate like a method but with the 'delegate' keyword before.
//We provide a return type (string), name (MyDelegate), and two parameters.
delegate string MyDelegate(string a, int b);

//You can now declare a variable whose type is the delegate name.
MyDelegate delegateVariable;

//Now declare a method that matches the return type and parameters of the delegate.
string AddNumberToString(string a, int b)
{
    return a + b;
}

//Since the method matches the delegate return type and parameters, we can assign the method
to the variable.
delegateVariable = AddNumberToString;

//The delegate variable can be called like a method.
delegateVariable("Hello World", 1);
```

In this example scenario, you might as well just call the method by its name directly, of course. An actual use case might be a custom UI system where a Button class exposes a delegate variable that is called when the button is clicked. When creating a button, we can supply any method that matches the delegate to be called when the button is clicked, making it easy to reuse the button for different purposes. We could even change the method that the delegate variable points to on the fly to change what occurs when the button is clicked.

Documentation Comments

C# defines a system of "documentation comments" that can be written before definitions such as classes, methods, variables, properties, and so on. These comments use a special syntax to define documentation for code, right within the lines of the code. Code editors and other software can read the comments and use their contents in useful ways. One purpose for this that you'll see used widely is the "summary" tag, which uses documentation comments to place a description of a definition which will then pop up when you mouse over that definition anywhere in the code editor, assuming the code editor supports it.

For example, you might write a summary before a class you declared. Sometime later, when you declare a variable with the class name as its type, you can mouse over the class name and see that description you wrote.

In fact, Unity provides a summary description for most of their built-in classes. If your code editor supports it, you've probably seen them when you leave your mouse hovering over a type or method name for a second.

The following code shows how to write a basic "summary" for one of our existing methods: the **WallIsNearby** method we declared for our Player in the last example project. Documentation comments always start with three slashes "///" instead of the two "//" that make up a normal comment. They contain "tags" inside them: an opening tag, like "<summary>", and then a closing tag of the same name but with a slash before it, like "</summary>". The text that belongs to the tag goes between those two tags:

```
/// <summary>
/// Checks if a wall is near enough to the player for them to wall jump off of it.
/// Returns true if there is a wall, false if there is not.
/// </summary>
private bool WallIsNearby()
{
    ...
}
```

As you can see, it always starts with "///", with a single space coming after the three slashes (because it looks prettier that way). We start the "<summary>" tag, write the text we wish to serve as the summary, and then write the closing tag "</summary>".

Documentation comments can also provide other kinds of data that is used in other ways. Methods can have a description provided for each of their parameters so that while you write out a method call, the description of each parameter is shown to you as you type. This is done with the "<param>" tag. Methods can also have a "<returns>" tag that gives a description of what the method returns (assuming it doesn't return void).

Some code editors, Visual Studio included, will automatically generate the basic tags for you when you type the three forward slashes "///" before a method declaration. Cleverly, they'll read the method declaration, and if it doesn't return "void", they'll create a "<returns>" tag. They'll also create "<param>" tags for each parameter declared in the method, if any.

Here is an example of "<param>" and "<returns>" tags, using our (somewhat useless) method we declared for our delegate a little bit ago:

```
/// <summary>
/// Describe what the method does here.
/// </summary>
/// <param name="a">Describe parameter 'a' here.</param>
/// <param name="b">Describe parameter 'b' here.</param>
/// <returns>Describe what the method returns here.</returns>
string AddNumberToString(string a, int b)
{
    return a + b;
}
```

This shows how to declare a parameter within a tag: the "param" tag has a "name=" passage within that is used to specify the name of the associated parameter.

You may be interested to know that this method of writing and formatting data with this "tag" syntax is widely used to represent various different kinds of data through text files and is known as **XML: Extensible Markup Language**. It's a flexible and readable way to declare text data.

In favor of keeping our code samples a bit less bulky, we haven't employed this custom throughout this book. However, you'll often see it if you look at other people's C# code. It can be useful to maintain since it allows you to get a description of a method on the fly just by hovering your mouse over it (assuming your code editor of choice supports this feature). This can make it easier to work with code you wrote a while ago, where the details on how to use it might have since slipped your mind. For example, you might forget what a method returns or the purpose of each parameter it declares. Having that information pop up as you type can make things clearer. It can also be useful when writing code that others are meant to use.

Exceptions

Many programming languages have control structures in place that revolve around reacting when code that you're running throws an **exception**. "Exception" is the technically correct C# term for "error." Any code that results in an error popping up in your Console in Unity is "throwing an exception."

Exceptions are actual data types that all inherit from a base class called **Exception**, which is in the **System** namespace. When an exception is thrown, it's done with a simple line of code: the **"throw"** keyword and then a constructor that creates an Exception instance. The most basic form is to use the base Exception class:

```
void DoSomething()
{
    if (a)
        throw new Exception("Failed to do something.");
    else
    {
        //...
    }
}
```

That example assumes you have a **"using System;"** at the top of your file; otherwise, you'd have to type "throw new System.Exception" instead.

However, more particular types exist that inherit from Exception, which make it clearer what went wrong and why the error occurred. For example, an **IndexOutOfRangeException** will be thrown if you try to get an index from a collection (array, List, etc.) that doesn't have that index stored in it, such as if the index is higher than the "Length" of an array or the "Count" of a List.

A control structure that you'll commonly see when coding is the **"try...catch...finally"**:

```
try
{
    //Run some code you think might produce an exception here in the 'try' block.
}
catch (Exception e)
{
    //If an exception occurs in the 'try', this code will run and the Exception will be
    'caught' so it isn't thrown as a message in the Console.
    //The 'Exception e' parameter will point to the Exception that was thrown, which may
    contain useful data.
}
```

```
finally
{
    //This code runs after the fact, no matter whether an exception occurred or not.
}
```

This can be used to define "fallback code" for what should occur if an exception was thrown while some code was running. Whatever type the "catch" block declares as its parameter, that's the type of Exception that will be handled. You can even declare multiple "catch" blocks, each one catching a different type of Exception. If your "try" block results in some Exception being thrown that is of a type that none of your "catch" blocks are expecting, the Exception will show up in the Console and is considered "uncaught" or "unhandled." But as long as the Exception is caught by one of your "catch" blocks, it won't end up in the Console.

Advanced C#

If you feel confident and want to further explore the nitty-gritty details of C#, this section will list some extra features and talking points that you may be interested in learning about, briefly explaining the basic concept so you can explore it on your own after.

Operator Overloading

Operator overloads are something like methods that can be declared in a class to write your own code that occurs when a certain kind of operator is used with your class instance. This allows you to, for example, permit two instances of your class to be operated on by a "+" operator. You could also allow some other type to be added to your class with the "+" operator, like an int or string. When the operator occurs, it'll be your code running and returning the result based on the operands (which is the technical term for "the values on either side of the operator").

Conversions

As well as overloading operators like "+", "-", "*", and so on, there are also **"conversion operators"** that you can declare within a class. They allow you to write code that determines what is returned when your class type is implicitly or explicitly converted to another type. If you have some data structures that are similar to each other, you can declare conversion operators to allow easy conversion from one type to the other.

An example of such a conversion within Unity's built-in types is that of **Vector2** and **Vector3**. The Vector2 type is just a vector with only an X and Y value. The Vector3 is pretty much the same, but it has the Z axis as well. A Vector2 can **implicitly** convert to a Vector3 – implicit meaning we don't have to tell it to convert, it just does it if necessary. A Vector3 can **explicitly** convert to a Vector2 – explicit meaning we must tell it to convert by using a conversion operator, because data will be lost when we convert it.

Both cases were implemented with a conversion operator declared in each vector class, specifying what to return when performing the conversion.

Generic Types

Generics are a somewhat confusing but very powerful feature. We already lightly explored generics during this book, but to give true justice to this concept, you may want to do some further digging. Learning how to declare classes and methods that use generic types can be a good way to gain further understanding so you don't just know how to work with generic types, but how to use them in your own classes and methods.

Structs

We went over the difference between classes and structs before, but we never learned how to declare structs and when you might consider using them.

Generally speaking, structs will give you more trouble than classes. If you don't quite know how to use them, you'll have your compiler throwing errors at you in no time. They can be a bit of a pain. That being said, knowing when and how to use them can get you a few steps ahead of the game.

Summary

Our final chapter has given you some ideas for further learning to pursue on your own, as well as some basic demonstrations. Here's a short summary:

- A **coroutine** is a method call that can **yield** on the spot, stopping its operation for a given amount of time and then resuming in the same state. This means you can yield in the middle of a loop and then continue at that same point in the loop.

- A **delegate** is something like a way to allow a variable to store a reference to a method. The delegate definition acts as a blueprint that a method must follow in order for it to be stored in such a variable.

- An **exception** is the C# word for "error." When code **throws** an exception, that means something went wrong and generated an error, like those seen in the Console window of Unity.

- Data types like classes and structs can declare **overloads** to allow specified **operators** (like "+" and "-") to be used with the type or to allow **conversions** to other types.

With these ideas in mind, it's now up to you to decide where to go – isn't that exciting? The concepts discussed briefly in this chapter are a good place to start. The more tools you have on your belt and the more experience you have with using them, the easier it will be to find clever solutions to the problems you face. If you encounter new syntax, don't be afraid to look for information on it and figure out how it works!

Index

© Casey Hardman 2024
C. Hardman, *Game Programming with Unity and C#*, https://doi.org/10.1007/978-1-4842-9720-9

■ X

■ Y

■ Z

Printed in the United States
by Baker & Taylor Publisher Services